THE PRESIDENT'S BOOK OF SECRETS

The

PRESIDENT'S
BOOK
of SECRETS

The Untold Story *of* Intelligence
Briefings *to* America's Presidents
from Kennedy *to* Obama

DAVID PRIESS

PublicAffairs
New York

PublicAffairs books are available at special discounts for bulk purchases in the
US by corporations, institutions, and other organizations. For more information,
please contact the Special Markets Department at the Perseus Books Group, 2300
Chestnut Street, Suite 200, Philadelphia, PA 19103, call (800) 810-4145, ext. 5000,
or e-mail special.markets@perseusbooks.com.

Book Design by Jack Lenzo
This book was typeset in ten point Meridien

Names: Priess, David, author.
Title: The president's book of secrets : the untold story of intelligence
   briefings to America's presidents from Kennedy to Obama / David Priess ;
   foreword by George H. W. Bush.
Description: New York, NY : PublicAffairs, 2016. | Includes bibliographical
   references and index.
Identifiers: LCCN 2015041833| ISBN 9781610395953 (hardback) | ISBN
   9781610395960 (e-book)
Subjects: LCSH: Intelligence service--United States--History. |
   Presidents--United States--History. | United States. Central Intelligence
   Agency--History. | National security--United States. | United
   States--Foreign relations. | BISAC: POLITICAL SCIENCE / Government /
   Executive Branch. | POLITICAL SCIENCE / Political Freedom & Security /
   Intelligence.
Classification: LCC JK468.I6 P745 2016 | DDC 327.1273--dc23 LC record available
at http://lccn.loc.gov/2015041833

First Edition

10 9 8 7 6 5 4 3 2

CONTENTS

FOREWORD
by George H. W. Bush

I AM OFTEN ASKED of all the jobs I've held in my now very long lifetime, which was my favorite. There is, of course, no greater honor than to be President of the United States of America. So I imagine that all of the men who preceded me in the job, and the three who succeeded me, would immediately agree that no job compares to sitting in the Oval Office.

But I am just as definite about the job next on my "Top 10" list: being Director of Central Intelligence. Sometimes that answer surprises people at first. They then immediately assume, mistakenly, that I loved heading the CIA because of what would commonly be called all "that cloak and dagger stuff." Nothing could be further from the truth.

My love of the job was all about the remarkable men and women who make up our intelligence community. Their dedication, their courage, and their determination match that of no others and inspired me every single day. Yet, their names are seldom known, and their accomplishments are rarely celebrated. But that is not why they do their jobs. Without any expectation of credit, they put extraordinary time and effort—and too often their lives—on the line every single day. It is all too easy to forget why they collect and interpret intelligence information: to provide accurate, timely, and objective information from all sources to help top decision-makers defend the United States and protect its interests abroad.

For presidents and their closest national security advisors, this Top Secret intelligence comes via daily delivery of a truly one-of-kind publication, the President's Daily Brief.

Each working day as president (which is most days), I invited CIA briefers to sit with me, enabling them to offer insights beyond those on the PDB's pages and to answer my questions. Without fail, they enriched my time with the PDB and helped me make more informed choices about world affairs.

Every experience with my daily book of secrets, and with those who produced and briefed it, reminded me how the PDB stands out as something both uniquely American and yet underappreciated by the very people it helps to ultimately protect.

That is why when David Priess asked me to write the foreword for this remarkable book, I immediately said yes. First, I should explain that I rarely write forewords any more. I like to tell people that at age ninety-one, I have more or less run out of things to say. But I am delighted to have this opportunity to help shine a spotlight on true American heroes, thanks to this book.

Despite being on both sides of the PDB—the provider and the recipient—I learned much from these pages about the fascinating history of the President's Daily Brief. As Priess deftly relates here, each president's relationship with his PDB has depended upon his background, his challenges in office, and the influence of his closest advisors.

By using the words of those closest to the PDB across its fifty-year history—presidents and vice presidents, CIA directors and National Security advisors, White House chiefs of staff and intelligence briefers—this book offers a rare window into an underappreciated institution of our foreign policy and national security system.

Uncovering and respectfully writing about so many previously unheralded tales of presidential intelligence requires an unusual mix of dedication, insight, and discretion. Priess combines them seamlessly. I appreciate the care and skill with which he protects the book's still-classified content while telling so many stories surrounding the PDB that *can* be told. Many of them call up happy recollections of my early morning sessions with intelligence briefers. Other ones bring up more somber memories of the most difficult moments commanders-in-chief face—deciding to send the brave members of our armed forces off to war.

Some of those who dedicated so much energy and time to this unique daily publication will finally, with this book, get a touch of the recognition they justly deserve. Many more must remain nameless. All of them have my respect and appreciation.

George H. W. Bush
41ST PRESIDENT OF THE UNITED STATES

PREFACE
Top Secret Delivery

THE PRESIDENT DESCENDS FROM the residence to the Oval Office to start his morning. After quickly reviewing the day's agenda with the chief of staff, he sits down and invites in his national security advisor, who tells him no crises have developed around the globe overnight. A few minutes later, his secretary pokes her head in.

"Mr. President, your briefer is here."

He leans back, takes a deep breath, and says, "All right. Let's go." The next appointment rarely brings good news.

His visitor walks in looking like she's been awake half the night. She has. In fact, her day started when most people have just gone to bed. Since getting to work at CIA headquarters just before 2:00 a.m., she has looked at late-breaking raw intelligence reports, studied each analytic assessment in the package now sitting securely in her locked bag, and spoken with analysts (from some of the seventeen organizations within the federal government that make up the intelligence community) who wrote those assessments. That way, she could learn about any related classified stories that hadn't made it into the ultimate text because of the gauntlet of reviewers and editors.

Opening the locked bag while she moves toward the desk, she reaches in and looks up at the commander in chief.

"Good morning, Mr. President. Here's your PDB."

THE PRESIDENT'S DAILY BRIEF contains the most sensitive intelligence reporting and analysis in the world. The Central Intelligence Agency's spies, the National Security Agency's listening posts, and the nation's reconnaissance satellites gather secrets for it, while America's enemies send undercover agents to try to unearth its classified content. Every working morning, intelligence briefers fan out from CIA headquarters to personally deliver copies of the PDB to the president and the handful of senior advisors he has designated to see its Top Secret pages. No major foreign policy decisions are made without it.

For the past fifty years, intelligence officers have made their way to the White House five or six days a week to hand-deliver the President's Daily Brief to the president—or, in some administrations, to the national security advisor, who then gets it to the president. Assessments from analysts at the CIA and, since 2005, the wider intelligence community prepare the president for foreign visits and overseas trips, anticipate national security threats, and identify global opportunities. What insiders simply call "the book" represents the highest fulfillment of the intelligence mission: to provide accurate, timely, and objective information from classified and unclassified sources alike to help the president defend the homeland and protect US interests abroad.

Yet its story has gone largely untold—until now.

Extraordinary efforts go into the drafting, editing, production, and delivery of the PDB. Analysts dig through wide-ranging raw intelligence reports: clandestine sources (human intelligence, or HUMINT), intercepted communications (signals intelligence, or SIGINT), scientific measurement and signature (MASINT), and open sources such as foreign media (OSINT). They find nuggets of likely interest to the president and synthesize the various sources into a document that is usually no longer than a single page, focused on what the president *needs* to know. Although the CIA has the majority of all-source analysts, these short articles get sent around much of the intelligence community under the direction of a small staff reporting to the director of national intelligence (DNI). This coordination process aims to ensure that each PDB piece includes all relevant information from anywhere in the US government, presents an analytic message clearly and concisely, offers major alternative explanations, and highlights implications for US interests.

Analytic managers in the lead author's agency evaluate the text for substance, structure, and style before editors working for the DNI judge whether it meets the threshold for publication in the PDB. If so, they polish it and send it along to a senior DNI or CIA official for a final look to ensure it hasn't been overtaken by sensitive policy decisions that only those most senior officials would be aware of. Through most of the PDB's history, the resulting articles were printed before dawn on high-quality paper and inserted into a leather binder; now they are uploaded to a Top Secret tablet computer.

From its birth in late 1964 during Lyndon Johnson's administration, the President's Daily Brief has seen its format, highly classified content, and mode of delivery tailored to the current commander in chief. The PDB's first three recipients alone demonstrated great variety in how they received it: Lyndon Johnson had his book delivered at night for his bedtime reading, Richard Nixon's legal-brief-styled PDB was screened the night before by national security advisor Henry Kissinger, and Gerald Ford during his first year as president had a working-level CIA officer brief him personally on it in the Oval Office. More recently, Barack Obama has received his PDB on an iPad. Yet for all the differences over the decades, the delivery of the President's Daily Brief every working day remains a rare constant.

Because the PDB has been the most tightly guarded daily publication on the face of the earth for the past half century, this book is a little like the biography of a recluse: only glimpses of the subject from long ago exist, with recent views more difficult to come by. These pages cannot include any classified information about intelligence sources and methods in the PDB. Documentary sources from presidential libraries and declassified government archives, while expanding steadily over time, remain limited. Yet a sense of the PDB's role and impact still emerges through stories of the high-stakes interactions among modern presidents, other PDB recipients, and intelligence officers of all ranks, often in their own words. Each living former president and vice president has shared reflections on the President's Daily Brief exclusively for this book, as has almost every living former CIA director and deputy director for intelligence and the vast majority of other living former recipients of the book.

The most fascinating issues about the PDB do not involve the exact substance of its articles but, instead, revolve around the personalities of its producers and its readers, the process of its creation and delivery, and the place it holds in the daily work of national security at the highest level. These topics are the heart of this book.

CHAPTER ONE

BEFORE THE BOOK

Intelligence Analysis for the President,
from Washington to Eisenhower

NO CHIEF EXECUTIVE IN the Republic's first 150 years received any objective analysis of international events from an independent intelligence service. Secretaries of state and other advisors may have offered assessments of various foreign developments, but reports tailored to the specific needs and style of each occupant of the White House simply didn't exist until the middle of the twentieth century. With no existential threats and limited global interests, the United States and its leaders could afford to go without them.

Early presidents did not avoid foreign intelligence altogether. George Washington brought to the nation's highest office a personal understanding of the business, dating from his days handling espionage duties against Great Britain while commander in chief of the Continental Army. Even without formal training, he demonstrated a good feel for the importance of objective intelligence analysis in an April 1782 letter to Continental Congress delegate James Lovell: "It is by comparing a variety of information, we are frequently enabled to investigate facts, which were so intricate or hidden, that no single clue could have led to the knowledge of them in this point of view, intelligence becomes interesting which but from its connection and collateral circumstances, would not be important." Washington had no analytic service to perform this duty, so he did it himself.

Many of Washington's successors during America's first century came to the presidency with significant international experience. Four of them—Thomas Jefferson, James Monroe, John Quincy Adams, and Martin Van Buren—served both as secretary of state and as ambassador to at least one other country before assuming the presidency. Two others, James Madison and James Buchanan, had been secretaries of state, while John Adams and William Henry Harrison had represented the United States abroad. All of these leaders' first-hand knowledge of the world helped them evaluate reports coming across their desks from the young nation's fledgling diplomatic service, but even they carried out their duties without an analytic cadre to assess foreign developments. Of course, they also lacked Washington's intimate knowledge of espionage.

Abraham Lincoln used Allen Pinkerton, co-founder of the Pinkerton National Detective Agency, to lead the nation's intelligence gathering during much of the Civil War. The duties and the operations of the "Pinkertons" and the short-lived Bureau of Military Information had little to do with overseas issues, however, emphasizing instead the clandestine collection of information about the Confederacy, to the neglect of what we today consider analysis. For the next fifty years, the US intelligence system continued to lag well behind the services of the world's other powers, and the nation's experience in World War I moved the ball forward only slightly. Woodrow Wilson allowed only a small US foreign intelligence collection capability to emerge during the war. He exhibited little interest in intelligence analysis as such—largely ignoring the small intelligence division tasked to support the American end-of-war peace conference delegation that he led. The analysis he did receive came not from US analysts but largely from the British intelligence chief in the United States. It would take the dual challenge of Nazi aggression in Europe and the surprise Japanese attack on the US Pacific Fleet at Pearl Harbor in Hawaii to plant the seeds for a new system of modern intelligence analysis and, eventually, a presidentially focused intelligence publication.

FRANKLIN D. ROOSEVELT IN 1941 established the nation's first foreign intelligence service: the Office of the Coordinator of Information, which morphed into the Office of Strategic Services (OSS) the following year. Led by the charismatic and adventurous William "Wild Bill"

Donovan, the OSS covered the gamut of intelligence activities—from the collection of human intelligence to propaganda and sabotage operations behind enemy lines—throughout World War II.

A lesser-known OSS component, the Office of Research and Analysis (R&A), emerged as the country's first nondepartmental analytic unit, collating information from diplomats, military reports, international media sources, and academic research. The initial division of R&A officers into isolated geographical, economic, and political units shifted in January 1943 to multidisciplinary groups that reflected the military's overseas theaters of operation. For the unprecedented effort, the government gathered a wide range of experts that Donovan referred to as "his professors," many of them prominent scholars from Yale, Harvard, Princeton, and other top universities. During the peak of the R&A effort, nearly a thousand of these political scientists, historians, economists, geographers, cartographers, and others produced about two thousand long reports, many more short memoranda, and stacks of generic handbooks about other countries.

Ray Cline, R&A's chief of current intelligence from 1944 until the dissolution of the OSS after the war, struggled to get the office's scholarly personnel to focus on immediate issues instead of academically interesting but policy-irrelevant research papers. He worked hard to get them to condense their assessments into readable articles suitable for the Joint Chiefs or the president. With scant feedback from Roosevelt, the analysts had no idea whether they had an eager reader in the Oval Office or a bored one.

Via the president's secretary, Donovan sent FDR some of R&A's assessments, covered by a memo that he wrote personally. These personal notes started out largely administrative but increasingly addressed substantive intelligence as the war progressed, and included some unedited intelligence tidbits from case officers in the field. Roosevelt appeared to like the OSS director's memos, which certainly offered more interesting prose than the thick bureaucratic text typically reaching his desk from others. Donovan's style embraced some decidedly nonacademic phrases such as "that old fox" and "the final death-bed contortions of a putrefied Nazi diplomacy."

A CIA retrospective calls the R&A analytic effort "one of the few original contributions to the craft of intelligence" by the United States. Yet even a veteran of the service such as Cline recognized that this initial foray into presidential intelligence fell short of its promise. Not only did wartime analysts lack access to foreigners' intercepted communications—SIGINT, in national security jargon—but also their publications tended to provide far more background information than actionable insights. For example, R&A officers in 1945 produced a civil affairs handbook on Germany that reached a whopping two thousand pages. Hopes faded for a rigorous system to gather and assess useful intelligence for the commander in chief.

HARRY TRUMAN, ONLY RECENTLY a senator from Missouri, faced a steep learning curve when he assumed the presidency in April 1945.

During his less than twelve weeks as Roosevelt's vice president, Truman had picked up virtually nothing from the longest-serving president in American history to prepare him for the national security burdens he now faced. The ailing leader had spent much of early 1945 away from Washington, limiting his direct contact with Truman, outside of cabinet gatherings, to two inconsequential meetings. He excluded his VP from major discussions of foreign affairs, including his vision for the postwar world and his ideas regarding a US intelligence infrastructure after hostilities ended. Roosevelt even neglected to tell Truman about the production of the atomic bomb.

Truman, of course, found out about the Manhattan Project after taking office, using its product within four months to prompt Japan's surrender and end the war. The new president, who disliked Donovan, almost immediately accepted a suggestion from his budget director to disband the OSS. By October 1, R&A officers who had neither returned to academia nor found other employment were transferred as a group to the State Department.

Nevertheless, Truman came to believe that the consolidation of intelligence, not just its collection, was crucial—and that the Japanese would not have surprised the United States at Pearl Harbor if his predecessor had established a more robust intelligence system. He observed in his memoirs that national security information that could not be presented in "an intelligent and understandable form" to its customers remained "useless."

So Truman created the Central Intelligence Group (CIG), under the leadership of Rear Admiral Sidney Souers—the first director of central intelligence (DCI). The president lightened the mood at the founding meeting of the organization at the White House on January 24, 1946, handing Souers and military advisor William Leahy black cloaks, black hats, and wooden daggers while he read to them his directive bringing the CIG into existence. Truman described the DCI's first duty as "the correlation and evaluation of intelligence relating to the national security, and the appropriate dissemination within the Government of the resulting strategic and national policy intelligence." Truman did not explicitly mention current intelligence, such as daily analytic support for the president, but he clearly wanted it, complaining when conflicting reports reached his desk without any attempt at coordination.

CIG's Office of Reports and Estimates (ORE) attempted to meet his need with the first daily analytic product targeted at the president personally: the Daily Summary, a classified compilation of reports from across the government. The first issue, on February 15, 1946, had just two pages with six items, covering Germany, Turkey, Yugoslavia, China, French Indochina, and the appearance in Europe of forged "secret protocols" allegedly signed in 1945 by Washington and Moscow. In the months to come, the Daily Summary regularly highlighted reports about the USSR's aggressive global activities.

Even this initial publication spurred bureaucratic conflict. First, despite Truman's wish for a publication including all departmental information, his new product initially lacked SIGINT; years went by before the Daily Summary's successor actually included information from decrypted communications. Second, at the inaugural meeting on February 5, 1946, of the National Intelligence Authority (designed to oversee CIG's fledgling intelligence activities), secretary of state James Byrnes asserted that, as the president's primary advisor on foreign affairs, only *he* could deliver analysis on international developments to Truman. DCI Souers, who stayed in the job for less than five months, said that Byrnes won the day: "The result was agreement that the daily summaries should be 'actual statements.' The Department of State prepared its own digest, and so the President had two summaries on his desk." An article in the CIA's in-house journal, *Studies in Intelligence*, acknowledges that early copies of the Daily Summary "probably did little but confuse the President."

If Truman felt baffled, it didn't show. He noted the Daily Summary in his memoirs but gave no sign that its largely factual nature,

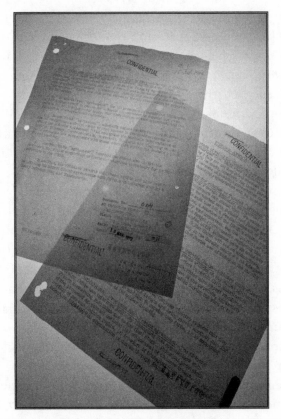

President Harry Truman's first Daily Summary, February 15, 1946. *Central Intelligence Agency website photo*

or the appearance of a more interpretive State Department cousin alongside it, troubled him. One of the document's earliest editors, R. Jack Smith, noted that Truman began asking for it almost daily.

Smith and his colleagues at ORE took the president's interest as license to push the boundaries. Under the more assertive leadership of a new DCI, Lieutenant General Hoyt Vandenberg, CIG's personnel expanded from roughly one hundred in June 1946 to more than eighteen hundred less than a year later. By the end of 1946, analysts occasionally complemented their raw reports with interpretations of the material. Hearing no objections from the Daily Summary's readers, during the following year they kept doing it, with increasing frequency. The lack of a direct feedback mechanism initially prevented anybody at CIG from knowing what Truman truly wanted. White House officials simply never informed Smith or his officers what they expected for the president. Finally, in 1947, presidential naval aide James Foskett told officers in ORE that "the President considers that he personally originated the *Daily*, that it is prepared in accordance with his own specifications, that it is well done, and that in its present form it satisfies his requirements."

Although aimed at Truman, the Daily Summary from the start also went to about fifteen other senior recipients. Some readers outside the White House dismissed the new publication. Secretary of state George Marshall read it for only two weeks after succeeding Byrnes in January 1947. Because most of the information in it came from State Department sources, which Marshall had already seen, his aide ended up showing him only two or three items from the *Daily* per week. An advisor to secretary of the navy James Forrestal said that his boss called the Daily Summary "valuable" but not "indispensable." One of the few senior officials around town who seemed to like it was secretary of war Robert Patterson, who read it "avidly and regularly."

It didn't take long for the existence of Truman's Daily Summary to hit the press. The *New York Times* in July 1946 said the president's new secret "newspaper" made him "the best informed Chief Executive in history on foreign affairs."

THE NATIONAL SECURITY ACT of 1947 restructured the US military services, established the National Security Council (NSC) and the Joint Chiefs of Staff, and created the Central Intelligence Agency on the foundation of the CIG. The law of the land codified analysts' duty: "to correlate and evaluate intelligence relating to the national security, and provide for the appropriate dissemination of such intelligence within the Government using where appropriate existing agencies and facilities." Led by Rear Admiral Roscoe Hillenkoetter—the third DCI, and the first to also serve as CIA director—the Agency thus kept producing the Daily Summary for Truman.* In a practice that most of Truman's successors would reject, the president frequently received his copy personally from the DCI.

---

* From 1947 to 2005, directors of central intelligence (DCIs) both managed the intelligence community and ran the Central Intelligence Agency. For convenience, references hereafter most often use the title "CIA director." In April 2005, the Intelligence Reform and Terrorism Prevention Act split these duties between a new position, the director of national intelligence (DNI), and the director of the CIA (DCIA).

Authors of pieces in the publication found themselves asked quickly to assess controversial topics for the president. During the war scare of early 1948—sparked by a cable from the US military governor in Germany warning the Pentagon about a coming Soviet attack on the West—analysts pushed back in the March 16 Daily Summary: "CIA does not believe that the USSR is presently prepared to risk war in the pursuit of its aims in Europe." Within months, as the Soviets ratcheted up pressure on the Western powers by blockading West Berlin, the Agency's experts similarly wrote for Truman: "The Soviet action . . . has two possible objectives: either to force the Western powers to negotiate on Soviet terms regarding Germany or, failing that, to force a Western power withdrawal from Berlin. The USSR does not seem ready to force a definite showdown." On June 26, 1950, the day after North Korea invaded the South, the Daily Summary included this text: "In sponsoring the aggression in Korea, the Kremlin probably calculated that no firm or effective countermeasures would be taken by the West. However, the Kremlin is not willing to undertake a global war at this time."

And yet daily intelligence reports for the president still lacked access to much US government information. In January 1949, the so-called Dulles-Jackson-Correa Committee, which the NSC had tasked to explore the effectiveness of the new intelligence system, found that "approximately ninety per cent of the contents of the *Daily Summary* is derived from State Department sources. . . . There are occasional comments by the Central Intelligence Agency on portions of the *Summary*, but these, for the most part, appear gratuitous and lend little weight to the material itself." Jack Smith, who directed the CIA's current intelligence unit, acknowledged in September 1950 that State Department cables dominated the Daily Summary. He laid the blame at the feet of other departments for withholding from the Agency sensitive materials, such as General MacArthur's reports from Tokyo and various messages sent in to the Joint Chiefs of Staff. Smith urged his bosses to "make urgent efforts on a high level, as I have repeatedly requested be done, to have the sensitive cables of the Defense Department made available to CIA."

Such high-level efforts would come sooner than expected. A new, widely respected DCI, General Walter Bedell "Beetle" Smith, took the Agency's reins in October 1950. He possessed the most impressive background yet for the office, having served as secretary of the General Staff under General George Marshall early in World War II, chief of staff for General Dwight Eisenhower from 1942 to 1945, and ambassador to the USSR. The only thing stronger than his resume was his legendary temper, which he used liberally to smash through bureaucratic obstacles.

Within three months of Beetle Smith's arrival at the CIA, the Office of Current Intelligence (OCI)—the Agency's collection of analysts who would provide daily intelligence to the president for almost thirty years—took shape and began revamping the Agency's finished product line. The Daily Summary ended on February 20, 1951, with an issue covering Soviet leader Joseph Stalin's comments in an interview, Prime Minister Josip Broz Tito's machinations in Yugoslavia, and the USSR's military operations in China. Each item passed on comments from US embassy cables or military attachés without any analysis.

The following week, the all-source Current Intelligence Bulletin debuted. From the start, it differed clearly from its predecessor. First of all, each item in the inaugural issue on February 28 included analytic commentary. All presidents from this point forward would consistently see in their daily intelligence book not only summaries of raw reports but also assessments from CIA experts. Second, four of this first edition's six pieces focused on information from communications intercepts; only two remained based on State Department reporting and foreign media information. Such SIGINT appeared regularly in daily intelligence for the president after this.

The Current Intelligence Bulletin initially went only to a select few top-tier officials, listed inside the front cover of the first issue: Truman, the secretary of state, the secretary of defense, the chairman of the Joint Chiefs of Staff, and the three service chiefs. Soon thereafter, thirteen copies went outside the Agency, including to General Dwight Eisenhower, supreme Allied commander in Europe (SACEUR). However, errors tainted the product's first few weeks. In a prominent example, one piece in March indicated that North Korea had missiles. A follow-up item a few days later admitted that upon retranslation, it was clear that the meaning of the Korean word was "radar," not "missiles." Despite such glitches, the new product pleased Truman, who wrote the same month to Smith: "Dear Bedel [*sic*], I have been reading the Intelligence Bulletin and I am highly impressed with it. I believe you have hit the jackpot with this one. Sincerely, Harry Truman."

OCI officers knew little about how Truman actually used the Current Intelligence Bulletin during his remaining two years in office. However, they were pleased when he told a group of CIA employees as he was departing:

> This agency puts the information of vital importance to the President in his hands. He has to know what is going on everywhere at home and abroad, so that he can intelligently make the decisions that are necessary to keep the government running. . . . Those of you who are deep in the Central Intelligence Agency know what goes on around the world—know what is necessary for the President to know every morning. I am briefed every day on all the world, on everything that takes place from one end of the world to the other, all the way around—by both the poles and the other way.

WAR HERO DWIGHT EISENHOWER entered the presidency in 1953 with orders of magnitude more international experience than Harry Truman had had some eight years earlier. He had served as SACEUR to close out the German theater in World War II, after earlier experience overseas in the Philippines and Central America. He had worked closely with British and French leaders and even traveled to Moscow after the war. For the first half of 1952, while serving as SACEUR, he joined the small (at that point) circle of readers of the top-level Current Intelligence Bulletin.

He also carried forward into his new job a rigid pattern for receiving and processing intelligence information and for making decisions—an approach that reduced the importance of the Agency's daily intelligence product for the next eight years. When asked how he wanted his CIA briefings, Eisenhower said, "I would much rather have it at the NSC level so all my staff and all of us can hear the same thing each time rather than to have a personal briefing." Thus, Agency analysts shifted their primary emphasis from writing presidentially relevant information in the Bulletin to preparing a steady stream of papers and briefing materials for the weekly NSC gathering, which Eisenhower chaired virtually every Thursday for eight years.

Robert Cutler, one of Eisenhower's national security advisors, asserts that his boss made the vast majority of his national security policy decisions through this formal process.

Although he and Eisenhower had shared a close relationship during the war, Smith did not regularly brief the president alone—a situation that continued under Allen Dulles, who succeeded Smith as CIA chief in February 1953. "Every President has his own system," Dulles noted. "Under Eisenhower the briefing system was quite largely developed around the meetings of the National Security Council." The director started each meeting with an intelligence presentation— which could take up 25 percent of the session—covering the world's hot spots, fielding questions from the NSC members, and then spending most of his time on that meeting's predetermined topic. An assistant took notes and produced charts or maps synchronized with the director's commentary.

Officers in the Directorate of Intelligence (DI), formed in early 1952 to consolidate analytic functions in the Agency, accordingly shifted their focus away from the Bulletin (which stayed in print, just with less focus on the president as a customer) and toward support for the director's frequent NSC briefings. The schedule of topics for forthcoming NSC sessions engendered an assembly line of policy papers that often had little to do with crises of the day. "I can remember an occasion when the newspaper headlines were along the lines of, 'NSC Meets as War Clouds Loom over Taiwan Strait,'" recalled Dick Lehman, who in the early 1950s was a young current intelligence analyst. "They were right: the NSC did meet, but it discussed a paper on policy toward Italy, which had been in gestation for six months, because that was the agenda, set months in advance."

Lehman got to see Eisenhower in action once, at an NSC meeting near the end of the president's term. Lehman sat in the back row of the Cabinet Room, behind Dulles's seat, where he could manipulate the maps and briefing boards to which Dulles would refer moments later. All rose as Eisenhower entered the room, and the briefing began with a discussion on Communist China's shelling of offshore islands controlled by the nationalists. The president looked at Dulles and asked, "What are the calibers of the Communist guns?"

Dulles looked behind him. The back-benching Lehman quickly replied, "Just small stuff, 75-mm or less." Eisenhower nodded, the meeting went on, and Lehman never spoke up again during this or any other NSC session during that administration. However, the young analyst believed that current intelligence publications could, and should, focus more effectively on the needs of the Agency's top customer. Lehman would translate thought into action during the next administration and, in so doing, influence how presidents have received daily assessments of foreign developments for the five decades since.

PRESIDENTIAL AIDE GENERAL ANDREW Goodpaster, in lieu of an Agency officer, briefed Eisenhower at least twice a week. He used the Current Intelligence Bulletin—along with products from the State Department, the Defense Department, and the Joint Chiefs of Staff—to develop an oral presentation because his boss avoided reading daily written reports himself. The Bulletin became seen less as a vehicle for getting intelligence analysis to the president than as a product for informing a wider cross section of national security officials. As a result, its distribution outside the Agency had expanded to thirty-three copies by 1954 and forty-eight copies by mid-1957.

Eisenhower grumbled in early 1954 that the intelligence coming to him lacked context for its assessments of the Soviet threat and failed to differentiate between the USSR's capabilities and its intentions. The first concern was understandable: analysts at the CIA typically spent more time focusing on reports relating to foreign targets than to comparisons of US and Allied postures to those targets. But the fact that his intelligence analysis failed to distinguish clearly between what the Soviets *could* do with their resources and what they were *likely* to do must have infuriated the man who would leave office warning the American people about the societal implications of assuming the worst merely from an enemy's capabilities.

In February 1956, Eisenhower established the President's Board of Consultants on Foreign Intelligence Activities—which, five years later, became the President's Foreign Intelligence Advisory Board. Goodpaster says that Eisenhower, concerned about the quality of intelligence reaching him, tasked this group of experts to examine the entire structure of US intelligence. A new focus was placed on long-form National Intelligence Estimates (NIEs), which found an easy place in the step-by-step NSC process. Even with the rise of the

NIE, director Allen Dulles took time to write an item for the Bulletin personally in 1957, an unusually speculative and long piece (more than two pages) relating the difficulties facing Cuban dictator Fulgencio Batista. But Eisenhower still seemed to avoid it. An OCI internal memo in October 1957 summed up the general frustration with the Bulletin's reception: "The present publication is not read by top officials. It is not established as 'must' reading. At best, portions of it may be conveyed to these officials by briefing officers."

Agency officers tried one more angle. In January 1958, they replaced the Current Intelligence Bulletin with the Central Intelligence Bulletin (CIB), a new-look document with more material. The first issue featured a "Daily Brief" section, with twelve items of six to eight lines each, followed by several pages of articles addressing many of these short items in more depth. The articles also broke new ground by showing source document numbers so readers could look up original reports themselves. Trying to appeal to Eisenhower's fondness for graphics, producers of the revamped CIB soon added a world map with red arrows indicating the areas covered by that issue's items. A CIA internal retrospective notes that the new CIB successfully forecasted developments such as anti-US demonstrations during Vice President Nixon's May 1958 trip to Latin America and the political crisis in France the same month that led to Charles de Gaulle's return to politics, but admits that it missed a few big calls: the Baathist coup in Iraq in July 1958, the time and manner of Batista's fall in Cuba at the end of 1958, and the Tibetan revolt starting in March 1959. Although the dissemination quickly rose to ninety copies outside of the Agency, there is no evidence that the president himself took an interest in it.

CHAPTER TWO

FOR THE PRESIDENT'S
EYES ONLY

JOHN F. KENNEDY ENTERED office in January 1961 with a decidedly different approach to national security decision making than his predecessor. Where Eisenhower had enforced a rigorous structure of briefings and National Security Council meetings before taking foreign policy actions, Kennedy adopted an improvisational style built around informal conversations. A top CIA analyst during Kennedy's term later likened the new president's less bureaucratic approach to a "pickup touch football game crossed with a Harvard seminar." Eisenhower relied heavily on formal input from the State Department and the Pentagon to prepare him for decisions. Kennedy, though, preferred ad hoc consultations with close aides to long papers and longer official procedures. Robert Amory, the CIA's deputy director for intelligence (DDI) until March 1962, said Kennedy "wasn't going to fool around with chain of command or logical places; he was going to go to human beings on problems."

The State Department drew Kennedy's particular ire. Just after his inauguration, he asked a friend how many people worked there. After hearing the answer, he offered his view: "Hell, they've got their own damned government over there. I'm not going to be able to change their thinking." Because the young president saw Washington's established bureaucracies as obstacles to quick policy formulation and execution, the relatively small and agile CIA looked good by comparison. "I don't care what it is," he told national security advisor McGeorge Bundy just after taking office, "CIA is the place I have to go. The State Department is four or five days to answer a simple yes or no."

Kennedy read voraciously, valuing the kind of crisp, insightful prose he had learned during his brief stint as a journalist for the *Chicago Herald-American* before entering politics. As commander in chief, he got the majority of his information not from classified intelligence analysis but from the public press. His military aide, Major General Chester "Ted" Clifton, noted that Kennedy started each day reading daily newspapers in bed: "He consumed five or six papers in his own special method of scanning, halting, exclaiming, studying." Quickly, Kennedy's cabinet and senior White House staff learned to scour these same dailies to prepare for his inevitable questions. One day, early in his service as special military assistant to the president, General Maxwell Taylor asked Clifton to put him on the distribution list for the newspaper summary that he assumed White House staffers prepared for Kennedy. Clifton replied that there was no such summary and told Taylor that everyone read the newspapers frantically just to keep up.

The president's ability to absorb so much, so rapidly—picked up in a month-long speed reading course, from which he claimed he could take in 1,200 words a minute—did not mean that he wanted to struggle with long, wordy documents. Instead, he preferred a text he could get through easily. After just one week on the job, he asked an assistant handing him a thick booklet of briefing papers, "Look, I've only got a half hour today. Do I have to read it all?" Soon after, Clifton urged the CIA's current intelligence chief to keep memoranda and reports for Kennedy double-spaced and down to about two pages. The message was clear: dense, bureaucratic prose had served Dwight Eisenhower just fine, but it would not fly with *this* president.

While Kennedy's loose, carefree style worked well on many issues, nothing spotlighted the downside to his approach more than Cuban exiles' failed invasion of their home island, with US funding and training, in April 1961 during the Bay of Pigs fiasco. Up to this point, he had great confidence asserting himself on domestic topics while grudgingly trusting the national security establishment on military and intelligence issues. He told aide Arthur Schlesinger that he assumed the professionals working those topics had "some secret skill not available to ordinary mortals." His takeaway from the Bay of Pigs was clear: an intelligence failure had led to bad advice, which in turn prompted a bad decision. The debacle, per Kennedy's counsel and primary speechwriter Ted Sorensen, changed the president's method of managing foreign policy. Presidential lawyer Clark Clifford said the event pushed Kennedy to question established truths as never before: "He might make mistakes in the future, but they would be *his* mistakes, not someone else's."

It also prompted a reexamination of how Kennedy should receive his intelligence analysis. Ted Clifton told the CIA's OCI chief, Huntington "Ting" Sheldon, that Kennedy had balked at continuing to receive his daily intelligence in the same way as before the Bay of Pigs crisis—setting in motion a new system that would eventually produce the President's Daily Brief.

ARMY VETERAN AND HARVARD graduate Dick Lehman never intended to work as a CIA analyst, much less as the Agency's "Mr. Current Intelligence," as he became known after decades in the business. When a recruiter came to Charlottesville, Virginia, in 1948 to find Russian-speakers for the CIA, Lehman had never even heard of the newly formed intelligence agency. The recruiter focused on Lehman's nearly completed master's degree in Russian studies from the University of Virginia, for which he had taken every course remotely related to the Soviet Union—including classes in the Russian language. His penchant for precise, clear writing, which would prove to be crucial in the years to come, added to his appeal. Lehman had not been considering an intelligence career—he was simply looking for a job—but the Agency's Directorate of Intelligence, where analysts informed their judgments about foreign threats with a wide array of classified intelligence reporting, looked like a fine place to start his civilian work.

Lehman's first boss told him bluntly, "Whatever you do, just remember one thing—the Soviet Union is up to no good." Starting as a P-1 (professional grade one) analyst of Soviet affairs, with a salary of $3,000 a year, he internalized the core message about the intelligence profession underlying that advice: a good analyst of foreign affairs is, above all, a skeptic who must look beyond the obvious for deeper

Dick Lehman, CIA's "Mr. Current Intelligence." *Courtesy David Lehman*

motives and implications. He was promoted four times by 1952, and during Eisenhower's second term he helped senior managers prepare Agency director Allen Dulles for National Security Council briefings. Managers noted his poise during the stressful process of developing and delivering daily presentations for the legendary Dulles, whose true love was not analysis but intelligence operations. During Lehman's briefings, Dulles would often lean back in his recliner and pay less attention to the assessments than to the baseball game on his television. He exasperated the junior analyst with outbursts like "Good pitcher—can't hit!" just as Lehman hit key points.

By the time Kennedy assumed the presidency in January 1961, Lehman stood tall as an analytic leader within the CIA's Office of Current Intelligence. But the new president presented a challenge. How do you serve a man whose entire approach to foreign policy clashes with existing institutions?

"THERE IS NO EXPERIENCE you can get that can possibly prepare you adequately for the Presidency," Kennedy told reporters in December 1962. The demands of the office—and Kennedy's bias for clarity and action, as opposed to waiting for the bureaucracy to work—certainly made it hard for his national security aides to help him. This was especially true given the president's propensity to jump into the weeds on pet topics. "Domestic policy," he said, "can only defeat us; foreign policy can kill us." For example, as the US government struggled with developments in Laos in the early months of the administration, Kennedy focused on the country obsessively. He created a task force, directed it to give him daily progress reports, and sent crisp orders to the US embassy in Vientiane, prompting Ambassador Winthrop Brown to remark how much clearer communication becomes "when the President is your desk officer."

White House officials soon identified a core problem: Kennedy was proving unable to stay in one place long enough for substantive national security discussions. NSC executive secretary Bromley Smith tried to give the president formal presentations, such as those Eisenhower had preferred, but Kennedy "was rocking in his chair" and nearly walked out of the sessions. "We couldn't say to President Kennedy: 'You just sit still and just listen.' This was an option the staff doesn't have. But we never tried briefing again because we were never certain he would not get up and walk out."

In the wake of the Bay of Pigs fiasco, an exasperated McGeorge Bundy finally vented to Kennedy, laying out his annoyance with the president's style. "I hope you'll be in a good mood," the national security advisor wrote. "We need some help from you so that we can serve you better." He offered his diagnosis: "We do have a problem of management; centrally it is a problem of your use of time and your use of your staff. You have revived the government, which is an enormous gain, but in the process you have overstrained your own calendar, limited your chances for thought, and used your staff incompletely." Bundy then proposed a new approach:

> First: you should set aside a real and regular time each day for national security discussion and action. This is not just a matter of intelligence briefing—though that is important and currently not well done by either Clifton or me (we can't get you to sit still, and we are not really professionals). . . . Truman and Eisenhower did their daily dozen in foreign affairs the first thing in the morning, and a couple of weeks ago you asked me to begin to meet you on this basis. I have succeeded in catching you on three mornings, for a total of about 8 minutes, and I conclude that this is not really how you like to begin the day. . . . Right now it is so hard to get to you with anything not urgent and immediate that about half the papers and reports you personally ask for are never shown to you because by the time you are available you clearly have lost interest in them.

Bundy's candid memo to the president ended with an appeal to Kennedy's obsession with efficiency: "All this, if it is done right, will strengthen, not weaken, your Secretary of State, your Secretary of Defense, and your head of CIA. But most of all it should be useful to you." He urged Kennedy to begin taking intelligence briefings, with Ted Clifton on hand, at least three times a week directly from a "professional" CIA officer.

Clifton shared Bundy's frustration. Up to this point, the military assistant had been assembling for the president every morning a stack of intelligence reading, including items from the Central Intelligence Bulletin and various State Department and Defense Department materials. Bundy or Clifton would take the large package into the Oval Office, where the imposing pile of paper often sat unread. Clifton found himself thinking there was simply too much screening of material each morning. Lacking background in the nuances of intelligence analysis, he felt increasingly uncomfortable trying to discern quickly which reports to bring to the president's attention.

The issue came to a head in spring 1961. Kennedy found himself blindsided by events that had been reported in the regular intelligence publications but had not made it through Clifton's screening. Kennedy told his brother Bobby, the attorney general, who in turn came down hard on Clifton for failing to get key information to the president. Clifton knew something had to change. After struggling over how best to serve Kennedy's intelligence needs, he reached out in June 1961 to Ting Sheldon, one of the CIA "professionals" whom Bundy had referred to in his memo. "Bring one of your writers over," he said.

SHELDON GRABBED DICK LEHMAN. The two career intelligence analysts visited Clifton at the White House on Thursday, June 15. After exchanging brief pleasantries, they watched quietly while Clifton opened a large folder, pulled out the Central Intelligence Bulletin, and dropped it on the table. He returned to the folder, removing a classified Department of Defense document. And then a State Department paper came out. To Lehman's surprise, Clifton kept going, bringing out report after report to show his visitors the mountain of intelligence products he received every day from the CIA and various other bureaus and departments. These papers, Clifton told them, competed every morning for his, and Kennedy's, time.

"What I need," he said, "is something that will have everything in it that is worth the President's attention, everything that is worth his knowing in all these things so I don't have to fuss with them."

Clifton painted a picture of what he wanted: a short document with minimal jargon and no annoying classification markers, both of which characterized virtually everything he saw from the intelligence community. And, knowing well from direct personal experience the president's inability to sit still for formal presentations—much less his full "daily dozen" in national security affairs, as Bundy had said—Clifton wanted a document that Kennedy could fold and carry around in his breast pocket, to read at his leisure between meetings during the day.

Lehman caught Sheldon's eye and resisted the urge to smirk. During the closing months of the Eisenhower administration, Lehman had mused about just such a potential CIA publication. Recently, in fact, he had been chatting with his OCI colleagues about a finished intelligence report specifically for the new president—a product so limited in distribution that it would include highly classified CIA operational reports and other sources deemed too sensitive for the Central Intelligence Bulletin. He envisioned something written in conversational language that would appeal to the young president much more than the "officialese" that regularly muddled other products.

Clifton's appeal was music to Lehman's ears. "What he asked us to do," he later recalled, "was what we wanted to do." Less than twenty-four hours later Clifton had in his hands a dry run of the new product: the President's Intelligence Checklist.

The development of the Checklist was only half the job. In most cases, getting the publication out of the CIA without any upper-level management interference would have been just as difficult. But in a rare coincidence, the three officials above Sheldon within the CIA hierarchy—director Dulles, deputy director General Charles Cabell, and DDI Robert Amory—were all out of town. So Sheldon boldly assumed the authority to communicate with the president, pushing the new product out the door before anyone above him in the management chain could weigh in or object. And it worked. Clifton liked what he saw so much that he took the first "live" issue of the Checklist to Kennedy the very next day.

STARTING A FEW WEEKS after John Kennedy's inauguration in January 1961, the First Family had been spending fewer weekends in Washington than at Glen Ora, their leased country retreat just south of Middleburg, Virginia. Only twenty-five minutes from the White House by helicopter—roughly an hour by car—the four-hundred-acre hunt-country estate appealed both to Jackie's horse-riding habit and to her desire to escape the White House. Renting Glen Ora had proven challenging. Clark Clifford, the president's lawyer, called on owner Gladys Tartiere three times before she agreed to let the Kennedys use the property. Ultimately, an appeal to her patriotism worked. Clifford convinced her that it would be downright un-American, given the presidency's great burdens, to refuse the Kennedys' request to use the estate.

Unlike the White House, which Jackie deridingly called "Washington," Glen Ora was the place she considered home—referring to it as her "salvation." The ample riding space gave her the freedom and peace she seldom had within the confines of the nation's capital. Within weeks of the Kennedys moving in, the Army Signal Corps set up a trailer with switchboards behind the stables to ensure that the president could instantly contact top aides in Washington and overseas even while relaxing in the countryside. Kennedy spent weekends at Glen Ora regularly enough that on the first day of the Bay of Pigs invasion (Saturday, April 17, 1961), he made a point to head there so the White House press corps would not presume something momentous was brewing.

Exactly two months later, on Saturday, June 17, Kennedy had been enjoying a morning dip in the estate's outdoor pool—he swam as often as twice a day, both at the White House and at his country retreat, to relax and to relieve his perennially aching back—when Clifton arrived with the inaugural, seven-page President's Intelligence Checklist in hand, finding Kennedy sitting on the diving board between laps. Lehman had designed and developed the document virtually overnight specifically for Kennedy, who flipped through the 8½-by-8-inch booklet, which held fourteen 2-sentence pieces, six slightly longer notes, and a few small maps. The Checklist was easy to skim and then set aside for reading in depth after a few more laps. It hooked Kennedy, and he approved the continued production of the Checklist on the spot.

Glen Ora's swimming pool, where Kennedy saw his first Checklist on June 17, 1961. *Courtesy John F. Kennedy Presidential Library*

Sheldon finally reported to his bosses on Monday what the current intelligence folks had been up to, after Lehman and his colleagues had ensured that the president had his second copy. Continuing the Checklist at that point was an easy sell to the CIA leadership, because Clifton had already told them to "go ahead—so far, so good."

Ted Sorensen said that wherever his boss went during his two and half remaining years as commander in chief, he would receive the Checklist, thereby spurring a dialogue between the president and intelligence analysts like nothing the country had ever seen.

SO THAT THE CHECKLIST could include analysis based on the most sensitive intelligence sources, only a handful of officers in the CIA's Office of Current Intelligence worked on it. And its distribution to actual readers remained extremely limited even after that first Kennedy-only weekend. The White House received one, of course. But while most other CIA products had wide dissemination, at least among leaders of the foreign policy establishment and the upper tier of Agency management, for several months the only other copies of the

Checklist went to the director, Allen Dulles (until November 1961, when John McCone replaced him), and into the official Agency production files. The PICL—as the President's Intelligence Checklist became known inside the CIA, leading to jokes that the OCI was a "pickle factory"—had no further internal distribution apart from Sheldon's boss, Robert Amory. Even then, Sheldon and Lehman let Amory see Checklist items only *after* they went to the president.

Lehman naturally led the effort to write or compile Checklist items. R. Jack Smith, who became the director of current intelligence during Kennedy's term, noted that Lehman's "warm, direct, somewhat Thoreau-like style" drove a uniquely readable product. Writing seemed to reside in his genes. His father, Edwin, had crafted poetry, editing a published anthology that included some of his own works, and his grandmother Margaret had a penchant for humorous doggerel. Lehman credited his Harvard introductory writing course for honing his skills. There, he had drafted an essay every day that was torn apart—sentence by sentence, word by word—teaching him that crisp prose came from precision and hard work.

The production of each day's issue began the day before, when OCI officers, initially just Lehman and another OCI analyst, modified analytic articles from other Agency publications, such as the Central Intelligence Bulletin, or wrote original products based on highly sensitive sources not approved for the Bulletin. Lehman or others might roll into the office before 5:00 a.m. to incorporate late-breaking developments into the Checklist and ensure that anything relevant coming into the Agency by 7:30 a.m. would make it to Kennedy. After a final edit, a senior OCI officer—usually OCI chief Sheldon, Lehman, or a colleague—hand-carried the Top Secret document in a locked bag to the White House to ensure that the president's top advisors saw it by 8:30. There was no actual briefing of the product: most of the time, Bundy, Clifton, and/or Bromley Smith would simply read the Checklist in the presence of the OCI officer, who sat there solely to answer questions or take queries back to the CIA for relevant experts to address later that day.

Kennedy usually awoke around 7:30 in his second-floor White House bedroom, read newspapers, placed a few calls, bathed, shaved, ate breakfast, and took an elevator to the first floor. After he arrived in the Oval Office (between 9:00 and 9:30 on most days), Bundy,

Clifton, or both would sit with the president as he read the Checklist, if he had time to do so in the morning. More often, they gathered his feedback on its content later in the day, after he had skimmed it during breaks in his schedule. Clifton would write a short memo with the president's reactions and taskings, and he or Bundy would call the OCI to let the Agency know what had happened. The Checklist's authors and editors occasionally waited until later in the week to hear how a particular edition went over with Kennedy because he held on to the Checklist for a day or two, waiting for the time to flip through it.

Regular, if indirect, interaction between intelligence analysts and the president had thus begun. Requests from the president for information and analysis started pouring into the CIA, usually via Clifton or Bromley Smith. Lieutenant General Marshall Carter, who took over as the CIA's deputy director in April 1962, asked the Agency's executive director about the standard operating procedures for such requests. "Almost all requests for memos," the reply said, "arise in the course of the daily 9 a.m. staff meetings in the White House which are attended by an OCI official who delivers the Checklist. Discussions and bull-sessions involving the staff lead to requests for memos and the OCI man gets tagged. Presidential requests for memos are usually laid on the OCI by General Clifton who sits with the President when the latter reads the *Checklist*."

ALLEN DULLES, the CIA's director for the first five months of the Checklist's existence, tellingly described the Checklist as "snappy, short, but fairly, at the same time, reasonably comprehensive . . . It might be four or five pages, and on these pages we'd say—here are the important things that have happened in the last twenty-four hours, if anything important had happened."

Kennedy learned a lot, quickly, about the previous day's developments around the globe from the snapshots in the Checklist, as one issue from February 1962 reveals. It includes nine short pieces ranging from one long sentence to nearly a full page, on a wide array of topics: Berlin (two pieces), the Soviet Union, France, Laos, West New Guinea, Soviet-Chinese relations, Congo, and Ghana. The Soviet-China item illustrates the product's terse style. A descriptive title ("Soviets and Chinese greet twelfth anniversary of their treaty of alliance with something less than enthusiasm") introduces this—only slightly longer—text: "In perfunctory ceremonies, the Chinese implied that Khrushchev rather than Mao was responsible for weakening of the alliance. The Soviets remarked that the USSR's great military power would be used to protect only 'friendly' Socialist countries. Last year, they had repeated Khrushchev's pledge of 1958 that the USSR would consider 'an attack on China as an attack on the Soviet Union.'"

After these nine short items, which fill only four pages, two other pages appear. First, a sheet titled "Notes" contains four separate blurbs of just one or two sentences each, such as "The Turkish government has begun a new series of arrests of Menderes supporters; this will please the army but will not contribute to political stability" and "We do not see any great significance in Castro's relinquishment of the presidency of the National Land Reform Institute." A page from the intelligence community's Watch Committee closes out this Checklist, listing brief assessments about the likelihood of Sino-Soviet military action, military moves tied to Berlin, Communist activity in Laos, and Viet Cong action in South Vietnam. Successive Checklists often contained such short notes pages, Watch Committee conclusions, or both. And occasionally Lehman and his colleagues even included "raw" documents, such as a cable from a US embassy or a report from a foreign intelligence asset, that the president might appreciate seeing.

OCI analysts kept their focus on the biggest foreign policy events of the roughly thousand-day Kennedy presidency, such as West Berlin (which continued to be a flash point after earlier Cold War crises), Soviet nuclear tests (especially when frequent tests resumed in 1962), Southeast Asia (centering on South Vietnam and Laos), and Cuba. Much of what appeared in early copies of the Checklist is largely descriptive, lacking what would qualify as insightful analysis. For example, Checklist authors reported in August 1962 about Cuba's reactions to small raids in just four sentences, ending with this pithy assertion: "These incidents have given Havana the jitters."

Although Lehman and his OCI colleagues used highly classified intercepted communications and intelligence reports from spies around the world to craft articles for the Checklist, only rarely did any item tell the president specifics about that reporting base. For example, the Checklist on July 12, 1962, noted, "The [Chinese] Nationalists are dropping hints that we should provide them with more advanced jets in view of the Communist air buildup along the coast." Left unanswered: What exactly were these "hints"? To whom were the Nationalists dropping them? Similarly, a Checklist several weeks earlier had related, "Nehru's daughter has admitted that he has a prostate condition, which she fears may be malignant, and thinks he may undergo surgery, possibly in September." To whom had Nehru's daughter admitted this? How did the CIA find out about it? Kennedy's frequent requests to the OCI for more information after reading Checklist items suggests that the analysts would have served the president better by including in the text richer details about their sources.

To remind the president that intelligence usually paints an incomplete picture, OCI analysts often included in Checklist articles language conveying their lack of full conviction regarding their own assessments. A great example is in the Checklist of June 19, 1962: "As time goes on and the extraordinary Chinese Communist military buildup continues, our confidence in the assessment that this movement is primarily defensive in purpose is dwindling. We are unable to find any fully satisfactory explanation for this large movement, and we therefore feel that the possibility of some offensive action (perhaps against the offshore islands) cannot be dismissed." The president understood that analysts believed Chinese offensive action had become more likely than before, but the text fell short of making a call about the prospects for a Chinese Communist attack, much less the probable time and place of any aggression. In other cases, Checklist pieces conveyed bottom lines more efficiently and with greater confidence, such as "President Goulart [of Brazil] will probably propose that foreign minster Dantas be moved up to prime minister" and "The Soviet airlift into Laos has fallen off sharply since late last week."

The Checklist's authors took seriously Clifton's appeals to write specifically for John Kennedy, with clearer prose than that in other intelligence offerings of the era. "The stuff for Kennedy was really very much leaving out any background at all," Lehman recalled. "You assumed that he knew everything that had gone before, so it was just the newest developments that you had to report to him and what they might mean." Gone are the long, clunky bureaucratic "word blocks" that dominated most formal government reports. Instead, Checklist articles were full of punchy words and phrases:

- On a simmering border conflict between Thailand and Cambodia: "The King of Thailand, besides calling publicly for even tempers on the temple issue, is doing what he can in private to hold back the hotheads."
- On South Vietnam and Cambodia: "Meanwhile, we are hearing once more that Diem's brother Nhu may be getting ready to go gunning for Sihanouk."
- On the aftermath of Peru's military coup: "As of now, the government is neither fish nor fowl, being somewhere between the constitution and a military dictatorship."
- On Egypt's intervention in the Yemeni civil war: "The Saudis, fed up with the unending overflights of their territory by Egyptian aircraft, have obliquely warned Cairo to knock it off."

FOR FOURTEEN DAYS IN October 1962, the world stood on the brink of superpower war. The discovery of Soviet nuclear missiles in Cuba brought the United States and the Soviet Union closer to a nuclear exchange than at any other time in history. The Checklist had covered that fall's increase of Soviet arms shipments to, and troops in, Cuba. But OCI analysts did not know, and left unaddressed for the president, the purpose of the buildup. We now know that the first Soviet missiles arrived in Cuba in early September, with surface-to-surface missile equipment getting to the outskirts of the western town of San Cristobal on September 17–18. The Soviets and Cubans had disguised their missile site scouting and construction activity during the spring and summer through an elaborate campaign to deny intelligence collection and deceive American watchers. The administration unwittingly assisted these efforts by standing down surveillance overflights of the island in the late summer and early fall, just when they would have been most useful.

Lehman and others in the OCI wrote frequently about overall activity in Cuba. On August 4, the Checklist reported, "Eleven Soviet merchant ships are on their way to Havana and we strongly suspect they are carrying arms. Such a delivery would not be far short of the total amount of arms delivered in the first half of 1962." No mention was made of what types of arms could be included. The text certainly fails to cite any missile cargo. A few days later, the Checklist authors wrote, "Soviet shipments to Cuba have been arriving on an unprecedented scale since mid-July. Some 32 vessels are involved;

at least half of these we believe to be carrying arms. Five passenger ships with a total capacity of about 3,000 persons have already arrived. Some of the personnel are said to be Soviet technicians, and we have no reason to doubt this. We do not believe there are any combat troops among them." In fact, the scale of the USSR's buildup dramatically exceeded that estimate provided in the Checklist: some forty thousand Soviet troops had arrived in Cuba by October. The CIA continued writing in the Checklist about developments related to the mysterious arrival of Soviet forces. On August 23, an item simply titled "Cuba" began:

a. Most of our information from within Cuba on the influx of Soviet equipment and technicians has come from Cuban sources. We now have several reports from the British Embassy whose people have been out looking.

b. They have spotted at least one camp southeast of Havana, where the number of vehicles suggested the presence of "many" more than the 200 presumed young Russians they did see, and where a radio antenna field had already been erected. This they think could be connected with radio monitoring.

c. Their information on the equipment coming in—some "hard" some not—leads them to suggest that "an expert might consider the possibility of anti-aircraft rockets and radar."

Additional items in the Checklists during the next week updated the president on things such as the increasing budget of the Soviet Chief Engineering Directorate's representative in Cuba—from $80,000 in July to at least $175,000 for August—but warned him, "We are not able on the basis of evidence available at this time to determine the precise nature or purpose of the intensified program of Bloc military assistance and construction in Cuba."

The earliest indication about missiles in Cuba that made it through to the current intelligence officers came from a single intercepted message on April 11, 1962, sent to a Russian on the island who had previously been at the Soviet Union's Kapustin Yar missile test range. CIA analysts judged that fragment—and, later, Cuban oppositionists' reports about unusual activity in Cuba—too weak to include in the daily publications. Later in the year, they could not write about such information even if they wanted to. Intelligence community leaders had interpreted presidential advisors' concerns over possible leaks of intelligence about offensive weapons in Cuba as a proscription on including *any* analysis of the topic in finished intelligence products. So they put a gag order on the analysts unless or until they heard differently from Kennedy himself. The assistant director of the CIA's Office of Current Intelligence on September 12 put on paper for OCI staff the guidance that had been understood for some time: "We are under a White House injunction *not* to print in any publication which goes outside CIA any intelligence bearing on Cuban offensive military weapons."

Lehman considered the Checklist exempt from the ban due to its highly controlled distribution, but the injunction still stifled what he could include. Its writers drew information on Cuba largely from the CIA's Cuban Daily Summary, to which the prohibition *did* apply. Later he wrote that this effectively "[cut] the *Checklist* off from information on offensive weapons." In any event, it would not have made a big difference in the Checklist because, as Lehman assessed in an internal postmortem about intelligence analysis before the Cuban missile crisis, "at most the President might have learned that there was suspicious activity around San Cristobal slightly more than a week before he apparently did."

Kennedy announced to the world on the evening of October 22 that the Soviets had put missiles in Cuba and that the United States would "quarantine" Cuba until they were removed. Although the Checklist had covered the earlier Soviet military buildup on the island, the president received most of his intelligence on crisis developments during the Cuban missile crisis itself outside of the Checklist. During those fourteen days, relatively few pieces addressed Cuba and the Soviet Union. One interesting Checklist item from October 18 titled simply "Cuba" highlights air defense missiles but not the more alarming offensive missiles that prompted the crisis:

a. Our latest photography has turned up two more SA-2 surface-to-air missile sites, both in Oriente province. One of these, near the town of Cabanas, is the first site within SA-2 range of the air approaches to Guantanamo.

b. The photography also shows that one of the previously confirmed sites has now been abandoned, making the present total
   twenty-one.

c. Seven of the twelve sites observed on this occasion now have missiles on launcher [sic]; some of these are probably operational.

Kennedy managed the actual crisis via an expanded version
of the NSC, which he called the Executive Committee (or simply
ExComm). Members of the ad hoc group, including a dozen of the
government's top national security officials and a few other advisors,
met frequently to discuss options and advise the president. Because
the ExComm received briefings directly from a CIA missile expert
and the director of the National Photographic Interpretation Center,
the CIA's analysts used the Checklist largely to keep the president up
to speed on other world events. As Lehman said, "Why summarize
what the President already knew?"

That does not mean that the OCI in general, and Lehman in
particular, were out of the loop. Military analysts in the office were
writing pieces about the ground truth in Cuba for the ExComm
after reviewing the photography from reconnaissance flights. And
the OCI's political analysts predicted Russian and Cuban moves. The
breakneck pace of developments made the Checklist's twenty-four-
hour cycle too slow for a president who wanted information *now*. One
political analyst in the OCI who picked up his ringing phone must
have nearly fallen out of his chair upon hearing the voice of President
Kennedy, who called directly to get an update faster than the bureaucracy could provide it.

The act of delivering the Checklist downtown every day still provided Lehman a unique window on history as it unfolded. He took the
daily edition to the White House on the morning of Saturday, October 27—the final day of the crisis—when the NSC's Bromley Smith
showed him the text of a letter that had come in from Nikita Khrushchev the night before. The Soviet leader's proposal for a way out of
the crisis, which the CIA had not received, contained his now-famous
impassioned plea to Kennedy: "You and I should not now pull on the
ends of the rope in which you have tied a knot of war, because the
harder you and I pull, the tighter the knot will become. And a time

may come when this knot is tied so tight that the person who tied it is no longer capable of untying it, and then the knot will have to be cut." Lehman read the note quickly, committing as much to memory as possible. On his ride back to Langley from the White House, he re-created the text to pass on to his bosses at CIA headquarters.

The crisis ended with Khrushchev's agreement to remove Russian missiles from Cuba. The president's meetings on Cuba remained comprehensive enough to obviate the need for extensive Cuba coverage in the Checklist or via supplemental intelligence documents. On November 1, Clifton noted for the record, "The President read the checklist for this date. I have made the assumption that the President is getting all the information he needs on Cuba, and thus have not put any of the Cuba material before him."

KENNEDY READ THE CHECKLIST not to entertain himself but to act. He might simply scan it, storing tidbits away for future action. Much more often, its updates and analysis drove him to instruct his cabinet officers and top aides at the White House. Kennedy's actions after reading various Checklist items included:

- Suggesting that senior military officers be brought into negotiations with Portugal about the use of the Azores.
- Seeking assurances from Bundy that he planned a more complete briefing on Berlin than the situational update in the Checklist.
- Ordering his staff to give information about Chinese Communist activity in northern India to a group of prominent senators.
- Asking for the precise vote in the Dutch lower house's rejection of a resolution regarding West New Guinea.
- Directing his staff to prepare a story on US nuclear-powered aircraft, which the administration had canceled, in case the Soviet Union announced its own such capability.
- Asking for details about the woman who interpreted during the visit of Soviet first deputy premier Anastas Mikoyan.
- Directing Clifton to ensure that the US government do "everything it could" to prevent Ethiopian leader Haile Selassie from removing his country's troops from the Congo.

Kennedy sent instructions not only through White House staff channels but also directly to CIA leaders. "There would be quite a barrage of questions," said Dulles. "You'd often get telephone calls and so forth. . . . Sometimes you'd get them personally; sometimes you'd get them from the particular aide who was working with him on the particular matter for the National Security Council." By February 1963, the Checklist and its accompanying materials spurred requests for additional information so often that the CIA's deputy director, Marshall Carter, told the DDI to give him and Dulles's successor, John McCone, copies of *everything* the Agency's briefing officer took to the White House. "The Director and I must be protected on intelligence items which are covered during the White House sessions when the Checklist is delivered," he wrote.

The CIA's top managers and OCI analysts were pleased that their efforts drove such frequent action and prompted numerous requests for more information. "We tried very hard to live up to his high views of us," noted DDI Robert Amory. "I don't mean just at the high level. This had a very good morale effect all down the line in the analytical side of the CIA establishment. People were willing to work long hours and to come in at 3 o'clock in the morning because they knew damn well what they produced was read personally by the President immediately upon its delivery to the White House." His successor as DDI, former OCI chief Jack Smith, wrote that Kennedy engaged "enthusiastically" with the Checklist's producers, alternating between praise and criticism, once even offering that "boondocks" was an inappropriate word. Intelligence analysts loved this level of presidential engagement.

Ray Cline, Smith's deputy, didn't always appreciate Kennedy's attention. The presidential calls that he received usually came after Kennedy had read something that angered him—or when he sought high-confidence judgments that Cline found difficult to provide. Kennedy, however, did like a touch of humor in the Checklist, which Cline said analysts were happy to provide when they found a way to do so properly. Kennedy's standard for what was appropriate was characteristically liberal. He enjoyed intimate details about foreign leaders—like a transcript of remarks by the German defense minister that revealed what he sounded like after a few drinks, and news that the Brazilian president ordered the murder of his wife's lover. Morale among OCI analysts writing for the president jumped even higher in September 1963, when Clifton passed back to the CIA Kennedy's personal expression of delight with "the book." The president valued the Checklist enough to miss it in the rare cases when it was not in the Oval Office upon his arrival.

The Checklist's success had an unintended consequence: it crowded out Agency leaders' actual face time with Kennedy. In November 1963, Bundy told the CIA's deputy director that neither he nor McCone needed to attend a national security meeting with the president in Hyannisport, saying that "the *Checklist* was all he needed." It is not hard to see why the Directorate of Intelligence, seeing senior-level briefings drop off, considered writing and delivering the Checklist as its bread-and-butter activity.

KENNEDY'S TENDENCY TO DIRECT actions while reading his Checklist revealed a crucial limitation of a document that came to him alone at the White House. On most national security issues, planning and execution necessarily involve the State and Defense Departments. Yet Kennedy surprised secretary of state Dean Rusk and secretary of defense Robert McNamara, along with other members of his cabinet, by asking questions based on Checklist items that the secretaries had not seen. So by December 1961, less than six months after the Checklist's debut, the president directed the CIA to provide copies of it to Rusk and McNamara. OCI officers dutifully delivered the Checklist to Foggy Bottom and the Pentagon, waiting for each new customer to read his copy before taking it back to a secure vault at the new CIA headquarters building in McLean, Virginia. By late 1963, the chairman of the Joint Chiefs of Staff had also begun receiving a copy.

In his memo telling the two secretaries they would start receiving the Checklist, Clifton shed light on how President Kennedy viewed it. "The report," he wrote, "includes more than intelligence items and is considered by the President as a daily communication between the Director of Central Intelligence and the President's office. Consequently, it includes comments, notes, and suggestions which the Director of Central Intelligence makes to the President." He told them that Kennedy did not read the report at a fixed time, instead working it into his schedule as the opportunity arose, and he reminded them to treat the document with the greatest care:

> Because the usefulness of the Checklist might be diminished if the report were too widely circulated, the Director of Central Intelligence should arrange delivery so that the report is read by the two Secretaries *only*. In the event that an Acting Secretary of State or an Acting Secretary of Defense is performing the Secretaries' duties, the respective Acting Secretary will be furnished the report. . . . The President's Checklist is a very closely held report in that it contains information of the most sensitive nature gathered from all sources available to the Government and for which very few individuals have the necessary clearances for all the types of information which it contains. Consequently, its handling must always meet these requirements.

Within the month, McCone sought the secretaries' reactions to the Checklist. In McNamara's absence, his deputy Roswell Gilpatric—who had taken advantage of the "acting secretary" clause to read it—replied, "I believe it is of definite value and should be continued. I particularly like the succinctness and clarity with which information is reported and evaluated." For his part, Rusk told McCone that he appreciated how the Checklist informed him of "developments which are being brought daily to the attention of the President through this informal channel. The format and content seem ideal for this purpose, and I have no suggestions for its improvement." Later in Kennedy's term, Rusk stated simply that it was "a damned useful document."

The CIA honored the White House's order to keep the briefing secure. Throughout Kennedy's time in office, his top national security aides received the Checklist either via direct, OCI-officer delivery or through encrypted channels. When McNamara went overseas in April 1962, for example, the Agency demanded that the Checklist go through the CIA's own secure communication network and avoid any undue attention. Cabell, the deputy director, told McNamara's assistant to inform the secretary that "what he received from our Station Chief would be identical with the 'President's Checklist' but would not, repeat not, in any way be identified as such."

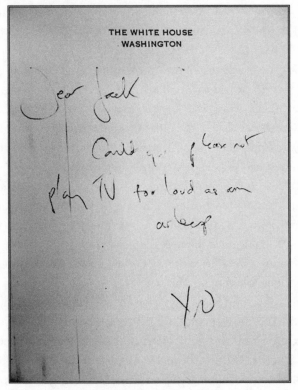

Jackie Kennedy's note to her husband—a bookmark in a May 1963 Checklist.
Courtesy John F. Kennedy Presidential Library

For his part, Kennedy kept his Checklist very close for reading at his convenience, day or night, for the rest of his time in office. In fact, when officials at the John F. Kennedy Presidential Library filed his papers years later, they found a handwritten note from Jackie Kennedy in a most unexpected place: stuck between two pages of a May 1963 Checklist.

CHAPTER THREE

THE BIRTH OF THE BOOK

ON THE AFTERNOON OF Friday, November 22, 1963, Lyndon Johnson stood in Air Force One on the tarmac of Love Field in Dallas to be sworn in as the thirty-sixth president of United States. Less than twenty-four hours later, he was back in Washington for his first morning in office, unsure what to expect from a White House and National Security Council staff that had treated him like a stranger for more than two years.

To say that relations between Kennedy and Johnson had been strained understates the depth of the animosity between the two former senators. The high-tension Democratic Party primaries in 1960 played a role. So did the simple fact that up to this point presidents had kept their vice presidents distant. Besides, the two men simply did not like each other, which showed in the way the president and his staff talked to the vice president: with disdain and, often, downright meanness.

Arthur Schlesinger claimed that Kennedy had taken great care to keep Johnson in the loop, but the historical record, including the fallen president's own words, contradicts him. Kennedy's friend Charles Bartlett recalled him saying more than once after the Cuban missile crisis that he would happily see three men from his crisis-handling ExComm—defense secretary Robert McNamara, treasury secretary Douglas Dillon, and his own brother, attorney general Bobby Kennedy—become president of the United States. Vice

President Johnson, who also had been on the ExComm, was conspic-uously left off the list.

Kennedy offered Bartlett a weak excuse for excluding Johnson from important meetings, such as a crucial mini-ExComm discussion near the end of the Cuban missile crisis. "When you get into these problems . . . you never even think of talking to anybody about them who hasn't read the cables. Lyndon hasn't read the cables." The presi-dent, of course, could have shown his vice president anything—from these specific cables all the way up to the tightly controlled President's Intelligence Checklist—whenever he wanted. He simply chose not to.

Johnson had begun his vice presidency in 1961 without any staff to support him on national security issues, a situation that Ken-nedy did nothing to rectify. NSC executive secretary Bromley Smith recalled the gap years later: "One of the assignments we picked up at this time was briefing Vice President Johnson. I felt a special respon-sibility for the Vice President, because the secretary of state, the sec-retary of defense, and the director of the CIA had huge staffs. They always came with briefing books and all kinds of papers. The Vice President had a small staff and there wasn't the attention given to briefing him that was given to every other participant in the Council." To help close the distance in situational awareness between Johnson and the other NSC members, Smith reached out to the vice presi-dent's military aide, Colonel Howard Burris, at least once a week— and always before a rare formal meeting of the NSC—to keep Burris, and thus the vice president, more up to speed.

Neither Allen Dulles nor John McCone, Kennedy's two CIA directors, provided finished intelligence or briefings directly to John-son. Richard Helms—at the time a senior officer in the Directorate of Plans (CIA's operations division), and later one of Johnson's CIA directors—recalled that Johnson had lacked any real contact with or interest in the Agency before his sudden rise to the presidency. Every day, the vice president's office received a copy of the CIA's Central Intelligence Bulletin, but there is no evidence that he read it. Even if he did, the Bulletin included less sensitive intelligence reporting than Kennedy's closely held Checklist.

The only attempt to give Johnson the Checklist came from Dick Lehman in the CIA's Office of Current Intelligence. Lehman had noticed an oddity back in December 1961, when Kennedy had told the

Agency to deliver his Checklist outside the White House, for the first time, to Dean Rusk at the State Department and Robert McNamara at the Pentagon. Three of the four statutory members of the National Security Council—the president, secretary of state, and secretary of defense—would now be seeing the Checklist every morning. But the fourth formal member of the NSC would remain ignorant of each day's most sensitive intelligence. Surprised, Lehman raised it with Bromley Smith at the White House, asking, "What about the Vice President?"

Smith's reply was firm and final: "Under no circumstances!"

Just under two years later, on November 22, 1963, Lehman was at CIA headquarters. Like everyone else that day, he was reeling from the news that President Kennedy had been shot in Dallas. He found little time to process the event, however, because DDI Ray Cline called him into his office to discuss how the OCI would support the new commander in chief, who, as far as anyone there knew, had still never even heard of the President's Intelligence Checklist.

JOHNSON THUS DID NOT know what to expect when John McCone came to meet with him on his first morning as president. The CIA director maneuvered his way onto the new president's schedule with a dash of deception. His assistant had called the White House just hours

The President's Intelligence Checklist from the day of John F. Kennedy's assassination. *Courtesy John F. Kennedy Presidential Library*

after Kennedy's death to confirm that Johnson would take the regular 9:00 a.m. intelligence briefing. He was bluffing: there was no such regular session.

McCone had indeed been a "very, very frequent visitor" to the West Wing, according to presidential advisor Carl Kaysen, but Kennedy had not seen his CIA director one-on-one often, and certainly not daily. McCone gambled that Johnson's general ignorance about Kennedy's intelligence briefing routines would render the new president unable to refuse the meeting. It worked.

Johnson, focused that morning on practical issues such as keeping Kennedy's aides from leaving en masse, found fifteen minutes for McCone around 9:15 a.m. Because the late president's staff had not yet cleared the Oval Office of Kennedy's effects, Johnson took the meeting downstairs in national security advisor McGeorge Bundy's basement office. The president told McCone he had long valued their personal friendship—quite a stretch, given their minimal relationship up to that point—and expressed respect for the CIA and for McCone's leadership of the intelligence community. McCone dutifully returned the niceties, declaring confidence in Johnson and a desire to support him "in every way." Concerned that the Soviet Union, Cuba, or others would exploit the nation's post-assassination confusion, the president began the substance of the session by asking about world developments. Years later, he recalled being relieved when the CIA director responded to him that the world was about as peaceful as it could be.

McCone then took a deep breath and revealed to Johnson the existence of the President's Intelligence Checklist, dodging any discussion of how Kennedy's staff had forbidden the CIA from showing it to him as vice president. The director reported back to OCI leaders that their hunch had been correct; Johnson's reaction to the Checklist confirmed that he "was not familiar" with the product. McCone then quickly gave him a global *tour d'horizon* highlighting potential and actual areas of concern.

That first day, the Checklist led with a summary of developments in South Vietnam, which extended to a rare length, for a single item, of almost two pages. "Vietnamese Communist efforts to discredit the new Saigon regime stayed in high gear this week," it began, followed by summaries of armed antigovernment attacks, South Vietnamese military operations against the insurgents, and leadership dynamics. Johnson also saw shorter pieces about Venezuela, Soviet advisors in Cuba, Soviet harassment of Allied access routes to West Berlin, and relations between Arab states. The Checklist package ended with two pages of brief notes, each one just a sentence or two about the USSR, Congo, Britain, Ecuador, and Thailand. Johnson asked a few questions but did not dwell on any particular story, and he agreed to see McCone every morning to review the Checklist with him personally.

The style of the very first Checklist Johnson saw already differed slightly from the ones Kennedy had enjoyed reading. Beginning on the afternoon of the assassination itself, analysts in the OCI started adding context to many analytic items to bring the new president up to speed on the things that his predecessor had been fully aware of. Lehman began writing "at great length in order to fill in some of the background, because the stuff for Kennedy was really very much leaving out any background at all." He described the OCI's mission as "trying to bridge the gap without having to talk down to him, which was difficult." Bromley Smith at the NSC signed off on the idea of offering such additional text but warned that analysts should not be too obvious in their efforts to educate the new president, who had proven sensitive to real or perceived condescension.

The lead article in Johnson's second Checklist bluntly laid out one of the most bedeviling issues for the five remaining years of Johnson's time in office: "The North Vietnamese have told the French they believe that sentiment is growing in the US for the withdrawal of US forces. They reportedly plan to keep the heat on to encourage it." Related articles on Laos and Cambodia followed. The heavy focus on Indochina probably kept Johnson's attention away from the other topics that day, ranging from Egypt's intervention in Yemen to Italy's parliamentary structure. These daily intelligence summaries, if nothing else, highlighted the wide range of international issues that Johnson needed to stay on top of. During his first week as president, the Checklist contained items analyzing thirty-seven countries. From strategic articles, such as one on Communist China's outreach to nations in Africa and Asia, to tactical pieces, including a readout of Venezuela's seizure of a large cache of weapons of Cuban origin, the Checklist brought information from far-flung corners of the world to the new president.

```
                            NOTES

A.   Oswald   Press stories to the effect that Lee Harvey
     Oswald recently visited Mexico City are true, accord-
     ing to our information.  Oswald visited both the
     Cuban and the Soviet embassies on 28 September.  He
     was trying, we are told, to arrange for visas so
     that he could travel to the USSR via Havana.  He
     returned to the US on 3 October.
```

Lee Harvey Oswald tops the Checklist's "Notes" page on November 25, 1963.
Courtesy Lyndon Baines Johnson Library

Standing out among the Checklist items during that first week is a brief note on Monday, November 25 titled simply "Oswald." It read: "Press stories to the effect that Lee Harvey Oswald recently visited Mexico City are true, according to our information. Oswald visited both the Cuban and the Soviet Embassies on 28 September. He was trying, we are told, to arrange for visas so that he could travel to the USSR via Havana. He returned to the US on 3 October." As part of a daily product covering *foreign* intelligence, this item solely about the travel of a US citizen stood out. It would take almost forty years— until after the al Qaida attacks on America on September 11, 2011— for intelligence involving US citizens to appear in the Checklist's direct descendant, the President's Daily Brief.

McCONE AND JOHNSON FAILED to click, despite the regular daily meetings, and within a few weeks the one-on-one sessions had shortened as Johnson's other priorities grew and his interest in daily intelligence declined. McCone lamented by December 9 that the meetings had become "very brief." Soon thereafter, briefings dropped off the president's regular schedule altogether, and OCI analysts began to miss the glory days of Kennedy's active engagement.

It is unlikely that anybody could have kept Johnson's interest. Richard Helms told future CIA director and secretary of defense Bob Gates that Johnson had once compared intelligence officers to a cow he had owned as a kid in Texas. "One day I'd worked hard and gotten a full pail of milk, but I wasn't paying attention, and old Bessie swung her shit-smeared tail through that bucket of milk. Now, you know, that's what these intelligence guys do. You work hard and get a good program or policy going, and they swing a shit-smeared tail through it." Another future director, William Colby, remembered that when he stepped forward during a meeting in the Cabinet Room to show the new president a photograph of a Vietnamese installation—the kind of hands-on intelligence collection Kennedy would have loved—Johnson failed to engage Colby except to warn him not to spill coffee as he reached over the table. Within the White House itself, national security advisor Bundy quickly adjusted, taking fewer issues to Johnson than had been his norm for Kennedy.

General Ted Clifton, who stayed on as the president's military assistant, confided to Lehman that those closest to the dead president would appreciate a tribute from the CIA. Lehman kicked an idea around the OCI: how about a memorial issue of the Checklist? McCone liked the idea, approving a limited distribution list of only Jackie, Bobby Kennedy, Bundy, Smith, and Clifton. So on December 4, the OCI chief delivered to the White House just five copies of a memorial Checklist, backdated to November 22, containing no substantive content. The main page sported a banner across the top: "In honor of President Kennedy for whom the President's Intelligence Checklist was first written on 17 June 1961." The text on the following pages was similarly brief:

> For this day, the Checklist Staff can find no words more fitting than a verse quoted by the president to a group of newspapermen the day he learned of the presence of Soviet missiles in Cuba.

> > *Bullfight critics ranked in rows*
> > *Crowd the enormous plaza full;*
> > *But only one is there who knows*
> > *And he's the man who fights the bull.*

As 1964 BEGAN, CLIFTON began fearing for the future of presidential intelligence. He warned OCI officers that he had been able to get the Checklist to Johnson only with "some regularity," a far cry from Kennedy's deep engagement. Clifton warned his CIA contacts that Johnson was "not getting a steady feed of intelligence on world situations" and instead only got what he or Bundy could tell him orally when they saw him, which was not often. Clifton told them at one point that the president, who he said was a "painfully slow reader," had not looked at any finished intelligence for the better part of a week. Johnson had tuned out. Clifton decided something had to change.

So in January he tasked the CIA to supplement the Checklist with a simple, less frequent booklet that would include "the shortest possible review of highlights of the intelligence-gathering effort for the 5-day period from Sunday to Thursday." OCI officers stepped up with the new Current Intelligence Review, which allowed Clifton to update the president with minimum effort. Clifton told Lehman on January 10 that the Review had "worked like a charm" at breakfast with Johnson, who soon told Clifton to keep it coming in its current form because he found it "very valuable."

This weekly offering reengaged the president with finished intelligence at a time when hopes for any real connection had dimmed. This came as good news to the CIA, and to the OCI in particular. On the other hand, because the Review pulled together a full week's worth of highlights into one document, Johnson found it even easier to push the Checklist to the bottom of his reading stack. Clifton nevertheless told the OCI to keep sending the Checklist because the president expected his triumvirate of national security aides—Bundy, Bromley Smith, and Clifton himself—to read it each day and be ready to brief him on its content. "The first day you stop," Clifton warned, "the President will ask for the Checklist or query us about something, and we will not have the answer."

McCone, increasingly frustrated by his lost face time with the president, worked with Bundy to expand the Checklist's distribution. Defense Intelligence Agency director Joseph Carroll had begun to see a copy, for his eyes only, a few weeks after Kennedy's assassination. In February, copies also started going to a set of next-tier officials, including undersecretaries of state George Ball and Averill Harriman, State Department assistant secretaries Gove Griffith Johnson and Thomas Hughes, deputy secretary of defense Cyrus Vance, assistant secretary of defense for international security affairs William Bundy (the national security advisor's brother), and the chairman of the Joint Chiefs of Staff, General Maxwell Taylor. The Checklist's content stayed the same; only the number of eyes on it each morning changed.

The recipient list was getting long enough, however, to cause angst. Bromley Smith sent McGeorge Bundy a scathing memo in late February complaining that the Checklist's expansion "makes it just another intelligence paper which has lost most of its value to the President. . . . With this many people fumbling with the Checklist, disseminating it," he added, "we might just as well print it in the *New York Times*." OCI leaders had followed McCone's orders to expand the Checklist's readership, but they resisted even wider distribution. For example, Jack Smith expressed "serious reservations" about supplying the Checklist to the US ambassador to the United Nations, Adlai Stevenson—citing how difficult it would be to keep the document secure at UN offices in New York—and the CIA never provided it to him.

Despite such concerns, McCone defended the Checklist's wider circulation, citing it to Bundy in April as "one effort to tighten the crucial relationship between policymaker and intelligence analyst." But he still chafed at being shut out of the Oval Office. By the spring of 1964, he was virtually begging Johnson's aides for greater access to the president. On April 22, he told Bundy that he was "highly dissatisfied over the fact that President Johnson did not get intelligence briefings from me," prompting the exasperated Bundy to tell McCone to raise it with the president directly. And McCone did just that during one of his increasingly rare meetings with Johnson one week later.

"I then said that I was concerned that the President was not getting sufficient and adequate intelligence briefings; that I was not seeing very much of him, and that this disturbed me," he wrote that day. "He said he was available any time that I wanted to see him. All I had to do was call up. I said that this had not been the case on several 'attempts.' . . . He invited me to bring to his attention any matters of special and particular interest; however he did not wish to be briefed just for the purpose of being briefed." To push McCone off, Johnson told him that his summary of Checklist items was "perfectly adequate."

By the time election day rolled around in November, Johnson had been on the stump for months. Word got back to the Agency that he was catching up on the Review upon returning from campaign trips but ignoring the Checklist, which became an anomaly: a document published specifically for the president but read only by other national security officials. Dean Rusk at the State Department fretted over the security implications of the Checklist's expanded readership, and McCone himself began to doubt the value of producing it if Johnson would never read it regularly again. White House National

Security Council staff members continued venting to Lehman and others at the CIA about the president's lack of interest in daily intelligence analysis.

So OCI analysts did what they should have done a year earlier, immediately after the easily slighted Johnson assumed the presidency: they gave him a new product that fit his reading habits, one he could truly call his own. They called it the President's Daily Brief.

By 1964, DDI RAY Cline had worked just about every angle of intelligence during his two decades in the profession. He had cracked Japanese codes while serving as a navy cryptanalyst starting in 1942. A year later he joined the CIA's World War II predecessor, the Office of Strategic Services, and dove into current intelligence, which he oversaw for the OSS from 1944 until its dissolution late in 1945. After an interlude researching and writing official histories of the army's World War II operations, he joined the newly formed CIA in 1949. A wide range of positions during the next fifteen years, both domestic and overseas, led to his appointment as DDI just a few months before the Cuban missile crisis. Cline, in fact, had been the CIA officer who called Bundy on the night of October 15, 1962, to tell him that the Soviet Union had placed nuclear missiles in Cuba.

Like the officers working for him in the CIA's analysis directorate, Cline went through 1964 missing the glory days of John Kennedy's intense engagement with his daily intelligence. He and his newly promoted deputy, Jack Smith, recognized that the Checklist's status as a Kennedy administration holdover left Johnson cold. So they directed the Office of Current Intelligence to create a new publication that would build on the foundation of the Checklist but allow Johnson's aides to tell him it was designed just for him. Having heard that Johnson tackled his serious reading in the evening, Smith suggested that the CIA publish this daily report in the afternoon instead of in the morning. Bundy approved the concept, and the OCI stopped publishing the Checklist and the biweekly Review in favor of the new product. The President's Daily Brief was born.

The debut on December 1, 1964, of the PDB—or "the book," as it has been called in CIA circles ever since—caught Johnson's eye. It was now a full-sized document, more suitable for his late-night bedtime reading than the odd, roughly square shape of Kennedy's Checklist. The PDB covered a similar range of global developments, but its items tended to be much shorter. Each day's edition had a simple cover containing a small CIA seal and "Central Intelligence Agency" printed at the top, "The President's Daily Brief" appearing alone in the center of the page, and "Top Secret" at the bottom right underneath the date. The first issue came to Johnson accompanied by a memo from Bundy: "Ray Cline of CIA and I have worked out this new form of a daily intelligence briefing on the premise that it is more useful to you if it comes in your evening reading." He stated his goal bluntly, telling the president that he hoped the PDB would be "more nearly responsive to your own interests than the papers we have been sending heretofore."

The new product worked. Jack Valenti, one of Johnson's closest aides, noted to Bundy, "Mac, the President likes this very much." Cline and his busy analysts in the OCI felt even better months later when presidential special assistant Bill Moyers passed word along that Johnson still continued to read the PDB "avidly."

PDBs from the first summer of the new publication's existence show that the OCI replaced the Checklist's typical six to eight pages of relatively long articles with only two pages of text (which contained just three items on each page), plus annexes. The language in the PDB remained accessible—less clunky than typical intelligence assessments—with bits such as "Despite Sukarno's long-standing kidney ailment, for which he delays proper treatment, he has seemed quite chipper lately." The graphics supplementing the text stand out, too, for their austerity. In the August 7, 1965, book, for example, a map of Communist China paired with an article on a Taiwan Strait naval clash looks crisp enough, but OCI analysts showed the president the location of the skirmish with a rough X—apparently scribbled on at the last minute with a plain black marker.

The PDB's brevity and simplicity turned Johnson into a regular daily intelligence reader again. Other recipients also appreciated the change. Deputy secretary of defense Vance told the CIA's deputy director in February 1965 that while the Checklist had left him cold, the daily product now was "the most helpful document" he was seeing from the intelligence community.

MARVIN WATSON HAD LONG been a Johnson Democrat. The son of an east Texas auto dealer, Watson served in the Marine Corps during World War II before volunteering for US Representative Lyndon Johnson's Senate campaign in 1948. After various business and government jobs, he became a member of the Texas State Democratic Committee in time to support Johnson's presidential bid in 1960. He resisted calls to come work for Johnson in the Senate, in the vice presidency, and even during his first year in the Oval Office. Then Johnson tapped Watson to oversee the Democratic National Convention in Atlantic City in 1964. By fending off an effort from Bobby Kennedy's supporters to steal Johnson's thunder, if not the nomination, Watson guaranteed Johnson's smooth sailing toward a landslide victory over Republican senator Barry Goldwater that November. His value to Johnson proven once again, Watson finally headed to Washington.

Johnson named him special assistant to the president, dropping in his lap a long list of duties now associated with a position that Johnson never formally filled: White House chief of staff. Watson had an unenviable job: managing one of the oddest workday patterns of any modern commander in chief. Rising by seven on most mornings, Johnson would sit in bed for hours, making phone calls, watching the morning news programs, and going through various newspapers and documents. Sitting bedside faithfully through it all was Watson, who had arrived at dawn to record the president's questions, decisions, and instructions to cabinet officers and White House staff. Around mid- to late morning, the president descended to the Oval Office for meetings and an early afternoon lunch. After spending a few hours each afternoon back in bed reading papers, talking to advisors, and working the phone—in pajamas but never actually napping, Watson claims—Johnson worked for the remainder of the afternoon and evening. He took a break around ten or eleven for dinner, a rubdown, and the late news on TV, and then stayed up well past midnight.

These late evening hours were filled with his "night reading," which Watson had compiled all day for his information or action. The foot-high stack of reports, correspondence, and other paperwork included responses to his previous queries and provided fodder for the hours of discussion and decisions the next morning, when Watson returned to the White House after four or five hours of sleep.

Johnson's late nights gave him, too, only a few hours of sleep before starting the cycle all over again. Controlling the massive paper flow from the president's nightly output required a precise system because Johnson remembered previous nights' documents down to the numbers that Watson had assigned them. "I don't think he was ever wrong," recalls the de facto chief of staff, who learned to serve his boss with ruthless efficiency. If candidate items for the president's night reading failed to reach Watson by 5:00 each afternoon, he would leave them out.

For more than two years after its creation, the President's Daily Brief made it into Johnson's night reading. Johnson even liked the PDB enough to start getting it seven days a week instead of six starting in 1966.

JOHN MCCONE HAD TOLD Johnson back in June 1964 that he intended to resign as soon as the president could identify a successor. But Johnson had sat on the request, effectively holding the CIA director in place indefinitely. As 1965 began, McCone thought the president's steady interest in the Agency's nightly PDB provided a rare opportunity to try to reconnect with him one-on-one. "McCone had one view of the CIA," Watson recalls, "and how important intelligence was at the moment." The president, he would learn, did not share this view. McCone showed up at the White House unannounced on February 1, 1965, Watson's very first day on the job. "I am Director McCone, CIA," he told the de facto chief of staff as he walked right into the Oval Office.

Within seconds, the phone on Watson's desk rang. The president barked, "Come in here!'"

Watson darted through the door. For having let McCone through, he got a nasty scowl from Johnson, who was lecturing the CIA director. "Now, I know what you have for me is important," Johnson said, "but we work on a schedule and a system here. And if you want to see me, you should call, and we'll try to arrange to have a vacant spot for you."

It was the end of the road for McCone, who came back and told CIA operations chief Richard Helms that his diminishing influence with the president left him little choice but to leave the Agency, which he finally did a couple of months later. Retired Vice Admiral

William "Red" Raborn, who had led the navy's Polaris missile project, was sworn in as McCone's successor in the dual-hatted role of director of central intelligence and CIA director on April 28, 1965. Johnson cajoled Raborn to come to Washington with a promise that he would serve only as a caretaker; Johnson had Helms in mind for the director position but felt that he needed seasoning as Raborn's deputy first. The career navy man accepted the president's offer but never earned the CIA workforce's respect; even his DDI, Ray Cline, found Johnson's choice of Raborn baffling. The new director wore his ignorance of intelligence on his sleeve, reportedly asking questions such as "Which tribe in Liberia are the oligarchs?"

He also learned a lesson that McCone had not: give the president plenty of space. Raborn said that Johnson had told him directly, "I'm sick and tired of John McCone's tugging at my shirttails. If I want to see you, Raborn, I'll telephone you!" So the new director instead took an active interest in the best channel for getting information to the president: the President's Daily Brief. Memos from CIA files reveal that he frequently told the OCI what to include in the book. Once he even forbade any changes to the PDB's scope and style without his explicit approval. And he learned to flaunt the CIA's daily service to the president to promote the organization's best interests. In December 1965, for example, Raborn took Cline's description of the extensive collection and analytic effort behind the PDB's reporting on Vietnam to discussions with the director of the Bureau of the Budget, the predecessor to today's Office of Management and Budget.

During the tenures of Raborn and, later, Helms—who succeeded Raborn in June 1966—President Johnson shared the PDB with other top officials in his administration. Hubert Humphrey assumed the vice presidency on January 20, 1965, after the job had gone vacant for fourteen months, and started receiving the President's Daily Brief shortly thereafter. By the summer, its distribution remained limited to fewer than a dozen people: Johnson, Humphrey, Bundy, Bromley Smith, Bill Moyers, Rusk, McNamara, and four others at the Defense Department. Once Checklist-era recipients attorney general Bobby Kennedy and treasury secretary Douglas Dillon had left office, the CIA (with Bundy's approval) had stopped delivering it to the Justice and Treasury departments. De facto chief of staff Marvin Watson, though not a formal recipient, also saw the book every day while preparing the president's night reading.

By SPRING 1965, US involvement in Vietnam had started taking more and more of Johnson's time. In February, he had begun receiving a daily Vietnam report from the CIA, obviating the need for the PDB to cover every detail on the topic, but the OCI still used the book to offer stand-back analysis on Vietnam. A good example comes from this lead PDB article on May 13, 1967:

> The North Vietnamese seem to want a war of attrition in the two provinces just south of the Demilitarized Zone. In a CIA assessment completed this week, we have wrung out the available evidence and we conclude that the enemy is not trying to "liberate" these provinces now. Instead, we feel, the Communists hope to create the illusion of "a war no one can win." Attacks will be aimed at spreading US forces thin and keeping them under constant pressure without offering the opportunity for a clear-cut allied victory. We believe up to five enemy divisions may now be involved along the zone and in the mountain redoubts to the south.

The PDB proved less useful in other cases. For example, analysts discounted field reports in early 1968 about a significant upcoming Viet Cong and North Vietnamese military operation in South Vietnam and thus failed to provide much advance warning of the Tet Offensive, which began on January 30. Helms says that despite Johnson's anger at the CIA over some of its Vietnam assessments, the president—unlike Johnson's staff—never pushed the CIA director to alter the Agency's finished intelligence products to reflect White House policy.

Many PDB recipients attended the "Tuesday lunches," Johnson's unique institution for discussing the situation in Vietnam and, occasionally, foreign policy more generally. Held in the White House's private dining room starting in early 1964, these meetings were less formal versions of National Security Council meetings. Johnson, for example, excluded Vice President Hubert Humphrey, a statutory NSC member. The lunches (which, despite their name, were not always held on Tuesday) gave the president a chance to kick policy ideas around with a trusted inner circle including his national security advisor, secretary of state, secretary of defense, and a few others. Dean Rusk said that it allowed the president's closest advisors to talk "in complete confidence and candor about the matters that were up for decision." He found them invaluable because "we all could be confident that everyone around the table would keep his mouth shut and wouldn't be running off to Georgetown cocktail parties and talking about it."

"The cabinet secretaries knew they always had access to the president at least every single week," noted Bromley Smith. "They knew they couldn't schedule anything else for Tuesday lunch. Once when one secretary couldn't come the President cancelled the luncheon. It was necessary to do that only once or twice. The group got the point." Walt Rostow, who succeeded Bundy as national security advisor in April 1966, said that Johnson arranged to have the director of central intelligence and the chairman of the Joint Chiefs added as regular members.

Richard Helms became a regular attendee after he succeeded the ineffective Red Raborn. Within a year, Helms also oversaw the return to delivering the PDB before the president woke up in the morning, ahead of his reading the daily newspapers, per a White House request. Dick Lehman, by then OCI director, happily obliged—even though it meant OCI analysts would have to publish the book by 5:00 every morning to ensure it was at the White House before dawn. "Johnson had his at 7:00 at the latest," Marvin Watson recalls. "And I think Johnson liked it. Now don't misunderstand me, he could have slept until 9:00, as far as I was concerned. But he wanted to be in front of everything instead of behind everything. That was just him."

The PDB's early morning timing and its basic format appear to have remained steady through the last two years of Johnson's presidency, with the book's producers following Helms's order that the change in delivery should affect neither the content nor the dissemination of the Agency's flagship publication.

THE PDB WARNED THE president in mid-May 1967 that Egypt's president, Gamal Abdel Nasser, would seek to expand the rising friction between Israel and Syria into a regional war by "going all out to show that his mutual security pact with Syria is something which the Israelis should take seriously." The PDB's writers assessed that Nasser probably felt that "his prestige in the Arab world would nosedive if he stood idly by while Israel mauled Syria again." As regional

President Lyndon Johnson and his family look over the PDB in 1967. *Central Intelligence Agency website photo*

tensions grew in late May, the PDB was delivered for five days via secure White House communications cable format to Johnson's Texas ranch to keep him up to speed with late-breaking updates.

The CIA analysts excelled during this period, not only providing policy makers with ample warning of the conflict but also predict-ing a quick Israeli victory—something the Israelis themselves were loath to forecast while they sought assurances of US military support. Early in May, Jack Smith—who had been promoted to DDI in Janu-ary 1966—told Helms at a daily staff meeting that Israel was likely to win the probable conflict in ten to fourteen days. Helms, who passed the assessment to Johnson and his closest advisors, claims that the analysts rescrubbed the data and shortened that time frame to judge that the coming war might end within seven days. Documentation supporting Helms's assertion about that precise prediction is lacking, but CIA analysis nevertheless prepared the White House well for the June 1967 conflict that became known as the Six-Day War. A CIA retrospective on the war summarizes the impact: "Although the anal-ysis ran contrary to the views initially held by senior policymakers, the President and his National Security team ultimately adopted policy based on intelligence analysis that alerted them to Arab troop movements, the thinking behind Egyptian plans regarding the Gulf of Aqaba, the likelihood of potential Soviet intervention in support of the Arabs, and Israel's ability to defeat Arab militaries." Helms put it this way: "I think that President Johnson came to understand what intelligence could do for him during the events leading up to the June War of 1967."

Starting on the day the war began, June 5, the President's Daily Brief every morning contained tactical developments and analysis of breaking events. On June 6, the PDB told Johnson that "Israel has gained an early and perhaps overwhelming victory in the air, but the progress of the war on the ground is unclear." Over the next few days, the PDB covered military developments, political machinations of the various players, and threats to US diplomatic facilities across the Arab world after the decisive Israeli successes in the war. This detailed attention to the war and its implications resonated with Johnson, who paid even more attention to the intelligence after this crucial time.

It was also during the Six-Day War that the President's Daily Brief printed a breaking news item that had eerie echoes more than forty-five years later in the attack that killed US ambassador Christopher Stevens on September 11, 2012. Appearing on the "Late Items" page of the June 5 PDB was this chilling text: "Libya: The US Embassy in Benghazi flashed word at 4:30 AM EDT that it was being attacked by a large mob. It is burning its papers."

THE TECHNOLOGY AND SCOPE of intelligence gathering and analysis have changed since the early 1960s. But the basics of writing for the president have not. CIA analysts coming to work each day spent hours looking over the previous night's information take related to their accounts—often the political, military, or economic situation in a particular country, sometimes a specific technological or transnational issue. The collected documents, all in hard copy, included diplomatic cables from embassies and consulates around the globe, clandestine reports from the CIA's recruited spies, intercepted foreign communications, and open-source material from news wires and major US and international print and broadcast media. Analysts and managers would cull this wealth of classified and unclassified paperwork for anything reaching the threshold of writing up a piece of finished intelligence for US policy makers. If so, analysts would write a draft within a few hours, coordinate it with peers in the Agency, clear it with a manager or two, and send it up to an editor for final review.

"Writing for the PDB—and, underneath it, the Central Intelligence Bulletin—was the reason for our existence," recalls Bob Gates, who was an OCI analyst during the Johnson years. "I remember the first PDB I wrote. The cigar-chomping editor handed me back my first piece for the PDB, and it looked like a bloody chicken had walked across it. That's where I learned to be succinct and put things together in a coherent way." He also remembers vividly that OCI officers included in the PDB what Lehman called "the occasional bag of dirt on foreign leaders." Johnson reveled in reading "the same kinds of dirt on his foreign counterparts that he enjoyed from J. Edgar Hoover on his domestic counterparts," Gates says. "He was very interested in any story about the peccadillos of other international leaders—those stories always sold well. It was a very politically incorrect time."

The CIA produced more than twelve hundred issues of the President's Daily Brief for Lyndon Johnson before he left office in January 1969. Brief glimpses into his daily intelligence reveal much about how the analysts' efforts came across to Johnson.

Often the text was abrupt, especially on issues outside of Vietnam and Soviet intentions in Europe, Johnson's core interests. On April 1, 1968, the PDB provided the simplest possible assessment of President Nasser's political reform program: "We doubt that it will amount to much." Analysts often explicitly acknowledged gaps in intelligence collection and analysis. A mid-1968 blurb about a postponed Soviet launch of a planned flight around the moon admitted, "We do not know just what caused the delay." Student protests against the Mexican government in the weeks leading up to the 1968 Summer Olympics in Mexico City received frequent but brief coverage in lines such as "Students are still in a defiant mood" and "It is hard to see how more trouble can be avoided."

As in Kennedy's Checklist, the assertions usually skipped specifics about the intelligence sources underlying the judgments. One pre-Olympics piece in the PDB said—without any insight into the quality or reliability of the information—that "the capital is rife with rumors of revolution and military takeover, and the government expects a major set of sabotage before the opening of the Olympics on 12 October." On occasion, Johnson's book included longer assessments to provide context for day-to-day developments. Just days after these Mexican student protest assessments, for example, the president could have read in his PDB a full-page annex comparing and contrasting student unrest across Latin American countries. The text told him that despite the absence of evidence that the Soviets or other foreign players were directing these protests, Communists were clearly taking advantage of the situation.

PDBs from Johnson's final six months in the White House also showed steady coverage of Soviet military and technological efforts. Predictions of Soviet rocket launches appeared regularly, as did assessments of the success or failure of ongoing Soviet space missions. The USSR finance minister's presentation of the defense budget to the Supreme Soviet in December 1968 received coverage both for its content, which revealed a relatively large increase in defense spending earmarked for scientific work, and for its insight into Moscow's intentions in strategic arms limitation discussions. Later that month, the PDB—citing analysis of satellite imagery of missile silos under construction—informed Johnson that in six months the USSR would be ready to operate the SS-13, its first solid-propellant intercontinental ballistic missile. During Johnson's final weeks in office, analysts put in his book updates on a new type of short-range missile fired from a Soviet nuclear attack submarine, the USSR's antisubmarine helicopter carrier capabilities, and the Soviets' first successful flight of a supersonic aircraft.

Helms was convinced that the book had sunk its teeth into the president. "I could tell from the questions he asked later that he did read it very carefully," the CIA director said just months after Johnson left office. Johnson himself never wrote by name about the President's Daily Brief after leaving office, but others who read the PDB during his administration have commented on the intelligence they received. Rusk at State and McNamara at Defense appreciated getting the PDB enough to have asked in September 1966 for it to be delivered to them during their travels to, respectively, New York (for the United Nations General Assembly) and Rome (for NATO matters).

The CIA eagerly met both requests. Rusk later said he found the analytic products "exceptionally good" and saw shortcomings as a necessary part of collecting and analyzing intelligence information.

Johnson's deputy national security advisor for two years, Francis Bator, has a mixed judgment about the PDB. On Western Europe, his main area of responsibility, he says the book "had little incremental value over what was in the newspapers and in Embassy cables. But on other issues, like the situation in the Congo, the incremental value on those issues was great." Regardless, Bator says, "I liked getting them because it was a very efficient way to see what the President was seeing on worldwide topics." Robert Pursley, military assistant to three secretaries of defense starting with McNamara in April 1966, said the PDB had value "primarily for seeing what the president was seeing early in the morning. On top of that, it didn't have much value." Pursley recalls that when Clark Clifford succeeded McNamara at the Pentagon in February 1968, he was so concerned with getting US troops out of Vietnam that it was hard to focus him on anything else, including the PDB.

CIA officials who regularly saw the book had fonder memories of it. Cline, who was DDI when the PDB started, praised its sophistication. His deputy and successor, former OCI chief Jack Smith, recalled the pride that intelligence analysts had in providing their assessments to the president and his top aides every day. Helms took time during an Agency senior staff meeting in September 1966 to note the difficulties that the OCI faced in covering complicated subjects in limited space and tell his assembled managers simply that the publication was "remarkably well done."

Chapter Four

OUT IN THE COLD

Richard Nixon held long grudges. Few of them grew greater than the one he harbored toward the Central Intelligence Agency.

In the 1960 presidential debates, Senator John Kennedy had exploited perceptions of a "missile gap"—the since-discredited claim that the outgoing Eisenhower-Nixon administration had allowed the Soviet Union to achieve strategic superiority over the United States. Richard Helms, who served as CIA director for both Lyndon Johnson and Nixon, believed that Nixon felt he lost the election because of the supposed missile gap, saw the CIA's hand behind Kennedy's charge, and "had it in for the Agency" as a result.

The president-elect's distrust of what he saw as the anti-Nixon East Coast establishment—which he believed the CIA's analysts to be part of—further poisoned the well. During his first post-election session with soon-to-be national security advisor Henry Kissinger, Nixon excoriated the Agency as a group of "Ivy League liberals" who lacked analytic integrity and "had always opposed him politically." Kissinger reflected and reinforced Nixon's mind-set. "I thought the analytic branch was occasionally a subdivision of the *New York Times* editorial page," Kissinger says, "biased very much to the liberal point of view."

Directorate of Intelligence officers had grown accustomed to seeing the President's Daily Brief read and even appreciated every day. Their faith that its value would be clear to anyone coming into the Oval Office would soon be dashed.

MANHATTAN, MID-NOVEMBER 1968: UNIDENTIFIED men sneak into the basement of a building along Park Avenue, space that had recently housed a chapel for the headquarters of the North American Missionary Alliance. Ignoring curious glances from tenants and passers-by, the shadowy figures rush broken office machines and debris out of the site before efficiently moving in large safes, utilitarian office furniture, and state-of-the-art communications equipment. They seal the air ducts leading to other floors and weld into place street-level grilles above brand-new window air conditioners. Within seventy-two hours the team leaves just as quietly as it had come.

Had Secret Service officers set up a stealthy command post for Richard Nixon's nearby transition offices? Did uncover FBI agents acquire the space to interrogate Soviet spies and turn them against their masters? Occupants of the building could only speculate.

The truth was simpler: the CIA, during a single weekend, had established an unprecedented, full-time support hub for the intelligence needs of President-elect Nixon and his top staff, just steps away from their offices in the Hotel Pierre next door. Paul Corscadden and Ken Rosen, two senior analysts from the CIA's Office of Current Intelligence, led a small logistics team in an outpost that they called "DDI New York."

The Agency's security office decreed the site would stay anonymous, with no public tie to the CIA—or anything else, for that matter—thus drawing to its mysterious personnel just as much attention as a formal intelligence office might have done. Before long, the staff of the Hotel Pierre's mailroom and the building's other residents alike began asking the new office's workers for help with diverse problems, including locating a missing television set and tasting canned hams that supporters had sent to Nixon as Christmas gifts.

On Tuesday, November 19, Corscadden and Rosen started their work. They focused on two tasks: getting the PDB to Nixon's office and providing intelligence support to his top national security staff. The former was simple enough. Every morning by 5:30, the DDI New York officers received the Top Secret President's Daily Brief, Central Intelligence Bulletin, and Vietnam Situation Report via a secure communication link from CIA headquarters. They stuffed the papers in an envelope marked "Eyes Only—the President-Elect" and delivered it to Nixon's secretary at the Pierre, Rose Mary Woods, to whom the Agency had given both the appropriate clearances and a suitable safe to store the classified material.

Corscadden and Rosen ten days later added the "Nixon Special," an all-source intelligence memorandum just for him. This new material would cover the gap between the content of the PDB—which, after all, remained Lyndon Johnson's personal document—and what Nixon required to get up to speed. But the CIA team, absent direct contact with Nixon, lacked confidence about exactly what the president-elect needed, and they found themselves guessing.

The intelligence officers had greater success, initially, with Nixon's staff. OCI guru Dick Lehman came up to New York to brief campaign manager and attorney general–designate John Mitchell, chief of staff Bob Haldeman, and domestic policy advisor John Ehrlichman on technical intelligence issues. Mitchell ended up meeting with a CIA officer almost daily between mid-December and mid-January. Part of the DDI New York space served as a classified reading room for the fifteen or so Nixon staffers who had received security clearances quickly. Several visited to review daily intelligence publications, National Intelligence Estimates, special memoranda, intelligence handbooks, and various visual aids.

Dick Allen—Nixon's primary foreign policy advisor during the campaign and immediately after the election—came by the reading room often and offered Corscadden his thoughts about how the PDB might work better for his boss. Such tidbits from Allen spurred the officers back at the OCI in Langley to develop an expanded transition version of the PDB for Nixon. His modified book soon contained three sections. First came "Major Developments," subdivided initially into coverage of Vietnam, the Middle East, Soviet Affairs, and Europe, but shifting as events warranted. The next section, "Other Important Developments," highlighted looming but not yet critical national security issues. The new format closed with annexes featuring analyses that were more speculative than what usually appeared in the book's pages. Corscadden, Rosen, and their support team printed each day's PDB, bound it at the top like a legal brief, and delivered it to Nixon's office.

They learned on December 18 that the president-elect had not looked at any of them. Allen, who was named deputy national security advisor by Nixon in December 1968 after serving as Nixon's foreign policy coordinator for the campaign, was unsurprised by his boss's lack of interest in the PDB. "Back in 1968," he says, "Richard Nixon was not especially trusting in what the Agency would give him during the transition. He didn't place a whole lot of inspiration and faith into Agency interpretations."

Nixon remained elusive as he wrapped up his transition operations in New York and relocated to Washington for the inauguration. By the time it closed up shop on January 17, 1969, DDI New York had sent or received 523 messages to and from CIA headquarters. Its officers had processed 2,179 pages of text in less than two months. Corscadden and Rosen nevertheless failed to arrange even a single face-to-face meeting with the president-elect. They soon confirmed their suspicions about the president-elect's lack of interest in the book. The feedback came in the form of a delivery from Nixon's office, a towering stack of the previous two months' PDB envelopes—all of them unopened. A dejected Dick Lehman captured the feeling of the Directorate of Intelligence, calling the DDI New York innovation "an impressive performance, but to what end?"

"ONCE I WAS IN office," Allen remembers, "I lost track of seeing the President's Daily Brief, nor was I consulted by the Agency about the construct of the PDB." Henry Kissinger had taken control of both the president's national security sessions and related papers going into the Oval Office, including the PDB. "He made it into a sacrosanct item that he wasn't going to share," according to Allen. Substantive memoranda written by NSC senior staffers were sent to Kissinger's office, with the originating staffer's name removed and Kissinger's substituted. Allen maintained a separate channel to the president, which he used only sparingly. The staff hired by Kissinger rarely saw the president, a source of substantial dissatisfaction. Although Allen carried on as deputy national security advisor—"against my better judgment," he now says—his reduced opportunities to influence policy led him to leave as Nixon completed his first year in office.

The seeds for Kissinger's dominance had been planted back on December 2, when Nixon announced that Kissinger, not Allen, would be the next national security advisor. "We were dealing with Kissinger rather than anyone else from then on," Lehman recalled. "He was suspicious of the Agency. I don't know how much of it was

Nixon's suspicion that he was reflecting, or his own sense that there might be a central source of power here if he didn't put his foot down fairly firmly." Within weeks, Kissinger had received several ad hoc briefings from the DDI New York staff and had spoken for the president on who should receive the PDB, when they should see it, and what the book should look like. Upon reading his first few issues of the book, Kissinger had complained about the product's elliptical prose, seemingly random topics, and lack of continuity, driving the OCI to add speculative annexes to the PDB to highlight issues likely to hit the Nixon administration once in office.

"Do you have a regional quota for reports?" Kissinger asked Smith and Lehman in New York, after leafing through material about Panama. "So many for Africa, so many for South America?"

Confused, Smith replied, "No, why?"

"I don't understand why you are paying so much attention to Panama."

Smith relayed his analysts' judgment that boiling political tensions there had threatened American national interests. Naturally, he pointed out, the DI wanted to present its assessment of the situation on the ground to Nixon and Kissinger.

"But if anything happens there," Kissinger declared, "I would simply turn it over to an assistant secretary of state." Looking at Smith and Lehman, he added, "Our attention, the attention of Mr. Nixon and myself, is going to be centered on the Soviet Union and Western Europe."

Smith suspected that events would prevent Nixon and Kissinger from staying so removed from emerging trouble spots, but he swallowed his rebuttal. Instead, he broadened the discussion. "If you want us to refocus on a special aspect, just tell us. But please do not try to rework the material yourself because intelligence evidence is tricky."

"Oh, no," Kissinger replied. "You are the intelligence fellows. I will leave all that to you."

Smith said years later, "I left feeling considerably more reassured than it turned out I should have."

IN FACT, KISSINGER CAME to dominate the PDB process like no other national security advisor to this day. Before Nixon's inauguration, Kissinger directed his military assistant, Alexander Haig, to discover, and recommend changes to, the outgoing administration's distribution and handling of the nation's most sensitive document. The PDB's distribution at the White House, in the waning days of LBJ's term, included the press secretary (whom Haig suggested dropping, or at least putting on the reading list after the president saw the book) and General Maxwell Taylor, Johnson's special military assistant (whom Haig thought should stay on the list). Kissinger cut both. At the White House, only he and President Nixon would formally receive the PDB.

Haig also learned that Johnson had been receiving the PDB in his early morning package, at or before 6:30 a.m.—giving him nearly up-to-the-minute information and analysis straight from the CIA's analytic directorate, but minimizing his national security staff's opportunity to prepare for follow-on taskings. Kissinger had something else in mind. Starting on Nixon's first day in office, a CIA briefer delivered the next day's PDB at 5:30 p.m. Haig reminded Kissinger that this approach would introduce a seventeen-hour delay in the PDB's content by the time Nixon read it the following morning. No matter; this was the price the president would have to pay to enable his national security advisor to avoid unwelcome early morning

On February 20, 1972, President Richard Nixon sits with national security advisor Henry Kissinger, who controlled the flow to the president of all intelligence—including the PDB. *Courtesy Richard Nixon Presidential Library*

surprises from the CIA. Besides, Kissinger said, current intelligence officers could just put late-breaking items into the next-tier Central Intelligence Bulletin and call such issues to his attention in the morning. "Henry is brilliant," his former personal assistant David Young says, "but there is also this side of him in terms of wanting to have covered all the bases."

The PDB was just one of many documents in the robust stack of national security material the president received very morning. A daily Pentagon brief and State Department report joined the book, all of them underneath a White House summary prepared by the Situation Room with input from National Security Council (NSC) staffers, signed by Kissinger. "The president," says Robert McFarlane, who started on the NSC staff during the Nixon administration, "was left with having to wade through not just the normally six to eight pages of the PDB, but a lot more—triple the volume. On top of it all would be Henry's paper that would have started in the Situation Room. And then, often they would put even another memo on top of it that said, 'Here's why State or Defense is wrong in their judgment.'" This gave Kissinger the opportunity to preempt pieces in the PDB that he disagreed with, but he denies using the cover memo to divert the president's attention from the book: "We may have commented on it, expanded on it—but it wouldn't have been normal or sensible to summarize the PDB."

We will never know exactly how much attention Nixon gave to the President's Daily Brief. His failure to mention it in his recorded White House conversations, memoirs, and post-presidency interviews suggests that his PDBs barely influenced his thinking, if he read them at all. Kissinger once wrote that Nixon "frequently ignored it," echoing an unsourced comment in a 1971 *Newsweek* report that the president let Kissinger summarize the highlights for him because he didn't bother to read it himself. This would parallel the fate of the State Department's Evening Report memorandum for the president. Although White House staffers routinely put that into Nixon's morning reading stack, he rarely read it, according to the State Department's own internal history.

Former CIA current intelligence officer John Hedley offers a view widely held by his colleagues, noting, "Nobody from the Agency saw him directly with the PDB. The PDB went to Kissinger, who came back and said, 'The president doesn't like this,' or 'The president isn't interested in that.' We got the general feeling that the president was not terribly interested." Other former analysts are even more blunt. "I remember the deep frustration of Dick Lehman," one says. "At times, probably biased and distorted information was going to President Richard Nixon." Another officer vents, "We had the impression as young analysts that basically Nixon and Kissinger didn't give a crap about the PDB."

Kissinger, though, has retracted his earlier skepticism about the president's inattention to the PDB. "I am sure that Nixon read it," he says. His assistant David Young agrees. "Kissinger must have had two copies, because he would leave one with the President. And then the President might read it in the afternoon or at night. If it was really hot, something he was really bugged about, he'd call Henry: 'I just read in the PDB' something or other." And in August 1969, a senior NSC staffer told the deputy director for intelligence that Nixon had appreciated the PDB during his recent travels. "My suspicion," says Jim Schlesinger, who would become Nixon's second CIA director in early 1973, "is that even though he thought the Agency put out a lot of crap, he peeked at it. He was curious." An Agency analyst who worked on the PDB staff echoes this. "Nixon, being the devious guy he was, probably wanted to make sure that Kissinger was not the only voice who had his ear. This was a way of making sure he wasn't being blindsided by Kissinger."

More than Nixon, who had minimal contact with any CIA officials, Kissinger became the primary target of current intelligence efforts. Yet soon after the administration started, DI managers vented to an NSC staffer that "decision-makers and/or their staffs want to become their own intelligence analysts." The PDB itself failed to excite Kissinger. "You have to remember," he says, "Nixon and I both really knew a lot about foreign policy—we were not novices. So we didn't need a daily newspaper. On the whole, I preferred to read raw intelligence reports in order to get a feel for the situation." Having independent assessments of world developments each morning ranked low for him. "Nixon and I probably thought our analysis was as good as the CIA's. The PDB was not a central document in our thinking. It was one input." The national security advisor seemed to care much more about a wealth of other finished intelligence products: specific reports that *he* had tasked personally. His voracious appetite for these assessments spurred hundreds of White House requests for focused studies. "The burden placed on the Agency by the White House and the Kissinger staff is just fantastic. I don't know what they do with all this stuff," a senior officer noted at the time. Analysts detected Machiavellian intent, perceiving Kissinger's constant taskings as his way of keeping the DI so busy on pet projects that it could not trouble the president with independent analysis. "Kissinger certainly had a sense of how to take control of a bureaucracy," Hedley recalls. "He tied up analysts with demands. He would give you topic after topic after topic to write on, and that kept you from ginning up things on your own because you were responding to *those*."

In sharp contrast with the Johnson years—when director Helms had alerted his deputies and assistants every morning about issues on the minds of the president and his top aides—Nixon and Kissinger restricted senior CIA officials' access to the most sensitive policy deliberations, blocking insight into what intelligence inputs would help most. "Nobody came in and briefed the president as such under Nixon," Kissinger says. "I came in every morning and went over the issues that he raised and the issues that I raised. He would call in others as the situation required." Nixon grew increasingly detached from the PDB and other analytic products prepared for him. He told his President's Foreign Intelligence Advisory Board (PFIAB) in late 1969 that he valued the raw intelligence he received but considered the CIA's intelligence estimates "virtually worthless." An internal OCI document in early 1970 reflected the lament among current intelligence officers: "The policymaker tends to take his intelligence for granted, like the paper at the door in the morning, unless he has specifically asked for something."

DDI Jack Smith tolerated this situation for less than eighteen months before leaving his post for an overseas position. Kissinger and Haig had made their disdain for the CIA's analysis explicit in a meeting with the PFIAB in December 1970, where they lamented receiving intelligence assessments they saw as "flavored by policy considerations so that factual data are distorted or omitted in favor of policy preconceptions."

OUTSIDE THE WHITE HOUSE, the President's Daily Brief initially got into the hands of just four other men: secretary of state William Rogers, secretary of defense Melvin Laird, attorney general John Mitchell, and chairman of the Joint Chiefs of Staff Admiral Thomas Moorer. At the start of the administration, Helms told these readers that Agency couriers would visit their offices each day to deliver the current PDB and pick up the previous day's edition—preserving the security of the document that, he wrote, contained "the most sensitive material at hand." By late 1970, Vice President Spiro Agnew, the undersecretary of state, and the deputy defense secretary had been added.

The silence from Nixon about the PDB led Agency analysts to appreciate attention from these other readers even more. Laird, who received the book through secure CIA channels even when traveling, says, "I would always read it. I never disregarded it." He remembers that the PDB's content drove discussions with Admiral Moorer, sparked conversations during staff meetings, and prompted direct calls to Helms. "In a friendly fashion," he recalls, "I said, 'Dick, where the hell did you get that information?' or 'I don't agree with you there.'" Laird, in fact, appreciated the President's Daily Brief enough to argue that his deputy should join the tight circle of readers. "I went to Helms," he recalls, "and said, 'I'd like David Packard to have a copy.' He could have mine any day, because I kept it on the left-hand corner of my desk. But I felt he should have access to it, particularly when I was not in the building."

His interest made an impression. Long-serving intelligence community officer Charlie Allen, a member of the PDB staff early in Nixon's term, remembers Laird as the only official who frequently commented in the book's margins and regularly raised questions, especially about Vietnam. Says Allen, "I remember we used to joke, 'At least we've got *one* good reader who actually reads the thing and asks relatively decent questions.'" Laird turned into such a fan of the book, in fact, that he says he kept reading it even after leaving the Pentagon in January 1973 to become Nixon's domestic counselor, a job with little need for the PDB's foreign intelligence content. "I'm not sure whether I asked or not," he recalls, "but I know I got it."

George Shultz, Nixon's first secretary of labor, had agreed in early 1970 to move over to run the Bureau of the Budget. "President Nixon said we'd never seen a comprehensive view of all the money we spend on intelligence—where it is and what for," he recalls. So Nixon tasked Shultz to pull it together. "The intelligence people decided I must be important when I started doing that, looking at their budgets, so they said, 'Why don't we give you the President's Daily Brief?'" They delivered it to him, but not for long. "I decided I was not reading anything useful to me," Shultz says. "I was better off not having it; I told them to stop."

Attorney general John Mitchell was no average cabinet official; he stood out as one of Richard Nixon's only close personal friends. Even before the inauguration, Lehman—by then the CIA's deputy director of current intelligence—anticipated the incoming AG's status as a virtual "Assistant President." Nixon, who sought his attorney general's insights on matters well beyond the law, called him "my most trusted friend and adviser." The Agency responded. "Mr. Mitchell will need much more extensive intelligence and foreign policy support than his predecessors," Lehman told his boss at the time, Jack Smith, noting that he had been directed to give Mitchell "the same intelligence Mr. Nixon gets, including the PDB." So he did, even getting a CIA analyst to sit with Mitchell as he read the book each day.

Overall, Mitchell seemed to enjoy leafing through each day's book, pipe hanging out of his mouth. "Mitchell was very affable," one of his regular OCI briefers recalls. "He would read the thing as I sat there, and occasionally he would ask for more details about something. I had a special box of material that people saved for me because I wanted to read up on stuff that might not be in the PDB that he might want to ask me about." Early in the administration, protests against the Vietnam War rolled through the streets of Washington. The Justice Department became a target, sometimes affecting Mitchell's PDB sessions. His briefer had no trouble getting into the building during the demonstrations, but awkward moments still intruded. During one protest directly under Mitchell's office window, the briefer recalls, he was sitting inside and struggling to hear over the shouting. "Mitchell walked over to the window, looked out, and said, 'They ought to round up all those people and send them off someplace.'"

Another morning, after an election in Malta, Mitchell griped to a substitute briefer, "I've never seen you guys call one of these right." In fact, the previous day's PDB *had* nailed the election result—but the briefer had forgotten to read the earlier assessment before setting out.

"Well," he replied, "we called the Allende election right."

The rejoinder was ill-advised. Referring to the Chilean election in 1970—which had frustrated the Nixon administration enough to later try to overturn the elected Allende government in Santiago covertly—went over like a lead balloon with the attorney general. He simply snapped, "Then why didn't you do something about it?"

"I FEEL THERE IS a real problem here," Andrew Marshall wrote to Kissinger in March 1970, "and it starts at your and the President's levels." The national security advisor had brought Marshall from the RAND Corporation to the NSC as a consultant to evaluate, among other things, the president's morning intelligence package. Marshall's report to Kissinger revealed just how concerned some national security officials had become about the process for producing and delivering daily intelligence.

He told Kissinger that his examination of the president's marginal notes showed that the cover memorandum prepared in the Situation Room "probably is the only part of the package which the President regularly reads." Most notably, he cited an overlap of more than 30 percent between Situation Room memo items and the same day's PDB articles. "The success of the Situation Room product probably has driven the CIA PDB out of the President's focus of attention . . . two-thirds of the items in the PDB the President may never see."

Understanding how Washington worked, Marshall realized it was only a matter of time before CIA's current intelligence officers discovered the situation. He warned Kissinger that the Agency might start putting less effort into the book, "hoping to live through the current situation and later regain the position the PDB had with Presidents Kennedy and Johnson." This section of the memo appears to have caught the national security advisor's attention more than anything else in it. Where Marshall wrote that DDI Jack Smith had told him CIA officers considered themselves "almost as part of the President's staff" because they have "no other natural superior," Kissinger jotted in the margin next to it: "Don't discourage too much."

This overlap problem, Marshall warned, could bite Kissinger in two other ways. First, if Nixon believed that all he *needed* to read each day came in the first memo on his morning reading stack, the president might blame the national security advisor and his staff if an important item in the CIA PDB, but not in the Situation Room product, slipped by him. Second, Agency briefers also delivered the PDB every day to customers such as the secretary of state and secretary of defense, who remained unaware of the Situation Room memo and its "displacement of the PDB," Marshall wrote. "This could lead to some misunderstandings." He boldly pointed to problems at the top. "Your style of work and that of the President," he wrote to Kissinger, "are not conducive to a lot of feedback." The absence of clear direction forced everyone to guess what Nixon wanted, complicating efforts to coordinate. "Today CIA writes a type of newspaper, the PDB, hoping it is interesting and relevant," he added. Some NSC staffers had told Marshall that they simply had "no feeling for what is read, whether the Situation Room product and/or the PDB."

The exhaustive study prompted just one small modification: Kissinger wanted to see a sample of a new format for the daily cover memo that reduced the number of analytic items and added a brief second section of short, merely descriptive items. But the fundamental problem remained unaddressed. Even three years later, senior Nixon staffers informed CIA officers that they were still drawing on PDB articles for their own cover memo.

In a more revolutionary proposal, which Kissinger ignored, Marshall appeared well ahead of his time. He recommended dropping hard-copy products in favor of a "flexible on-line reading program," which would allow the national security advisor (and, eventually, the president) to select the level of detail he wanted for each morning intelligence item, read the result on a computer monitor, request additional material with a button, and have staffers automatically informed of the topics selected and how much attention they received. "This would have been totally wasted on me," reflects Kissinger. "Neither Nixon or I would have had interest. You have to consider that both Nixon and I were technologically challenged; I wouldn't have known what a computer was at that point." After Kissinger's pocket veto, the idea would only come to pass forty years later, in a different form, when President Barack Obama started receiving his PDB on an iPad.

THE BEST WINDOW INTO the president's thinking about the President's Daily Brief as the administration started came not from Henry Kissinger or Nixon himself, but from John Mitchell.

CIA director Helms, concerned that Nixon's disregard for the PDB while in New York might continue now that he was in office, sent Jack Smith to Kissinger to discuss current intelligence support. When Smith arrived in the national security advisor's basement office, Kissinger fortuitously was sitting with Mitchell—who rose to leave as Smith raised the PDB. Kissinger stopped him, recognizing his unparalleled insight into Nixon's mind, and asked him to weigh in. Mitchell said the PDB too casually mixed information with analytic interpretations. "The President is a lawyer," he said between puffs on his pipe, "and a lawyer wants facts."

It was precious little to go on. But the quip stood out as the most useful tip anyone had given Smith about the reclusive president. So Smith ordered OCI analysts to start separating facts and opinions in PDB items, inserting commentary into the text only after citing the relevant intelligence reporting. Officers of the time recall clearly the new format. "You started out with a factual lead," John Hedley notes, "and then it would go into italics because this is our comment or our analysis. Presumably, Kissinger knew why we did that and pointed out to Nixon why it was that way."

The approach didn't last long. By August 1969, the PDB's text lacked any such italics or stylistic innovations. Instead, Nixon got a strict, no-frills appearance: simple paragraphs and short supporting points. On August 19, 1969, the PDB's three pages included short items on the scale of Communist attacks in Vietnam, Israeli Labor Party dynamics, West Germany's stance on the Non-Proliferation Treaty, the United Kingdom's efforts to deal with violence in Northern Ireland, Sino-Soviet border skirmishes, India's hotly contested presidential election, and the appointment of two Pakistani military officers as governors. Some of the material appears overly tentative and full of caveats: "Sporadic enemy activity marked the Vietnamese Communist holiday of 19 August. The attacks fell far short of what had been forecast in intelligence reports during the past few weeks. Allied spoiling operations may account for part of the shortfall, but the original Communist objectives probably were overinflated in many cases."

The next day's book, which featured analysis on Soviet relations with Czechoslovakia and China as well as Soviet space developments, shows an emphasis on openly available sources and a lack of analysis, as in this short piece: "The Chinese chose the eve of the anniversary of the Soviet invasion to issue another lengthy attack on the USSR as the aggressor in the prolonged border dispute. The note charges the Soviets with more than 400 provocations during June and July, and denounces Moscow for talking about normalizing the situation while actually adopting measures which intensify tensions. Moscow meanwhile pointedly commemorated the thirtieth anniversary of a victory over the Japanese on the Manchurian border." Marshall's fears that the Agency would reduce its PDB effort if substantive feedback from its top customers remained lacking seemed to have come true. "The PDB is something that happened to an item that you might have written for other products," recalls one analyst who started during the Nixon administration. "You did the other work, and PDBs happened by chance."

Current intelligence analysts found themselves thinking less about the president than about the pet peeves of DI reviewers who *did* care about the product. Memos circulating in the OCI told writers that editors "prune some articles of excess verbiage, add a paragraph or two of interpretation to some, and rewrite a few others to make the message more pointed." Such bland information left analysts vulnerable to the cantankerous editors who reviewed all analytic articles. "My lessons in clear writing came when I had slaved away on a piece down on my black-key Royal typewriter," one officer says. After getting his PDB article through his branch chief's and group chief's reviews, he went upstairs to the editing staff.

> I'm standing in line, about three back, reading my piece. And the editor in front—smoking a cigarette, sleeves rolled up, about as old school as you could get—has some poor wretch up there, whose piece is in front of the guy. And he's editing it with a ballpoint pen.
>
> Suddenly he looks up, to nobody in particular and everybody, and barks, "There's not one fucking active verb in this whole fucking piece!" I look down at my draft, and it's full of passive voice. So I slipped out of there, went back down to my office, and retyped it.

Lyndon Johnson had vouched for Helms as a nonpartisan, merit appointment during the transition, prompting the incoming president to keep him on the job. But the relationship between Nixon and Helms began roughly. While incoming defense secretary Melvin Laird helped kill Nixon's plan to exclude his CIA director from meetings of the NSC, the president still dismissed Helms from such sessions immediately after the factual intelligence briefings—reducing the director's ability to identify additional opportunities for the PDB to support presidential policies. Helms bluntly called Nixon "perpetually cranky" when dealing with the Agency.

"There was not very much opportunity to talk with him personally," Helms later said about Nixon. "He liked to deal through Kissinger and Haig, and so we had an arrangement whereby written reports were sent to him and he read them. When necessary, one could talk to him, obviously, but it was a more stylized and formal arrangement." Because Kissinger's monopoly of the president's national security time prevented direct substantive meetings between Nixon and Helms, the national security advisor became the CIA director's main point of contact. Kissinger says he regularly called Helms to ask him what he thought.

Nixon's criticisms of the CIA at NSC meetings hit harder. Helms said Nixon repeatedly would "pick on the Agency" and "make nasty remarks." In a June 1969 NSC meeting, he accused analysts of trying to "use intelligence to *support* conclusions, rather than to *arrive* at conclusions."

The president's attitude grew more vitriolic as his time in office progressed. He brags in his memoirs about mocking Agency officers in March 1970, in the presence of secretary of state Rogers, for failing to predict that anti-Communist military officer Lon Nol would overthrow Cambodian leader Prince Sihanouk: "What the hell do those clowns do out there in Langley?" The following year, he ranted to a roomful of federal officials assembled to discuss the budget, "The CIA tells me nothing I don't read three days earlier in the *New York Times*. . . . The CIA isn't worth a damn." He went on to lament the billions of dollars spent on intelligence issues to "learn nothing."

His attacks often returned to the same themes that he had carried with him for many years. In describing the Agency to Haldeman in May 1972 as a "muscle-bound bureaucracy which has completely paralyzed its brain," Nixon suggested that its workforce remained "primarily Ivy League and the Georgetown set rather than the type of people that we get in the services and the FBI." In one of many directives that the chief of staff simply ignored, Nixon then ordered Haldeman to get rid of half of all senior CIA officers by the end of the year "so that we can move to get in some better people." He added, "In filling our needs I want you to give first priority to those schools who have presidents or faculty members who have wired us or written us their support of what we have done in Vietnam."

FOR YEARS, HELMS AVOIDED rocking the boat—which kept him in office but left him vulnerable to White House manipulation. In a memo to Kissinger in November 1970, Haig had written, "Helms will play whatever role the President wants him to play." Nixon also felt that Helms owed him one for a minor favor: the president had told his CIA director he would back any legal action Helms took to prevent two former Agency officers from publishing a tell-all book.

Despite Haig's assessment that the holdover CIA director would always do what the president wanted, Helms had a limit. Not long after news broke in 1972 about the break-in at the Watergate Hotel, Helms was asked to give the FBI a national security excuse for it to cut off the budding investigation. Helms and his deputy, General Vernon Walters, steadfastly refused. Longtime senior analyst and manager Ray Cline said nobody could have handled the sticky situation better than Helms. The director even earned praise from Kissinger, who called him responsible with his authority and "meticulously fair and discreet."

Helms took Nixon's scorn for more than four years before the president pushed him out, ending a difficult relationship for both sides. After his reelection in November 1972, the president had called on all top officers to submit their resignation letters—without letting anyone know which ones he planned to accept. Viewing his appointment as nonpolitical, Helms ignored the order and directed Walters to follow suit. No reaction came for two weeks. Then Nixon invited the CIA director to join him at Camp David on November 20. Helms guessed the president wanted to discuss the CIA's budget. Instead, Nixon fired him.

Seemingly on the spur of the moment, Nixon offered him an ambassadorship, which Helms would soon accept (eventually moving to Tehran to serve as US ambassador to Iran starting in April 1973). Helms thought the president had agreed to let him stay at the CIA until the end of March, when he would turn sixty and qualify for Agency retirement, but the president either missed the point or changed his mind. He shocked Helms by waiting only a few weeks before nominating his successor: James Schlesinger, chairman of the Atomic Energy Commission.

The brash, forty-four-year-old Schlesinger had completed a study on the intelligence community for the president back in 1971, when he had been serving as deputy director of the Bureau of the Budget. "One time I flew up to Camp David with the President in his helicopter," he recalls. "Nixon looked down at the parking lot at the CIA facility and said, 'Look at them, what the hell are they all doing?'" Schlesinger generally shared the president's views of the Agency, especially about the need for a change in direction at the top.

With a strong mandate to take on the Agency's elite, Schlesinger ruffled feathers early. He barked at senior staff, "God damn it, what you people don't understand is that you work for the United States government." His grumpiness targeted analysts most. Just before his confirmation, he told the CIA's operations chief that he planned to dismantle the Directorate of Intelligence. Although he dropped the threat, he often lectured DI managers about how to serve PDB readers: "Remember who you are dealing with," he recalls telling them. "Think of how you are saying things. All of these people have predilections. Think of ways of saying things that don't trip them up. You raise hackles because of your wording."

If Schlesinger's tough stance with current intelligence officers aimed to improve the president's impressions of the PDB, it failed. A group of senior White House staffers told DI leaders in March 1973 that Nixon and Kissinger remained dissatisfied with current intelligence overall. They noted, in particular, that "the PDB consistently fails to meet the intelligence requirements/interests of the President." One of the White House officials said he had "no confidence that the PDB will improve." Around the same time, Kissinger told a CIA officer that on an Arab-Israeli issue, he wanted assessments only from Agency operations officers—collectors of raw intelligence—not from "those DI bastards."

Nixon barely let Schlesinger get settled at Langley before yanking him, too, by nominating him to replace Elliot Richardson as secretary of defense. "I was only effectively at the CIA for four months," Schlesinger recalls. And by June, the Agency—and its PDB—fell again into limbo.

DESPITE TUMULTUOUS ANTI–VIETNAM WAR protests that focused on William Colby's role in the CIA's "pacification" efforts while serving as an operations officer and senior manager of covert actions, he received Senate confirmation as CIA director in July. He started briefing the president at formal national security meetings, but his relationship to Nixon remained just as distant as his predecessors' had been. In more than a year as director, Colby received *one* call from the president, an out-of-the-blue question about China. He focused instead on reenergizing current intelligence.

On one front, Colby pressed Kissinger—who had taken his close-to-the-vest style with him to the State Department in September 1973, when he became secretary of state as well as national security advisor—to give CIA analysts more inside information for their assessments. He wanted them to see copies of no-distribution (NODIS) cable traffic, the State Department's most sensitive reporting, about Middle East peace negotiations. The lack of analytic insight into Kissinger's secretive diplomatic efforts had been raised before. A senior Agency official warned an NSC staffer back in October 1972 that Agency frustrations raged even then. "I pointed out that if he [Kissinger] should leave this world tomorrow or even leave the Government at some point, there would be a large vacuum to represent all that he had experienced." Referring to Nixon, he added, "One of these days, you can bet your hat, he will ask why we don't know more about Brezhnev and we will be in a nice position to come back and say because [Kissinger] never told us!" Deputy national security advisor Brent Scowcroft told Kissinger at the end of 1973 that he saw no reason to reject the director's request for NODIS cables, given they had handled other sensitive matters "with discretion." Kissinger approved the change. But Colby said that within weeks, CIA analysts would be excluded from NODIS material again because of a new policy initiative.

Colby also went big, revolutionizing the CIA's product line. He started with the Central Intelligence Bulletin. Its diverse readership had led by 1968 to a trifurcated sub-PDB product, with different customers and varying levels of classification. The exclusive "Black Book," classified at the Top Secret level and including satellite imagery, went to the three dozen or so seniormost customers below the president, some (but not all) of whom also saw the PDB. Then came the Top Secret "Red Book," which lacked clandestine photography and was delivered to roughly 150 next-tier officials as well as to Kissinger and White House military assistant General Maxwell Taylor. Finally, the Secret-level "White Book" made its way to about a thousand readers but avoided sensitive intelligence sources. As deputy director early in 1973, Colby had found himself confused and frustrated by the analytic differences among the three CIBs and the PDB. He asked DI officers why they bothered to issue the lowest-level CIB version at all.

In September, just days after being sworn in, he revisited a proposal he'd offered as a junior officer in the 1950s and seen rejected by director Allen Dulles: reformatting the CIB as a fold-out newspaper (instead of a standard-sized bound document) that would offer readers a choice on each item between a succinct headline and an in-depth article, in a product incorporating more input from other parts of the US intelligence community.

Kissinger had encouraged Colby to experiment, but he turned against what Colby named the National Intelligence Daily, or NID. "I'm going to get that thing abolished!" he told Colby at a White House meeting several months after the NID's debut. "I just can't take seriously anything that looks like a newspaper!" Most other recipients, however, warmed to the idea.

The shift to the NID in late 1973 and early 1974 drove Agency leaders to streamline the distribution of all current intelligence publications. Lehman dropped many lower-level recipients from the CIB's distribution, making the new National Intelligence Daily an elite publication. Fewer than fifty copies of the NID would be distributed to the former PDB readership, the NSC staff, and a few other national security officials. "It is no hyperbole to say that, with the DCI's decision to proceed with the *National Intelligence Daily*, OCI is moving into the most ambitious current intelligence project ever undertaken in

Washington," Lehman told colleagues. "A few years ago, there were complaints that our analysts were under-employed. I do not believe we need worry about this any longer. We will all have to work like hell."

The birth of the NID allowed CIA to return the President's Daily Brief to the most exclusive status it had seen since the first days of John Kennedy's President's Intelligence Checklist. With most senior policy makers now getting the NID, the OCI started delivering the PDB exclusively to the White House for the president and the national security advisor only. Bob Haldeman, still Nixon's chief of staff, informed the director in 1973 that the PDB worked fine in that format. He suggested that its authors keep the prose as concise as possible and maintain wide margins for notes despite the lack of any evidence that Nixon wrote much on the PDBs themselves. Without feedback to the contrary about the PDB, Lehman in late 1973 told his current intelligence workforce that Nixon "specifically does not want it changed." He assured Colby a few months later that he still operated under Haldeman's guidance that the president "likes the PDB as it is."

The perception, accurate or not, that the book remained adequate in Nixon's eyes prompted Lehman to spend more time working on Colby's new NID than on the president's book.

AT ITS BEST, THE President's Daily Brief grants to the president and his closest circle of advisors unique insights into foreign leaders' actions, national security threats, and international opportunities. At its worst, the PDB swings and misses. And on October 6, 1973, just a month after Colby had replaced Schlesinger, the analysis in the book was completely, disastrously, and embarrassingly wrong.

Charlie Allen had been a current intelligence officer since joining the Agency in the late 1950s. His experience included writing pieces for the President's Daily Brief and what was still the Central Intelligence Bulletin and managing military intelligence production in the DI's Office of Strategic Research. By the fall of 1973, when perennially tense relations between Israel and its Arab neighbors deteriorated further, he had moved to the current intelligence production staff to watch over the daily development and production of the PDB and the CIB.

Israeli and US intelligence agencies alike had judged that Egypt and Syria, facing an overwhelmingly superior Israeli military, would not start a new war. For example, a few months earlier, Schlesinger had told Kissinger that Egyptian leaders had tasked their military's General Staff to plan a Suez Canal crossing to attack Israeli positions in the occupied Sinai Peninsula. But Schlesinger added his analysts' conclusion that any preparations appearing to set the stage for such an attack would serve only psychological purposes and would, in fact, reveal nothing about true Egyptian actions. In early October, after the Soviet Union removed its official advisors' dependents from Egypt—historically, a strong indicator of pending hostilities—a CIA Middle Eastern chief of station sent in a seven-page appraisal concluding that Egypt would not go to war. "In my view," a Middle East analyst of the time recalls, "the game was over at that point. For Washington-based analysts to go up against the guy on the ground was a very steep mountain to climb."

"On October 5," Allen says, "I spent a good deal of the day working with the analysts . . . on a Central Intelligence Bulletin, from which a President's Daily Brief was written, on the continuing military activity in both Egypt and Syria. We assessed that the state of activity in Egypt—including the alert of Egyptian air, defense, and air forces, as well as their ground and naval shipments—was worrying. We rationalized, however, that Cairo usually conducts such activities in the fall and the spring."

Allen remembers finishing his work on the current intelligence products around 8:00 on Friday evening. He swung through the CIA's Operations Center, where a watch officer reported that Fatah, the Palestinian resistance wing led by Yasser Arafat, had gone on a war footing. "This worried me a bit," he recalls. "I thought about calling in analysts to take a look at this and other material that seemed to be flowing, in increased volume, into the Ops Center. But it was Friday. It had been a long week. So I went home."

It fell to another current intelligence officer, Dick Kovar, to stick around a little longer to update the daily publications, as necessary, based on new intelligence reports or late-breaking world events. "I was waiting for a final input, which was going to come directly from the horse's mouth, because it was going to come from the chiefs of Israeli intelligence," Kovar remembers. The document that finally came in ended with the Israeli assessment that the chances of any action remained low. So Kovar signed off on the final draft and left. "I was so

President Nixon meets with Kissinger, House majority leader/vice president–designate Gerald Ford, and chief of staff Al Haig, October 13, 1973. *Courtesy Richard Nixon Presidential Library*

sure, if the Israelis said nothing is going to happen, nothing is going to happen. I went out to dinner, got home late, and went to bed."

Scowcroft recalls hearing, immediately upon his arrival at the White House the next morning, that the Egyptians had attacked Israel. "And then I opened the PDB," he says, "and it said that the maneuvers this year were particularly realistic." Indeed, that Saturday, the president and his top advisors' daily intelligence report said: "The exercise and the activities underway in Egypt may be on a somewhat larger scale and more realistic than previous exercises, but they do not appear to be preparations for a military offensive against Israel." Nixon wrote that news of the attack shocked him, in part because of such Agency assessments about the nature of Egypt's military movements.

Kissinger remembers it clearly, too, but avoids shifting the blame entirely to the Agency: "Look—they were wrong on everything. But so was I. We just didn't think they had the balls to attack the Israelis. And we all thought the Israelis would kill them quickly, and therefore they wouldn't do it. So we were all wrong." Like his boss, Scowcroft understood why the analysis missed the mark. Looking back, he reflects, "Logic says it won't happen. What they didn't figure out is what Sadat had in mind: just a quick attack to give him some negotiating space. From his standpoint, it made great sense. Not from an overall military assessment of trying to destroy Israel—but that wasn't what he had in mind."

Bob Gates, then a young intelligence officer advising an arms control delegation in Geneva, remembers that the failure of the PDB and other daily publications before the Egyptian invasion led to his most embarrassing moment as an analyst. The products from CIA headquarters—which he delivered dutifully to his delegation chief, the legendary elder statesman Paul Nitze—stated clearly that Egypt would not invade. Nitze saw the text and bluntly asked Gates if he had listened to the radio while coming into the office that morning. Gates said no, and learned from Nitze only then what everyone in the world but him seemed to know: hostilities had already begun.

A ringing telephone had awoken Charlie Allen's wife before dawn. She pushed the phone to her husband, who heard a DI manager say that new reports made it clear Egypt and Syria would invade Israel within a few hours—leaving Israel, which needed seventy-two hours to mobilize its defense forces, too little time to stop the attack. "Come to work," the senior officer ordered. "Report to Dick Lehman."

"In the years that followed," Allen says, "I felt a personal responsibility for contributing to the failure to warn." The lesson he took remained a common one for DI analysts after missed calls in decades to come: "I swore that I would always work a lot harder in re-examining my assumptions and views."

While continuing to write for the president and other senior policy officials, analysts also stepped up their support via a Middle East Task Force (METF). The surged team of intelligence officers, hastily assembled to provide around-the-clock support to senior officials at the Agency and downtown, prepared an initial take on the situation that first morning in time for a 9:00 a.m. meeting at the White House. Every half hour thereafter, the principal CIA office passing assessments to the White House received updates from the METF, which continued to produce situation reports up to four times a day throughout the height of the fighting.

Within a couple of days, director Colby brought back to the Agency news that Kissinger had held up the most recent situation report during a meeting at the White House, saying, "Have you all seen this?" After everyone nodded, he said, "Then we can dispense with the briefing." The task force received a memorandum from Colby relaying Nixon's and Kissinger's praise and thanks for its work.

"HEY, WINSTON, THERE'S A task force going on," the young analyst's boss barked. "Go upstairs, stand in the corner, and watch. Don't touch anything—because you'll probably break it. Just see what happens."

It was late July 1974. Winston Wiley was about to receive his first view of an essential part of the CIA's analytic mission. For on this summer day, while the Supreme Court debated whether President Nixon had to turn over his recordings of White House conversations related to the Watergate investigation, Washington's national security bureaucracy was dealing with the Turkish invasion of Cyprus.

Following orders, Wiley ran up to the seventh floor, which housed the Agency's executive suites and its Operations Center, where the Cyprus task force had found a makeshift home. Slipping into one of the few open spots afforded by the crowded space, he saw a rapidly repurposed conference room. Frantic analysts manned an oversized table that groaned under the weight of a dozen typewriters. Officers ran in, attaching new stacks of raw intelligence reports to clipboards spread throughout the room. Others darted out, carrying various situation reports and memoranda for distribution to CIA leaders and senior policy makers.

Awestruck, Wiley stood for a few minutes, watching the spectacle playing out in front of him. Making eye contact with one of the less frenzied people in the room, he said, "What are you guys doing now?"

"We're writing the sit rep that's going down to the White House, and it's going right to the president," the chief of the ad hoc group replied. Looking his questioner straight in the eye, he added slowly, "Because that's what we do."

Wiley had no time to respond. A watch officer from the main floor of the adjoining Ops Center threw the door open and yelled, "The Supreme Court says he's got to give up the tapes!" Everyone in the room dropped what he was doing. As one, the assembled officers let out a resounding "Yay!" And then, just as quickly, their heads went back down to the intelligence reports in front of them.

"Clearly, the majority sentiment in the room was 'Get the bum out,'" Wiley says. "It was a five-second interruption, at most. This was the apolitical nature and the ethic of the place."

For the young Wiley, who would rise to become the deputy director for intelligence from 2000 to 2002, the episode brought home a key message: the profession demands that analysts put aside their politics when assessing foreign events and presenting assessments. Respect for the positions that policy makers hold requires objective analysis, free from personal bias, even during a constitutional crisis. In this case, the president would resign within weeks and leave the Oval Office to a man Americans had never elected to national office. Yet CIA officers just kept producing the intelligence publications— immune, by all appearances, to the storm of controversy sweeping through the nation's capital.

CHAPTER FIVE

FACE-TO-FACE

GERALD FORD NEVER ASPIRED to an office higher than Speaker of the House of Representatives. So when Vice President Spiro Agnew resigned in disgrace in October 1973 to face tax evasion charges, Ford had little interest in succeeding him. He also started out low on embattled President Richard Nixon's list of candidates for the open position. The president preferred to nominate John Connally, who had served as both governor of Texas and US treasury secretary. Nixon even quipped, in the Oval Office, to then New York governor Nelson Rockefeller, "Can you imagine Jerry Ford sitting in this chair?" But his advisors and congressional allies eventually convinced him that only Ford—the congressman from Michigan with universally acknowledged integrity and friends on both sides of the aisle—would receive confirmation in the wake of the Watergate scandal.

Ford's experience had prepared him to appreciate and use the highest level of intelligence. Starting as a young representative more than two decades earlier, Ford had served on the House Defense Appropriations Subcommittee. He had been one of a handful of representatives who kept an eye on the CIA long before the establishment of formal oversight committees in the late 1970s. Sitting on the Foreign Operations Appropriations Subcommittee and serving nearly nine years as House minority leader, he attended numerous briefings from intelligence and other international affairs officials. His work took him to Europe and Southeast Asia. He engaged secretaries of state, secretaries of defense, and CIA directors.

Nevertheless, Ford lacked executive experience. He thus knew nothing about any of the top-tier current intelligence for senior policy makers. That would change quickly as he became the nation's second in command.

FORD BECAME THE FORTIETH vice president of the United States on December 6, 1973. Almost immediately he began receiving regular national security support, building on his interest in such issues as well as the growing realization among Nixon's inner circle that the president's chances of completing his second term had become dim. Henry Kissinger, who wore both the national security advisor *and* secretary of state hats starting in September 1973, briefed Ford about leading international developments every two weeks. Then Brent Scowcroft, Kissinger's deputy for managing the NSC process and staff, began sitting with Ford for an hour or two every week. Additionally, CIA director William Colby visited the vice president right after he took office to get him up to speed on a full range of intelligence issues.

On June 12, 1974, Ford visited CIA headquarters to receive wide-ranging presentations about intelligence analysis and operations. During a break from the substantive sessions, Colby walked the vice president through the building to show him artifacts from the Agency's history and pop him into a few offices to witness intelligence officers at work. Ford visited the Office of Current Intelligence, where analysts produced the newly created National Intelligence Daily (NID), which the vice president had been seeing every day, and the PDB. Ford asked about the latter, prompting Colby to describe the highly sensitive daily book—and then offer it to the vice president.

A CIA-published retrospective suggests the PDB exposure was "innocent" and "inadvertent," but Colby recalled thinking at the time, "We should get the PDB to the Vice President so that he would know everything the President knew. We didn't want another situation like when Truman was unaware of the Manhattan project." In fact, a memo to Ford's defense assistant, Jack Marsh, that Colby wrote the day *before* the visit included a brief biography of the "analyst we propose to offer to service the Vice President's special interests in publications or briefing on intelligence matters, if Mr. Ford feels that would be useful." Whatever Colby's intent, the White House added Ford to the short list of authorized PDB recipients.

"Mr. Ford accepted my suggestion that the PDB be brought to him directly," says Dave Peterson, an experienced senior current intelligence officer selected to facilitate intelligence support to the vice president. Ford accepted, according to Peterson, "acknowledging that this would be the most secure way to receive the sensitive document." This would be Peterson's sole duty; allowing one person to devote all of his energy to meeting the vice president's needs was a novel move. Peterson told colleagues that he got tapped for this simply because he was between jobs and the powers that be could not find a better fit at the time for someone at his high pay grade. More likely, Agency leaders matched Peterson to Ford because of their shared roots in the upper Midwest—the vice president was from Michigan, while Peterson was from Minnesota—and their similar personalities. Peterson had impressed colleagues and policy makers alike with his pleasant manner, suggesting he would hit it off with the similarly down-to-earth Ford and develop what Dick Lehman called a "comfortable relationship."

Ford elected to get the PDB early each morning, as his first business item each day, starting on July 1. The personalized PDB sessions—often in the backseat of Ford's car as he was driven downtown, sometimes at the kitchen table of Ford's modest home in Alexandria, Virginia—went well from the start. Peterson said Ford was always a gracious host, making instant coffee for his guest. The VP seemed to truly enjoy hearing Peterson's stories about intelligence as well as his analytic insights about items in the President's Daily Brief. Sessions held downtown, in Ford's office, could go quite long; Ford's schedule from July 1, 1974, shows that he spent a full hour discussing current intelligence with Peterson and Marsh.

On days when he briefed Ford in the car, such as when the vice president was traveling to a morning speaking engagement or to the airport, Peterson arranged for a CIA car to drive behind the vice president's Secret Service chase cars. That way he could get back to CIA headquarters after Ford had finished reading the PDB. One day Peterson jumped out of Ford's car, raced back to the car behind it, and leaped in. In the front seat, where he expected to find his Agency driver, sat someone he had never seen before: a woman commuting into the city. She was rather surprised to find a man with a locked briefcase hopping into her car without warning.

Colby's deft maneuver made Ford the first vice president to receive the PDB directly from a CIA briefer. Even on days when Ford could not take the briefing, such as when he met early with President Nixon or traveled to an event out of town, Peterson supported him by passing pertinent information to Marsh so that *he* could bring Ford up to speed. For example, a declassified CIA memo from late July 1974 reveals that Peterson informed Marsh, not Ford, ahead of an announcement in Athens that Greece's military ruler, Brigadier General Dimitrios Ioannides, was being removed from power.

Not everyone loved Ford's PDB briefing procedure. Peterson later heard that when Kissinger, who had kept a tight leash on national security arrangements in the White House since 1969, learned after the fact about the daily briefing routine with Ford, he was "furious."

THE SUPREME COURT'S RULING on July 24, 1974, that Richard Nixon had to release the "smoking gun" White House tape from June 23, 1972— during which he could be heard agreeing to obstruct the FBI investigation into the Watergate break-in—virtually guaranteed that he would be impeached by the House of Representatives and convicted by the Senate. After wrestling with the momentous decision for a couple of weeks, the president resigned his office on August 9, 1974, thereby elevating to the presidency the very man he had mocked as undeserving of the office less than a year earlier. Gerald Ford became president despite never being elected to anything beyond the representative of a few hundred thousand people in Michigan's Fifth Congressional District.

Suddenly Ford faced much greater demands on his time than he had just hours earlier, along with intense pressure to tighten his schedule. The daily PDB session with Peterson seemed a likely casualty. But Ford calmly resisted the temptation to drop it.

On his first night as president, he told his transition team and key advisors that he would continue to start his business each day with Peterson a little before 8:00 a.m., before any other substantive meetings or office work. As if to preempt questions about why he would take time with a CIA briefer every day instead of just going through the PDB on his own, he told those in the room that he was a better listener than a reader. "Ford was a very diligent president," recalls Bud McFarlane, who at the time was an NSC staffer. "He knew what he didn't know, and he was trying to do his best to absorb quite a bit of information."

"That Saturday morning," Peterson notes, "Mr. Ford seemed as awed as I was when he entered the Oval Office to begin his first full day as Chief Executive." He found the Oval Office surreal, a pale imitation of its usual glory. "The walls and the furniture in the Office were bare—thanks to the removal of Mr. Nixon's pictures and possessions." Even the desk sat empty but for a telephone.

Ford—joined that day by Nixon's chief of staff Alexander Haig, who stayed close to Ford during the transition—sat behind the desk, joking with Haig that he would rely on him to ensure his desk stayed so clean. Peterson updated the new president on a sensitive operation, handed him the President's Daily Brief, and then answered a few of Ford's questions. Ford declared that he liked this routine for his PDB and would keep it to help him prepare for his morning meetings with Kissinger.

"The initial session in the Oval Office ended on a mildly embarrassing note for me," Peterson recalls. "I exited the Office through the nearest door—only to find myself at a dead end. A second door, which I later learned led to a smaller, more private office for the president, was locked, trapping me in the passageway." Finding no way out other than via the door he had just shut, he timidly returned to the Oval Office—where Ford and Haig remained in discussion. "I knocked, opened the door with my apologies and sheepishly explained my predicament." Ford laughed, said he didn't know his way around the West Wing very well either, and directed Peterson to the proper door. One of Peterson's colleagues says the president soothed his nervous briefer by saying, "The first time I tried to leave this office, that's what *I* did."

During his senior staff meeting the next Monday morning, Ford asked his advisors if they thought deputy national security advisor Brent Scowcroft should join the president's PDB session. Scowcroft, after all, was reading the PDB every day at the White House, in a separate meeting with Peterson, while he stood in for Kissinger. Haig—surely shocked that Ford was taking an in-person CIA briefing at all, diverging so dramatically from Nixon administration practice—quickly said yes. Nobody disagreed and Ford concurred, so Scowcroft added the meetings with Peterson to his own morning schedule. Later that week, Kissinger gave his blessing to the Peterson-Scowcroft briefing arrangement; it remains unclear whether any objection he raised would have mattered at all to Ford, who had become quite attached to his daily PDB briefing.

"Scowcroft's presence undoubtedly enhanced the value of the intelligence briefing for Mr. Ford," Peterson recalls. The deputy national security advisor would either immediately answer the president's questions about the policy implications of the PDB material or request follow-on assessments. Either way, his presence minimized the possibility that Peterson, whether purposely or inadvertently, would unduly influence the president's national security decisions instead of merely informing them. "No previous President had derived such prompt benefit from the Agency's current intelligence reports," adds Peterson. And by carrying the book away after Ford had read it, Peterson notes, the CIA kept "complete control of his copy of the publication." The wide White House staff exposure that the PDB had seen during much of President Nixon's administration disappeared.

The DI, by then, had already begun tailoring the PDB to the new president. Emboldened by their tighter distribution of the book, Agency leaders now included information based on extremely sensitive human intelligence sources, from highly classified intercepted communications, and about CIA operational activities that had not made it into print before. Designated officers typed these special supplements on separate pages, stapling them into only the White House copies of the book to prevent too many eyes even at Langley from seeing them. Current intelligence managers also informed their analysts, within days of Ford's ascendance, that the new president preferred "short sentences, short paragraphs, and simple language." The shift seemed to do the trick. Peterson reported to his DI managers a few weeks later that the president was reading both the President's Daily Brief and the next-level-down National Intelligence Daily every day.

Every day immediately after the briefing, Peterson called the director of the OCI, his boss back at CIA headquarters, to ensure that the president's queries about and comments on PDB items made it to the director's daily senior staff meeting at 9:00 a.m. He then visited the White House Situation Room to give personnel there insight into any presidential interests and concerns that had emerged from the morning's briefing. The PDB staff at CIA headquarters also started telling the Situation Room the night before each day's book what topics it would include—to help avoid double coverage of them in the Situation Room's morning summary of overnight developments for the president. Ford recognized, however, that the PDB rarely started his day on a good note, telling Peterson that "when there is more to report that usually means you have bad news."

"IT CANNOT BE THAT the president and the secretary of state have nothing to talk about," Henry Kissinger says. "We had to get into each other's head. We had to know how we would react in a crisis. So I saw President Ford for at least half an hour every day."

Kissinger made his way to the Oval Office after Peterson's early morning briefings, having started each day at his Department of State office. But he remained national security advisor, too, firmly inside the tight President's Daily Brief circle and reading Scowcroft's copy of the book upon arriving at the White House. Ford and Kissinger, usually joined by Scowcroft, would often discuss the PDB. In early 1975, the Agency began delivering to Kissinger his own copy via an aide, who would then ensure that an Agency officer returned it securely to CIA headquarters.

Ford rarely saw CIA director Colby outside of formal meetings, so he came to rely on his secretary of state for discussions of intelligence as well as foreign policy more generally. Kissinger remained far from a champion of the PDB: "You shouldn't see it as we were waiting every morning to read that product. It was one of many products, but a little higher status because of the people who were reading it." Kissinger's feelings about the PDB came out during an Oval Office meeting with Ford and Scowcroft on July 7, 1975. The president noted that he had just read in the PDB that the Turks and Romanians continued to resist expanding the role of the Conference on Security and Cooperation in Europe. Unimpressed that Ford merely cited reports that he had already seen at the State Department, Kissinger brusquely replied, "That shows what the CIA brief is—just a distillation of State cables."

Despite the aftermath of Turkey's invasion of Cyprus and other pressing world events, foreign intelligence took relatively little of Ford's time during his frenetic first few weeks in office. Domestic diversions—such as managing tensions between Nixon's staff and his own incoming team while building public confidence in an unelected chief executive—dominated his attention. Most of all, he and his advisors struggled with the legal and political issues still revolving around his predecessor, culminating with Ford's "full, free, and absolute" pardon of Richard Nixon on September 8 for any crimes he had committed or might have committed while in the presidency.

He also faced the need to nominate, and get through an intrusive congressional confirmation process, a new vice president. After considering a range of options, including a young George H. W. Bush, Ford in late August put forward Republican Party icon Nelson Rockefeller. The grandson of wealthy Standard Oil co-founder John D. Rockefeller Sr., he was no stranger to international affairs, having served increasingly important national-security-related roles for presidents Roosevelt, Truman, and Eisenhower. But that was back in the 1950s. In fact, he had been serving as governor of New York from 1959 to 1973, far away from Washington.

In early January 1975, just a couple of weeks after his swearing-in, Rockefeller received his first major assignment from Ford: he would chair the executive commission looking into allegations that the CIA's domestic activities had exceeded its statutory authority. Starting with a December 1974 exposé in the *New York Times* by reporter Seymour Hersh, cascading reports accused the Agency of breaking into US citizens' homes and offices, listening to their phone calls, and reading their mail. In response, CIA director Colby informed congressional leaders and President Ford about the "Family Jewels"—the dossier of internally reported potential Agency violations of the law first compiled by his predecessor, Jim Schlesinger.

What came to be known as the Rockefeller Commission included national security veterans—such as former secretary of the treasury and undersecretary of state Douglas Dillon and former chairman of the Joint Chiefs of Staff Lyman Lemnitzer—as well as prominent up-and-comers on the national scene, such as departing California governor Ronald Reagan. Like the congressional investigatory committees led by Frank Church in the Senate and by first Lucien Nedzi and then Otis Pike in the House of Representatives, the VP's commission expanded its mandate to investigate a wide swath of intelligence operations.

The commission released its report in June. Unfortunately for the administration, the swirl of politics, intelligence, and sensationalist media headlines just intensified. By midyear, the Church Committee in the Senate, and what became the Pike Committee in the House, had latched onto an off-the-record comment Ford had made to reporters that the CIA had plotted to assassinate foreign leaders in the 1950s and 1960s. "That blew the roof," director William Colby later said. "It was also clear that we were in that period of revolt in the Congress where that group elected in '74 were some pretty strong-minded younger people out to throw over the old, cozy system." It became known as the "Year of Intelligence," or, inside the intelligence community, as the "Time of Troubles."

For his first six months in office, Vice President Rockefeller spent far less time on the President's Daily Brief and current intelligence than on uncovering the truth about decades-old covert operations. The CIA, at the start, tried to establish a regular morning briefing pattern. But the vice president avoided any set schedule and, regardless of when he arrived at his office, found himself routinely besieged by his staff regarding more pressing matters. So Agency leaders suggested that a current intelligence officer could brief him in the car on the way to the office. That failed, too, so Rockefeller's military assistant, Jon Howe, briefed him on intelligence every morning as they rode to the office. Howe told his CIA contact that Rockefeller gave his full attention to intelligence during the ride, reading the National Intelligence Daily "religiously." A senior CIA officer would carry intelligence items deemed too sensitive to appear in the NID directly to the vice president in his office, waiting for any brief window to see him with the highly classified material.

Rockefeller did not yet see the PDB, and he might not have found out about it at all without Agency action. The dissemination of the President's Daily Brief at the time included only Ford, Kissinger, and Scowcroft. Not even the secretary of defense, James Schlesinger, himself a former CIA director, received the book. But in the summer of 1975, the Agency provided a cable version of the PDB to inform Rockefeller while he traveled in Europe. He liked the PDB so much during his trip that Howe reported back to Langley that the VP wanted to see it regularly during his morning car briefing. Agency leaders resisted, preferring the highly controlled delivery mechanism in place at the

White House for the book's few recipients, but eventually consented to giving Howe the PDB. He received it at the Executive Office Building each morning around 7:30 a.m., which enabled him to get to the vice president's residence and brief Rockefeller while they rode back to the office together. Howe agreed that particularly sensitive items would be left out of his copy and briefed directly to the vice president by a CIA officer. Colby himself approved the plan on July 11.

A quick reader, Rockefeller would tear through the PDB and the NID, often asking questions or starting discussions with Howe that would continue even after they arrived at the office. Other than NSC meetings, occasional meetings with foreign leaders, and conversations with the president, however, Rockefeller had little need for the highly sensitive intelligence. Nevertheless, Howe recalls that the vice president kept reading the PDB and "thought that it was a good use of his time, a high-quality publication."

"WITH FORD," KISSINGER REMEMBERS, "what you saw was what you got. He was a normal human being." This earnestness gave Ford a distinct advantage in his personal diplomacy. "He wanted to know about people and how they reacted to different approaches," recalls Scowcroft. Ford's lack of depth in foreign policy, at least compared to Kissinger, drove him to want to learn more. "He had a very easy demeanor with foreigners," adds Scowcroft. "No guile, no nothing. He was very good at that—and it was very effective, because it tended to be disarming for his foreign interlocutors."

Advisors who worked for both Nixon and Ford have described briefing the latter as the more pleasant and rewarding experience. "He would sort of listen to people and distill their thoughts," Kissinger says. "He treated them in an open and trusting manner." Also, Ford showed no embarrassment when he lacked knowledge about international affairs. If something sparked his curiosity, he would simply ask. During a discussion one day with Scowcroft, for example, he asked point-blank what UNESCO did. After Scowcroft described the educational, scientific, and cultural activities of the United Nations–linked organization, Ford thanked him and moved right on.

With CIA officers, too, Ford's respectful and guileless demeanor replaced Nixon's condescension. The most animated that Peterson recalled Ford getting during their PDB briefings was one day when the president's golden retriever, Liberty, joined the men in the Oval Office. Peterson scratched her neck to stop her from pacing back and forth between himself and Scowcroft. Appreciating the gesture, she wagged her tail with enough gusto to rattle Ford's prized pipe rack. "The clatter of pipes and other smoking paraphernalia brought swift Presidential retribution," Peterson says. "Liberty was banished, never to appear again during a PDB meeting."

Those writing the President's Daily Brief for Ford also felt the change and stood eager to help. After years of apparent neglect, the PDB now had a primary reader who not only read the book intently—confirmed every working day by Peterson—but also appreciated the very writing style the book tended to contain. Ford's easy-going manner granted Agency writers more flexibility on the types of items included in the PDB, as long as they kept their writing clear and direct. Analyst John McLaughlin, who ended his CIA career as deputy director during the George W. Bush administration, recalls the Ford-era PDB having "very few rigid guidelines," which allowed CIA experts to create many longer pieces.

For some analysts and managers, this openness came with a downside. Dick Kerr—who would go on to brief President Reagan

President Ford, with his golden retriever, Liberty, looking on, confers with secretary of state and national security advisor Henry Kissinger and deputy national security advisor Brent Scowcroft on October 8, 1974. *Courtesy Gerald R. Ford Presidential Library*

personally on the PDB and then serve as deputy director—thought that this freedom, combined with Agency demographics, weakened the PDB. "A lot of our old-timers," he says, "had gone—the Jack Smiths and the Ray Clines and a lot of the people who were editors. We got into a period in the '70s of laissez-faire, and the product lost a lot of its class. It seemed like it was not nearly as disciplined."

As the administration progressed, the Agency updated the content of the PDB to match Ford's maturing interests. For example, Colby directed the OCI in November 1974 to expand the PDB's coverage of international economics—probably reflecting increased policy attention to such matters after the 1973 OPEC oil embargo—and include more charts. Deputy director of intelligence Ed Proctor passed Colby's order on to his troops, noting, "The readers of the PDB probably need a lot more education on the real difficulties of solving economic problems and why some of the solutions may call for actions that counter established political and defense relationships." Peterson notes that he would occasionally add summaries of National Intelligence Estimates or intelligence memoranda to the actual PDB.

The CIA also introduced a visual medium to help communicate information during the briefings. On November 13, Peterson brought with him to the White House a short film on Soviet leader Leonid Brezhnev to show to Ford, Scowcroft, and chief of staff Don Rumsfeld. Such video supplements would expand under presidents Carter and, especially, Reagan.

AFTER MORE THAN A year in office, Ford had gained plenty of confidence in his use of intelligence, prompting a shift in how he received it. Rumsfeld and his deputy, Dick Cheney, sent a memo to Ford on October 24, 1975, suggesting that he discontinue his daily morning meeting with Scowcroft and Peterson and, instead, just read the PDB, alone.

The logic was simple. First, the president had gotten well up to speed on foreign affairs by then, and his advisors believed he no longer truly needed the full session every day. If he had questions about items in the PDB, he could still follow up. Second, the 1976 presidential campaign loomed large and tightened Ford's schedule. Ronald Reagan had announced he would challenge Ford for the Republican nomination, forcing the president to invest more time in the primaries than he had hoped. Politics may have also influenced the choice in another way: it certainly didn't hurt Ford to put distance between himself and the CIA during the peak of the highly charged congressional investigations of Agency activities.

Whatever the president's reasoning, Rumsfeld and Cheney's arguments won the day. Rumsfeld told Scowcroft on October 28 that Ford now wanted the PDB on his desk in the Oval Office before he got there. "He will not need you or Dave Peterson to sit in with him," their memo said. "If Dave wishes to bring it over, he can sit in the outer office while the President reads it but any questions that the President has, he can get the answers from Dave if he needs them, by calling him in or by talking to you or Henry later in the day." Scowcroft's early morning meetings with Ford—and with them, the CIA's in-person PDB briefings—thus went away. Peterson now handed the book each morning to Scowcroft, who took it to Ford's personal secretary for Oval Office delivery and retrieval. As a result, even Scowcroft lost insight into the president's immediate reactions to items in his PDB. But annotations on the book and on other material passed to Ford let the NSC staff know that the president continued to read the intelligence package.

That same week, Ford decided to shake up his national security team. He had kept Nixon's appointees in place for more than a year, citing their individual strengths as well as the value of continuity in foreign affairs during the domestic turmoil after Watergate. Over time, though, Ford tired of managing relationships with men he had not selected. The overhaul he announced on November 4—replacing Colby at the CIA with George H. W. Bush, firing secretary of defense Schlesinger in favor of Rumsfeld, and giving Kissinger's national security advisor hat to Scowcroft—became known as the "Halloween Massacre."

Ford called Colby in and told him that he appreciated his work at the Agency but wanted to replace him anyway. Scowcroft notes that the president's move was merciful: Colby's repeated trips to Capitol Hill had tainted him, leaving him unable to effectively lead the CIA or deal with Congress. Ford proposed that the spy chief now take an ambassadorship to Norway or NATO. Colby said he would resign as asked, but declined the offer of another post.

Ford's annoyance with Schlesinger's condescending attitude provided the backdrop for the shift at Defense. Schlesinger grated on the generally amiable Ford by talking down to him and adopting an overly casual vibe, even slinging his leg over the armrest of an Oval Office chair. At one NSC meeting about arms negotiations with the Soviets, the president challenged one of the secretary's remarks, prompting Schlesinger to snap back in front of everyone. Scowcroft advised him that his constant slouching and patronizing tone would rub the down-to-earth Ford the wrong way, but he failed to adjust. "President Ford and Jim Schlesinger simply did not get along," Scowcroft says.

Ford also tired of the toxic relationship between Kissinger and Schlesinger. Kissinger recalls that he once said to Ford, "It's a pity that you have to keep adjudicating disputes between Schlesinger and me." The president replied, "He thinks I'm a dummy, and he thinks I have to be run by somebody, and he thinks you're running me. And this won't stop until either I make him believe he's running me, or I fire him." Schlesinger's disregard for presidential directives sealed his fate. In April 1975, for example, the administration prepared to extricate from South Vietnam all remaining Americans (and as many friendly Vietnamese as possible) before North Vietnamese forces overran it. Ford ordered Schlesinger to fly planes into Saigon and bring out everyone who could fit on board, Americans and Vietnamese alike, but the defense secretary disregarded his orders and allowed some planes to leave Vietnam empty.

Ford's meeting with Schlesinger on Sunday, November 2 to let him go went as poorly as one would expect based on their tense history. Ford told him bluntly that he was out and offered him another post. The surprised Schlesinger tried to argue his way back in, emphasizing the value of his service. The president wouldn't budge, saying, "This is my decision. We're going to have another Secretary of Defense." Some accounts relate that Schlesinger fought back for almost an hour, trying in vain to persuade the president that he should stay in this job. Ford later asserted that the disagreeable exchange only made him more certain that firing the secretary of defense had been the right call.

A bitter Schlesinger channeled his disappointment into helping Ford's political foes. First he advised Ronald Reagan, who was now trying to take the president's spot on the Republican ticket in 1976. After Reagan's bid failed, Schlesinger switched to the camp of Democratic candidate Jimmy Carter. The move paid off: Carter defeated Ford, and the new president named Schlesinger the first secretary of energy in August 1977.

Ford also took away Kissinger's original national security advisor role—naming his three-year deputy, Brent Scowcroft, to the position—while keeping him on board as secretary of state, a move that he knew would bruise Kissinger's ego. Indeed, Kissinger considered leaving, thinking that foreigners would view the move as a reduction of his status within the administration, but agreed to stay on, writing years later that resigning in protest would have been immature. The elevation of Scowcroft to run the NSC formally—as he had been doing in practice for two years—worked well for the plain-dealing president, who appreciated Scowcroft's succinctness and competence.

"THE PRESIDENT ASKS THAT you consent to his nominating you as the new Director of the Central Intelligence Agency."

The cable from Kissinger on November 1 surprised George H. W. Bush, the de facto ambassador of the United States to the People's Republic of China. By late 1975, the former oilman, two-term congressman from Texas, ambassador to the United Nations, and Republican National Committee chairman had already enjoyed a full year in Beijing, an experience he found challenging and rewarding. He had earned high marks for both his work in China and his earlier assignment at the United Nations; the two roles had turned him on to international politics. So Bush looked forward to continuing his overseas role for a while—if for no other reason than to maintain a safe political distance from the rocky post-Watergate political climate back home.

"When President Ford asked me to head up the CIA," he says, "I did not want to do it for two very specific reasons: (1) I was happily serving as our country's envoy to China and was not ready to leave that post; (2) I was still interested in politics, and heading up the CIA would likely derail those ambitions." The Agency indeed looked like a dead end. No politician had ever run the intelligence community; no CIA director had ever won an election. That trend seemed especially unlikely to change after the recent congressional investigations, which would make life difficult for any incoming director. Plus, the

Bush children had already lived through their father running the Republican Party during the peak of the Watergate scandal. Given the public battering that the CIA had taken in the past year, did he really want his family to suffer further?

"When the cable came in," Bush wrote later, "I thought of Dad [Prescott Bush]. What would he do? What would he tell his kids? And I think he would have said, 'It's your duty.'" Kissinger triggered this sense of responsibility by including in his message a phrase that meant a lot to Bush: "The President asks." As a former World War II naval aviator—the youngest in the entire US Navy at the time—Bush learned to take his commander in chief's wishes as orders. In fact, when President Nixon had asked him to lead the Republican Party in 1973, just as the Watergate scandal was heating up, Bush had dismissed his wife Barbara's comment that he was better off doing any job but that one by declaring, "You can't turn a president down."

That principle of duty triumphed the next day when he replied to President Ford, via Kissinger, "My Dad inculcated into his sons a set of values that have served me well in my own short public life. One of these values quite simply is that one should serve his country and his President. And so if this is what the President wants me to do the answer is a firm 'YES.'" Years later, Kissinger called Bush's approach a rare classy moment during a generally "dismal period of maneuvering."

After a brief delay to wrap up preparations in China for Ford's early 1976 trip there, Bush came back and took up the reins at Langley. Dick Lehman and three other senior CIA officers wrote him a memo titled "Where You Should Sit." They urged him to avoid the Agency's small office near the White House, warning him that locating there would be seen as dissociating himself from the workforce— potentially crushing Agency morale at a time when the CIA remained the butt of public attacks and late-night jokes. Bush agreed with the logic and settled in at CIA headquarters. At Bush's confirmation hearings, New Hampshire senator Thomas McIntyre had asked him what he would do if President Ford directed him to spy on primary party rival Ronald Reagan. Bush said he would easily refuse any such request because he felt his political days were behind him. Once confirmed as director, Bush sought to avoid political entanglements during private meetings at the White House. He attended cabinet

President Ford meets with CIA director-designate George H. W. Bush in the Oval Office, December 17, 1975. *Courtesy Gerald R. Ford Presidential Library*

meetings, for example, only when the agenda included national security items. Even then, he would leave the room whenever conversations drifted away from national security topics.

President Ford supported Bush's focus on the intelligence mission from the start. Instead of putting distance between the Oval Office and the intelligence community by skipping Bush's swearing-in ceremony, he instead made it a media event—bolstering the embattled Agency, its new leader, and the PDB. He announced to a cheering crowd at the event: "I depend on you as one of America's first lines of defense. Every morning, as a result of your efforts, an intelligence report is delivered to my desk which is complete, concise, perceptive, and responsible. . . . [L]et me express my personal gratitude for this fine work."

Bush's ties to Ford proved valuable in helping the Agency fend off challenges to its authority in the wake of the Church and Pike investigations. In one case, senior CIA officer and future deputy director John McMahon approached Bush early in his tenure to warn him that the Pentagon and State Department had begun encroaching on CIA prerogatives. "And when I did," McMahon recalls, "he picked up the phone and got a hold of Don Rumsfeld, who was then secretary of defense. When Rumsfeld came on, Bush had a few words of small talk but then acknowledged that some of his people were trying to grab DCI responsibilities. And he asked if Rumsfeld could take care of it, or should both of them go see Jerry? Meaning President Ford. Rumsfeld allowed that he'd take care of it, and, indeed, the door slammed shut on the Pentagon's ventures shortly thereafter. It was then that I realized that having a DCI who can call the President by his first name was well worthy of the assignment." CIA workers' initial skepticism about their first "political" director morphed quickly into respect.

Although Ford had just ceased his daily briefings with Peterson, choosing to read his President's Daily Brief alone, Bush probably could have convinced Ford to see him every day to discuss the PDB one-on-one. But he did not even try. In an extra step to avoid even the appearance of politicization, he avoided direct participation in the editing, review, and briefing of the PDB. Instead, he read it in the car alone on the way to Langley each morning. "I deferred to the intelligence people and did not try to get into the process," he recalls. "I had the utmost respect for the career intelligence officers, who never got enough credit."

"Bush," Lehman said, "made his meetings a 'band of brothers.'" Three days after taking over from Colby, in fact, Bush hosted a regular senior staff meeting that addressed negative newspaper stories about the CIA. A senior intelligence officer cited a particular accusation made in the press that day, prompting Bush to look around and say to his new crew, "What are they trying to do to us?" After that, Colby later noted, "he had the place in the palm of his hand." His leadership of the Agency workforce lasted less than a year—one of the shortest tenures of any DCI—but it seemed to affect him deeply. He wrote to a friend in early 1976 that he'd neither worked harder nor had a more interesting position, which he said allowed him to dive into intriguing subject matter alongside superb people.

INSTEAD OF GETTING HEAVILY involved in the details of the President's Daily Brief, and thus risking perceptions of politicization, Bush stuck to strategic issues involving the book. For example, because Ford had kept his first secretary of defense, Jim Schlesinger, out of the PDB loop, new Pentagon chief Don Rumsfeld was not seeing the book. "I was getting a briefing from DIA [Defense Intelligence Agency]," he recalls. "I probably knew most of what he was getting just from that."

But history and common sense suggested he should be seeing the PDB. Rumsfeld raised the anomaly with newly arrived director Bush—who was surprised that the book was not going to the defense secretary and said he would arrange it. Because it was the president's decision to make, Bush held off on providing it to Rumsfeld until Ford personally signed off on the request in mid-March 1976—allowing the PDB back into the Pentagon after an absence of more than two years.

The line was held there. A declassified internal Agency memo from the next month shows that treasury secretary William Simon received CIA publications such as the National Intelligence Daily and a weekly economic intelligence product. But he did not get the President's Daily Brief.

One of Bush's few conditions for taking the CIA job, which Ford granted, was direct access to the president. Every Thursday or Friday when he and Ford were both in town they met in the Oval Office, with Scowcroft attending. Bush saw value in the personal sessions, writing to Ford several weeks after starting the job that their meetings were "very, very important to the entire Intelligence Community." He also took advantage of the opportunity to show off the Agency's abilities. The president was better off, in his view, hearing directly from the CIA's technical experts than listening to him try to effectively convey their content, so he would sometimes bring along working-level officers to brief Ford. Scowcroft agrees. "Ford loved it—and I think it was a way for the DCI to give his people a pat on the back. Good all the way around."

Scowcroft remembers the PDB taking second place as a predictor of trouble on the foreign policy horizon to a simpler indicator: Bush's whereabouts. It seemed that whenever the CIA director took one of his frequent weekend trips to the Bush family house in Kennebunkport, Maine, some overseas crisis broke out. Bush seems to have appreciated the national security advisor's talents as well as his humor. Upon becoming president more than ten years later, Bush convinced Scowcroft to return as *his* national security advisor.

Reflecting on his CIA experience, Bush now says, "All these years later, serving as DCI for one short year still stands out as my favorite job ever, outside of being President. I loved the challenge. But I mainly loved the people. They were smart, professional, dedicated, loyal, and patriotic. And they received credit for none of that."

CHAPTER SIX

PLAINS AND SIMPLE

To CELEBRATE THE NATION's birthday in 1976, the CIA's Dick Lehman spent the evening watching the spectacular bicentennial fireworks show from the National Mall in Washington, D.C. Lehman fought outrageous crowds to escape downtown, finally arriving home at 3:00 a.m.—just in time to take a call from George H. W. Bush.

"I want you to meet me in Bar Harbor tomorrow in the afternoon," the CIA director said. "We are going down to Hershey to brief Carter. Will you pull the stuff together and come on up?"

Within hours, the Agency's Gulfstream flew Lehman and a healthy stack of highly classified material to Maine. To show off the capabilities of the prized KH-9 satellite, for example, Lehman brought along one swing of its imagery, showing a stretch of the southeastern United States from the Atlantic Ocean into Mississippi—featuring a small town called Plains, Georgia. Bush and Lehman then made their way to Hershey, Pennsylvania, where Carter was meeting with Democratic governors.

Carter had requested an intelligence briefing from the CIA even *before* the Democratic National Convention, where a week later he would receive his party's nomination for the presidency. After consulting Bush and national security advisor Brent Scowcroft, Ford sent Bush himself to meet with the man who would, it turns out, defeat him in the November election. Ford set clear ground rules for his CIA director: this initial session, coming before the convention, should cover only arrangements for the Agency's intelligence support to Carter after he officially became the Democratic nominee.

Bush exceeded his mandate. The discussion ended up covering "virtually the entire field of intelligence," according to Lehman, who remembered Carter as "terribly interested" in the intelligence products and satellite imagery shown to him. The presumptive nominee asked his guests about issues ranging from Agency workers' morale to the future of Rhodesia, soon to become Zimbabwe. He requested more intelligence-related sessions, to include additional details on Soviet strategic programs, every week to ten days after the convention. Later he described himself as "very honored" by Bush's personal attendance at this early meeting.

The first post-convention session came on Wednesday, July 28, in Plains, at Carter's brick rambler. Because Agency pilots could not find anywhere close to Carter's farm capable of taking the Gulfstream, Bush and Lehman arrived via helicopter from a more distant airfield, accompanied by two CIA analysts. Carter and his vice presidential nominee, Senator Walter Mondale—who had frequently criticized the CIA during the previous two years' scandals—absorbed briefings on Lebanon, Iraqi-Syrian relations, Egyptian-Libyan strains, tensions between China and Taiwan, Rhodesia, Uganda, and the Cuban presence in Angola before spending most of the day hearing about the USSR's nuclear weapons, delivery systems, defense capabilities, and compliance with the SALT treaty.

Lehman said Carter sat "very intent, totally concentrating and taking it all in." The future president and vice president both jumped in with questions. Mondale, in fact, grilled the briefers on arms control details and delved into sensitive areas such as the CIA's collection techniques and its ties to other countries' intelligence services. Georgia's summer temperatures overwhelmed the small air-conditioning unit in the study where Carter received the analysts. "We all sat around in straight wooden chairs, and it was hotter than hell," Lehman said. "In order to be able to hear you had to shut off the air conditioner. The temperature was unbearable and your clothes stuck to the back of the chairs." Only one interruption provided relief during the six-hour session: Carter's wife, Rosalynn, delivered peaches to the attendees late in the afternoon.

The CIA team prevented Mondale aide David Aaron—who would become deputy national security advisor but lacked security clearances at the time—from attending. "We could see him prowling around outside," Lehman said. "I don't think he ever forgave us for that." Carter, however, clearly got over it. His senior aide, Stuart Eizenstat, informed Lehman the next day that the "extremely pleased" nominee wanted the same kind of marathon sessions for future pre-election briefings.

For a second six-hour session in Plains on Thursday, August 12, Carter and Mondale added Eizenstat and a relieved Aaron. Bush brought eight experts to discuss topics addressed earlier (including Soviet strategic programs, arms control negotiating issues, and the dispute between Egypt and Libya) as well as Soviet conventional forces, Chinese issues, Greek-Turkish tensions, a Rhodesian incursion into Mozambique, the Korean demilitarized zone, Somalia, Djibouti, and Lebanon. Mondale avoided overly inquisitive lines of questioning, which in the first Plains session had worried Bush and Lehman enough to warn Eizenstat about the difficulties inherent in addressing such issues while the presidential election campaign continued. Lehman had explained that Bush would prefer not being put in a position requiring him to refuse to answer off-limits queries. Perhaps as a result of the warning, Mondale in this second session surprised Bush and the others by noting recent CIA reforms and expressing his respect for the organization.

"I was impressed with Carter," one of the Agency briefers says. "He was a very, very quick study, able to digest immediately everything we gave him—fact after fact. He seemed to have a photographic memory and would often repeat back to us the points we had made to be absolutely sure that he understood." Carter left happy, too. "I wanted the long briefings in Plains," he said. "I wanted particularly not to make any inadvertent mistake that would complicate things for President Ford . . . or later for me."

FORD AUTHORIZED BUSH TO start giving Carter the PDB every day after he won the White House in the closest electoral college ballot since Woodrow Wilson's reelection some sixty years earlier. So on November 19, Bush brought a copy of the book on his next trip to Plains, where he described to Carter and Mondale its current distribution and sensitivity as part of a nearly hour-long private session.

"As I look back on it," Bush wrote a few days later, "there is one strange thing. There was no comment and almost no questions. . . . Perhaps it was because he knew that there was a full plate waiting for him in the next room of several more hours of briefings." But the formal meeting, in which Lehman and a team of Agency briefers picked up where the pre-election sessions' substantive briefings had left off, ended without Carter committing to receive the President's Daily Brief during the rest of the transition. So Lehman took charge. As the briefing ended, he cornered the president-elect and suggested that he get the PDB directly from a briefer in Plains. Carter agreed, noting that the sample copy Bush had shown him appeared "useful."

Ten days later, the CIA began daily, on-site support. A midlevel imagery analyst, John Biddiscomb, received the PDB via secure fax every morning at 6:30 and took it by hand at 8:00 to Carter, who spent thirty to forty-five minutes reading through the book and accompanying materials. Because the book still focused on Ford's interests, Biddiscomb also gave Carter a wide array of Agency products, including detailed write-ups of international crises, foreign government reactions to the incoming administration, and profiles of world leaders whom Carter would be meeting soon.

Right away, Carter began scrawling on the PDB, putting his initials on copies he had read and even jotting questions in the margins. His oral and written remarks informed Biddiscomb's daily calls to Lehman back at CIA headquarters, to help current intelligence officers prepare follow-on material. Although Carter maintained a formal, detached air with Biddiscomb, the Agency welcomed the daily interaction.

"I WENT DOWN TO the house and walked through the Secret Service cordon that had been thrown around the house," Lehman said about his follow-up visit to Plains in early December. "Carter was alone—he had no help, and the Secret Service was kept back from the house, so he was completely by himself."

To Lehman's surprise, Carter told him that the President's Daily Brief disappointed him. He complained about the PDB's heavy coverage of newspaper items; as a "voracious reader of the press," he said, he did not need that. The president-elect understood his ideas for changes would have to wait because the PDB was not yet *his* document, but that didn't stop him from venting. Lehman left him four samples of previous PDB formats to consider. He took Carter's requests for longer backgrounders on issues such as Middle East peace negotiations, including "insights into proposals that might be coming from other countries," and more material on foreign leaders. "Meanwhile," Lehman said, "he wanted to talk and, well, I talked. For nigh on two hours."

Carter and Lehman met again on December 10, this time at Blair House in Washington. Trying to hook Carter on a daily briefing habit, Lehman introduced Dave Peterson—who had taken the PDB to Ford daily for over a year—and told the president-elect that Peterson would present the PDB to him when he returned to Washington. Carter seemed more relaxed than he had in Plains, even laughing about Libyan strongman Muammar Qaddafi's positive remarks on the incoming White House team. His enduring impatience about waiting until inauguration to receive the PDB in the format that he wanted it gave Lehman an idea for the remainder of the transition. He told his current intelligence staff to print the add-on material for the president-elect in the same format as the existing PDB until he took office, when they would just put everything into the PDB itself, tailored to Carter's wishes.

During the last of his pre-inauguration intelligence sessions at Blair House, Carter settled on a simple PDB format, with more white space than text on each page, allowing plenty of room for him to write notes. "I wanted to extract the essence of the PDB," Carter says, "from the former wordy and rambling collection of non-essential and verbose text." This guidance, along with insights from Lehman and Biddiscomb, allowed current intelligence officers at the CIA to tailor the book to the new president. "I wanted it to be as thorough as possible," Carter says, "but also wanted it to be separated so that I could read the headlines, in effect, and then go back and more thoroughly pursue the details on issues that I needed to have at that time."

On January 6, incoming national security advisor Zbigniew Brzezinski asked for a sample of the new PDB to show Carter the following week, emphasizing it should give the incoming president "a comprehensive but extremely succinct daily summary, with emphasis given to intelligence material and with sensitive material clearly indicated by some typographic device."

ON INAUGURATION DAY, JANUARY 20, Peterson dutifully hand-carried the reformatted President's Daily Brief to Carter. It was the first time a CIA officer would deliver the PDB to the president during the four-year term. It was also the last time.

Starting the very next day, the intelligence briefings fell instead to Brzezinski. He had met Carter, then Georgia governor, in 1975, while serving as the Trilateral Commission's executive director in North America. They stayed in touch and quickly developed a relationship of solid rapport and blunt honesty. "Long before I ever was elected President," Carter says, "I recognized Zbig's strengths and some of his possible weaknesses." Brzezinski, for his part, supported the president during group meetings and in public but proved willing to push him when they found themselves alone. "In private, you have the obligation to tell him that he's wrong," he says. "And I did that repeatedly, and the President wanted me to."

Peterson's job defaulted to what it had been during the final fifteen months of Ford's term. Each day he briefed the national

President Jimmy Carter and National Security Advisor Zbigniew Brzezinski discuss the PDB in the Oval Office, January 21, 1977. *Courtesy Jimmy Carter Presidential Library*

security advisor on the book, provided supplementary information, and grabbed the previous day's copy to return it to Langley. Early on, he spent some extra time bringing Brzezinski up to speed about the PDB and its content—given that the new national security advisor had barely seen it during the transition—and began recording anything Brzezinski said about Carter's reactions.

By the time he went to see the president, Brzezinski had thus read the PDB and talked to Peterson or another CIA briefer. "I would come to my office fairly early," he says. "It could be any time from six to seven on—seven would be late." He had scanned, and perhaps added to the president's reading stack, foreign communications intercepts, leading international editorials, newspaper articles from different papers abroad, and the State Department's Secretary's Morning Summary (produced by the Bureau of Intelligence and Research for the secretary of state, but also sent to other top officials around town). Settling on the most important issues from the PDB and other sources to highlight, he tied items to the president's schedule, when possible, or other upcoming events. Then he jotted down three or four main points, walked down the hall for the fifteen-to-thirty-minute meeting, and delivered more than double the PDB's amount of paper.

"In general, Zbig and I discussed most of the PDB items verbally that were included for the first time," Carter notes. "On some occasions I would retain it to read an item more thoroughly after he left." Brzezinski knew that the president would look at everything. "We discovered before too long," he says, "that if we gave him, let's say, a 100-page document with a cover note saying, 'Please read the introduction, just the marked pages, and the conclusion,' the whole document would come back annotated from beginning to end."

HANK KNOCHE, THE AGENCY's deputy director under George H. W. Bush, served as acting director between Bush's resignation on January 20 and early March. In that role, he didn't have the institutional power or personal ties to Carter to challenge Brzezinski's dominance of the intelligence briefings. But Admiral Stansfield Turner, Carter's next choice to lead the Agency, made it through confirmation easily and took the helm in March.

Turner should have entered the president's inner circle with ease. After all, Carter's connection with him went back further than his ties to any other national security aide: they had entered the United States Naval Academy together in 1943. Although the two had not been close while in Annapolis—Turner does not recall even meeting Carter until their twenty-fifth class reunion—the incoming president seemed to admire the career navy officer. He had graduated with even better marks than Carter did, reached top naval ranks, and served in senior navy positions by the time the new president called him back to Washington to serve as CIA director. Brzezinski later said Carter had claimed to a group of senior officials that Turner had enough talent to serve as an exceptional secretary of state.

Turner heard from Carter early on that he loved the PDB and didn't want anybody "messing around" with its current format, prompting him to wonder why *he* wasn't the one briefing the president on the PDB each morning. He visited the national security advisor and staked his claim, noting how peculiar it seemed to him that the president's chief intelligence advisor had been shut out of the daily intelligence sessions. Brzezinski found a quick bureaucratic solution. He simply changed Carter's schedule to reflect that he would get a "national security briefing" instead of an "intelligence briefing," and told Turner there was nothing left to discuss.

"Brzezinski was very domineering," Turner comments. "He wanted to be in control of every minute of the president's time and all the flow of information to the president." This worked fine for Carter, who later said, "Zbig was enough day-to-day. I read the PDB and the Secretary of State's Morning Report. I wanted Brzezinski to draw to my attention things I needed to do something about."

The president told the members of his National Security Council during their first meeting on January 22 that Ford's PDB, which he had been reading during the transition, had struck him as bland and lacking the best intelligence—a condition he attributed to Ford having allowed too many people to see the book. He said that *his* PDB had "sharpened in focus" after he put a tight cap on its distribution to ensure that the most sensitive information and analysis made it to him each day. Now the PDB would go only to himself, Brzezinski, Vice President Mondale, secretary of state Cyrus Vance, and secretary of defense Harold Brown—no deputies, no aides, no assistants. "It wasn't necessary for all the cabinet members and their deputies to know the most highly sensitive information," Carter now says, "and it was obvious that with a large circulation, the Intelligence Community just deleted this material from the information they gave to me and the officials who needed it." He told the CIA to put its "very best intelligence in it," said Knoche. The limited distribution worked well enough to keep its few readers interested. "The most important thing about it for me," Brown says, "was that other people—and especially the President—who were my closest interlocutors and collaborators were reading it that morning. So I had to read it."

Carter resisted calls to add additional formal PDB recipients. Just after inauguration, one of treasury secretary W. Michael Blumenthal's assistants called the NSC staff to get his boss on the book's dissemination list after CIA leaders had refused to do it. The treasury secretary, after all, was being added to the National Security Council, so shouldn't he have the same daily intelligence information as its other members? Carter stood firm; Blumenthal did not get the President's Daily Brief. Even a year into the administration, Brzezinski kept even the acting secretaries of state and defense from seeing the PDB.

CARTER ENTERED THE WHITE House determined to give his vice president more access and influence than any of his predecessors had experienced and to bring him into the whole range of governing. To start, he insisted that Walter Mondale attend his Joint Chiefs of Staff briefing about nuclear attack procedures. Carter spent the most valuable coin of the realm—real estate physically close to the president—when he gave Mondale space adjacent to the Oval Office. Richard Moe, Mondale's chief of staff during his four years as vice president, recalls three other ways in which Carter followed through on his promise to involve Mondale more deeply than his predecessors had done: unimpeded access to the president, including an open invitation to any presidential meeting; service as an across-the-board advisor, freed from narrow assignments that would impede his ability to move where emerging events demanded; and full access to everything the president saw.

To fulfill that third commitment, the PDB made it to the VP from the start. And Mondale saw not just any copy of the book; he received the president's own PDB. "The President would read it," he says, "and then I would see it with his written comments." Typically, as soon as Carter finished reading the President's Daily Brief, the president's personal secretary would deliver it directly to Brzezinski's special assistant, who in turn would let vice presidential national security advisor Denis Clift know that it was ready for Mondale's eyes. No other vice president to that point had had such insight into the president's thinking about his daily intelligence report.

Mondale followed a strict regimen to protect the president's copy of the PDB. If the vice president stepped out of his White House office, his secretary would lock the book up in a safe. If he had not yet read the PDB before leaving the office for the day, he had it hand-carried back to Brzezinski's office for overnight secure storage. The president himself liked how it worked out, saying that he kept Mondale in the loop on even highly compartmented topics because he had faith in his "judgment, honesty, and frankness."

The vice president would also see a copy of the PDB, albeit without the president's handwritten comments and questions, when he traveled. The CIA station nearest to Mondale's destination would receive a White House directive to get the PDB to Clift at a set time and place. Clift recalls what this meant for him. "I would inevitably be shaving, have a towel around my waist, and there would be a knock on my hotel door at 5:30 or 6:00 in the morning, and the PDB would arrive. We'd have a few sentences of greeting, and thank you. Then I would take it." Even without elaborate security protocols, the document remained secure. "It impressed me," Clift says, "that we handled it very professionally, in that there weren't great receipts to be signed. CIA is an operational organization, and they understand ops." After Mondale read the book and discussed with Clift any of the issues it raised, he returned it for destruction via shredder or for personal delivery in a sealed envelope back to a station officer.

"I read the PDB carefully every day," Mondale recalls. "It was an important help to those of us who were on the highly selective reading list." But even while acknowledging that it added value by anticipating short-term developments, he wishes it had conveyed even more secrets, and in more depth. "Many of items appearing in the Brief I had heard about or read about in the better newspapers and from leading journalists," he notes. "Sometimes they would miss issues or discuss them in a way that just introduced the issue without really explaining it. That is a problem, of course, inherent in a document that was kept as abbreviated and terse as possible."

The vice president also regularly attended Carter's Friday foreign policy breakfasts, a relaxed forum that started just a few months after inauguration to expand on the daily meetings with Brzezinski only. These meetings in the Cabinet Room—held without note takers and, probably as a direct result, with few leaks—continued throughout his term. Bob Gates, who had a window on the preparation for and follow-up from the sessions while serving as Brzezinski's special assistant in 1979, says, "Most of the most important foreign policy decisions in the Carter administration were made in the Friday morning breakfast."

The absence of formal agendas or official notes led to a perennial problem. The breakfast attendees—who soon included all five PDB principals (the president, vice president, secretaries of state and defense, and national security advisor), the White House chief of staff and, later, a few senior White House aides—disagreed on the details of presidential orders emerging from the chats. Only after the spring of 1980, when officials bungled the president's wishes about a United Nations vote on the status of Jerusalem, did Carter allow Brzezinski to circulate definitive summaries of presidential guidance from the breakfasts.

Stansfield Turner, however, remained excluded. Brzezinski repeatedly argued with Carter to add him, leading the president to bluntly tell his national security advisor to stop asking. So the CIA director remained the only major national security official absent from the crucial meetings. The CIA's role in the breakfasts was reduced to the President's Daily Brief. "The commonly read PDB," Carter says, "abbreviated our discussions and made it possible for us to cover a lot of ground during these times together. It obviously helped for us to be 'preaching from the same text.'"

TURNER HAD STARTED THE job on the wrong foot, entering the CIA director's suite with some naval aides—which Agency officers interpreted as a lack of trust in their own ability to serve the new director. Careerists felt the new crew prioritized reform over support for ongoing operations and analysis. He also went forward with personnel cuts that had been proposed, but not implemented, long before his arrival. Most of the cuts came through attrition, and the operations directorate took the bulk of them. Still, the event sent a chill across the Agency.

Soon after starting, Turner circulated to the analytic wing of the Agency a paper raising two provocative questions: "Why the products of the Community—and in particular the CIA—are shallower, more often wrong, much less relevant than consumers need and can reasonably expect," and "What a determined Director might do to achieve an order of magnitude improvement in the quality of estimates and analyses used in policymaking." Not surprisingly, a management advisory group from the Directorate of Intelligence complained to Turner a few months later about a variety of perceived sins: the lack of timely and substantive communication to analysts from the director and his staff, uncertainty over what Turner wanted and how he wanted it, and late-night changes to the analysis in the President's Daily Brief without coordinating these changes with the analysts.

Turner still defends his hands-on approach. "I always felt a tremendous responsibility toward the PDB. [The president] was probably the busiest man in the world. You can't waste his time in reading about it and thinking about it. You don't want to fill up his head with miscellaneous stuff that isn't important." He feels that editing the book every night was proper because *he* would take the calls from Carter, Brzezinski, or other senior officials if pieces in the book confused or annoyed them. His careful eye looked for one thing above all: "I was very concerned that we be absolutely clear. That was my main thought—to be sure there was nothing stuck in there that could be interpreted two ways, or three or four. I certainly felt that I couldn't send anything to the president that I had not checked and felt was worthwhile. Sometimes the content was too thin to be worth the president's time. That was my main concern: Was there enough meat in this paragraph to be worth a minute of the president's time? If not, generally I would just delete it."

The head of the CIA's Directorate of Intelligence during the Carter era, Bruce Clarke, says Turner engaged in the PDB review process in "a far more direct and involved way than his predecessors." Bob Gates, who served as Turner's executive assistant for much of his tenure, says, "Stan essentially reviewed the PDB every single night. I can't remember a single director who, in essence, edited the PDB before he signed off on it and let it go down to the White House. I felt Admiral Turner had gone too far in 'red-inking' the PDB on a daily basis."

Turner also pushed analysts to put certain material into the PDB. For example, in April 1980, he sent a memo to analysts working on Vietnam's offensive against the brutal Pol Pot regime in Kampuchea (Cambodia): "I believe we should get the point across to the President that this troublesome situation has taken a little different turn than we anticipated a few months ago and that we might see some rather different approaches to it by the Chinese, the Thais, and the Vietnamese over the next year." A senior DI officer who managed the Iran Task Force during the hostage crisis remembers that Turner emphasized the PDB personally. "In fact," he says, "he would tell us around noon what he thought we should put in the book. He'd call us and say, 'What are you guys going to do?' And we'd try it out. And he'd say, 'Well, here's what I think you ought to do,' based on what he'd heard downtown."

Once they got over the annoyance of a new layer of senior review and hands-on direction of what to include in the PDB, many analysts appreciated that Turner actually engaged them about their assessments, more so than most of his predecessors. A senior budget officer of the time noted that the new director's interest in analytic techniques and emphasis on quality in the written product led him to approve funding for "anything requested for analysis." Gates asserts that most analysts seemed "happy to have a director that cared about analysis" and who spent significant time on it. "I didn't get the sense that the analysts were offended or felt like their work was being politicized."

Turner feels that despite his heavy editing hand, he got the balance right because he would provide insight into *why* he changed their text. "I tried to make sure the analysts knew as much as was appropriate about what the president was saying, or what his reactions were to the material we were sending him. Often I would pass the thing on without necessarily attributing it to the president. 'In the draft of the PDB yesterday, did you really think about this aspect of it?' And it was not my idea—it was the president's idea—but I didn't always attribute it to him."

BRZEZINSKI'S SWIFT EDITING OF the president's schedule had precluded Turner from seeing Carter every day, but the CIA director received a consolation prize that most other senior officials could only dream about: frequent, regular meetings with the president.

"On occasion," Carter says, "a brief outline in the PDB would not fulfill my desire for a more thorough understanding. One example was my desire to understand the difference between Sunni and Shia beliefs during the Iraq-Iran war." Along with other PDB topics that left Carter wanting more—like religious and political divisions in Lebanon, a new imagery collection system, and the South African nuclear program—this spurred extended presidential discussions with Turner.

Turner claims that Carter suggested up to three thirty-minute intelligence briefings per week. They settled on two sessions each week to start. The CIA director says he studied up to twelve hours for each half-hour meeting, which Brzezinski almost always attended. Turner recalls one notable exception, when he asked the national security advisor to leave the room. "I just told the president that if it got out that we had this source, say, inside the Kremlin, that was the end of him," he says. "When the life of a source was possibly at stake, you felt great responsibility, so you would not tell one more person than absolutely needed to know. If the president wanted to share it with Brzezinski, that was his choice, not mine."

One day, a midlevel analyst's presentation in Turner's seventh-floor Agency office impressed the director enough to say, "I want you to be here at 8:00 tomorrow morning and go with me to the White House to give that briefing to the president of the United States." The stunned analyst stared back at Turner for a few seconds, avoiding the glare of his direct supervisor, who sat right next to him but who had *not* been invited. The next morning, the director went into the Oval Office and told Carter, "This analyst has got a briefing that is so good, I wanted you to hear it, sir." The young officer dutifully informed the president about his topic, answered a few questions, and left after Turner thanked him. The old Naval Academy classmates and Brzezinski then went on with the rest of the event.

"I felt it was, number one, good for the president to hear from somebody else," Turner says about taking working-level analysts to the briefings. "Jimmy Carter was just a sponge at absorbing information; he would have a give-and take with them. I don't remember him ever complaining that we shouldn't have brought somebody in. Also, it was great for the analyst. If you're a low-level analyst out there, you almost never get to see the director—let alone the president of the United States. It really pumped up their morale."

These briefings, in turn, provided fodder for material going into the PDB. "If he questioned something today," Turner recalls, "I would be sure that in the next morning's brief I had somebody cover that subject. I would ask myself, 'Is there more I can follow up on? Have we covered it as well as we possibly can?'" In an example from the CIA's newly declassified files, the president asked if an Agency estimate that oil production and demand curves would cross in 1982 represented a drastic change from previous assessments. Turner then directed the head of the CIA's analytic branch to put a piece into the President's Daily Brief comparing older estimates to the new one. Analysts felt that regular and personal contact between the director and the president was the next best thing to one of their own briefing him directly, especially when Turner's time with Carter generated clear advice for the PDB's preparation.

But Turner continued to keep some things out of the PDB. In October 1978, he informed Brzezinski that the personal-opinion approach he had taken with Carter in a recent briefing, which the national security advisor liked and wanted more of, would stay solely in the briefing sessions. "Even with limited distribution of the PDB," he told Brzezinski, "somebody would probably file an objection if I took too speculative an attack" by putting his own opinion directly in the PDB.

His briefings worked well enough for the president that they soon dropped to once a week—and, eventually, down to twice a month—but they did not go away entirely. Turner probably viewed this as a success. Carter's emphasis on efficiency suggests he would not have tolerated briefings for nearly four years that wasted his time. "Stan was outstanding in making sufficient and definitive analyses of complex subjects," he recalls. Carter says he appreciated the opportunity to examine intelligence issues "more thoroughly through verbal exchange" than he could through the printed PDB alone.

AGENCY OFFICERS MISSED THE daily contact with the president about the PDB that Dave Peterson had enjoyed for the first half of the Ford administration. But they got something from Carter that his predecessors never provided: frequent written comments.

"That was a habit that I maintained throughout my time both as governor and president," Carter says. "When I was reading not just the PDB but any sort of extensive memorandum from my cabinet officers or top people in the White House, I would make my queries in writing—sometimes in the margins and sometimes at the top of the front page—with a specific question or comment. Just something like, 'I approve of this,' or 'Why do we need to do this?' or 'I don't understand what this means.'"

To give the president plenty of room for his notations, the CIA kept printing the PDB in the simple format he had requested, featuring wide margins. A national security official who regularly saw Carter's copy of the book recalls, "He penned, with his beautiful, engineer's hand, his comments on the page, either making observations or requesting additional information or giving guidance." These written reactions changed the PDB's chain of custody. Peterson on January 31, 1978, told his bosses back at Langley that Brzezinski had determined that *any* notation from Carter transformed that day's book into a presidential document. From that point on, such copies of the PDB remained in secure storage at the White House. The national security advisor followed through on his pledge to show Carter's written questions and reactions to Peterson, ensuring that the Agency would gain necessary insights into the president's needs. The system not only kept Carter's comments highly secure but offered assurances that Brzezinski wasn't exploiting his exclusive access. "If a cabinet member or Stan Turner sent me something," Carter notes, "and I handwrote a question back, they knew that it was from me and not from Brzezinski or somebody else."

Any reaction written on the PDB made its way right to the director, as Turner recalls. "There was no way anything from the president would come to my office that I wouldn't want to see." Carter's intent usually made sense, such as when he corrected spelling errors that somehow made it through the PDB's rigorous editing gauntlet. But deciphering some of his marginalia took extra effort. For example, Agency officers only gradually realized that a question mark did not require an immediate answer; instead, it reflected the president's doubts about a point in the text.

Early on, Carter and Brzezinski expressed appreciation for the effort that went into the PDB. Carter in April 1977 told his cabinet that the CIA had dispelled his concern during the campaign about its reputation and professionalism, leaving him "highly impressed" with the accurate, unbiased, and complete analysis he received. Specifically, he said the Agency's responses to his questions, routinely printed in the PDB the day after he jotted a question in the margin, had been "prompt and meaningful." He told CIA employees during a visit to Langley in August that they had done "a superb job," noting his appreciation for "the high professionalism, training, education, experience that you bring to your job and which you demonstrate every day with your good work." Early the next year, he praised the "professionalism and the competence of the collection and analysis and distribution of intelligence information to me and to other consumers in the Federal Government." And Turner told DI leaders soon thereafter that the defense secretary, secretary of state, and national security advisor had *all* made specific reference to recent PDB items during a senior-level meeting at the White House.

Brzezinski echoed this overall satisfaction with the daily intelligence report years later. "The *President's Daily Brief,* I think, was very helpful to the president on some major issues, notably arms control and the strategic dimension. By and large, the quality of the reporting was excellent. It was informative. It was detailed." As the person best placed to know, he confirmed that Carter "would follow it in great detail."

THE BOOK RECEIVED NEGATIVE feedback, too. "Of the three Administrations I served at the NSC," Bob Gates wrote in the late 1980s, "the Carter team worked most conscientiously to inform the CIA of the analytical needs of the president and constructively to advise the Agency of perceived shortcomings in its analysis, especially with respect to subject, timing and form." Many officers felt that these constructive criticisms failed to provide enough specificity to help them serve the book's readers better.

Comments about the PDB's failings came in several forms. For one, President Carter relayed his concerns and criticisms directly. It started less than two months into his term, when he told intelligence officials he was "disappointed" with the analysis he received on foreign political trends and intentions and wanted more "divergent views," even in the PDB. Soon, it got more pointed. "Carter sent a note to us, saying, 'We're not happy with the PDB,'" recalls senior CIA analytic manager Dick Kerr. "The president actually wrote it on the PDB. He just felt it was not as valuable as it could be and there should be some changes." Kerr laments that the president's feedback lacked specifics. "It's typical of a consumer—'I'm not happy with it, but I don't know what I'm not happy with.' Carter just said words like, 'I'm not happy, I think we could do better.'"

"What struck me about the PDBs," Brzezinski says, "was that they were informative specifically, but not enlightening generally." He says he never sensed that the current intelligence came to him "contaminated by political preferences or leanings," but he remained largely unhappy with the book's assessments of foreign leaders and their policy intentions, especially because such analytic pieces usually lacked synchronization with primary Oval Office concerns. The national security advisor lamented the absence of "broad, sweeping, bold insights into the future," specifically about Soviet planning. By late 1978, he told Turner that the PDB's usefulness had dropped because it carried "too much gisting of cables" without enough "additional information or insights." Turner told his troops that Brzezinski "expects something a little more startling or secretive . . . he thinks of the PDB as an opportunity to stir the President to think about significant issues more than to substitute for forwarding cables to him."

Brzezinski admitted that top-level feedback to the Agency should have been clearer. He remembers, "Very often we were critical of what we were getting, but we weren't very clear in demanding what we needed." He regrets his lack of specificity: "I know that the Agency would have been more helpful if it had been more deliberately tasked, very specifically tasked, with clearer emphasis on what was needed, and perhaps with greater identification, earlier, of what really is not all that helpful to the top policymakers."

The lack of clear guidance, combined with the alternative praise and criticism of the PDB, took its toll. Two of the Agency's most senior analysts wrote, "We had spent the past few years trying to divine exactly what President Carter wanted in the way of current support— the feedback was as mixed as it was sparse—and we were never sure our efforts were on the mark. He eventually took time to visit Headquarters and thank us specifically for the President's Daily Brief (PDB), but we were not convinced that he really valued it." For some, the criticisms completely blocked the previous positive comments out of memory. "Carter and Brzezinski," one analyst recalls, "crapped all over all political reporting and the PDB."

It came to a head in November 1978. Protests in Iran against US ally Shah Mohammad Reza Pahlavi spiraled out of control. PDB customers felt poorly served by the analysis in the book and other sources. The secretary of state, Cyrus Vance, noted that he felt comforted that Agency analysts joined his own experts and the ambassador on the ground in the belief that even though the shah might be required to make political compromises, the Iranian leader did not face a severe threat to his rule. Defense secretary Harold Brown says, "Our intelligence apparatus did not function in Iran—and that meant that neither the PDB nor the other intelligence entities were providing well-based knowledge, let alone an ability to anticipate what was going to happen." Vice President Mondale recalls, "The material about Iran tended to be late and I believe crippled by what I remember to have been an understanding that our agents were instructed not to talk with opponents of the Shah." And for Brzezinski, it sharpened his disappointment in the raw intelligence on Iran, and in the Agency's analytic assessments overall. He urged Carter to write a personal note about the unacceptable situation to Turner, Vance, and himself—with Turner and the CIA being the main target.

The president followed his national security advisor's advice despite a busy calendar. "That day," he says, "I was dealing with China normalization, strikes in Iran, SALT discussions with the Soviets, and promises by Israel to move on peace. Also we decided to invite Gen. Zia from Pakistan over for a visit. That is when I made this request." He handwrote: "To Cy, Zbig, Stan—I am not satisfied with the quality of our political intelligence. Assess our assets and, as soon as possible, give me a report concerning our abilities in the most important areas of the world. Make a joint recommendation on what we should do to improve your ability to give me political information and advice."

Brzezinski followed the note two days later with a memo to Turner and Vance saying, "The attached note makes clear the President's determination to improve our political intelligence. I believe we should give the political intelligence problem our highest priority attention. . . . I am concerned that this not turn out to be another bureaucratic exercise that is long on words and short on implementation of meaningful action." An immediate result was the Political Intelligence Working Group, which established senior-level collaboration to improve intelligence collection from the CIA, State Department, and military attachés.

Although a private note to only three people, the swipe at the Agency's efforts (and, to a lesser degree, the State Department's collection) hit the newspapers within a few days, and Turner took it hard. He thought the president had been pushed into sending the note. "I was very upset. But I was mainly upset with Brzezinski because I assumed he had engineered this thing." Carter firmly disagrees that manipulation drove his action. "When people write about who orchestrated my decisions, I think they are completely wrong. I was not a puppet that Brzezinski would come in and say, 'Mr. President, you have got to do this.' The final decision on every issue that I ever decided was mine."

Regardless of who spurred the note, Turner recognized there had been lapses in the Agency's analysis. "We in the CIA were not well enough versed in the mores, the character, the cultures of the Middle East," he said years later, "and I don't think we gave adequate advice to the President taking into account the longer-term aspects as opposed to just dealing with the current aspects. . . . We ought to have done a better job in giving the President advice based on a longer-term perspective."

He knew he needed to show improvement within the CIA. "There was nothing I could do but swallow it and try to improve. It made me more conscious each day of scrutinizing the PDB before it went to the president to make sure it was as clear as we could make it." The director spun the incident as a net positive when speaking to the workforce in 1979. "It was just a year ago now that we had the so-called intelligence failure in Iran and the president wrote a note to the Secretary of State, Dr. Brzezinski and myself suggesting that we could improve political intelligence reporting," he told a full crowd in the CIA's auditorium.

> The President didn't say, nor is it true, that that situation represented an intelligence failure. That was coined by the American media and was an exaggeration. We would have liked to have done better, but there was no failure.

The President's suggestions have helped us improve for the future. . . . Put the shoe on the other foot. If we had not done quite as well as we would have liked in Iran, and the President had said nothing to me, and incidentally that wasn't the first time he made a suggestion to me, think of the implications of that. To me that would have implied that he wasn't concerned, that he wasn't reading and depending on his intelligence input. The fact that he was concerned and interested is indicative of how important he regards what we do for him. Six mornings a week we give him a Presidential Daily Brief—the PDB—and I guarantee you it is the highest quality intelligence product in this or any town.

THE PDB's BIGGEST CONTENT change in two decades began with someone who wasn't even supposed to be seeing the book. "I read the PDB, to the degree I did, because I looked at it as I was walking between the offices," says Denis Clift, the vice president's national security advisor. "I wasn't supposed to do that, but for me to be able to work with Mondale, I did. If there were hot issues, he would discuss them with me."

Mondale would occasionally raise items from the President's Daily Brief directly with Clift to help his aide complete the necessary material for the VP's weekly meetings with Carter, frequent National Security Council meetings, and assorted other foreign policy events. Even then, Clift recalls, his discussions with the vice president never explicitly mentioned the president's notations on the PDB, for one simple reason: Mondale's unprecedented role in White House decision making included an understanding that he would *not* pass on to others what he and the president had privately discussed, a category in which he included Carter's scribbles in the PDB's margins. "He's a very conscientious man, a man of integrity," Clift says of Mondale, "and he didn't want to violate his ground rules with Carter on this new role."

By the fall of 1979, Clift had become increasingly disappointed in the CIA's efforts. "I found the PDB to be flatly inadequate," Clift says. "I saw some articles that I thought were too long, and it left most of the world unaddressed." He remembers shaking his head at the missed opportunity. "You were writing this for the leader of the free world, who was dealing with stuff going on everywhere. The president needs to know about all of it because his calendar, his telephone calls, and his interactions are such that the globe is spinning in front of him every day."

One morning he saw PDB articles that, as far as he was concerned, were "essentially irrelevant." He'd had enough. "This is what was being given to the president by the crack intelligence agency of the United States? I was professionally disgusted and had to get it off my chest." After showing the PDB to Mondale, he returned to his office, sat down at the typewriter, and hammered out a Top Secret memo to the CIA's deputy director, Frank Carlucci, that laid out his assessment of the PDB's gross failings in four single-spaced pages. "It wasn't just a ramble; I had a lot of very specific points I was making. I didn't just say, 'This stinks.' I was offering constructive criticism, saying, 'This is the way to make it better.'"

Clift suggested a new approach toward the PDB's content. First, he thought the book should provide quick updates on more places around the globe, delivering a true worldwide survey instead of just a few long articles drilling down on countries because new intelligence reporting had come in. "Not every one of the world's key spots may be jumping that day," he recalls writing, "but you have to tell the president what's going on across the world, even to say, 'Nothing's going on here that you have to worry about.' Let him know what's going on, and where there are hot issues in hot places." Second, Clift's experience with the president and vice president over more than two years convinced him that brevity worked better for them then comprehensiveness. "I saw some articles that were too long—deep analytical pieces. Don't make him go through an encyclopedia each day; keep it tight. Tell him when there's good photography, tell him when there's other good sources of information, and you can rocket that to Brzezinski or whomever as soon as he asks for it."

The next thing Clift knew, senior DI officers invited him to the CIA to discuss what he had set out. They hosted him for a long discussion of his observations and insights, during which he both reiterated the points he had made in his memo and emphasized the human element. "Let's be a little Machiavellian," he said to them. "The president is dealing with leaders around the world every day, discussing with them issues of importance to the United States. If I were writing this document, I'd let him know when a prime minister, president, or crowned head was in some domestic difficulty, something that really had him or her tied up. I said that I would use the PDB to tell the president, 'This might be the perfect time to go to that person and push your issue.'"

Instead of brushing off the senior aide, the DI's leadership relished the detailed input. After all, other recent feedback on the PDB had been less than encouraging and frustratingly vague. They had heard in early 1980 from defense secretary Harold Brown that "it sounded in recent months more as though we were 'not on the inside.'" "Their reaction to me was extraordinarily positive," Clift says. "We talked it through at some length." Realizing that the absence of a briefer gave them little else but the president's scribbles on the PDB to work from, they took Clift's advice as an opportunity.

"First of all," says Dick Kerr, who managed the PDB at the time, "we thought he was more interested in detail, so we started to do pieces with a little more richness and substance to them. We tried some format changes, trying to make it a little more attractive and easier to read. We put a few more graphics in it, charts and maps and photos and things that were a little more helpful. They still wanted a very limited number of pages, a quick read, so we very seldom would do more than two or three longer pieces, half a dozen intermediate-size ones, and then some quick little updates. I don't think it ever went more than ten pages long."

The mantra for the refocused PDB was "Today's News Today," with a renewed effort to get inputs as late as 4:00 a.m. into the book that Carter would read just a few hours later. The current intelligence officers impressed director Turner with their quick turnaround, which added demands on analysts for broader coverage for what he called "a significant departure from the publication we have been sending the President for the last three years." The Agency put the new-look PDB before Carter for the first time on March 26. The new book stood out enough with the president for him to discuss it with Turner, noting that its content that day included an article on the demographic deterioration of Kampuchea (Cambodia) and an assessment that there was a 50 percent chance that the Soviets had used poisonous gas in Afghanistan.

The instigator of the effort was not forgotten. Director Turner sent this personal note of thanks to Vice President Mondale: "I want you to be aware that Denis Clift provided very useful insight and a number of helpful suggestions on ways to improve the PDB. A number of Denis' suggestions have been incorporated into the revised PDB. Please convey to Denis my appreciation for the time and effort he very kindly volunteered to assist us." Many years later, one of Clift's contacts at the CIA surprised him, saying, "You know, Denis, the changes that you introduced to the PDB lasted twenty years. You reshaped the document, and it lasted."

"My recollection is that I was pleased," Carter says about the new PDB. Mondale is more direct: "I believe the PDB was fundamentally improved."

CHAPTER SEVEN

WRITE ONE FOR THE GIPPER

RIGHT AFTER RONALD REAGAN's election in November 1980, President Jimmy Carter authorized the CIA to deliver the President's Daily Brief to both the newly elected president and the vice president–elect, George H. W. Bush. Despite the bitter campaign fight, a decades-long principle prevailed: national security trumps partisanship when it comes to preparing the next commander in chief for his solemn duties ahead. Dick Lehman, who had more experience with person-alizing finished intelligence for presidents than anyone else at the CIA, had become chairman of the National Intelligence Council (NIC), a high-level unit established recently to bridge the intelligence, academic, and policy communities, and Lehman reached out to the Reagan camp. He quickly called Dick Allen—Reagan's top foreign policy advisor, who had served briefly in the Nixon administration more than a decade earlier—to discuss the Agency's support to the incoming administration, including PDB logistics.

CIA officers began briefing Allen across the Washington area: in his office, in his car, and even during breakfast at the Madison Hotel. Just nine days after the election, Allen was joined by campaign man-ager Bill Casey and top advisor Ed Meese—both of whom would take prominent positions as the administration started—in a session with CIA director Stansfield Turner, his executive assistant Bob Gates, dep-uty director Frank Carlucci, and Lehman. Turner showed the PDB to Reagan's advisors, telling them the Agency would use the next two months to determine how the president-elect wanted his intelligence presented to him. Only two important pieces of PDB-related guidance emerged from this early session: direct all intelligence support for the president and his staff through Allen, not through the formal transition team, and enlarge the book's typeface to make it easier for Reagan to read.

Allen invited Agency briefers in mid-November to two tightly structured sessions with Reagan himself at Blair House, the president's official guest residence, just across Pennsylvania Avenue from the White House, before Reagan flew back to the West Coast. Agendas for the sessions certainly included intelligence, for which CIA briefers remember Reagan being "extremely alert," but Allen's broader national security business dominated. By contrast, the vice president–elect began receiving daily, in-person PDB briefings from Agency officers at the nearby Jackson Place townhouse, which former presidents had been using for the past decade. Compared to the straitlaced, formal meetings Reagan was holding, Bush's sessions were animated and loose, a result of his personality and his experience as a CIA director.

Both factors led CIA officer Peter Dixon "Dix" Davis, who had been briefing Bush, to boldly ask him to encourage Reagan to accept daily PDB briefings upon his return to California. Bush accepted, and he found the perfect opportunity to lobby Reagan: their ride together to Andrews Air Force Base before Reagan's flight home. "I felt it was very important for the President to not only read the PDB every day," Bush recalls, "but to do so in the presence of briefers who could answer questions and get more information if required." The vice president–elect's efforts paid off; while Reagan's plane was in the air, Ed Meese informed the CIA that his boss was expecting to see an Agency briefing officer at his home in Pacific Palisades—the very next morning.

WITHIN HOURS, DICK KERR was flying to Southern California. Kerr's intellect and keen analytic instincts stood out almost as much as his towering frame and booming voice. Decades of experience as a current intelligence analyst and manager in the DI prepared him to represent the Agency to the new president. His plane landed early enough for him to drive to an Agency facility in Los Angeles and prepare the next day's briefing. Just a few hours later, in the wee hours of the morning, a CIA security officer picked up Kerr and the locked bag holding the President's Daily Brief and drove to a narrow street with a closed-off driveway. Flashing his CIA card to the Secret Service agent guarding the house, Kerr got in without any questions or even a cursory search. He cooled his heels for a few minutes in a lower-level recreation room until he was escorted up to the main level and introduced to Reagan.

After meeting Nancy Reagan—and telling an inquisitive security officer that the briefing was for Reagan only—Kerr accompanied the president-elect into a den for the PDB session. Colleagues back at CIA headquarters, led by Dix Davis, had provided Kerr with not only the PDB itself but also supporting documents, hoping they would help Reagan gain the deeper background necessary to get up to speed quickly on the world situation. On that first day, Kerr recalls, "Reagan read the PDB carefully, asking an occasional question, and then read the other material." Reagan liked what he saw enough to agree that he would receive a roughly twenty-minute briefing each morning, except for holidays, unless pressing business intervened.

To stay fresh for the president-elect and to keep tabs on the analytic office he ran at home, Kerr started splitting the briefing duties with Davis, who flew out to California every other week to relieve his colleague. They made an unlikely-looking pair. Kerr cut an imposing figure at nearly six and a half feet tall; Davis was slim and barely topped five feet. Kerr always radiated a casual vibe, even in suit and tie. He even came to the office on Halloween dressed as Big Bird. Davis, by contrast, dressed impeccably and remains unmatched in Agency lore for his dapper attire. Both briefers, however, had sterling reputations as good-humored experts who enjoyed their work and brought out the best in others.

While in California, Kerr and Davis operated with little supervision from CIA headquarters. Director Stansfield Turner, in fact, "never asked us what was going on," they later said. The deputy director for intelligence, Bruce Clarke, served as the briefers' upper-level management point of contact, but even he avoided micromanaging the briefers' efforts. His instructions to Kerr before the first session with the president were focused on style instead of substance: "Get a black belt to go with that blue suit—the brown one is not appropriate." Kerr promptly bought himself the belt. The communication was

Dick Kerr (left) and Dick Lehman (center) at Lehman's CIA retirement ceremony; future CIA director/secretary of defense Bob Gates appears at the far
right. *Central Intelligence Agency website photo*

decidedly heavier in the *other* direction, with Kerr and Davis sending
memoranda about the substance of the sessions back to the Directorate of Intelligence, along with requests for follow-up information.

Between late November and mid-January, Reagan received more
than two dozen briefings. The Agency learned much about their
soon-to-be top customer from these sessions. "As a rule, Reagan was a
studious reader," Kerr and Davis recall, "going over each item deliberately and with considerable concentration." But this did not mean he
agreed with the Agency's analytic assessments. Davis found Reagan's
thoughts on most topics firm and fixed, noting that Reagan "knew
what he thought about everything." The two briefers declined to send
back to headquarters inside scoops about Reagan's style or his interactions with aides. "The only things we were going to pass back were
substantive things," Kerr says. "We didn't do any of the chatter, like
what they say to each other and how they talk. We were extraordinarily careful about that, because we figured that would kill the
thing immediately if it got out that we were going back and saying, 'I

talked to the president and the president thinks that so-and-so is an idiot.' We didn't even tell any of our bosses. Absolutely not."

The briefers' discretion impressed Reagan enough that after another trip to Washington, in mid-January, he brought Davis on his plane back to California. While on the DC-9, Davis gave Reagan his first in-flight intelligence briefing, introducing both the day's PDB and a special report on various anti-Israeli Palestinian groups and leaders, covering factions both inside and outside the Palestinian Liberation Organization (PLO). He took ten minutes to read the extensive report. Then Reagan looked at Davis and confirmed the briefer's growing suspicion that the daily intelligence briefings were failing to expand the president-elect's views by saying, "But they are all terrorists, aren't they?"

Kerr and Davis had supplemented Reagan's copy of the current PDB to bring him up to speed on issues that Carter had been reading about regularly for months or years. Working with Allen to determine topics worthy of the president's special attention, Agency officers came up with a list: Kampuchea (Cambodia), Lebanon, the Philippines, Pakistan, Somalia, Morocco, Zimbabwe, North and South Yemen, Turkey, and Namibia. The PDB itself continued to treat at length developments in the Soviet Union, Poland, Iran, and Israel. Of all the issues he saw, the president-elect seemed most interested in accounts of Soviet consumer frustration and economic difficulties, strategic arms control issues, foreign leaders' intentions for dealing with his incoming administration, the disposition of Soviet nuclear weapons, and the brewing crisis in Poland—where, just a few months earlier, labor unrest had spurred the creation of the Solidarity trade union. And Bush encouraged the Agency's briefers to use time with Reagan also to educate him about the intelligence community and the covert collection of sensitive intelligence. After leaving office, Reagan recalled this entire pre-inauguration period generically but fondly: "My memory is of being completely satisfied with the briefings I received during the transition."

Back at headquarters others in the analytic wing of the Agency also focused their efforts on the new team. "It was an interesting situation," Kerr and Davis noted. "We were still producing the PDB for President Carter, although we had no contact with him or with senior officials in the administration. The incoming group had captured our attention."

THE NATIONAL SECURITY ADVISOR designate, Dick Allen, came back to Washington with Reagan lacking positive memories about the President's Daily Brief. Twelve years earlier, he had taken the lead on intelligence issues for President-elect Richard Nixon's transition team—and he notes that the PDB was "a source of very interesting information, but none of it profound enough to affect broad policy decisions or implementation in the short term." To refresh himself on the PDB and determine what additional backgrounders Reagan needed, Allen in mid-November had begun getting his own daily intelligence briefings. By early January 1981, he sat down with Kerr to review various PDB formats from the previous sixteen years, hoping to find one that impressed him more than what he had been reading for almost two months. He saw nothing he liked better.

But the opinion of someone else mattered more: Ronald Reagan himself. Kerr had asked the incoming president about his preferences for the PDB's look and composition. To everyone's surprise, Reagan said that its current format, length, and specificity satisfied him. Whether his approval reflected his true feelings or merely politeness, Reagan's PDB would end up closely resembling Carter's book, reshaped just slightly by Allen and CIA director designate Bill Casey based on how *they* wanted the president to see it.

"By Inauguration Day," Kerr and Davis recall, "the daily briefing system was so well established that it seemed natural to all involved that it would simply continue." Indeed, the daily sessions with Kerr or Davis went on, but with one vital difference: Allen ensured before inauguration that *he* would receive the daily, in-person briefing, and then *he* would deliver the President's Daily Brief to Reagan without a CIA briefer present. "We had a very good relationship with Allen," Kerr recalls. "We spent a lot of time together. And we won him over." Allen became an avid customer of intelligence, recognizing the value of the in-person briefing enough to keep seeing a PDB briefer each morning as long as he held the job. "Allen was one-on-one, always," Kerr says. "Probably a half hour. We tried to keep it short because that was the beginning of his day and we did it fairly early."

President Ronald Reagan with the first of his six national security advisors, Dick Allen, June 8, 1981. *Courtesy Ronald Reagan Presidential Library*

The day after the inauguration, Reagan and his national security advisor started the daily pattern that would remain largely consistent for two full terms, well beyond Allen's departure less than a year into the administration. "On a typical morning," Allen says, "I'd go up and hand him the PDB and sit at the opposite corner of the desk while he read it. And if he wanted something elaborated upon, I'd make a note of that and have it elaborated upon for him." The familiar 8-by-10½-inch book usually included four or five single-page articles with facing-page maps or pictures, a page or two with wide-ranging bullets of information (colloquially called "snowflakes") about world events, and a single two-page article. Raw intelligence reports, foreign press articles, and other documents from Allen or his National Security Council staff would often supplement the core six-to-ten-page book. Agency analysts included, generally on Saturdays, a "Selects" page listing about a half dozen CIA reports for Reagan to mark if he wanted to see them. On one early Saturday, Reagan had checked a few report titles and scrawled right on the PDB page, "Can I have these?" Then, as if realizing that the president need not *ask* for such service, he crossed out those words and wrote in their place, "Have Sit Room send to me routinely."

Allen recalls that the overall PDB package worked well for Reagan, who preferred "a straightforward presentation without too many parentheses and/or footnotes." By contrast, he says, the president from the start "couldn't abide what the State Department produced, wall to wall on long memoranda of 8.5" × 11" paper: Courier font, dreary, droning, bad indentation, poor English—on and on and on it went." So he left the daily State Department intelligence report, called the Secretary's Morning Summary, out of the president's daily folder.

White House chief of staff James Baker, deputy chief of staff Mike Deaver, and counselor Ed Meese—Reagan's senior staff triumvirate, which the press soon labeled the "troika"—usually joined Allen's national security session with Reagan. Baker remembers reading a copy of the President's Daily Brief every day in his office before the national security briefing, allowing him to duck out of the national security session if pressing business arose elsewhere in the West Wing. The book was "more like *Reader's Digest* than *War and Peace*," Meese recalls, noting, "The PDB gave the President a broad overview of what was going on."

BUSH, AS HIS SCHEDULE permitted, would attend Reagan's sessions after an Agency officer had already briefed him independently at his Naval Observatory residence. Focusing on the intelligence during his own personalized briefing allowed him to use the Oval Office time to build his relationship with the president. "The Vice President learned early on that President Reagan liked a good story," remembers Robert "Bud" McFarlane, the longest-serving of Reagan's six national security advisors. "He almost always came with some kind of joke or story or anecdote—and he would take fifteen minutes out of my briefing time at least once or twice a week, leaving me with fifteen minutes instead of a half hour. It was kind of annoying. However, you could go over, and we often did."

As a former CIA director, Bush knew the value of having a working-level briefer in the room when going over the PDB, and he insisted upon having one come to him during his entire eight years as vice president. The intelligence officer brought extensive supplemental information, ranging from details of Agency operations to analytic insights that had been left on the cutting room floor as PDB pieces made their way through the Agency's editing gauntlet. One of Bush's

briefers, Doug MacEachin—who would go on to run the Directorate of Intelligence in the 1990s—recalls that Bush was a particularly
energetic customer. "He read it, he wrote on it. I'd take it back and
there would be all kinds of marks all over the borders. Tons and tons
of questions. A really good, active exchange."

Bush and an assistant or two who joined him for the briefing
interacted extensively with the briefers. Donald Gregg, a CIA officer
who had shifted over to become the vice president's national security
advisor, remembers, "If I saw a particularly piquant piece of intelligence, I'd ask for the sourcing: Does this come from a human source
or an intercept? Many days it brought some unique input." Gregg
notes that Bush was particularly fond of the PDB's graphics, such as
maps showing the ebb and flow of the war between Iran and Iraq
that endured for most of the Reagan presidency, and he would often
ensure that President Reagan read particularly insightful PDB items.

The vice president's comfort with the PDB was so high that he
took liberties with it that others would not. "He was a very down-to-
earth guy," one of his briefers recalls. "There were a couple of times
on a beautiful spring day that he'd say, 'Let's go out on the balcony.'
And the mess steward would bring us some orange juice and coffee.
And I'd think, 'They are paying me to do this?'"

MacEachin recalls one morning later in the administration
when James Baker—a good friend of the vice president—had joined
Bush for his session. After handing over the book, the briefer only got
a few words in before Bush interrupted him.

"I've got to go downstairs to the men's room. Do you mind if I
take this with me?"

"Not at all, Mr. Vice President."

Bush exited, PDB in hand. MacEachin shrugged and glanced at
Baker, who leaned over and whispered, "Well, now we've got black-
mail on him."

Vice President Bush's insistence on having a CIA briefer personally brief him on the PDB every day emboldened the Agency to suggest the same practice for other recipients of the book. They accepted,
setting a precedent that PDB customers in future administrations,
with few exceptions, have followed. This meant that CIA briefers
delivered PDB copies to Allen, for Reagan's briefing, as well as all
around town.

Chuck Peters and John Hedley were the officers tapped to take over the morning deliveries. Although nearly opposite in style—Peters was blunt, bordering on gruff, whereas Hedley was personable and courteous—both took seriously the burden of briefing the book to multiple customers. They first tried trading off: every other day, one of them would come in late and stay as long as it took to review the next day's book. Analysts usually compiled their drafts by 6:00 p.m., but Peters or Hedley would stay until 8:30 or 9:00 to chat with the analysts or their managers, get PDB articles typed and retyped, and oversee substantive changes. Whoever put the book to bed would also brief its recipients the following morning. This meant getting into the office well before dawn to peruse the cables related to PDB items that the Operations Center's senior duty officer had collected overnight. After briefing, one by one, every recipient of the book other than the president himself, the briefer would return to CIA headquarters to tell director Casey and other Agency leaders about principals' reactions and attend the production meeting for the next day's book; then he could go home early while his partner took over for the next day. It was not long before everyone realized that the every-other-day schedule was unsustainable. Peters and Hedley each began briefing a few customers every day instead.

The first two additional PDB customers, secretary of state Al Haig and secretary of defense Caspar Weinberger, had begun receiving briefings back on inauguration day. Kerr remembers getting frequent earfuls from Haig during each morning's car briefing as the secretary was driven from his home to the State Department: "We'd get into big arguments about substantive issues, which I always thought was a great thing." Haig did not hesitate to disagree with the analysis he read, especially on terrorism. "You were going to get a lecture on that," Kerr recalls, "because when he had been CINCEUR [commander in chief, European Command], the Red Brigade tried to blow him up and killed one of his drivers and a military aide. So he had a personal interest in it." Haig also saw a Soviet hand behind most threats to US interests overseas, including terrorism, leading to heated disagreements with Kerr about the CIA's analysis that other forces were at play, too.

"There are the Soviets doing it again," Haig growled to Kerr in the backseat of his limo one morning after reading another piece in the President's Daily Brief about one of the world's persistent terrorist threats.

"Well, I don't think that's an accurate way to describe it," Kerr said, pushing back. Haig raised an eyebrow and glanced over at the briefer as Kerr continued. "The Soviets have an interest in the outcome, and they may turn a blind eye to some of it, but the idea that they are behind every piece of terrorism in the world is giving them far more credit than they deserve."

Haig guffawed. "You don't know what you're talking about."

"Well, I think we do!"

Haig held Kerr's gaze briefly before smiling and turning to the next subject in that day's book. Kerr took it as a friendly argument, not a personal attack. Such was the life of a briefer.

Weinberger, fortunately, liked his briefing early. Seeing him at the Pentagon at 7:00 a.m. allowed the briefer enough time to finish with him and then scurry across the river to see the other recipients. The secretary would sometimes postpone other meetings to finish reading the PDB, which he considered the most useful product he got because of the "quality of the product and availability of the briefer for discussion." Briefer John Hedley describes Weinberger as less of a talker than Haig but a "wonderful guy, a very eager recipient." He still recalls their intimate sessions with the PDB: "I handed it over to him, and sat kind of beside him in his office at the Pentagon, just the two of us—nobody else ever in there. There was a young fellow outside, his military assistant, who I would chat with sometimes, an officer named Colin Powell. He knew he wasn't entitled to see the PDB, but he knew why we were there." But on Weinberger's overseas trips—which the CIA briefer did not join—the secretary of defense had Powell secure the PDB and bring it to him.

RONALD REAGAN'S MORNING ON Monday, March 30, 1981, started much like the others of his young presidency. After having breakfast with Nancy in the residence, he entered the Oval Office between 8:45 and 9:00 for a quick staff meeting to preview his day, get through some paperwork, and prepare for a 9:15 phone call with West German chancellor Helmut Schmidt. Allen arrived just before the call to give the president last-minute talking points and sit in on the conversation. When the call ended, Allen began his regular national security session with the PDB. That day, the discussion touched on a potential Saudi Arabian purchase of military aircraft and the movement of arms to Central American Communist guerillas. The usual White House senior staff officers attended, but the vice president did not. He skipped the national security session in the Oval Office that day because he was flying to Texas, requiring him to leave his Naval Observatory residence around 8:30 by helicopter for Andrews Air Force Base.

Bush thus missed not only the president's session but also the most dramatic event of the young presidency: John Hinckley shot at Reagan as he left the Washington Hilton hotel, nearly killing him and permanently disabling press secretary James Brady. Reagan's daily schedule came to a standstill as he recovered from serious injuries for nearly two weeks at George Washington University Hospital. The book continued to go to its other recipients—and the troika of Baker, Meese, and Deaver continued to meet with the president every day in the hospital—but Reagan himself remained out of the current intelligence loop. Allen recalls only one national security briefing for Reagan at the hospital, with even that one being "light."

After Reagan returned to the White House on April 11 and began a reduced work schedule from the residence, Allen still proceeded gingerly. Soon after, the senior staff decided the president should resume his national security briefing, in condensed form, upstairs in the residence. That night, Allen returned home, spending time at the dining room table with his wife and seven children before they went to bed. He recalls one of them asking how the president looked.

"He's fine," Allen replied. "He's getting along well. In fact, I'm going to see him privately on Wednesday morning."

His youngest daughter, Kim, was in kindergarten. With a look of awe, she asked, "You are?"

"Yes, I'm going to give him his briefing."

The conversation ended there, with his kids having little idea what he even meant by a "briefing." In fact, he forgot about the exchange entirely until the following night, when he returned home to find Kim pulling something out a bag for him.

"Here!" she declared proudly. He saw in her hands twenty-five get-well cards, hand-drawn for the president by Kim and her classmates and topped by a note from the teacher. "Will you make sure the president sees these?"

Allen sighed, not wanting to waste precious time during Reagan's first session back by pushing some kindergartners' cards on him. Choosing his words carefully, he told Kim that he would take them to the president's briefing. Early the next morning, he carried the cards into the office and, true to his word, stuffed them inside his own copy of the briefing folder. He had no intention of showing them, but he would keep his precise promise: Kim's cards would indeed go into Reagan's national security session that day. As he ascended to the residence for his scheduled meeting, Allen felt better seeing only Nancy Reagan and Mike Deaver with the president, reducing the chances that anyone would note his bulging briefing folder.

"Good morning, Mr. President," he said, handing the reclining Reagan the primary copy of the PDB.

"Good morning," Reagan replied. Although his energy had rebounded quite a bit, his full strength and attention had not yet returned. Reagan glanced down at the briefing folder, paused, and then opened it. Slowly he looked back to Allen and sighed.

He clearly doesn't want to read anything this morning, Allen thought. *So we're done.* Reaching across the president's body, he closed Reagan's folder and took it back, saying, "Thank you very much, Mr. President. You've had your briefing for today."

Reagan looked up at Allen and flashed one of his mischievous grins. "Well, thanks, Dick."

Allen returned the president's smile while slipping Reagan's book on top of his own, preparing to leave. But some of the get-well cards slipped a bit from his grasp as he stood up. Reagan noticed and stopped him.

"What's that?"

"Nothing, Mr. President."

Reagan scowled at his national security advisor and repeated himself. "Dick—what is it?"

Realizing that the president wasn't going to let this go, he replied, "Those are some cards that the kindergarten kids at Oakridge Elementary School in Arlington made for you, sir. I promised that I would bring them with me."

"Let me see them."

Allen sheepishly handed the cards to the president. He looked at them, one by one, beaming as he made his way through the stack.

National security advisor Dick Allen slipped this card from his daughter along with the PDB into the national security briefing in April 1981, when President Reagan began receiving such briefings again; Reagan signed the card for Allen to take home to her. *Courtesy Dick Allen*

After reading every card and then the teacher's note at the bottom, Reagan asked Allen, "So, which one is your daughter's?"

"It's in there, somewhere, Mr. President. I'll tell her you asked about it."

The scowl returned. "Which one is your daughter's, Dick?"

Allen did not need to hear it a third time. He shuffled through the stack until he found Kim's card, then handed it to the president.

"Give me your pen," Reagan said.

Allen watched as the president wrote, "Dear Kim—Forgive me for using your card for my answer but I wanted to let you know how very much I appreciate your good wishes and your lovely card. Love, Ronald Reagan."

REAGAN'S FIRST CIA DIRECTOR, Bill Casey, declined the DI's offer to brief him daily on the President's Daily Brief. A speedy and voracious reader, he probably wanted to avoid having to tell a briefer—who would be eager to impress the boss with additional insights—to shut up and let him focus on what the president was seeing in the book. Indeed, Casey read the PDB first thing every morning while his security detail drove him from his residence in Washington across the river to CIA headquarters in Langley. He told the DI to take precious time during his daily staff meeting only if there were late items that had not appeared in the daily publications and would be discussed orally with PDB recipients.

This did not reflect disinterest in analysis. Originally, in fact, Casey had wanted to personally review the book late each night before it was printed for Reagan. "I warned Casey against doing that because, frankly, I felt Admiral Turner had gone too far in red-inking the PDB on a daily basis," says Bob Gates, who continued as executive assistant to the director when Casey replaced Stansfield Turner in January 1981. He told his new boss, "It may give the impression that you are politicizing it, that you are putting your spin on what's in the current intelligence. Let the DDI review it. And then if you've got a problem with it, take it up with the DDI." Gates's words sank in. Casey ended up devoting much more attention to arguing with analysts about long-form National Intelligence Estimates than about current intelligence.

That said, Casey remained in the PDB loop. He wanted to hear the feedback that the daily intelligence briefers brought back from the book's restricted readership. "We would always come back and go see Casey," John Hedley recalls. "He never asked to see anything before it went to the president; he didn't want to sign off on it. He just wanted us to tell him what *they* thought about it." The director used these fifteen-to-thirty-minute feedback sessions with the briefers to suggest additional material for the PDB. He also used the PDB's daily delivery to send private messages to the president, letters that Reagan would read later in the day. Despite conventional wisdom that Reagan and Casey were close, the two rarely met outside of wider White House meetings and kept a professional relationship rather than a personal one. Gates recalls, "I've always believed that Casey's closeness to Reagan has been exaggerated. I think they were fairly close for the first several months after the election, when Reagan still had some sense of obligation to Casey for having helped get him elected. . . . Casey could see the President whenever he wanted, but Reagan really had a hard time understanding Casey and the relationship really wasn't that close in my view."

Casey's biggest impact on the PDB was indirect, via impressions that he would "politicize" assessments, or override experts' views to put them more in line with what policy makers wanted to see. Many analysts felt that Casey pushed his preferred conclusions on them, rather than letting them base their conclusions on an unbiased assessment of the facts on the ground. Objectivity ranks among the highest standards for intelligence analysts; decades of intelligence theory and practice suggest that policy makers lacking independent, impartial intelligence assessments formulate less successful national security policy. But Casey did not hesitate to express his strong policy views. He sat on Reagan's cabinet while CIA director and rarely withheld his opinions on what Reagan should do. When he accepted the CIA job after being passed over for secretary of state, Casey reportedly told Reagan that while he intended to present intelligence assessments objectively, he planned to engage fully on policy issues, too.

An intelligence analyst with regional or topical expertise naturally objects when a senior manager, who understands the details of virtually any topic much less, changes her bottom-line judgment. This sensitivity can lead analysts to view as politicization even standard editing of their products to make them easier for policy makers to read and understand. There is a fine line between adjusting a written product's style to make it more presentable and altering its analytic judgments to make it more palatable to policy customers. Casey frequently walked this line, disagreeing with analysts forcefully both in handwritten notes and in person. Gates, who became Casey's DDI in January 1982 and deputy director in April 1986, noted that analysts who had risen in their careers under generally less assertive directors disliked Casey's in-your-face style and his strong thoughts on proper analytic focus, particularly on assessments of the Soviet Union—about which he was more hawkish than just about anyone in Washington.

More often than not, Casey appears to have confronted analysts simply because he found their assessments wordy and equivocal. After only a few months in office, he had sent a letter to the president lamenting the "academic, soft, [and] not sufficiently relevant and realistic" analysis coming out of his own agency. He reportedly told analysts that he hated their wishy-washy judgments, which he saw as ducking the CIA's duty to provide policy makers with clear conclusions. Even Bobby Ray Inman—Casey's first deputy, who disagreed with him often—gave Casey the benefit of the doubt on this score. While noting that the director annoyed analysts by criticizing their writing style, Inman asserted that claims about Casey distorting assessments to support his personal views are "pure bunk."

Casey shook up the analytic wing of the Agency early on. First, he moved John McMahon, the tough but respected deputy director for operations, over to lead the DI—a rare lateral assignment at that level for someone with no significant analytic exposure. Second, Casey and McMahon reorganized the DI into geographically oriented offices, which took current intelligence out of the hands of an elite office and passed responsibility for the PDB and other daily products to the analysis directorate as a whole. Only nine months after McMahon took the job, he was promoted to become Casey's deputy.

His replacement as DDI, Bob Gates, quickly decreed that analytic items in the PDB, as well as in the more widely distributed National Intelligence Daily, would henceforth be split into two sections, like Richard Nixon's PDB had been. Information from clandestine reporting, intercepted communications, diplomatic cables, or world press now stayed together in every current intelligence piece, clearly delineated from analysts' judgments about the situation. "Analysis and evidence were jumbled together in a way that made it impossible to tell what is the evidence and what is the author's opinion," Gates said thirty years later. "That's when I divided each piece in the PDB up into two pieces: What's the evidence on whatever we are talking about? Then, what's your analysis of it? So it was clear to the policy maker. I think that was the biggest change that I made on the PDB while I was there." Many analysts recoiled, feeling that Gates was questioning their expert assessments, but he tried to emphasize that "the question was not their judgment; it was making clear to the policy maker what is your judgment and what are the facts."

Just under a year later, Gates gathered DI officers in the Agency's auditorium to address the angst that analysts still felt about these significant changes—and sell them on the benefit these reforms had brought. He called the 1981 restructuring of the DI the "most far-reaching reorganization in this Directorate's history" and "an absolutely necessary foundation for further efforts to improve the quality of analysis." As for splitting current intelligence pieces into evidence and opinion, he told the troops, "No other single change we have made has elicited as many favorable comments from consumers as this. As a whole, the Directorate is much more aggressive in following up on current intelligence and the publications show it."

WITH RARE EXCEPTIONS IN American history, the inner circle around the president has swirled with intrigue and backstabbing. Reagan's senior staff and cabinet took it to a new level, playing out their skirmishes in the halls of the West Wing and through the national press. The most affected position was national security advisor, which hosted a record of *six* occupants during the president's two terms. Before reaching his three-year mark in office, Reagan had already moved from Dick Allen to Bill Clark, in January 1982, and then from Clark to Bud McFarlane the following fall.

Bill Clark had been a rancher in California, like Reagan. "He was a coolheaded, evenhanded, affable guy," says John Hedley, who saw Clark at the White House early in the morning before racing to brief Vice President Bush. "And we had very good rapport." Clark often demonstrated his commonsense approach and congenial personality. One day the former judge read a PDB item about Nicaragua, which noted an information gap about Soviet ships in a Nicaraguan harbor. "Damn it, John—I'm going in to see the president and I know he's going to ask about this," Clark said to Hedley. "Can't you have somebody just sitting in a goddamn café or bar and look out at the harbor and see if there is a Soviet ship out there or not? Why is it so hard to find out?" Clark quickly reversed himself. "You know, forget it," he said as he returned to his preparation for briefing the president. "It's not you, I'm just venting."

Although Clark usually just left the PDB with Reagan for him to read during the day, once or twice a week he would point the president to something particularly noteworthy in the book. Reagan was so interested in Soviet issues that these dominated Clark's CIA briefings, but his briefers dutifully kept him apprised of other global hot spots such as Poland, Lebanon, and Mexico. Poland, in fact, became the focus of a special supplement in the President's Daily Brief—ordered up by Clark and CIA director Casey, according to a *Time* magazine report—to keep Reagan up to speed on the democracy movement there.

Bud McFarlane, who had served as Clark's deputy, continued the same basic approach to the PDB when he stepped up to the job in October 1983. Each morning, he read the book before checking in with the CIA briefer at the White House for additional insights. He then carried Reagan's National Security Briefing Information folder into the Oval Office, almost always at 9:30, accompanied by other reports and policy papers for the president to sign. Occasionally, in addition to the PDB, the CIA would offer longer reports. For example, in the run-up to Reagan's first meeting with Mikhail Gorbachev in Geneva in November 1985, the president wanted to know more about the Soviet leader's personality. The CIA sent, along with the PDB, a paper on Gorbachev, his roots, his history in the party, and so forth.

The White House infighting that contributed to the revolving door of national security advisors also affected the security of the President's Daily Brief itself. Those who put their eyes on the restricted document used that access to inflate their importance to the press. "For those who are allowed to read it," Dick Allen noted years later, "it is a source of bragging rights. Curious staff members everywhere sneak a peek if they can." The problem was acute during the nearly twelve months Allen served in the White House. "There were copies for the president, the vice president, for me, for Casey, for SecDef, and for a few others—and then one for the *Washington Post*, for as far as I was concerned, it wouldn't take that long to leak."

Senior White House staffers were tasked to assemble and then later take apart the National Security Briefing folder, which meant they could see the PDB before and after the national security advisor and the president did. When the president finished with the folder in the afternoon or evening, NSC staffers would record any notations he had made, call the CIA with any feedback, and then pass the PDB to the supervisor of the White House Situation Room, who would hold on to the book until an Agency officer picked it up the following day.

"I read it every morning to try to stay abreast of what was going on," said Reagan-era White House Situation Room director Mike Bohn. "The PDB had a cachet—having access to the PDB was like having access to the president." Bohn also recalls making copies at the national security advisor's direction for not only the White House chief of staff but also, by the time Don Regan held that job in 1985, some of his assistants who were not formal PDB recipients. One official on the distribution list was careless enough to store copies of the book in his home garage—until the national security advisor discovered the practice and had the copies returned and destroyed.

The absence of good security practices in the White House, particularly the lax handling of the PDB, distressed one senior official more than any other: Vice President Bush. He asked Casey less than three months into the first term to lecture the next meeting of the

National Security Council about how to handle sensitive information in public statements. His national security assistant, Don Gregg, recalls that Bush soon thereafter saw a list of all the people who had access to the PDB and was "amazed." As a former CIA director, Bush knew more than most the damage a loose PDB could do. "Some West Wingers left it lying around. It really disturbed and upset me," he said. It surely failed to surprise Bush, then, that leaks from the PDB and its casual treatment at the White House made the CIA more hesitant to include in it especially sensitive information or details about intelligence sources.

The Agency's concerns about the PDB's security led its senior officers to try to stem its expanded distribution and rein in NSC leaks. In April 1983, Casey's staff lobbied him to push back against pressure from the Pentagon to get the PDB to the chairman of the Joint Chiefs of Staff, General John Vessey. But Casey ended up agreeing with national security advisor Bill Clark in late July that Vessey should indeed start getting PDB briefings. As a safeguard, he insisted that no others would be present and no copies would be retained. The White House itself remained a problem. "The national security advisors were pretty much letting it go out to the staff and we were having trouble getting copies back," Dick Kerr recalls. "It was never formally going beyond the principals. But there was pretty clear evidence—we'd hear back from people who saw it on the National Security staff."

So in November 1985, Casey and his deputy John McMahon went to the White House to harangue the NSC about continuing leaks. Casey told Bud McFarlane that his sources had reported White House staffers were making ten copies of the PDB, including particularly sensitive "red stripers," which required strict handling controls even within classified spaces at the CIA. McFarlane denied the Agency charge of rampant unauthorized distribution, but Admiral John Poindexter—McFarlane's deputy and successor in December 1985—admitted he made a copy of every PDB for his files.

Some managers in the Directorate of Intelligence went an extra step to protect the President's Daily Brief on their end of the process. Many analysts from the era remember their bosses telling them the book was off-limits for discussion, even within the intelligence community. A career analyst and manager who started early in the Reagan era recalls, "It was explicit: you don't acknowledge its existence to

National security advisor Robert "Bud" McFarlane, with the president's national security briefing folder on the table in front of him, briefs Reagan and Vice President George H. W. Bush in the Oval Office, August 9, 1985. *Courtesy Ronald Reagan Presidential Library*

anybody that's outside of the Agency. I had friends from the Defense Intelligence Agency saying, 'Come on, tell us about the PDB.' And I'd say, 'About *what*?' It was just horrible. It was an open secret, but you kept it."

One CIA graduate fellow from the 1980s recalls hearing that the three words "President's Daily Brief," when used together, were classified. Even decades later, an article in the Agency's in-house newsletter asserted that the fact of the existence of the PDB remained classified until the early 1990s—a claim echoed to this day by CIA historians, who say that Bob Gates declassified the PDB's existence and title after he became director during George H. W. Bush's presidency.

This seems odd, given the relatively free discussion and correspondence about the PDB at the senior levels of the intelligence community during the Reagan administration. A casual comfort—or, at least, the absence of heightened sensitivity—existed about acknowledging the existence of the PDB. In May 1984, deputy director McMahon mentioned the PDB without any introduction or mystery in a letter to Defense Intelligence Agency director Jim Williams. In late 1987, deputy director Gates referred to the PDB and its distribution list without fanfare in an article published in the prominent journal *Foreign Affairs.*

Not only that, but senior policy makers had referenced the PDB publicly for years up to and through the Reagan administration. President Johnson had been shown in news photos in 1967 reading the document, with the words "President's Daily Brief" clearly on the cover. Henry Kissinger in 1975 told a press conference that President Ford received "daily, unabbreviated and without a covering summary, the *President's Daily Brief.*" In the 1980s, memoirs from President Jimmy Carter and his national security advisor, Zbigniew Brzezinski, both mentioned the PDB by name. More recently, Gates told the author bluntly: "I don't remember anything about declassifying the existence of the PDB. I figured it was already declassified."

DESPITE CONVENTIONAL WISDOM THAT Reagan did not read a lot of anything, much less serious material such as current intelligence, he took his PDBs and accompanying intelligence reading quite seriously. His first four national security advisors—Dick Allen, William Clark, Bud McFarlane, and John Poindexter—each insisted that he read with diligence not only the PDB but also other national security papers they put in front of him. By the beginning of Reagan's second term in 1985, he often wrote notes in the PDB—occasionally underlining misspellings or syntax errors—which senior NSC staffers dutifully recorded and sent back to the Agency. The public, lacking these officials' windows on the president's diligent reading, formed impressions about Reagan's reading habits largely from his public misstatements about the titles of books he had read, including even those he quoted often.

CIA historian Nicholas Dujmovic reviewed the first one thousand or so of Reagan's PDBs—which, like all previous PDBs, the CIA keeps in secure classified storage—covering almost half of the Reagan presidency. He found markings or notations in the president's hand on about 10 percent of the copies, despite Dick Allen's guidance to Reagan early on to avoid writing on the PDBs to protect himself from leaks. The president's notes included everything from simple marks of interest—checks, underlined words, brackets, double brackets, and exclamation points—to questions and full sentences. When one day's PDB left out the horizontal line across the page that had appeared in previous PDBs to delineate the end of an analytic item, Reagan scribbled, "I like line after item ends" and drew it back in himself. He occasionally showed that he wanted more analysis by writing "and?" or "but what else?" after the text ended. Once, after reading a PDB article about one country's possible violation of its arms control treaty obligations, he scrawled "breakout?" right on the text, suggesting he understood well that this might allow the country to achieve a new weapons capability.

The president did some of his own work in the margins of his PDB copy when he felt that the text was incomplete or unclear. An analytic piece covering Soviet support to a client state failed to add together the Soviet military forces moving in, so Reagan did it himself, jotting "5000 SOVIETS" next to the text. On an illustration of a Soviet mobile missile launcher, the president wrote "SCUD." He even caught a mistake on at least one occasion, in a featured article about Soviet arms control strategy. The text on the bottom of the first page told Reagan that the Soviets believed something, but the next page noted that another country's leaders, "unlike the Soviets," believed that same thing. Reagan underlined both phrases and asked in the margin, "Is this a misprint? See previous page."

A weekly PDB supplement from the Defense Intelligence Agency—the Saturday-only Defense Intelligence Supplement, which started in June 1982—competed for the president's attention. The product, which typically ran six to eight pages and focused overwhelmingly on the Soviet military, began when senior NSC staffers concluded that the president needed more intelligence on military issues. Bob Gates, who was DDI at the time, recalls:

> They were talking about having DIA [Defense Intelligence Agency] do a separate PDB, allowing the NSC to do some picking and choosing, from both publications, what they wanted to send in to the president. DIA was not set up to produce a daily report for the president like that, and I knew it. But the opportunity and the prestige were such that I knew they couldn't pass it up if given the opportunity. My willingness, my agreement, to do the Saturday supplement was an effort to preempt the effort by some at the White House for DIA to have a full-fledged daily PDB of their own—and to try to protect the preeminence of the PDB itself.

But the Defense Intelligence Supplement interested the president less than the core PDB. Dujmovic's review of more than three years of Reagan's daily intelligence packages failed to find a presidential mark on *any* of the supplements. This may have been due, more than anything else, to the total package's length on Saturdays. With the defense supplement added, the PDB would reach or even exceed twenty pages.

THE DIRECTORATE OF INTELLIGENCE's managers and editors worked every day to ensure that the next day's President's Daily Brief would be full and relevant to Reagan's needs. An example of the twenty-four-hour process of writing for the PDB comes from the night of October 30, 1984. Word came in over the newswires around midnight that revered Indian prime minister Indira Gandhi had been assassinated in India, where it was the morning of the thirty-first. The Ops Center swung into action, calling the manager overseeing South Asian analysis. He and an analyst raced in. By 3:30 a.m. they had handed an article to the PDB's overnight staff, which put it in the book.

When Bill Casey stepped into the car outside his Washington residence the next morning to ride to work, the radio in the car informed him of Gandhi's death. The hard-to-please director quickly opened his copy of the President's Daily Brief, expecting at most a short blurb announcing the fact of the assassination. Instead he found a full report on the attack and an analysis of its implications.

As DDI for the majority of Reagan's first term, Bob Gates left the bulk of the PDB's editing to its professional staff but still reviewed the next day's book every night. It was clear that the President's Daily Brief mattered a lot to him. "As much as anything," he says, "I wanted to know what was going to be in the PDB because I knew Casey would be on the phone to me first thing in the morning if there were something he didn't like. And occasionally I would want to forewarn him that something was going to be in the PDB that he wasn't going to like—or that folks downtown weren't going to like."

One afternoon back in December 1982, before Gates had finished his first year as DDI, a junior analyst named Carmen had her first PDB article running in the next morning's book. Senior managers summoned her to the Agency's seventh floor to meet with Gates. As she entered the conference room precisely at 6:00, with her copy of the draft article in hand, her heart raced; Gates's reputation as an exacting editor intimidated even experienced analysts. He first turned to another analyst's piece on Soviet submarines, featuring an eye-catching drawing of a sub. Gates looked over the article, scanned the image, and began asking the non-expert PDB editors technical questions, which they could not answer. He sighed and looked around the room.

"Where's the author?"

No one spoke. Carmen simply looked down at the table during the awkward silence. Just as Gates was about to ask again, an editor spoke up meekly. "He's at his office's Christmas party."

Gates's steely gaze froze the room. Slowly, quietly, he said to nobody in particular, "Hasn't anybody told this person that when you have a piece running in the PDB, you do *not* go to your office's Christmas party?"

Carmen considered jumping in to shout, "Well, *I'm* here!" But her discretion prevailed. Thankfully, she passed Gates's test on her first piece: he read it and had no comments at all.

GEORGE SHULTZ AND BOB Gates made an odd pair. Shultz already had an impressive "elder statesman" resume when he replaced Al Haig as secretary of state in July 1982. He had served as a staff economist on President Eisenhower's Council of Economic Advisors in the 1950s and then had led three cabinet-level units—the Office of Management and Budget, the Department of Labor, and the Treasury Department—under President Nixon. In 1973, a year before returning to private business for eight years, Shultz had founded the so-called Library Group of finance ministers, which evolved into the G7 and, after the Cold War ended, the G8.

Gates, by contrast, was a young rising star at the CIA. After a few years as an intelligence analyst, he had taken several assignments outside CIA headquarters, serving three different presidents on the National Security Council staff in the 1970s. Gates returned to become executive assistant to two directors, Stansfield Turner and Bill Casey. He was only thirty-eight years old when he skipped many levels of management in the DI to become the Agency's deputy director for intelligence in January 1982, just six months before Shultz's return to government.

Shultz dove into current intelligence when President Reagan convinced him to return to Washington. Even before his confirmation, he had seen parts of the PDB, courtesy of national security advisor Bill Clark—who urged the CIA to get Shultz the full PDB immediately after he was sworn in as secretary. "The PDB was one of the first things that happened when I got there," Shultz remembers. "You read the PDB partly for its content and partly because that tells you what's being told to the president. I thought it was always worth reading. It was well done, well produced." Within a month, a senior DI officer told Casey that Shultz spent more time reading his PDB articles than any other recipient of the book. And the secretary of state was not shy about following up on items in the president's book.

As his years in office went on, however, Shultz grew increasingly skeptical about the CIA's objectivity. He spoke more often and more loudly about what he viewed as Casey's politicization of assessments—and analysts' willingness to cave in to Casey's preferred judgments. "I felt after a while that he had too much of an agenda," Shultz says. "I've always felt it's a mistake for the CIA to have an agenda. They're supposed to produce intelligence. If they have an agenda, the intelligence can get slanted or you can worry that it might be slanted." Aware of Shultz's views from briefers' feedback and from comments during meetings, Gates tried to calm the secretary of state's frustrations by sending personal notes inside his PDB package.

After hearing Shultz disparage the DI's analysis over and over again, Gates finally got fed up. In late 1985, he included in the secretary of state's copy of the PDB a note requesting a meeting to air their differences. The two sat down in January 1986 for an hour-long chat beside the fireplace in the secretary's formal office. Shultz told Gates that he felt manipulated by the finished intelligence coming to him and by analysts' apparent willingness to color their analysis to protect or defend the CIA's covert operations—so much so that he no longer trusted the intelligence community.

Gates listened carefully, focusing on the substance of Shultz's words rather than the emotion behind them. He first acknowledged that Casey had not been shy about expressing policy views in White House meetings but said finished intelligence products remained pure. He told the secretary of state bluntly that the conspiracy he envisioned among analysts and operations officers did not exist, describing how analysts remained largely unaware of the secret operations that their colleagues were managing in separate vaults just down the hall. Likewise, he noted that covert operations managers at the CIA didn't even see the draft articles before they went out.

"I suspect no senior CIA official and Secretary of State had ever had a conversation like it," Gates reflects. The discussion failed to change either man's mind at the time: Shultz felt that Gates presented an idealized version of the intelligence world, while Gates continued to defend Agency analysts' integrity against charges of politicization. But one good thing came out of that candid meeting: renewed mutual admiration. Shultz agreed to give Gates the chance to win him over, and the relationship improved. He recalls, "I had a very good relationship with Bob Gates and I have a huge respect for him." Gates, reciprocating, calls Shultz the "best senior user of intelligence I ever encountered," with the possible exception of George H. W. Bush, because "he spent time with us, tasked and used us, met with our analysts and case officers, was willing to be debriefed by them, all to a degree unprecedented at the Cabinet level."

Gates was still thinking about the accusations of politicization near the end of the Reagan administration, enough to publish an article on the topic for all to see in *Foreign Affairs*. He wrote that the CIA would continue to "tell it as it is," despite perceived or real pressure from national security principals to change assessments. "Policymakers may not like the message they hear from us, especially if they have a different point of view. My position is that in the preparation of intelligence judgments, particularly in national intelligence estimates, we will provide them for the use of policy makers. They can be used in whole or in part. They can be ignored, or torn up, or thrown away, but they may not be changed." One can imagine Shultz reading the article and nodding along.

THE AGENCY OCCASIONALLY SUPPLEMENTED Reagan's PDB with short films of foreign places and leaders. They looked much like footage from the nightly news or overseas broadcasts, but with one crucial difference: their narration contained information from Top Secret clandestine sources to supplement material from the open press. Observers often attribute Reagan's fondness for this method to his comfort with movies from his time in Hollywood. But it was the CIA itself, not Reagan or his advisors, that started the video ball rolling during Reagan's first year in office.

This president was more of a people person than a head-in-a-book intellectual. "Reagan always focused on the human dimension of foreign policy," Bud McFarlane remembers, "wanting to know more about everybody from Thatcher to Kohl to Mitterrand to Craxi to Nakasone. How many kids do they have? What are their interests?" Indeed, press reporting from his first year in office cited videos, containing voice-overs with classified intelligence, about foreign leaders such as Israeli prime minister Menachem Begin, King Hussein of Jordan, and former Egyptian president Anwar el-Sadat. His national security advisors knew that the president got a good sense of a person by seeing the way that he or she moved and spoke. "Would it be better for me to sit there and attempt to describe it?" Dick Allen asks rhetorically. "A president who is smart would want to watch it."

McFarlane similarly asked for a video before every visit to give the president insight into the personal history, cultural setting, and institutional nature of the foreign leader's rise to power. He recalls two movies in particular on the Soviet Union—one on Gorbachev and one on the bigger picture of Soviet history—that Reagan loved. After seeing one of them, the president made a rare call to Casey and said, "Bill, that was a great film." Reagan himself praised the CIA's videos on Libya's Muammar Qaddafi and India's Rajiv Gandhi in his diary. He wrote in June 1985 that the Gandhi film offered "a sense of having met him before."

Putting these movies together was no easy task for intelligence analysts. Even with its global resources, the CIA struggled to get extensive visual material from closed societies beyond their own propaganda films. Independent video footage of China's leaders, for example, was far less prevalent than similar clips from more open countries. One analyst of the era recalls the challenge of matching the pictures and the script when doing a video of Chinese premier Zhou Ziyang, who had been involved in land reform. "There are two visual images you can use for land reform, and they have different reactions. One is landlords getting shot in the back of the head; the other is peasants out there with strings marking out land." That choice would make a huge difference for the video's eventual viewers: the first image would convey the horror of the reforms, while the second image would instead emphasize their progressive nature. The extra effort to pick the right images generally worked, according to Ed Meese: "The briefings for these meetings with foreign leaders—the State Department would have a brochure about two inches thick, and he'd try to wade through a lot of that stuff. That's why the movies were very helpful to him."

Former federal judge and FBI director William Webster, who took over as CIA director in May 1987 after Casey's death, continued sending classified videos to Reagan at the White House: "He was very appreciative of anything we did to help him be comfortable with people he didn't know or understand, or wanted to know and understand better. What I remember clearly is that, if he were traveling or if Nancy Reagan was traveling, we often gave them an inside look at places they would be taken to. And, of course, the textual material was designed to capture the personalities of people as best we could."

Webster's presence had refreshed analysts and policy makers alike. He was well aware of charges from Shultz and others that Casey had manipulated intelligence assessments, and he was determined to avoid even the appearance of politicization. During a late March White House meeting with President Reagan and a few top advisors about taking the new position, Webster suggested that he should not sit in the president's cabinet, saying that it would not be "necessary or desirable" to continue Casey's status there. The president immediately approved Webster's recommendation. He also avoided micromanaging the president's book. "I got the PDB at 10:00 in the evening wherever I was," he recalls. "And that gave me a chance to look at it, and the test I applied was, 'Does this raise questions that could easily be answered by a little more information or clarification in the PDB, so as to make it easy on the president as he was reading it, anticipate his questions a little, maybe even answer them for him?' So that's what I saw as my mission at 10:00 at night: I looked it over, made notes, and phoned in my thoughts to the Operations Center."

Respect for the new director extended throughout the organization. Gates, who served as Webster's deputy and succeeded him in 1991, says, "I then had and still have enormous respect and affection for Webster and I always believed that he does not get the credit he deserves for the job he did at CIA. I think he is one of the great patriots of our time." Dick Kerr, who had taken over for Gates as DDI in 1986, also lauded Webster with words that one cannot imagine being used for Casey: "an easy, relaxed person to deal with." A manager within the DI during the 1980s says, "In contrast with Casey, Webster—though always courteous and interested—was somewhat detached. He never pretended that he was the analytic expert."

WEBSTER PRESIDED OVER THE CIA as awareness grew within the intelligence and policy communities of fundamental economic, societal, and political challenges within the Soviet Union—leading within a few years to its disintegration and the end of the Cold War. The CIA had provided current intelligence and longer analytic products to policy makers about the deteriorating Soviet economy and weakening social cohesion back to the mid-1970s. One of the CIA's congressional oversight committees, the House Permanent Select Committee on Intelligence, in 1991 directed a team of nongovernmental economists to evaluate the CIA's assessments of the economic situation in the USSR. That team examined the relevant analyses and determined that they were "accurate, illuminating, and timely." They found consistency between the classified reports and unclassified releases to the general public, noting that both sets "regularly reported on the steady decline in the Soviet growth rate and called attention to the deep and structural problems that pointed to continued decline and possibly to stagnation."

Nevertheless, some policy makers and congressional critics of the Agency did not feel well served by this analysis. Part of the problem was that analysts' estimates of economic growth in the USSR included military production and raw quantities of wasteful output, seemingly inflating the economy's health despite outward signs of fundamental difficulties. Gates reflected years later that the CIA's Soviet sector analysis and macro analysis were "right on the mark" over the years: "Every President from Lyndon Johnson on made policy toward the Soviet Union with the knowledge and the conviction that growing Soviet economic problems were an ace in the hole for the United States." But he admitted that the CIA failed to model the Soviet economy well enough for policy makers:

The Department of Defense, because they wanted estimates of what portion of the Soviet economy was being spent on the military, insisted on the Agency building an economic model of the Soviet Union, of the Soviet economy. And we did. Beginning in the '70s. And this model was built on the same principles that models of western economies were built on. But, what the model couldn't take into account was how do you assign a value to a million pair of shoes that nobody wants to buy. And so the statistical analysis of the Soviet economy, while in its trend lines showed the same thing as the macro analysis and sector analysis, did show a Soviet economy that was stronger than in fact existed in reality.

The record shows that the CIA tried to answer crucial intelligence questions about the USSR for the president and his top advisors in the 1980s: How would Soviet leaders deal with the country's socioeconomic challenges? Would their measures succeed? What changes to the political system, and to the USSR's very existence, would result? Looking back at National Intelligence Estimates and long-form reports—whose themes, if not exact language, would have been echoed in the President's Daily Brief—Doug MacEachin found that CIA products in the Reagan years described in detail Mikhail Gorbachev's political and economic restructuring (perestroika), the inherent tensions in his approach, and Gorbachev's eventual realization of the need for more radical change to the system. In the mid-1980s, analysts produced current intelligence that correctly judged that the Soviet economy would be unable to support current and proposed military projects, driving Gorbachev to make deep strategic arms and troop cuts. Gates remembers a CIA analyst telling Reagan in November 1985, before the president met Gorbachev in Geneva, that "the system can't last, the domestic stresses are too great, can't pick the date, can't tell you when, but it is doomed."

But many of the written reports addressing these questions look like poster children for Casey's attacks on "iffy conclusions" in DI analysis. In December 1982, a DI paper laying out the ills in Soviet society said, "Precisely how these internal problems will ultimately challenge and affect the regime, however, is open to debate and considerable uncertainty. Some observers believe that the regime will have little trouble coping with the negative mood among the populace. Others believe that economic mismanagement will aggravate internal problems and ultimately erode the regime's credibility, increasing the long-term prospects for fundamental political change." The CIA's defenders could later claim that this showed foresight about "fundamental political change"; its detractors can point to the many phrases along the lines of "open to debate," "considerable uncertainty," and "others believe" as wishy-washy statements failing to predict anything at all. In September 1985, a DI report presented the daunting array of economic problems facing Gorbachev, but then limply assessed that he "could employ various options to address these issues," without asserting if any options were more likely than others.

Although Reagan and his top advisors received intelligence warnings about the rotting core of the Soviet state, some of them felt disappointed by the Agency's inflated figures of the size of the economy and by its failure to fully predict Gorbachev's radical opening of the political space (glasnost) in the late 1980s—unleashing forces that broke the Soviet Union apart in 1991. After the administration ended, George Shultz said bluntly, "The reports we got from CIA were all, 'The economy is strong.' But that turned out to be wrong." More recently, he took a more conciliatory line—and offered a reason for feeling that CIA analysis was fallible. "There was a distinct difference of opinion about how to interpret what was going on in the Soviet Union. I remember on one occasion they wrote a personality sketch of Gorbachev that I didn't agree with. And they said, 'We interviewed a lot of people about it.' And I said, 'Well, I've logged more time with him than any other American, and you didn't interview me. If you had, I would have told you this, this, and this.'"

THE PRESIDENT HAD CLEANED house after news broke in November 1986 about the Iran-Contra scandal, in which some of Reagan's senior aides illegally used proceeds of covert arms shipments to Iran to fund anti-Communist rebels in Nicaragua. The widely respected Frank Carlucci replaced national security advisor John Poindexter, bringing in as his deputy a young lieutenant general named Colin Powell. Powell was shocked at the degree to which Reagan delegated national security decisions, giving only general guidance and expecting his aides to interpret his desires. He walked out of one Oval Office meeting early in his tenure and said to Carlucci, "Frank, I didn't know we signed on to run the world." Powell would become Reagan's sixth and final national security advisor in November 1987, when Carlucci left to replace secretary of defense Caspar Weinberger. Chief of staff Don Regan had also been ousted, in favor of the highly regarded senator Howard Baker, with Ken Duberstein as *his* number two and eventual successor in July 1988.

In the Reagan administration's first term, many senior aides lacked trust in each other. George Shultz, for example, reacted to leaks from the National Security Council soon after he became secretary of state by saying in a subsequent meeting, "I'm never speaking in one of these meetings again because everything I say ends up in the newspapers." And he held firm for the next two or three NSC discussions, crossing his arms and sitting in silence as others debated key foreign policy issues. Earlier officials even seemed to enjoy denigrating each other in their public statements and memoirs after leaving office. A representative example is Casper Weinberger's swipe at Al Haig for habitually making his points with much "passion and intensity" combined with "a deep suspicion of the competence and motives of anyone who did not share his opinions."

By contrast, the team that ran Reagan's White House operations and foreign policy at the close of his presidency cannot seem to say enough good things about each other's abilities and actions. Despite some key early policy differences with Frank Carlucci, George Shultz said he found him to be a man of high principles and great skill. Carlucci, in another example, says, "Howard Baker is one of the finest people I have ever worked with. There was no envy or jealousy between us. I trusted him completely, and he trusted me." The key, according to Ken Duberstein, was open and honest communication between those with access to Reagan. "One of the things that Frank and Howard recognized, and that Colin and I certainly recognized, was that the national security advisor has a direct line to the president. But Colin never once communicated with the president without touching base with me. Often it was, 'C'mon, I have to go see the president. This is what it's about; why don't you join me?' Or me to him: 'Colin, we are discussing the potential defense reauthorization bill veto. You'd better come with me to see the president.'"

With the president increasingly distant from tactical decision making during his final year in office, the triumvirate of Shultz at

State, Carlucci at Defense, and Powell in the White House effectively ran the foreign policy of the United States. Carlucci recalls:

> When Colin succeeded me, and George and I had buried the hatchet, the three of us made a conscious decision. George said, "Ronald Reagan has had the landing lights on and the flaps down for the last year. Now we're going to have to step up to the plate on foreign policy. The only way it's going to work is for the three of us to agree." That's when we had seven o'clock meetings every day. It was just the three of us, no agenda, no substitutes. We worked through the day's events, trying to forge agreement. George and I changed positions a number of times in those meetings because we decided if the three of us agreed, we knew we had Ronald Reagan. That's the way foreign policy was basically conducted. . . . Colin would simply brief him "Sir, this is what we're doing, if you have no objections." Invariably, he wouldn't. The concept was to try and keep the issues off his desk.

Carlucci remained concerned about the president's ability to focus. "Sometimes he would take out his earphones and look at the squirrels outside the window. You never knew how much he was absorbing."

Career diplomat John Negroponte joined this cohesive team in late 1987 as Powell's deputy. Since joining the Foreign Service more than twenty-five years earlier, he had been posted to Southeast Asia, Latin America, and Europe and served in several senior roles within the State Department bureaucracy. His experience as an NSC staffer, covering Vietnam in the Nixon White House, helped make him a fitting partner for career military man Powell during the final fourteen months of Reagan's second term. Under Powell and Negroponte, the morning national security briefing remained a steady presence in the president's daily routine. Almost religiously from 9:30 to 10:00, both men—or just one, if travel kept one away—and the White House chief of staff and his deputy met in the Oval Office to get the president up to speed on world events and his foreign-policy-related schedule.

Powell was away on September 26, 1988, so Negroponte led the session. The intelligence for the president had recently been addressing coca growth and cocaine production in South America as he sought the passage of the Anti-Drug Abuse Act, which created the Office of National Drug Control Policy. That day, the deputy national security advisor had highlighted the Upper Huallaga Valley when he told the president about the piece on Peru in his leather folder.

"Mr. President," Negroponte began, "the way the American drug enforcement people refer to this—because they fly in the helicopters and then all of a sudden they come to the valley, and they look at it and see it just covered in cocaine fields—they say, 'Oh shit,' and they call it the 'Oh Shit Valley.'"

Reagan noted that day in his diary, citing the 40 percent figure that Negroponte gave him about the valley's cocaine production as a percentage of the world total. More than twenty-five years later, Negroponte suspects Reagan's precise diary notation had less to do with his own storytelling skills than the simple fact that the president neither used nor tolerated profanity in the Oval Office. "I'm sure *that*'s why he remembered it."

ON JANUARY 20, 1989, eight years to the day after Reagan was sworn in as the nation's fortieth president, Duberstein drove with national security advisor Colin Powell through the White House gates, because Duberstein still had his official car and driver, but Powell did not. On this day, the first president since Dwight Eisenhower to serve two full terms would become private citizen Ronald Reagan at the moment George H. W. Bush would be sworn in as the forty-first president. Even on a day dominated by ceremony, the president's staff kept their morning routine, including the daily national security briefing.

"I made a mistake," Duberstein recalls, "not recognizing that on the night of the nineteenth, the General Services Administration had cleared out all furniture and furnishings from the Oval Office." He entered the nearly empty room, looked around in horror, and said to Powell, "Oh my God. His last time here, and *this*."

Just then, Reagan entered the Oval Office for the last time as president. He noticed right away that it was, as he remarked in his diary, "pretty bare." He saw his two advisors in the open space and reached into his pocket to remove the nuclear code card. "Here, guys—I don't need this anymore," he said. Powell and Duberstein refused to take it, reminding Reagan that he remained commander in chief until noon. So the nuclear codes went back in his pocket.

Duberstein previewed the day's inaugural schedule and movements. Only one piece of business awaited: the national security briefing.

Duberstein and Powell had read the PDB earlier that morning, just as carefully as ever. But on this day, Powell's instincts told him that nothing required Reagan's attention. "Mr. President," he said plainly, "the world is quiet today."

CHAPTER EIGHT

THE SPYMASTER PRESIDENT

"WHEN I WAS PRESIDENT," Bush says, "one of my favorite times of day was when I would sit down with a briefer and read through the PDB." The interaction with the briefer both worked best for his style and encouraged intelligence officers to do their best. "I think it helped those who were working night and day out there in Langley on preparing the PDB to know that their product was being looked at by the President himself. I think it helped a little bit with the morale of that section of the CIA that works so hard to put this book together."

Bush's daily intelligence routine remained remarkably consistent through his term. Every morning he was in Washington, his first scheduled meeting in the Oval Office included national security advisor Brent Scowcroft and/or his deputy (first Bob Gates and then, less often, Jon Howe), chief of staff John Sununu and his successors, sometimes his CIA director (Webster, followed by Gates)—and always his CIA intelligence briefer. "The real payoff is having the Agency briefer there to follow up," he says. "But having too many people around creates a problem. . . . If the group grows, pretty soon word gets out that 'He's considering bombing Bosnia' or whatever."

"He would start at page one and read through," Webster says. "He didn't hesitate to ask for more information about something after he read it." The briefer would not only provide additional detail as requested but also direct Bush toward specific items in the PDB or add insights from analysts studying the issue, operations officers collecting clandestine human reports, or other sensitive intelligence sources. Most days the president welcomed such a dialogue with his briefer, especially about the sources underlying the information in the book. "Generally," Sununu says, "the president took a quick look as to how big the book was today and what the headlines were, and then came back and said, 'Go.' The briefer would then tee it up—and then they would go."

For most of the Bush presidency, daily briefing duty fell to either Chuck Peters or Hank Applebaum. The two veteran analysts left very different impressions. Peters, once Bob Gates's branch chief in the CIA's Office of Current Intelligence, developed a reputation for asking PDB authors hard, direct questions about their assessments. "You're the analyst, and you care about this—but nobody else does," an economic expert of the era recalls Peters saying to him about a draft PDB article. "He would make you exceedingly uncomfortable if you weren't up to those questions," says a former officer who covered the Middle East, "like a gruff old city editor would." Michael Morell— then a young analyst, eventually George W. Bush's PDB briefer and the CIA's deputy director—says that although he eventually learned Peters was willing to have a discussion to ensure that a piece was as good as it could be, initially he found him "incredibly intimidating."

Applebaum, by contrast, came across as less intense, quieter, and easier to approach. "Hank was always such a gentleman, more like your favorite college professor," the former Middle East analyst says. "Absolutely smart enough to be completely into what you gave him, but more deferential and reserved—less likely to point a finger in your face and say, 'You need to do *this*.' I always felt tested by Chuck but not by Hank. One scared analysts. The other didn't."

Their different styles seemed to work well each morning for the intimidating Oval Office crowd. Scowcroft calls them "very skilled, outstanding people." "I would have been pretty daunted being a briefer coming down," says Gates, "knowing that you were going to first have to get through Scowcroft and the former DDI and DDCI and then have to go through the former DCI in the Oval Office. Probably uniquely in the history of the PDB, that was a gauntlet of experience and inside knowledge about intelligence that would be hard to replicate." Sununu thought that it must have been difficult when the briefer didn't have answers off the top of his head to the president's questions, but he saw the briefers grow more comfortable with the process as time went on. Gates agrees that Peters and Applebaum adjusted. "They quickly realized that if they didn't know the answer, the easiest thing to do was just to say, 'I don't know the answer; let me get it for you.' They played it absolutely straight."

Their comfort in the Oval Office built on their extensive familiarity with the book. Peters and Applebaum not only delivered the PDB every day but also personally edited each book the night before. Peters typically took it a step beyond cursory review. "Chuck rewrote almost everything that went into the PDB," a CIA expert on European affairs says. "No matter how hard you tried—and we all tried so hard—I remember just beating my head against the desk, saying, 'I'll get it right *this* time,' but he would almost always rewrite it."

A new officer covering East Asia received a call to run up to Peters's office to "read off," inside slang for approving changes made to the PDB article he had sent up that morning. "I'm standing there in this smoke-filled room—the rules didn't apply to the president's briefer—and he sat there, making me wait. He put on his glasses, picked up my piece and edited it in front of me, circling this and cutting that."

Peters finally pushed the article across the table. "What do you think?"

Quickly scanning the completely revised language, the young analyst replied, "Well, that part that you just cut out is really important."

"Look, the president already knows this." Peters's tone brooked no disagreement; his confidence came from seeing Bush every day. So the newbie moved on, questioning a second change that Peters had made in his original language.

"The president doesn't care about that," Peters snapped. "That's not important. What's important is what's right *there*," he said while pointing to his own choice of words.

The lesson this officer took away? Unless Peters's edits dramatically altered the substantive meaning, he shouldn't argue. "This wasn't the director's book; it was Chuck Peters's book." On nights when Applebaum edited the book instead, things went much easier, even for the editors in the PDB staff who took a first cut at incoming draft articles before passing them to the briefers for their final look.

"Hank was so predictable," one of them says. "One time, to see what would happen, I made a piece up. Hank just changed a word or two and moved it on."

But the layers of review within the analytic offices and then in the PDB staff tended to remove pieces' flavor. John McLaughlin, then an analytic manager and later the CIA's deputy director, remembers sending in a long article from Romania right after the 1989 revolution there. "I said something like, 'I'm walking around streets filled with broken glass, the smell of oil in the air—revolutionaries with knives stuck in their belts and guns firing off.' Everyone at headquarters loved it. They said, 'Put this in the PDB!' By the time it got into the PDB, all the blood was drained out of it. It read like a travel ad for Viking River Cruises." Scowcroft noticed the dry style. "The PDB was not always as exciting to read as the *New York Times*. But I had more faith in it."

The PDB's "snowflakes," short blurbs of information taking just two or three lines of text, had been distilled down from full-page assessments to update continuing stories or give Bush quick factoids. Having read the entire piece from which they came, Peters and Applebaum would weave fuller stories out of them on the spot as presidential interests demanded. One officer new to the DI recalls Peters asking him to get his piece down to thirty-two words. "He took it, sat down, and rewrote every single word," the officer remembers. "He got it to 32 again, but they were totally different words." After the snowflakes, Bush saw about a half dozen articles of a page or less with fuller treatment of world developments, occasionally followed by longer assessments.

John Helgerson, who supervised Peters and Applebaum as the deputy director for intelligence and looked at the PDB every morning before it went downtown, says, "We almost never got any complaints about the book, and certainly not about the briefers." Later, he felt grateful that he never had any need to move them from their positions. "I don't think the president would have let me."

"I ALWAYS ASSUMED THE president knew more about the PDB than I did," says Scowcroft, who was happy to let Bush take the lead with Peters and Applebaum in the Oval Office. It helped that the CIA briefers earlier had briefed Scowcroft and his deputy, Bob Gates, who says he and Scowcroft would have already given the briefer a "real grilling," asking questions like "Why do you think that?" and "Do you have any

President George H. W. Bush started each day with his PDB briefing in the Oval Office; on February 15, 1989, attendees included (clockwise from Bush) CIA briefer Chuck Peters, CIA director William Webster, White House chief of staff John Sununu, deputy national security advisor Bob Gates, and national security advisor Brent Scowcroft. *Courtesy George Bush Presidential Library*

evidence for that?" Scowcroft sometimes queried Bush's briefer again during the Oval Office session to better understand issues that Bush seemed to focus on or to ensure that the president heard something that Scowcroft had been told in that earlier session.

The principals would chat about policy after Peters or Applebaum (and the CIA director, if he had attended that day) left the room. Sometimes the book prompted immediate presidential action, as Scowcroft recalls. Bush might be reading the PDB and say, "Well, you know what Mitterrand just did! Why don't I call him about that?" Knowing how much value Bush put on the PDB, Scowcroft put effort into the morning meeting follow-up. When he finally exited the Oval Office—leaving the president, vice president, and chief of staff to discuss domestic and political issues—Scowcroft called the secretary of state, the defense secretary, or both to inform them what had just been discussed. He also passed any presidential comments related to the PDB that came up later in the day to someone at the CIA, sometimes adding his own opinions with lines like "I thought the way you handled this issue was not exactly right."

On a few occasions, he says, he asked the CIA to put something on a particular topic into the PDB to introduce what *he* wanted to discuss. This particularly helped when Bush traveled, because either the national security advisor or his deputy would receive the PDB through a secure communications channel and brief the president on it himself. But the more the national security advisor directed the Agency to include things in the PDB the next morning, the less this president appreciated it. Bush let the Agency know one day that a particular piece he had seen in the PDB seemed odd, asking a senior DI officer, "Why is that there?" The answer—that Scowcroft had wanted it there—didn't please the president. Bush viewed the PDB as *his* book, lecturing his CIA briefers, "Don't let anybody else tell you what the President wants or needs in the PDB—ask him."

Trying to get an article on a certain topic in front of the president was the limit of Scowcroft's intervention. Everyone surrounding the PDB during Bush's term agrees that the national security advisor never sought to manipulate the analytic assessments in the PDB. He was "the most honest broker I ever knew," Webster says. "He carried out his functions in the most professional way. Every now and then, he said, 'I thought that was pretty strong,' or something like that. And my response was always to say, 'Brent, you know the rules: You can use it or not use it. You can tear it up or throw it away. The one thing you can't do is ask us to change it.' And he never did." Bush clearly admired his national security advisor: "There is nobody to whom I am more indebted than Brent for advice, for counsel, for wisdom, for caring," he said after leaving office. "He's the very best."

A window into Scowcroft's view of the PDB emerged during the crisis in Panama in late 1989, which led to a US invasion of the country that December. Sununu, who was new to the President's Daily Brief and received little foreign intelligence information other than the book, says, "We never got enough information out of the PDB to give us a comfortable feeling as to what the intentions of the Panamanians were. I guess what surprised me is that of all the places that were important topics, it seemed to me that Panama would be the easiest place to gather data." Scowcroft's more nuanced view emphasized the value of the in-person briefings more than the book itself. "The PDB on rapidly moving tactical situations—it wasn't designed for that. If you had a good briefer, he would supplement what was in the PDB. If it were a really hot, fast-moving situation, he would say something like, 'Since this went to press, we've heard this and this and this.' In fact, that's really the reason for the briefer—to give more background on the pieces in the book and to answer any questions."

Another reader inside the White House complex saw the PDB daily: Vice President Dan Quayle. Bush had told him as they came into office that he could attend any of his meetings or intelligence briefings. "You need to know exactly what I know," Quayle recalls Bush saying. He attributes the president's insistence on keeping him in the loop to Bush's own eight years as VP, which included John Hinckley's assassination attempt on Ronald Reagan. Quayle often walked into the Oval Office PDB briefings, usually right as they wrapped up—not out of disrespect, but because the CIA had established a separate intelligence support protocol. "We had made arrangements for him to see the briefs ahead of time and ask questions ahead of time," says Webster, "so the morning session would be primarily the president's. We had such a narrow window that we thought it would be better not to have too many people getting informed when they could get informed before the session."

Quayle actually saw the PDB before the president did, usually at 7:30 or 7:45 each morning. A CIA briefer delivered the book to his White House office—or to his house before any day trips—to discuss its contents with the VP and his national security advisor (Carnes Lord to start, followed by Karl Jackson) for thirty to forty-five minutes. His daily briefer ensured that the vice president looked at the same PDB pieces and raw intelligence that the president saw in the Oval Office session, highlighting certain articles in the book for Quayle, who would ask questions as he went through the PDB. "The people who briefed me," Quayle says, "were very knowledgeable and very conversational. They were pros."

He didn't limit himself to the book, asking questions about issues of interest outside the PDB, especially during the conflicts in Panama and Iraq. "When I asked questions that weren't part of the PDB, the briefers would answer or get back to me the next day." Then he made his way to the Oval Office to discuss intelligence and other foreign policy issues with Bush, Scowcroft, and Sununu, who were usually finishing up their own PDB briefing and dismissing the CIA crew. Bush used such informal meetings more than statutory National Security Council meetings to make policy.

Quayle says he would have preferred deeper, more specific assessments in the book. "The PDB was thorough and covered the world, a lot of different topics," he says, "but the only time there was a really deep dive is when you asked for it." In one area that the president handed to Quayle, space policy, the book helped more—especially at one crucial moment. "In one of my meetings with Gorbachev, we talked extensively about space cooperation," the former vice president says. "The PDB was helpful."

ALMOST FIFTEEN YEARS AFTER George H. W. Bush left office, retired vice admiral Mike McConnell became the second director of national intelligence for his son George W. Bush, the forty-third president, supervising the production and dissemination of the President's Daily Brief. But back in 1990, as the intelligence chief (J2) for the Joint Chiefs of Staff, McConnell found that the strict PDB controls imposed by the elder Bush ensured that he couldn't even look at Chairman Colin Powell's PDB. "General Powell was always very well informed. He had a perspective and context that was just different from what I was struggling with. Traditionally, when I served senior people, I knew more about intelligence sources and methods, as well as substance, than they did; I was usually educating them. But I found he knew more than I knew."

"What's happening here?'" he finally asked Powell.

"Well," came the reply, "I have the advantage of the PDB."

McConnell paused. "As the J2, shouldn't I see it?"

"Presidential policy—no way."

Bush's direct personal interest in the book's physical security was unprecedented. He ordered the CIA to deliver the PDB by hand every day not only to the few senior White House officials attending the daily intelligence meeting in the Oval Office but also to the chairman of the Joint Chiefs, the secretary of state, and the secretary of defense. Bush insisted that each of these recipients follow his own method of receiving the PDB: a CIA officer would deliver each principal's copy of the PDB directly to him, stand by to answer any of his questions (or take them back for Agency experts to answer the next day), and return the book immediately to Langley. "So the PDB was never left," Gates says. "Same thing at the White House."

Bush instructed the Agency to inform PDB readers which information in the book came from highly sensitive sources to help prevent inadvertent disclosures of such material. Having seen the PDB "floating around" at the Reagan White House, he resolved to do better. "We tried to protect the distribution of the PDB because we knew very well that once it was faxed or put through a Xerox machine, then the people preparing it, with their oath to protect sources and methods, would be inclined to pull back and not give the President the frankest possible intelligence assessments presenting the best possible intelligence."

James Baker recalls hearing the president say, "I want you and Dick and Colin Powell to see the PDB every day—but I don't want it left with you. I want it briefed to you." Baker's briefer followed through, staying every day while the secretary of state read the book but getting few queries from him. "I would only ask questions if I found an item in there I wanted to drill down deeper on," Baker says.

Defense secretary Dick Cheney elected to look at his copy of the PDB during his daily limo ride into work from his townhouse in McLean. He remembers keeping his briefer "largely a courier" in those days because he sought to avoid highly classified conversations about the book's content while his driver and security detail sat just feet away. Instead, he saved most of his PDB-related comments for discussions later in the day with other recipients, such as Joint Chiefs chairman Powell. The plethora of classified publications from the Defense Intelligence Agency and the services' intelligence shops that hit Cheney's desk nevertheless minimized the impact of the president's book. "Because I had so many more sources," he says, "the PDB didn't stand out as *the* product the way it does when you're sitting over in the West Wing."

One substitute briefer's first day taking the book to Cheney proved more eye-opening than he'd expected. His Agency driver took him to Cheney's townhouse. "I went up and knocked on the door," the briefer says. But instead of the secretary of defense or a member of his family, a woman in a negligee appeared. She seemed to understand immediately that the man with the briefcase, stunned into silence by the sight in front of him, had the wrong house. Pointing him next door, she tried to make the gawking briefer feel better. "It happens all the time," she said—which only made him wonder why she continued opening the door dressed so scantily.

CIA officers posted overseas had to provide the book to PDB recipients traveling through their turf, often in a hurry, while protecting its highly classified content. "The first time with [secretary of state Lawrence] Eagleburger," a DI officer who served in Europe recalls, "I showed up in the morning at his nice hotel in the capital. The place was a mess—activity going on and everyone disorganized. His handler said, 'Can you just leave me the PDB and come back tonight and pick it up?' I made a tough decision and said, 'Yes, I will leave it.' I was *not* going to refuse the secretary of state the PDB!"

Her choice almost backfired. When she returned that afternoon to retrieve the book from the secure room in the hotel, no one knew its whereabouts. "I stood in the corridor," she recalls, "and I saw three rooms being torn up. Finally they found it. That would have been an awkward cable to send back to Langley."

A different logistical challenge arose soon thereafter when Cheney finished his business in the same intelligence officer's capital and prepared to fly onward to Russia. Her task from headquarters, getting the PDB to the defense secretary, came with explicit directions: "Under no condition is this to travel to Moscow!"

She showed up at Cheney's hotel and his handler asked, "Can we keep it?" This time she held the line.

"No. You are not allowed to keep it."

"Maybe he can read it on the way to the airport," the handler replied.

"Well, then, I'm going to have to ride in one of those cars."

Cheney's lead security officer chimed in. "I hope you're not squeamish. He will be in one of the back cars—and we *cannot* lose that car."

Seeing no other option, she just got in—and endured thirty minutes of the worst high-speed, stop-and-go ride of her life. "We got to the tarmac, he returned the book, and I went home."

"We collected them all," Webster recalls, "except from the president, the only one with the privilege of holding on to his for a while. We ultimately retrieved them all."

BUSH'S INTEREST IN THE nuts and bolts of spycraft spurred Webster to occasionally bring additional intelligence officers to the morning briefings, adding a distinctly personal element to the material the president read every day in the pages of the President's Daily Brief. Most of these extra participants served as case officers, collecting human intelligence around the world. One of them really stood out for Bush. "I won't refer by name to the person Bill Webster brought in," he says, "but I'll never forget that meeting until the day I die. It was with a woman in the operations end of the business, who literally had her life on the line day in and day out in intelligence gathering—human intelligence. It brought home to me the necessity of protecting people like that and saluting them because they serve without ever getting the prestige or honor that they deserve." Others brought less drama—but great visuals. "We had some situations where we brought in imagery," Webster says. "And sometimes the imagery had to be accompanied by a courier, somebody to explain what it was all about." After all, pictures collected from far above the earth's surface often reveal little to those without the training and experience to interpret the images—and thus to see what enemies are trying desperately to hide.

Those supplements to the briefings set up a unique way to entertain as well as inform the president. Early in Bush's term, Jonna Goeser—who two years later married Tony Mendez, played by Ben Affleck in the hit movie *Argo*—became chief of the CIA's disguise unit. Under her watchful eye, a contractor had started making "advanced disguise systems," the precise details of which remain classified. "When they started moving out of production, one of the first ones was made for me." She can reveal only that it changed her gender and ethnicity, not how it worked.

Goeser took the disguise to successive managers. Each of them thought it looked so good that the next manager up the ladder needed to see it in person. Eventually, in spring 1989, she walked into the director's office as a dark-skinned man.

"I love this," said Webster, who had become a strong believer in disguises. "In the right places, under the right circumstances, they were helpful in getting us into places where we wouldn't attract attention," he recalls. The director also sensed an opportunity to have some fun. "This is great! Let's take this to the White House."

She recoiled. "I can't. There's no way I can talk like I look right now!"

"Well, make another one," Webster replied.

It wasn't that easy. But a direct order from the director had a way of moving the CIA bureaucracy quickly. Soon Goeser could appear as a much younger woman, sporting hair very different from her natural blond locks. She took her new disguise to Webster's house early in the morning on the day that he wanted her to join him at the White House.

"His security detail sent me right in with my little bag," she says. "He had a little dog that didn't like me. It was barking at me."

Webster, drinking coffee in his dining room, pointed her to the bathroom. "When you're done, come out and have coffee with me," he said.

"I came out and then the dog was fine," she says.

Webster liked it, too. "It wasn't all that perfect up close," he remembers, "but it was good for getting somebody in for a meeting." And, he thought, it looked good enough to show off to the president.

"We went out to the car, and I was a different person," she says. "I think his security noticed—but they were very discreet." During the drive to the White House, Webster read his copy of the PDB in silence as her apprehension rose. She remained all too aware that she hadn't used this disguise before and wondered if she could pull off the ruse. Then, just as they pulled into the executive mansion complex, she remembered a crucial detail.

"Sir! I don't have any ID that matches!"

He thought about it for a few seconds, then reassured her, "We'll be fine—just hold on to my coattails." Sure enough, they walked right in.

They went into the holding room where Scowcroft, Gates, Sununu, and the PDB briefer waited for word that Bush was ready. As usual, a friendly mood prevailed, which made everyone comfortable, except Goeser. "Everybody was telling jokes," she says. "But I couldn't talk too much, and I certainly couldn't laugh because of limitations imposed by the disguise. So I'm sitting there, chewing on my pencil, looking down." She dwelled on the advice her future husband, Tony—one of only two technical services officers who had been in the Oval Office before—had given her: pay close attention to the

THE SPYMASTER PRESIDENT – 177

door you enter through, because the stress of the moment will make it easy to forget. "It was frightening to use any disguise for the first time," she says. "Debuting this new technology in the Oval Office only ramped up the pucker factor."

The call came to join the president. Webster took her in, pretending that she was the courier for some space imagery. The session started normally as the briefer distributed copies of the PDB. All of the attendees settled into their seats and put their heads down, focusing immediately on the Top Secret books in front of them. The young "courier" sat quietly, waiting for her part to begin.

In fact, the former spymaster behind the desk had already noticed something amiss. "He was the only one who picked up on it," Webster says. "He communicated without saying anything. He was reading, and he looked up at her. He looked down again, but then back up—and then to me with a little tip of the head and a quizzical look. Sort of like he was saying, 'Is that? . . . Is she? . . . Is that what I think it is?' He didn't interrupt or anything, just made eye contact with me. It was clear that he was on to it. But nobody else noticed."

Webster played it straight, introducing Goeser under a false name and telling Bush, "She has a subject you'll be interested in." She talked to the president briefly, and then stood up to hand him a file. In it was a picture of a disguise the Agency had done for Bush when he was director. "Everyone but the president and Judge Webster were looking down at the PDB," she says, "and not really paying too much attention."

So she focused on Bush. "I know you've been exposed to our disguises and our technical officers. But we've made some advances since then. I've brought our latest disguise with me. In fact, I'm wearing it now."

He stopped and stared. The others finally looked up. She returned to her seat and prepared to take her disguise off.

"No, wait!" the president said. He got up, walked around the large desk, and tiptoed right up to her. Without saying a word, he bent over to get a close look from various angles. Then he slowly sat down again.

"OK," he finally said. "Take it off."

She did, with a bit of dramatic flair. The artful reveal made Sununu, who had been totally wrapped up in the PDB, nearly jump

CIA disguise expert Jonna Goeser surprises President Bush and other attendees of his PDB session with a new device—airbrushed out of the original White House photo for security reasons. *Courtesy Tony and Jonna Mendez*

out of his seat. "She did it very well," Webster says. "The president got a big kick out of it." After a quick expression of thanks from Bush, who put his head right back into the PDB, her role ended.

Stepping outside, Goeser saw the president's secretary, who was holding court with the Bush family dog Millie and her puppies, and the White House photographer, who had clicked away during the whole event. Goeser acknowledged her, saying, "You must have the best job." But the photographer, completely mesmerized by what she had just seen happen in the Oval Office, could only ask, "What did you just do?"

"I think you photographed it."

"But . . . what did you *do*?"

Goeser chuckled. "It's classified."

A YEAR LATER, BUSH read a PDB article carefully and then raised his head to look one of his regular PDB briefers in the eye. "I'll bet you an ice cream cone that you're wrong," he said.

Nicaragua, in April 1990, was holding its first internationally monitored, free presidential election. Sandinista strongman (and Reagan administration bête noire) Daniel Ortega sought to keep the reins of power against opposition leader Violeta Chamorro. The CIA analysts' assessment was that Ortega's control of the levers of power would prove too much for the anti-Sandinista movement to overcome, and they predicted Chamorro would lose. Bush, who sized up the situation differently, challenged his briefer to the wager on the election's outcome.

The briefer accepted. And when Chamorro defeated Ortega, he paid up by delivering an ice cream cone personally to the president in the Oval Office.

Bush had shown from the start of his term that the deadly serious nature of the nation's intelligence did not preclude a lighter touch. He told Chuck Peters on the very first day after his inauguration that the PDB looked good—but "there is one area in which you'll just have to do better." Webster, attending that session, braced for bad news. Instead, the president told Peters, "The Office of Comic Relief will have to step up its output." Peters assured Bush the Agency's analysts would do their best. He also assured Webster later that the president's remark did not require a frantic search of the Agency's organization chart; it was typical of Bush's relaxed asides during his intelligence sessions.

The briefers during the next few years met Bush's wish for humorous perspectives on world affairs with a recurring feature called "Signs of the Times." One former PDB editor remembers a whimsical title on an article about the withdrawal of Soviet forces from East Germany: "Tanks for the Memories." Yet Bush's request for more material from the "Office of Comic Relief" met stiff resistance from the most implacable of enemies, institutional culture. "We tried—more often than I care to remember—to get some humorous items into the book," Peters says. "But satisfying several layers of bureaucracy that a story is funny, in good taste, and not demeaning to the overall product is no easy task." Another supplement, a one-page addition to the PDB on Fridays or Saturdays that officers called the "Club of Kings," gave Bush intelligence about foreign leaders' personalities and their pressing challenges. It usually led the president through a handful of international figures and what they had coming up on their schedules that weekend, bolstered by analysts' speculation about what was probably on their minds.

Bush repaid the analysts who wrote for his PDB by giving useable feedback to Peters and Applebaum and even by calling analysts directly. Scowcroft, who sat deskside during such chats, thinks that the president hoped such calls motivated analysts to produce a useful product for him every day. "He was a serious and avid consumer of intelligence, and he wanted to get the best intelligence he could out of the PDB." Analysts ate it up. "He was the easiest brief in the world," says John Gannon, who became deputy director for intelligence in the 1990s. "He just loved to have a gaggle of analysts around him. I remember at Kennebunkport, he asked, 'Does anyone want some cinnamon toast?' And he'd go and make it. He was just an absolutely delightful guy."

A different kind of creative effort to supplement the PDB fared less well. Dick Kerr, who moved from DDI as the administration started up to serve as deputy director for the majority of Bush's term, pushed intelligence officers to produce what he called a "Red Book" PDB. He noticed that mainstream analysis had typically examined Cold War issues from a US perspective and thought it would be interesting to turn that around. "If you're surrounded by the US," he wondered, "and you've got the US doing all of these things—successes all around—what is it like if you're sitting in Moscow?" He prodded the Directorate of Intelligence's Russia experts to analyze the world situation, and write analytic pieces, from the Russian point of view. "What kind of PDB would you get? What would it say about what the US was doing and what the world looked like?"

His initiative brought a frosty reception from the workforce. "I had a terrible time getting the analysts to do it," Kerr says. "I finally had to say, 'We're going to do it—I don't give a damn if you want to do it or not. Just do it.' Maybe that was part of the problem—I thought it was a creative way to think about the problem, but their hearts weren't in it." He produced a couple of issues of the Red Book but received little interest from readers. "It was so much trouble to get going and so difficult to get the Soviet division to do it, so I gave up on the idea."

ANALYSTS DODGED THE RED Book concept but continued writing traditional PDB articles about world developments, including the defining one for the Bush administration: the 1990 conflict between Iraq and Kuwait.

Saddam Hussein concluded eight years of war with Iran in August 1988. He decided less than two years later to extort his Gulf

Arab neighbors, which he purported to have saved from the aggressive Shia Islamic Republic across the narrow Gulf. Agency analysts informed policy makers about Saddam's demands for Kuwaiti territory, the emirate's efforts to resist, and the massing of Iraqi troops along the border. "We followed that pretty well in the PDB," says Kerr. The book remained in line with what policy makers were hearing from contacts in the region. "We had been assured by everybody over there, the locals, that Saddam would never invade," Cheney recalls. "He was just trying to scare the hell out of the Kuwaitis and leverage OPEC prices and so forth."

"We all felt, and I'm sure our intelligence was helping us get there, that he would not be foolish enough to do what he did," says former secretary of state James Baker. He took a call—while meeting in Siberia with Soviet foreign minister Eduard Shevarnadze—from undersecretary for political affairs Bob Kimmitt, who was getting up-to-the-minute intelligence back in Washington.

"We've got disturbing reports that the Iraqis are massing on the borders of Kuwait," Kimmitt told his boss. "You might want to ask your interlocutor if he knows anything about that." Baker raised it.

"Oh, they wouldn't be foolish enough to do that," Shevardnadze replied. "There's no way."

"Well, we've got reports that they are. You might want to check with the KGB and see what you can find out."

Shevarnadze came back from lunch and told Baker, "No way they are going to do that. They may be looking at that oil field, but there is no way they are going to invade."

Iraq, of course, did invade, as Saddam attempted to get through force what he could not obtain through hardball diplomacy alone. Overnight on August 1, the CIA's assessment shifted to indicate that Iraq would invade, and soon—providing Bush with his first news of what was coming. The NSC's Middle East chief, Richard Haass, advised the president to call Saddam to try to walk him back. But before Bush could even get to the phone, the US embassy in Kuwait City reported shooting in the capital. "So much for calling Saddam," Bush said. Scowcroft soon confirmed that the invasion was under way.

The next morning, before 5:00 a.m., Scowcroft brought the president new information about Iraq's blatant attack. Two and a half hours later, Hank Applebaum and Webster brought Bush the day's

PDB. During the briefing, Bush and Scowcroft called Baker, who had flown to Mongolia after his meetings with Shevardnadze. The Soviet foreign minster's assurances to Baker the day before, however wrong, proved valuable. "That was the beginning of the coalition that kicked Iraq out of Kuwait," Baker says, "because Shevardnadze was so embarrassed about that. When I called him from Mongolia, he agreed to meet me at an airport in Moscow, stand shoulder to shoulder with me, and condemn that invasion. Without the Soviets, we never would have been able to get the UN resolution for the use of force." Webster stuck around after the PDB session to provide updates on developments in Kuwait (and on other countries' reactions to the invasion) to a formal meeting of the National Security Council—whose other members had already received their own daily PDB briefings. Cheney's briefer had told him, for example, that the invasion had gone off "like clockwork."

Throughout the buildup of US and coalition forces in Saudi Arabia starting in 1990 (Operation Desert Shield) and, eventually, the liberation of Kuwait in early 1991 (Operation Desert Storm), the Agency's experts on the region updated the PDB. Learning a lesson from the Panama crisis—which had spurred higher Oval Office interest in granular details not normally in the book—the PDB staff began regularly including more tactical information in the book in January and February 1991. The president read, in addition to analysis of worldwide developments and updates on diplomatic and military developments in Iraq and Kuwait, detailed accounts of the progress of an oil slick in Gulf waters and the status of assessed Iraqi chemical warheads for its Scud missiles.

The transition from Desert Shield to Desert Storm set the stage for the most public debate of the PDB's contents during Bush's term. The president and his top aides had decided to start with an air campaign to substantially degrade Iraqi forces before launching a ground attack to liberate Kuwait. Specifically, Cheney says, "we'd set for ourselves a benchmark—we wanted to take out half of the Iraqi armor before we launched. We got to the point where our guys were convinced that we had done that. We'd set the date for launching the ground war."

Agency analysts fed battle-damage assessments, including information from high-resolution satellite imagery, into the PDB—but their numbers for destroyed Iraqi equipment differed from in-theater appraisals by US Central Command (CENTCOM) analysts, who initially emphasized reports from the attacking pilots themselves. This made great sense for CENTCOM, which needed to rapidly plan follow-on missions before satellite imagery analysis could be brought to bear, but it opened up a divergence between CENTCOM's cumulative assessments of damage to Iraqi ground forces and those appearing in the PDB.

As the decision to initiate the ground war approached, the gap in these estimates expanded. CENTCOM by February 5 counted 151 tanks in the Republican Guard's mechanized division destroyed, but CIA analysts reported in current intelligence publications on February 9 that they detected just five. CENTCOM was in the process of updating its own numbers. Officers there began incorporating high-quality but slow-to-process U-2 photography for cumulative assessments—and discovered that the pilot reports needed to be adjusted downward to better reflect actual damage. Even when they began crediting only one-third of A-10 pilot reports and one-half of F-111 pilot reports, the battlefield picture still looked much rosier to them than to Washington-based analysts.

Differences emerged between the CIA-only PDB and the intelligence-community-coordinated NID. Imagery and military analysts at the Agency at that time got observations more quickly than other community elements, allowing the PDB to have up-to-the-minute information. NID versions of the same assessments often carried footnotes from the Defense Intelligence Agency, objecting to numbers that analysts there were uncomfortable with because they had not yet seen the same information that drove CIA analysis. "We consistently were saying it was larger than DIA was saying," recalls CIA manager Bruce Riedel. "And, consistently, they would acknowledge several days later that we were right." At one point, analysis chief John Helgerson sent Riedel to meet with the director of DIA. "He essentially accused us of having a secret source that we were not giving to the Pentagon," Riedel says. "I was shocked; it had never occurred to me that that would be the way they saw the problem." The garbled situation left customers such as Joint Chiefs chairman Colin Powell scratching his head when he saw different conclusions in the PDB and in the NID.

Military commanders deployed in the Middle East and working at CENTCOM headquarters in Tampa, Florida, believed that a CIA plot to delay the ground war was behind the judgments that Iraqi tanks and armored vehicles had not been degraded as much as in-theater analysts assessed. CENTCOM commander General Norman Schwarzkopf wrote that if he had postponed operations to wait for the CIA to agree with him, "we'd still be in Saudi Arabia." Webster remains shocked to this day that others perceived an Agency agenda. "We reported on what we were seeing. And that was all we were doing— we weren't saying we were not ready." CIA deputy director Dick Kerr recognized only later the thin ice his experts had walked onto. "In the first part of the war, we were probably right. But I don't think we understood the political risk we were putting ourselves in."

As tensions rose, Webster decided that Bush needed to know about the dispute. "It was not hostile," Webster says. "It was just a question of how to do this, because it was important from the standpoint of when they launched the ground war." On February 21, within a few days of the planned start of the ground offensive, he saved an article highlighting the different CIA and CENTCOM methodologies and damage assessments, and briefed Bush personally about it after the regular PDB session.

"Look, we're having some problems," he recalls telling the president. "We are seeing different numbers here, and we're trying to work them out."

"You mean, pilot euphoria," replied Bush, a former navy pilot.

"I can't say that," Webster said. "But our numbers do not match theirs. And their curve is going up and ours is staying pretty flat."

The president asked Scowcroft to host a follow-on meeting to get to the bottom of the issue. "I got a hurry-up phone call from the West Wing," Cheney recalls. "And I took Colin Powell and McConnell and I went over and met with Scowcroft and Webster, and Bill brought in one or two analysts from the Agency. We had a debate." By that point, just before ground operations began, CENTCOM judged that 425 tanks in the three Republican Guard divisions had been destroyed (about 43 percent of the total before the air war started), while the CIA assessment was that only 145 tanks had been destroyed (less than 20 percent of the prewar total). "It got to be a heated argument," Scowcroft says, "because that was the basis on which we would decide when D-Day was." The conflicting assessments leaked to the press, drawing national attention to the issue—and to the president's intelligence briefings. "Someone in Congress had been kept informed," Webster says, "and someone was leaking."

The president went forward with the ground war, and coalition forces routed their Iraqi counterparts quickly once Desert Storm started. Misperceptions lingered about the air war's attrition of Iraqi tanks and armored vehicles. A CENTCOM draft paper in November 1991 claimed that "Bomb Damage Assessment produced by CENTCOM tended to be more useful and accurate" than CIA estimates—and that "the rapid defeat of division after division in the ground phase of Operation Desert Storm" proved that CENTCOM's methodology had been superior. Some participants in this saga, including Schwarzkopf, remained adamant that the in-theater appraisals emerged as most accurate. Powell asserts that the Agency's assessments failed to consider the entire battlefield picture. Cheney remembers, "The conclusion was that we were right and the Agency was wrong."

The coalition's ability to demolish Iraqi forces so handily during the ground war, of course, neither confirms nor denies the accuracy of either the CIA or the CENTCOM methodology for counting disabled vehicles. More useful was an exhaustive survey of the theater done after the cease-fire. This report used unimpeded high-quality aerial photography to count Republican Guard tanks that had redeployed to face the coalition ground offensive and those that had retreated north of the ceasefire line, versus those that remained in revetments occupied before Desert Storm started (and thus were assumed to have been disabled during the air attacks). The study found that the air war had destroyed only 166 Republican Guard tanks—21 percent of the prewar force—compared to CENTCOM's estimate of 43 percent, while later ground operations had disabled or forced the abandonment of 29 percent more of the tanks. Thus, coalition forces actually had taken out about half of the Republican Guard tanks—but only *after* the ground offensive had begun, not *before* starting it.

"We were right, and time proved that we were right," says Riedel. Scowcroft, the man in the West Wing who mattered most because he had to convey the issue to the president, agrees. "I assumed Defense was more accurate because they had mostly pilot reports, and they would say, 'We killed this.' But CIA turned out to be more accurate."

EXPERTS WITHIN THE INTELLIGENCE community, along with other observers in the US government and internationally, disagreed about what was happening inside the Soviet Union and what the United States should (or even could) do about it. During these momentous times, Bush didn't rely only on the PDB's text for his intelligence needs. "There was so much information coming in that it wasn't necessarily going to be in intelligence analysis," says deputy national security advisor Jon Howe. "We never relied just on the PDB."

As Boris Yeltsin entered the stage as an independent force in Moscow, Scowcroft brought analysts with differing opinions into the Oval Office and "let them set forth their theses in front of the President." He says that the White House team looked for opportunities to push events in the most advantageous direction for American interests. "Did we use all the intelligence? Yes we did, but the intelligence was extremely confused at this period. As a guide to action, what it did clearly say is: Things are getting worse. They're not getting better. Gorbachev has set things in motion he can't control. He's not likely to be able to hold on."

Soviet troops withdrew peacefully from Warsaw Pact satellites. Communist regimes across Eastern Europe collapsed without major conflict. The USSR imploded without civil war. Any of those situations could have turned ugly with little notice. The direst event was the attempted putsch against Gorbachev in August 1991, which ended up failing due to stubborn resistance from Russian leader Boris Yeltsin and the coup plotters' own incompetence. "The Agency's forecast of serious trouble ahead for the Soviet Union and the possibility of a coup against Gorbachev," Gates says, "led us at the National Security Council to begin—on a close-hold basis—contingency planning for the collapse of the Soviet Union. This prediction took place in the fall of 1989, almost two years before it actually happened."

In the summer of 1991, the Soviet leader was preparing to sign a treaty transferring significant authority to the constituent republics of the USSR, rendering the USSR effectively impotent. On Saturday, August 17, President Bush was vacationing at his home in Kennebunkport, Maine. Without a PDB briefer when he traveled, Bush received his book that day from Gates, the senior NSC staff officer on the trip.

Gates remembers eating pancakes with the president on his ocean-view porch. "He was reading the President's daily brief," Gates says, which included an article conveying the CIA's assessment that "there was very likely to be a coup attempt" before the treaty's signing on August 20 because it would be much harder for Gorbachev's opponents to act after that. The PDB piece concluded with an assessment that anti-Gorbachev forces were increasingly likely to instigate a confrontation that would allow them to intervene with force.

After reading this assessment, Bush looked up from his book. "Should I take this seriously?"

"Yes," Gates replied, "and here's why." He reviewed the warnings that the CIA experts had been putting out for some time. Although Gates had no inside scoop on the precise moves the Soviet conservatives would make, or when, the message for the president was clear: Gorbachev's position had weakened. Indeed, within twenty-four hours of that briefing, a cabal of Gorbachev's opponents locked him into his dacha and seized control of the institutions of Soviet state power.

Did the PDB fail or succeed? CIA leaders defend the book's coverage in 1991. "We did the coup against Gorbachev rather well," says Dick Kerr, who had experience with providing crisis-related intelligence to the president since the days of John Kennedy. "We were on top of that. All in all, the PDB during this period was pretty good. Our assessments of Gorbachev and Yeltsin were right on."

Even experienced foreign policy hands who have learned the hard way how difficult it is to predict conspiracies overseas find themselves frustrated by coups that occur without warning from the intelligence community. Scowcroft, certainly a savvy intelligence customer by 1991, says that the coup's timing and details came as "a complete surprise." However, he also acknowledges, "I don't know how you do something like this other than to show trends. To predict a specific end of something—either a coup or that somebody's going to lose power—is awfully hard to do. It seems to me that they did their job." Baker concurs. "I don't think you could characterize that as an intelligence failure. Hell, we just didn't know it."

Within days, the Soviet hardliners failed to consolidate power, in part due to Yeltsin's strong posturing. "I think the biggest puzzle for all of us, at the time and afterward, was just how incompetently it had been carried out," Gates says. "This is one of those places where CIA had a huge influence during the course of the day. . . . Dick Kerr was talking about what hadn't happened in terms of the alerting of military forces or movement of military forces, in terms of the fact that telephone lines, telexes, faxes, were all still up and available, and many of the dissidents and potential oppositionists to the coup had not been arrested or taken into custody. So Dick sort of went through this litany. He said, 'This thing may not work.' And that was really the first indication that we had gotten that this thing was maybe not a done deal."

One senior customer missed the intelligence entirely on that crucial day of the coup attempt. Defense secretary Cheney was in British Columbia, satisfying his yen for fishing. "I didn't see that particular PDB," he says. "I was standing in the middle of the Dean River in chest waders, and the guy next to me had just caught a twenty-pound steelhead. I had a communicator and a security guy with me. And they hollered at me to come ashore because they had something. I did, and they told me, 'Sir, there's been a coup in the Soviet Union.'" They set up Cheney's satellite link to his deputy at the Pentagon, who advised him to return right away. "We hauled ass that whole day getting back to Washington. I remember getting off the Gulfstream at Andrews with my fly rod in hand."

THE GULF WAR BATTLE damage assessment dispute, the tension over what would happen in the Soviet Union, and related stresses brought Webster's time running the Agency to a close. During the Gulf War he remained out of the "Gang of Eight" that ran the war: Bush, Quayle, Scowcroft, Gates, Baker, Cheney, Powell, and Sununu. He had announced his departure in May 1991 but stayed on until the end of August, ending thirteen and a half years of service as head of the FBI and then of the CIA.

Bob Gates, who succeeded Webster and brought more hands-on experience with the PDB than any of his predecessors, ended up minimizing his contact with the president's daily book. His previous confirmation hearings—in 1987, when Ronald Reagan nominated him to succeed the deceased Bill Casey—had crashed on the rocks of concerns about his role in the Iran-Contra affair. In 1991, his hearings became even more contentious, as several former subordinates accused him of politicization, the mortal sin of the intelligence profession. Witnesses before the Senate Select Committee on Intelligence said Gates had changed assessments to fit Reagan administration policy preferences; he claimed that his hands-on approach, while serving as deputy director for intelligence and then as CIA's deputy director, merely reflected his desire to see the logic and evidence of analytic arguments expressed more clearly. He ultimately received the Senate's confirmation after vowing to avoid even the appearance of politicization. During his tenure as director, he followed through by initiating measures that exist to this day, including an annual survey on politicization and an active CIA ombudsman to investigate potential distortions of analytic conclusions.

To preempt future accusations involving the PDB, Gates stayed informed about the book but avoided touching its content before publication each day. "I wanted a brick wall there," says Gates, who let DDI Helgerson run the PDB show. "Bob had gone through so much in getting himself confirmed that he made a forceful point of *not* being involved in the review," Helgerson says. "Very occasionally, I would see a piece late in the day or early evening, and I would think there was some reason Bob would want to see it. So I would carry it down the hall and try to show it to him. More than once, he said, 'John, I don't do that job anymore. You're the DDI. I don't even want to see it; I'll read it in the morning.'"

That said, the director's duty as the president's top intelligence advisor required him to know if a highly charged topic would appear in the next day's PDB. "John would do for me what I did for Casey," says Gates. "He'd give me [a] heads-up if there was going to be a piece that would stir the waters downtown." Helgerson agrees that once in a while there would be an article that Gates "really needed to know about, and in such a case he would read it," but remembers Gates making it easy for him to avoid that most of the time. "It was extremely rare that he ever looked at a draft PDB—or evinced any eagerness to do so."

Like Webster before him, Gates attended the daily PDB sessions once or twice a week, usually on days that he went to see Scowcroft before the Oval Office briefings and just stuck around. "I'd just drop in and sit with the President and leave with the PDB briefer." Because, as Gates said, Bush seemed to understand better than previous presidents the value and the limits of intelligence, being his CIA director could have been difficult, or at least awkward. But Bush did not intrude into his management of intelligence, even though unexpected foreign events prompted him, like all presidents, to grumble.

Gates stayed less then fifteen months in the job that his career had been building toward since the late 1960s. He had decided to retire as Bush's term ended—even if President-elect Bill Clinton wanted to keep him on—because he had no ties to Clinton to match those he had developed with Bush. "I believe that the most important thing that a DCI brings to the table is his relationship with the President," he says. "You can have a deputy who knows intelligence. You can have a deputy who knows all the ins and outs and knows all of the foreign policy issues and so on, but if the DCI can't get in to see the President, everybody in the world knows it and it has a huge impact on the effectiveness of the Agency."

GEORGE H. W. BUSH had a more intimate relationship with his daily, personalized intelligence report than any of his predecessors had. "I wouldn't have wanted to try tackling any of the many issues that we confronted without the input from the intelligence community," he says. "Not for one second." His time each morning with the CIA's briefers stands out so much to him that, even twenty years after leaving office, he says, "My relationship with these men and women is one of the most satisfying of my life. I hope they all know how much I have appreciated them, and the excellent product they produced."

The Agency returned the love. In April 1999, George Tenet—appointed CIA director by Bill Clinton, who had defeated Bush's reelection bid seven years earlier—oversaw the designation of the CIA's headquarters compound in Langley, Virginia, as the George Bush Center for Intelligence.

CHAPTER NINE

EBB AND FLOW

WASHINGTON NEWCOMER BILL CLINTON—like Jimmy Carter and Ronald Reagan before him—used the time between his election as president in November 1992 and his inauguration in January 1993 to familiarize himself with the President's Daily Brief. Ten days after the election, DDI John Helgerson showed Clinton his first PDB in Little Rock, where the Arkansas governor had established his transition center.

Helgerson says Clinton and Vice President–elect Al Gore read every word in the book, "obviously intrigued to see what it contained." The biggest challenge was time. Clinton and Gore delved so deeply into their initial PDB that they took almost an hour, within a tightly structured day, to discuss its content and procedures.

The president-elect agreed to several things right away. First, to get up to speed, he agreed to receive a personalized supplement. Some of its pieces provided background on the content in Bush's book. Many others addressed areas likely to grab his attention quickly once in office: proliferation, Somalia, Bosnia, and especially Haiti, which Clinton's top national security aide, Sandy Berger, remembers being the biggest issue during the transition. He says the PDB relayed information, which soon followed in other sources, that thousands of Haitians were "ripping their roofs off their houses to build boats to come to the United States"—and that the intelligence reporting and analysis spurred Clinton to shift his policy toward the Caribbean nation.

Second, Clinton wanted to expand the range of issues included in what would become his book. "I became convinced early on that economics was going to be increasingly tied to security and that a part of that would be environmental issues," he says. "So Al Gore and I asked the CIA to include in the PDB any salient information on economic developments and environmental developments." Third, he established an initial plan to distribute the President's Daily Brief more widely than his predecessor had done, including to the treasury secretary.

That briefing on November 13 thus previewed much of the PDB experience for the next eight years: An active reader in the Oval Office. A vice president hooked on intelligence. Wider topical coverage. Expanded distribution. And, most of all, difficulty keeping the president on schedule—which ended up minimizing CIA officers' face-to-face contact in the Oval Office, a privilege they had started to take for granted during the previous four years.

CLINTON INTENDED TO RECEIVE intelligence briefings each day upon taking office. While in Little Rock between his first PDB exposure in mid-November and his inauguration, in fact, he had seemed to enjoy not only the CIA's dedicated daily briefing support—focusing on Russia, Somalia, Yugoslavia, Iraq, GATT talks in Europe, Lebanon, and Haiti—but also supplements, such as an Agency-produced video on Mexican president Carlos Salinas ahead of Clinton's meeting with him in Texas. The impressions he left with his post-election intelligence briefers echoed the one he made on the chairman of the Joint Chiefs of Staff, Colin Powell, who found Clinton had "an interest in everything and the kind of memory that never forgets anything."

Chief of staff Mack McLarty, national security advisor Tony Lake, his deputy (Sandy Berger), Vice President Gore, and *his* national security advisor (Leon Fuerth) attended Clinton's first PDB briefing after the inauguration. One piece that day addressed an adversary's chemical weapons (CW) program, prompting Clinton to blurt out that he had a steep learning curve because back in Arkansas, CW meant country and western music. The new president, in fact, seemed the ideal briefing customer—interested, engaged, and free with his comments—except that the meeting started late and the atmosphere in and around the Oval Office was chaotic.

Clinton's strengths as a leader famously did not include sticking to a fixed schedule. As the president's oldest friend among the White House staff—going back to a shared kindergarten class in Hope, Arkansas, more than forty years earlier—McLarty knew Clinton's habits well: "The president had a great natural tendency to want to understand what he was dealing with—ask questions, get into more detail, probe the accuracy of the information being presented to him. That just was his normal MO; it was in his DNA."

At least the briefers actually made it into the Oval Office for that first session. On many other days to follow, they would show up in the West Wing and just wait. The president's scheduler frequently warned his briefers that Clinton was running behind and begged them to keep their sessions short. Increasingly, when Tony Lake or Sandy Berger had particularly important policy matters to discuss with the president during his national security time, the CIA briefing fell off the schedule altogether.

This proved especially difficult for Clinton's first CIA director, Jim Woolsey, who had joined many of those early PDB sessions. Unlike the lower-ranking officers, whose workdays could easily bend around Clinton Time, the director had a tight schedule of his own that required recalibration every time the president's time frame shifted. "We just sat outside the Oval Office waiting to get in," Woolsey recalls. "Tony Lake would say, 'I'm sorry, he's just not going to have time today.' And, after a while, it became quite clear they wouldn't do that. Why? First of all, his background and his interest were almost exclusively on the domestic side. And, the United States in those post–Cold War years, as Shakespeare said of Caesar, bestrode the world like a colossus." When it became common for someone to pop his head out of the Oval Office to say, "Could you hand us the briefing?" and take the PDB in without Woolsey or the briefers, the CIA director simply stopped going to the White House.

Clinton offers a different explanation for skipping face-to-face intelligence sessions. "As I got more comfortable with the brief and working with the intelligence officers, I found it more fruitful and more practical on most days to read it myself early in the morning— and then to make, as I almost invariably did, a set of notes actually on the PDB for what further information I wanted or what I wanted to make sure that the National Security Council (NSC) staff had read."

He denies that letting the briefings drop off reflected disinterest in the book: "I really tried to read the PDB carefully, seriously, and thoroughly—and write on it—to use it as a tool to follow up on."

Others around Clinton support his claim. Berger, who served as Lake's deputy for four years before taking over as national security advisor for the next four, says the president from the start was "quite an avaricious consumer of intelligence. He would read the PDB in the morning in the Oval Office when he came in, and he would write questions on it and send it back to us. 'Why is this?' 'What is this?'" John Podesta, who served as the NSC staff secretary early in the administration and thus saw all of the national security paperwork coming to and from the president, says, "He would underline things and annotate the PDB with his questions. You rarely got it out with nothing written on it." A senior DI manager attending an NSC Principals Committee meeting soon after saw clear evidence that the president took the book seriously. Clinton, who chaired the session, specifically cited what he'd read in the PDB that morning about a developing issue in the Middle East. "That was the real Clinton interest in the book," the manager says, "not the myth that he had no time or interest for this stuff."

This practice created a different version of the two-way communication that the live briefings had provided. In February 1994, for example, the President's Daily Brief contained an article about Africa. Clinton read the book alone but wrote in the margin, "See attached magazine article." Sure enough, the president of the United States attached to his PDB a copy of something he had just read—Robert Kaplan's article in the *Atlantic*, "The Coming Anarchy"—for delivery back to the analysts at Langley. "As a result of that," says Woolsey, "we got together with Gore, which was the way he wanted to handle it, and had a little study group on potential chaos in developing countries."

The president recognized the value of the written document: "By reading the PDB, I got the distilled essence of everything that I could have learned if I read every newspaper article prepared on it plus whatever intelligence we had from the day before."

On such days, the PDB would almost certainly play a prominent role in Clinton's regular national security meeting with senior White House national security aides—led by Lake, who received regular

PDB briefings every day from a CIA briefer. Other, less urgent pieces in the book still gave Clinton areas to explore with the vice president, the national security advisor, and other foreign policy officials during the course of daily business. "On the days when there wasn't some blockbuster intelligence finding in it—most days—it served to organize and concentrate the attention and the resources of the White House for whatever the main issues were," notes Clinton.

However, the book also exasperated Clinton—"all the time," he says—because he wanted more than it could provide. He told the 9/11 Commission in April 2004 that he found the Secretary's Morning Summary from the State Department's Bureau of Intelligence and Research (INR) more helpful than the PDB at providing context for developments overseas. As Berger puts it, the PDB contained "more snapshots than movies." Rather than blaming the PDB's authors and editors, Clinton appreciated their open acknowledgment of the Agency's blind spots. "The frustration that I felt was a good thing for the CIA because it made the credibility of what made it into the PDB higher. When they would just 'fess up and say, 'We don't know this or that or the other thing—we can't find that out yet,' we'd ask them to try. The Agency was always really great working with us on that and giving us more information. It proved that the people who did the PDB were being honest."

One example from late in Clinton's term highlights the cumulative value of the daily PDB material for the man who came into office with minimal knowledge of foreign affairs. As he chatted on the phone one morning with the leader of a small country, who blathered on and on about his country's rough-and-tumble domestic affairs, he put his hand over the receiver and turned his head to a White House official standing nearby and monitoring the conversation.

"You know," the president said, "I understand his politics better than *he* does."

Returning to the call, Clinton proceeded to explain quite effectively that leader's own political situation to him. "He was getting the message across indirectly," recalls the official, "saying, 'Couldn't it be that? . . . Isn't it possible that? . . .' He was such a quick study, with such a memory, and he had a skill—an ability to really understand the other guy's situation."

"MACK," CLINTON SAID TO his first chief of staff right before the inauguration, "I want Al Gore to be the most effective, engaged vice president in history. We ran as a team, and that's the way I want to govern."

Clinton invited Gore to attend any national security briefings he wanted to, including the PDB sessions. "The vice president was always present when he was in town," McLarty says. Even as Clinton's in-person briefings became irregular, Gore's briefings remained steady—so the president often turned to his VP to follow up on issues raised by the book. "There were days when the most important thing about the PDB was not the lead article; it was one of the smaller articles that were almost like teasers," Clinton says. "But they contained things that the people putting it together thought the president ought to be aware of, or they raised red flags that might be coming down the road. Very often, I would talk to Al Gore about it—and I would ask him to go read the raw intelligence, go dig deeper."

For his entire vice presidency, Gore eagerly took on this task, making daily intelligence—led by the PDB—a top priority. "I read it religiously every morning—six mornings a week, because they didn't bring it on Sundays—and I spent a lot of time with it," recalls Gore. "I directed follow-up questions and frequently called items to President Clinton's attention." Gore says drilling down on pet issues brought real value. "Some of the most useful items were in follow-up to such inquiries. And I got the distinct impression that the people running the machinery really liked that—they liked to get feedback and direction."

An Agency officer saw the vice president every day he was in town, often during his car ride into the office (to avoid the inevitable distractions that would arise once he arrived in the West Wing). Gore's CIA briefers describe him as very focused during these short drives, polite but not chatty. They learned to wait until he showed them he was ready for the PDB. "He wanted to sit down, get comfortable, and start his breakfast," one briefer recalls. "After a minute or two, he would stretch his hand out, without any words spoken—my job was to wait for the cue. Then I would give him his material, and he would read whatever he wanted." Saturdays felt more comfortable because the official schedule usually remained light, allowing Gore to dig deeper into that day's intelligence as well as catch up on longer intelligence papers in the comfort of the vice presidential residence.

"The briefers were typically people who had high intelligence, insights into the culture of the intelligence establishment, intuition, impressions—which all helped me understand something," Gore says. "It was not unusual for them to add some layer of understanding that I would not have gotten otherwise." He adds that they learned to admit when they didn't have a particular answer and would instead offer to bring more information back with them the next day, typically in a memo. The briefers also added scuttlebutt they had picked up in conversations with the experts working the topic. "It was the single smartest collection of men and women that I've worked with in the government."

Gore's briefers soon discovered that his interests ranged both wide and deep. Recognizing him as a strategic thinker with the whole world as his portfolio, they learned to augment the PDB with a wide array of other material, often linked to his upcoming meetings or decisions. His longest-serving briefer, Denny Watson, recalls passing the VP a classified report about a foreign government official the vice president had developed close ties to. The information showed that this "friendly" official had, in fact, fomented domestic disturbances during events Gore spoke at. The vice president called the CIA director personally to thank him for the useful service. "It told him something critical about his relationship with that human being," notes Watson. "It made him think in a different way about where that relationship was going."

Most often, the vice president kept his opinions of the PDB's content to himself. He just read the book's assessments and moved on, Watson recalls, only occasionally posing follow-up queries. "When there *was* a question," she says, "it was always worth waiting for. It was clearly something he had been chewing on and thinking about for a while." Gore says that the DI's answers generally satisfied him— eventually. "If it was weak or based on a flawed understanding, then they corrected it. I don't remember a time when I felt like they were intentionally obfuscating or holding back. I never knew them to provide a weak response twice."

Over time, Gore's relationships with the CIA officers who served him grew warmer. One of his regular briefers convinced headquarters analysts to create a mock PDB for the vice president on his birthday. The idea carried risk; he might have had a particularly rough morning, leaving him in no mood for humor. When the briefer handed him the PDB straight, as if it were the regular book Clinton was seeing at the same time, the VP read it normally until he came across a farcical piece about penguins that prompted him to laugh out loud. "I loved it," Gore says. "Often, people with high intelligence have really good senses of humor. Those things don't *always* go together, but it was a sign of good emotional health at the Agency that they went together in the PDB team."

The worst part of the daily drives for Watson had less to do with the PDB's content than with her pregnancy. Suffering from frequent morning sickness during the entire nine months, the experience of reading and chatting in a moving car's backseat bordered on excruciating. "When I made the change from the Agency motor pool car to his limo," she remembers, "he'd have his breakfast: toast and a really smelly grapefruit. I thought I was going to vomit." From that point forward, Watson left for the briefing an hour early, allowing her to get her stomach back under control in the back of the parked Agency car before moving to Gore's car, where the sickness would reemerge. Seeing her job as a customer service position, where the VP's comfort mattered more than her own, she kept her feelings to herself. "If I had known that," Gore now says, "I would have changed the routine and had her come over earlier. Whatever I had waiting for me at the White House would have waited!"

On one typical weekday during this period, the vice president's limo made its way toward the White House, between a lead car and a chase vehicle. As they all neared the end of a parkway on-ramp, the lead car edged out. Gore's own limo driver, looking over to merge, failed to notice that the first car had suddenly stopped—so he rear-ended it. "I went flying," Watson recalls, "and with my belly I had no balance, so I went right onto the floor. The security guy looked back, and Gore calmly said, 'It's OK. We're OK back here.' Thankfully, I was."

As Watson's due date approached she faced an awkward question from the lead Secret Service agent, just as Gore entered the car.

"So, are you going to keep on coming, or what? We're getting kind of nervous."

"That's OK," Gore cut in. He had four children himself, and his eldest daughter had just delivered his first grandchild. "She can keep on coming—we know how to do babies back here."

During his eight years as vice president, Gore would endure political opponents and pundits calling him many things. But few of the epithets hurled at him compared to the one from his PDB's briefer's daughter. Watson took her to meet the vice president one day, forgetting how a kindergartner who has just discovered knock-knock jokes jumps at any opportunity to apply that knowledge.

"Knock knock!"

"Who's there?" Gore kindly replied.

"Banana."

"Banana who?"

"You're a banana head!"

FOREIGN POLICY DISASTER STRUCK the administration in 1994. In support of a United Nations mission in Somalia, US forces faced fierce resistance trying to arrest militia leader Mohamed Farrah Aidid and his henchmen in Mogadishu. Somali forces on October 3 downed two US Black Hawk helicopters, trapping their occupants in enemy territory and spurring a difficult overnight rescue mission that left eighteen Americans killed, many more wounded, and hundreds of Somalis dead. The events of October 3–4 became known as "Black Hawk Down."

Investigations by the press and Clinton's own President's Foreign Intelligence Advisory Board revealed that policy makers received warnings from the CIA about Somali plans to set a trap for American soldiers, embarrass the United States, and ultimately force foreign troops' withdrawal from Somalia. According to the head of the PFIAB, retired chairman of the Joint Chiefs of Staff William Crowe, the board determined there had been crucial errors—but not on the part of the CIA or any other intelligence agency. The original draft PFIAB report started with the assertion that the president could not have been surprised after what he had seen in his daily intelligence leading up to the crisis. "The intelligence failure in Somalia was right in the National Security Council," Crowe says. "There were a number of people handling Somalian affairs that expected way too much from intelligence. They expected intelligence to make their decisions for them, not just give them information about what was going on there. . . . It made for considerable confusion right at the top."

Doug MacEachin, the DDI at the time, recalls that the flow of intelligence to Clinton was in flux during that period, and he speculates that the president might not have even seen the PDB because Lake wasn't showing it to him. Clinton, however, offers no excuses, saying he read "a lot on Somalia" in the PDB before Black Hawk Down. He remembers seeing a regularly updated map showing the extent of Aidid's control of the Somali capital. "For weeks," he says, "Aidid had had 20 percent of Mogadishu. All of a sudden one day, the map showed him having 75 percent of Mogadishu. I looked at the briefer, and I said, 'Boy, he had a heck of a night last night!' Of course, I knew that wasn't what happened. Different intelligence had come in; it was a human enterprise."

Regardless, the PFIAB's recommendations to the president included getting the PDB delivered personally again. And, sure enough, face-to-face-briefings picked up at that point. "I was still learning my way and trying to pay attention," Clinton says. "It was a very sobering moment for me." Senior sources soon were telling the *Washington Post* that the White House had regularized the national security briefing, which featured a revamped PDB with bolder head-lines and punchier text. For a time, Clinton saw his CIA briefer more often, two or three times a week. Clinton himself told *Time* magazine late in 1994 that he had allocated more time for his national security

President Bill Clinton and Vice President Al Gore reading the PDB in the Oval Office on September 21, 1994, joined by CIA PDB briefer John Brennan. *Courtesy William J. Clinton Presidential Library*

briefing, taking it to a full forty-five minutes every day. And the CIA delivered the goods in his daily intelligence briefings by warning of the first Chechen war in 1994, calling the outcome of various foreign elections in 1995–96, and keeping ahead of the curve in anticipation of Boris Yeltsin's various government shake-ups in Russia.

Old habits, however, die hard. Before long, the president's inability to hold to a firm schedule again precluded regular intelligence sessions. The CIA officer sent every day to the White House would manage to get in to brief Clinton every few days, then once a week, and eventually only a few times a month. "I used to sit, and I did a lot of reading. I tried to write a lot of notes there to make good use of the time," the briefer says. He still did what he could in the West Wing, meeting with Lake or Berger almost every morning and seeing Gore's top aide, Leon Fuerth, each day. And this enabled *something* from the CIA briefer to get into the Oval Office via Lake or Berger.

"I DIDN'T HAVE A *bad* relationship with President Clinton," CIA director Jim Woolsey says. "I just didn't have one at all."

As Clinton approached his third year in office, Woolsey rarely came to the White House. He recalls meeting with the president alone only once—before his nomination to lead the intelligence community—and afterward seeing him two-on-two only twice, once at the Agency and once in the Oval Office. "Tony Lake was basically my boss. The PDB daily briefing didn't exist, so the way I was to get information in to Clinton was through Tony. I lived with that for two years." He cannot recall a single case where the PDB prompted a call from Clinton, the secretary of state, or the defense secretary. His face time with principals, including the president, remained limited to larger settings, such as meetings of the NSC, which historically have begun with intelligence briefings to ensure that the president and his foreign policy team debated policy based on objective assessments of the situation on the ground.

The presence at these meetings of White House press and public relations officials, often lacking Top Secret clearances, frustrated Woolsey. He recalls being invited to deliver an intelligence overview to kick off an NSC meeting about Somalia that had been designated as highly sensitive—meaning he should come alone, without staff backup. When he arrived, the Cabinet Room overflowed with not only the usual NSC principals but also about a dozen others, including PR staffers. The assembled officials shocked him by skipping the intelligence briefing, cutting right to their plan to send someone over to Somalia to set up a coalition government.

George Stephanopoulos and Dee Dee Myers, sitting at the far end of the table across from each another, started going back and forth about who would background the *Washington Post* and the *New York Times* and who would go on the Sunday talk shows. That went on, without interruption, for several minutes. Everybody else watched them blurt out ideas for media appearances, from one to the other like a table tennis match.

"Mr. President," Woolsey finally cut in, bringing the discussion back to Somalia, "this country has been engaged in clan warfare for a long time. I think pretty much everybody at the Agency who watches it would tell you it's going to be engaged in clan warfare for a long time into the future. And the chance of *any* coalition government between these warlords holding together is pretty much zero."

The room went still. Presidential advisor David Gergen waited for others to speak up. Seeing no takers, he stated the obvious: "Well, look—if what Jim just said is true, none of this that we're talking about makes any sense."

The Cabinet Room froze in another awkward moment of silence. Then Stephanopoulos and Myers picked their conversation up right where they'd left off, figuring out who would speak to which press outlets.

"Nobody frowned at me," Woolsey says.

> Nobody came over afterward and said, "Jim, you took the meeting off in an unfortunate direction." Nothing like that. I just was not on point. It was exactly as if I had intervened to say, "Mr. President, I would like everybody here to know that last Saturday, I had two of my sons up in southern Pennsylvania and we were able to take ten nice trout before 9:00 in the morning. I'm going back this Saturday; if anybody would like to join me, I'd be delighted to have them." People would have thought, "Well, it's odd that Jim is bringing up fishing in the middle of this NSC meeting, but Jim *is* a little odd—we'll just sit here for a minute."

I had departed from the PR meeting to talk about the underlying substantive issue. What was interesting about that? It was an
NSC meeting!

His deputy, Admiral William Studeman, conveyed the same
impression. "I do not think we have been successful with the current
administration in even being defined as being a relevant part of the
national security team," he told CIA's in-house journal during the
Clinton years. "And I am sure the DCIs have been frustrated by it.
When you have CNN announcing that the president is meeting with
his national security team and you know intelligence is not represented, that is a source of concern."

Fighting for face time with the president wasn't Woolsey's style,
and he had plenty of other things to keep him busy—he kept 205
appointments on Capitol Hill in 1993, when Congress was only in
session 195 days. Delving deeply into the PDB fell by the wayside. He
started each day by reading the book at his house, in his basement
command post. He recalls the PDB as "good and sound, a bit more
vivid than intelligence reports often are," but he ended up spending
much more time as CIA director on counterintelligence (due to the
arrest of Soviet spy Aldrich Ames during his tenure) and on his true
love, science and technology issues.

Woolsey's lack of access to the president made him the butt of jokes
inside the Beltway. The most prominent one evolved from a serious incident: Frank Corder's attempt to fly a stolen Cessna into the White House
early on the morning of September 12, 1994. Apparently inspired by
Mathias Rust—the German pilot who flew from Finland all the way
to Moscow in May 1987, landing near Red Square without Soviet military intervention—Corder plopped his two-seat aircraft down on the
South Lawn, just fifty yards from the Oval Office, killing himself in the
process. Clinton and his family, who had all gone to sleep that night at
Blair House while workers renovated the executive mansion, escaped
unharmed. Woolsey's pride did not, especially when Tony Lake shared
with him the gag running around the White House staff: the pilot must
have been Woolsey trying to get an appointment with Clinton.

"At first, I was kind of teed off," Woolsey says. But as he reflected
on it, he came to think, *What the hell—it's pretty accurate*. The story

remains his favorite characterization of his relationship with the president. He stayed in the job until December 1994 and then resigned. After the nomination of retired air force general Michael Carns to replace Woolsey stalled, Clinton sent the skeptical John Deutch to run the CIA.

Deutch had been seeing the PDB each morning for most of the past two years as undersecretary and then deputy secretary of defense, part of an expansion of the book's dissemination to more than a dozen recipients. He recalls seeing it with secretary of defense Les Aspin— and not being impressed. "I flipped quickly through it," Deutch says. "There was very little emphasis on the sources on which the intelligence was based. That's not useful." He nevertheless took no action as CIA director to change the PDB, probably because he perceived little interest from the top. During his eighteen-month tenure as director, which ended in December 1996, he says that he *never* briefed the president on the PDB. In fact, it would take a reengineering of the book and a third CIA director, George Tenet, to get the CIA front office more interested.

NOT LONG BEFORE DEUTCH left, the vice president's briefer noticed Gore's annoyance with the overlapping content between the PDB and another Agency product, which covered economic intelligence issues. He spoke up, asking the VP, "Do you think we should do something about it?"

Gore shot the briefer a look that spoke louder than words: *If you asked the question, then you know the answer.*

The briefer returned to Langley determined to act. "We've got to do something about this," he told his bosses. "Gore is getting tired." They quickly created a product that would cover key non-PDB items, tailored to match the wide portfolio that Clinton had given the vice president. "I asked them so many damned questions every day," Gore laughs, "I guess they worried about cluttering the President's Daily Brief."

The result was a de facto second PDB tailored to Al Gore's schedule and interests, the Vice President's Supplement. It focused on environmental, economic, technological, and humanitarian topics as well as on issues related to the bilateral commissions that Gore was responsible for, such as those with Russia, South Africa, Egypt, Ukraine, and Kazakhstan. Answers to his questions started appearing as articles in the new publication, which soon became known simply as the VPS. Analysts stepped up their efforts because they knew they had a vehicle to a senior customer whose daily engagement with his briefers provided rich feedback. "Every day," says briefer Denny Watson, "I went through every single piece in the VPS and I wrote a note to every author."

Editors of the Vice President's Supplement also learned to time the appearance of pieces in the new book explicitly to Gore's schedule. "Once we figured out what that sweet spot was," Watson recalls, "he loved it. All of a sudden, he's customer number one. He'd read the Supplement first." Gore calls himself a big fan of both the VPS and the people who produced it. "If there was something weak about it, I wouldn't hesitate to give them my opinion," he says. "Not that I was always right, far from it. But they would sure as hell react and incorporate whatever suggestions that I had." He also remembers being "universally impressed" with analysts' efforts to take on less traditional topics such as the environment and global technology.

Leon Fuerth, Gore's tenacious national security advisor, also received the VPS to ensure he would be up to speed on the issues that his boss worked on. After serving in the late 1960s and 1970s as a Foreign Service officer, Fuerth had worked on national security issues with Gore when the latter was first a congressman and then a senator, then moved with him to the executive branch. Clinton's expansion of the vice president's role in foreign affairs and intelligence gave Fuerth the broadest impact yet for someone in his position: he attended not only all meetings of the NSC's Deputies Committee but also most of the Principals Committee sessions, alongside the secretary of state, the defense secretary, and Clinton's own national security advisor. "As a consequence," Gore says, "he learned, and he remembered, a *lot*. He served me very well."

Fuerth's privileges extended not only to the VPS but also to the president's book. "What was shown to the vice president would be shown to me also," he says. "There was never a time in the transition and the administration that I did not get the PDB." The book's content initially left him cold—he remembers thinking, when he first saw the book after the inauguration, *Is this all?*—and he still laments that the PDB focused so much on what he calls the "raw statement of fact, to the point where insight was missing." But over time he found it a relevant piece of the complete intelligence package—including the VPS, which he called "enriching," particularly on the environmental side. He would continue his daily interaction with the material and his various briefers until the last day of the administration.

Agency leaders saw Fuerth as an exceptional customer in his own right, someone who brought out the best in Agency analysis. George Tenet said he stood out as the Clinton administration's "most thoughtful, most engaged, most task-oriented" policy customer, while a senior DI manager called him "the most demanding and most sophisticated user of intelligence" he worked with during his thirty-five-year career. Gore certainly noticed. "Leon could efficiently direct my inquiries to the right places—because he knew the entire intelligence community. I was very fortunate in having him as my national security adviser."

The impact of the Vice President's Supplement went beyond Gore's and Fuerth's satisfaction to affect the PDB itself. Watson recalls that soon after the president asked to see the VPS, Clinton was acting on its content as much as he did on PDB articles. Inadvertently, this highly personalized production served as a test run for a major reform of the president's book. As Watson puts it, "This was the first penguin in the water, and it lived. The sea lions didn't kill it."

THE LACK OF REGULAR, direct access to the president had troubled DI leaders since the start of the administration. The sense of indifference they got from the Oval Office toward their flagship product, the President's Daily Brief—especially compared to the hearty reception for the Vice President's Supplement—sharpened the feeling. The feedback they *did* get on the book tended toward the negative, especially from readers such as Fuerth, who didn't shy away from offering critiques.

Late in Clinton's first term, analytic leaders decided to reengineer the PDB, hoping to motivate their workforce to put more effort into the book and, as a result, again excite its namesake customer.

"We had a realization that we were writing this book largely for ourselves," says Agency manager Michael Morell. He gives the example of a full-page, two-column PDB piece on China, the precise details of which remain classified even now. A full three-quarters of the text covered what the analysts thought was going on in Chinese politics.

Only at the bottom of the second column, in the final short paragraph, did the analysts include policy implications. Fuerth pushed back, saying, "You guys just don't get it. You think what's important is what's going on in China. It's not. What's important is what this means for the United States."

Indeed, DDI John Gannon observed that authors of PDB pieces lacked a consistent connection to the intelligence needs and wishes of the president. He and the briefers tended to receive more commentary about Clinton's book from readers at the *bottom* of the book's dissemination list than from those at the *top*. Many offices within the DI by this time treated senior directors on the National Security Council staff or assistant secretaries of state or defense as their primary customers. In an era of declining intelligence budgets, however, it would be hard to continue to defend offices of hundreds of analysts and managers dedicated to serving officials well down in departmental bureaucracies.

It all welled up for Gannon one night as he reviewed a particularly weak edition of the PDB for delivery the next day. He remembers that the lead piece that day covered a breaking development but said very little. "It was not what you would have expected from an agency with our resources," he says. "I had so many capable analysts in the directorate who excelled at what they did; I just couldn't believe that *this* is what we were sending to the president of the United States." Around the same time, he received a spur from national security advisor Tony Lake to make the PDB more relevant to the daily agenda in the Oval Office. Realizing that he required thinking beyond that likely to emerge from in-house, conference-room meetings, Gannon sent senior DI officer Mike Barry and a team of analysts off with a private contractor for months to explore options.

"We interviewed a lot of people about it, but we had a hell of a time trying to figure out what to do differently," Barry says. "We were told not to talk to the White House. Like all customers, if they had known what they wanted, they'd have told us. The basic question I asked the DI front office and office directors: 'Is the president our most important customer?' And there was not a consensus about the answer to that."

Gannon, who drove the change, thought that analysts *should* focus on the top. He approved the study group's proposal: a "First

Customer" campaign to encourage the Directorate of Intelligence to renew its efforts for the president. For the first time in the CIA's history, the leaders of all analytic offices gathered each morning to decide what items should go into the next day's PDB.

Gannon also created the President's Analytic Support Staff (PASS), which reported directly to him, and put Barry in charge, authorized to change the way the entire directorate thought about current intelligence. "For the first time," recalls Barry, "analysts wrote for the PDB and in the PDB style—no matter what they were writing. For thirty years, analysts had always written primarily for the NID, and before that the Current Intelligence Bulletin." The First Customer initiative "changed the mentality," says Morell, who became Barry's deputy in the new office. "It changed from 'What is going on in a particular situation overseas?' to 'What does the president need to know about this situation?' It was a critically important change in mind-set."

PASS also required analysts to fit each of their assessments, however complex, onto one sheet of paper. Barry cited a higher authority for the limit, relaying that national security advisor Lake had told him, "For the president, there is no such thing as a second page." Editors rigidly broke their text into rectangular paragraphs and bullets, based on a study Barry consulted about how different formats affected how readers moved their eyes across the page and retained information. "We usually had a 3-2 cadence in the PDB: three sentences in each paragraph, followed by two bullets. It could be 3-1, or 2-1, but there would always be some bullets." Standardizing the style that Clinton would see each day, Barry at one point even outlawed adverbs from the PDB, finding that analysts would then use the word "because" more often and, as a result, explain more clearly the reasons behind their judgments.

To get more *from* analysts, the powers that be knew they had to give more *to* analysts. As part of the deal, PDB briefers now returned to CIA headquarters every morning after meeting with their customers and provided more nuanced feedback to DI managers. Some senior officers, who had grown up in a culture that emphasized top-down information flow, resisted passing details to working-level analysts. Barry often brought analysts up to PASS directly when he or the briefers felt that they needed to convey something that hadn't reached analysts through normal feedback channels. "How are you going to get analysts to buy in," he asks, "if they are dealing with a black box?" Gannon, who wanted analysts to be more energized to contribute to the PDB process, by 1997 had streamlined the directorate's organization to better enable such efforts. "I wanted our expertise to be more reflected, more engaged, and more present in the book every day. And then I wanted the feedback from the consumers to be available on a continuing basis to the producers, the analysts themselves."

By that point, reduced funding and personnel cuts had taken their toll on morale at the Agency. By 1995, the CIA's analytic cadre had shrunk by 17 percent from what it had been in 1990. Over the same period, the office overseeing Soviet (later Russian) affairs had shrunk almost in half. To better motivate and incentivize analysts, Barry and his team ramped up the First Customer campaign, including pins and stickers for authors of certain PDB articles. The marketing effort struck many in the DI as a patronizing gimmick. One manager of analysts in the mid-1990s quickly became irritated that his analysts spent so much time crafting pieces aiming at a "mysterious presidential appetite" while direct feedback from Clinton himself remained limited. He says the whole effort struck him as "throwing darts while blindfolded, not knowing where the dartboard is." Even Morell, who helped run the office pushing this presidential focus, admits, "We were still missing the mark because we weren't in the Oval Office every day. If you are there, then you *know* what the president wants as well as what he needs."

Despite these concerns, the elevation of the PDB to a top priority across the DI slowly began to take hold. "It didn't change things overnight," Morell says. "It was a gradual thing as the directorate came around." Analysts put more effort into pieces explicitly for the PDB, editors and senior reviewers renewed their focus on consistency and quality, and briefers felt better about the product they showed each day. Corporate culture started rewarding analysts for their PDB production beyond stickers and pins, with bonuses and promotions. A few years later, the 9/11 Commission found that in this period during the 1990s, DI managers indeed started putting "particular value" on writing for the President's Daily Brief.

Of course, the First Customer initiative had a goal grander than enriching analysts' experience: serving Clinton's intelligence needs

One of the "First Customer" stickers used to incentivize CIA analysts to write for the PDB during the book's re-engineering for President Bill Clinton's second term. *Courtesy Mike Barry*

more effectively. If CIA leaders hoped to rekindle face-to-face contact with the president, they failed. He wavered for the rest of his second term between receiving occasional in-person PDB briefings and just reading the book. In fact, briefings became even less regular, and the CIA officer sent downtown every morning to brief at the White House settled for daily briefings with second-term national security advisor Sandy Berger. He also began stapling handwritten notes into Clinton's PDB with insights or observations that he *would* have brought up with the president directly if only he had been given the time to do so.

Clinton continued to appreciate the book, now with even greater interest. "I thought that the longer I stayed there, the PDB got better," he says. Berger has asserted that Clinton consumed more intelligence than any other president in history. A deputy national security advisor told one of the White House briefers at the time, "You guys are the only ones in government who throw something over the transom that the president picks up that doesn't go through anyone else. That's a very serious responsibility—and I know that you take it as such."

One of the Clinton-era Situation Room directors used an example to convince a visiting CIA officer that the president cared about his PDB. "You know," she said, "the president reads the book every day."

EBB AND FLOW – 211

"How do you know that?"

"Because he calls me directly and says, 'Where's my PDB?'"

Clinton chuckled at the Agency's salesmanship when someone from the CIA showed him one of the First Customer pins that analysts were earning for producing content for his book. The phrase nevertheless sank into Clinton's mind. While visiting CIA headquarters in September 1997 to celebrate the Agency's fiftieth birthday, he told assembled officers, "As your first customer, let me reiterate, I depend upon unique, accurate intelligence more than ever."

On his own fiftieth birthday in 1996, Clinton certainly found his PDB unique. He remembers to this day picking up that book and reading about how things he had just said and done had sparked crises around the globe. "They tried to convince me the world had gone to hell in a handbasket just in twenty-four hours—and it was all my fault! I was totally, completely blindsided. I don't remember how long I read it before I figured out they were pulling my leg." He also recalls a couple of April Fools' Day versions of the PDB—"I was primed for crazy things happening on April 1," he says—but the fake birthday PDB came as a total surprise.

Despite, or perhaps because of, the Agency's ability to occasionally supplement the serious drumbeat of the PDB with humor, Clinton found the book "incredibly valuable, steadily better over time." He says that even on an uneventful day, he still got from it 90 percent of what he needed to make good decisions across a range of issues: "I can't imagine any president not taking it seriously, not reading it carefully, and then using it as a learning tool and an information leader to follow up on things that you need more on."

CLINTON ALLOWED THE BOOK to be distributed more widely within the White House than any previous president had. CIA leaders, too, widened the circle of PDB readers around town—eventually to more than two dozen people, including deputies and other nontraditional principals.

Secretary of state Warren Christopher read the PDB so carefully that he spotted the only typo that Barry remembers getting through his gauntlet of editors and proofreaders. It was during a Saturday morning briefing at Christopher's house. He eagerly pointed out the error to his briefer: "I'm so proud of myself—I've finally found one!"

Christopher also reportedly ripped pages out of the book to ensure that his assistants would follow up on important issues. Strobe Talbott, who served as deputy secretary of state for most of the Clinton presidency, looked through the PDB daily as part of his morning routine but tended to rely more on products from the State Department's own intelligence office. "The PDB would sometimes trigger things I'd want more on," he says, "and that I'd get from INR."

When Madeleine Albright replaced Christopher in early 1997, she continued the daily briefing service. She recalls reading the PDB mostly to ensure that she knew what the CIA was telling Clinton that day. For her, the book was part of a deluge of information coming across her desk each morning, including the NID and an information packet from the INR, which proved overwhelming even for a foreign policy junkie like herself. She recalls feeling the need to take it all in but not having enough time to read every word of every product. And she engaged her briefer less fully then her predecessor had. "I used to get irritated that the CIA person stayed there in the room with me," she says, "because I thought she was watching me to see if I moved my lips when I read."

Briefers also made their way to the Pentagon to brief Clinton's three secretaries of defense (Les Aspin, William Perry, and William Cohen), their deputies, the chairmen of the Joint Chiefs of Staff (Colin Powell, John Shalikashvili, and Hugh Shelton), and, soon, also the vice chairmen. Deputy secretary John Hamre, whom briefers recall as one of the best listeners among their Pentagon customers, spent his car ride into the office each morning on the PDB because he wanted to know what his boss and counterparts would be worried about that day. He remembers PDB articles coming up "rather consistently" in meetings of the NSC Deputies Committee and playing a role in "every one" of the daily meetings that the secretary and deputy secretary of defense held with the chairman and vice chairman of the Joint Chiefs. But the document didn't impress him much: "Well over half the time, the material was in the *New York Times* or *Wall Street Journal*; the PDB editors had a tendency to chase the news. I came to realize that this highly classified document was classified not because of the news but because all of us at senior levels of government were reading it and thinking it was important. That made it classified." Another PDB principal during the Clinton era says, "I seldom got stuff in the

PDB that was not also captured in a lot of other documents that I received in the course of the morning. The same intelligence is passed around fourteen different ways."

Shelton, conversely, notes that the PDB went beyond other products by providing more specific information about intelligence sources. He recalls asking his briefer for clarifications on PDB items, sometimes for follow-up the same day. Even the Joint Chiefs' intelligence guru, the J2, started seeing the PDB every morning so that he wouldn't be surprised by something the chairman brought up with him later in the day.

Various White House senior staffers who also become regular briefing recipients appreciated the book's wide coverage. John Podesta says that he often had only five or ten minutes a day for intelligence when he became deputy chief of staff in January 1997 and then chief of staff in October 1998. "The PDB distilled down what you absolutely needed to know. We were getting all the raw junk on a daily basis. That can cause you to overreact to trivia and bad information. So the value of having it vetted was clear." One briefing session for an expanded-distribution customer in the West Wing ended up annoying the First Customer. While discussing that day's book in an office abutting the president's private study, the CIA briefer and a deputy chief of staff began telling jokes—each one more raucous than the last. Suddenly Clinton's personal secretary poked her head in. "The president wonders if you two could use your *inside* voices!"

Neither Woolsey nor Deutch, however, remembers a single call about the book from any member of this wider readership. "The PDB was irrelevant to my role as director," says Deutch. "A lot of stuff didn't make it into the PDB because it would have leaked."

Briefers' agility often obviated the need for follow-up memos from analysts. In one case, the White House chief of staff stopped his briefer when she said the Pakistani press reaction to a development in the Indian subcontinent was "vituperative."

"What was that word you used?"

"Vituperative."

"Well," he said, "my momma taught me that if I didn't understand a word somebody used, I should just stop them and learn that word. What does it mean?"

"Well, they're angry—hot, incensed."

The chief of staff stood up and grabbed a dictionary. Opening it as he returned to his seat, he quickly found the definition and nodded his satisfaction. To confirm his mastery of the word, he then proceeded to use it in three different sentences—all of them related to his wife.

GEORGE TENET WORKED ON the staff of the Senate Select Committee on Intelligence for three years before rising to become its staff director in 1988. After Bill Clinton entered the Oval Office in 1993, Tenet moved over to the executive branch, serving as the NSC staff's senior director for intelligence programs until taking over as the CIA's deputy director in July 1995. When Deutch stepped down in December 1996, Tenet served as acting director for an unusually long period, seven months, because Tony Lake, Clinton's first nominee to replace Deutch, withdrew before his congressional confirmation hearings. Finally, in June 1997, Tenet took over as director.

He kept the seat that Deutch had held in the cabinet, giving him regular contact with the president in large group settings. But Tenet says smaller sessions with Clinton remained infrequent, and he played no direct role in the irregular PDB briefings at the White House. Most mornings, in fact, he just went straight to his office at CIA headquarters and avoided the West Wing altogether. From there, he still kept an eye on the DI's effort—to "make sure the president was treated differently"—and listened each day to what the White House briefer reported back about the book's reception that morning.

Tenet didn't worry much that the president tended to read the PDB in place of actual briefings. "Clinton used to write lots of questions to us," he says. "We had an engaged consumer who took the time to ask questions. See him or don't see him . . . I think people make more of that than they should. That's a function of how the president likes to acquire data. It matters to the extent you can provide historical context on an issue—an operational backdrop as to how data was collected, and other things that are happening around an issue—but Sandy and Tony were quite engaged, so they got the texture they needed."

As a PDB customer himself, Tenet started slowly. One former senior officer in the Directorate of Intelligence remembers having a conversation with him during his tenure as deputy director.

In the course of telling Tenet about a subject his analysts had been following, the DI manager pointed out that the topic had appeared in a recent edition of the book. Tenet looked back and said, "You're right—I should pay more attention to the PDB."

As director, Tenet found his interest growing. Early each morning on his ride into the office, his briefer showed him the PDB and other material that ranged from press clippings to highly sensitive raw intelligence reports, all pulled together from skimming through the overnight feed and talking to authors of PDB pieces in the early morning hours. To direct Tenet to key points, the briefer scribbled arrows on the director's copy or wrote short notes on the side of the PDB's page. "He was always a reader," says Rodney Faraon, Tenet's longest-serving briefer during the Clinton administration, "so I would time my interjections to where he was on the paper." On a good day, Faraon had answers ready for Tenet's typical questions—such as the identities of cooperative foreign intelligence services whose information made it into the book's articles.

His best insights on what to bring up with the director came when the DI's experts would visit the Agency's seventh floor early in the morning to "pre-brief" the briefers. For example, after NATO accidentally bombed the Chinese embassy in Belgrade in May 1999, due to a CIA database's incorrect address for a nearby Yugoslavian military facility, US and Chinese negotiators eventually settled on a multimillion-dollar compensation figure. The next day, an analyst working the issue came in early to tell the briefers interesting factoids about the agreed-upon amount.

Later that morning in the car, Tenet read through the related piece and asked, "What do you think about that number?"

"Well, for one thing," Faraon said, "in Cantonese numerology, it can mean 'easy money.'"

The director stopped, put down the book, and thought about it. Looking up at his briefer, he said, "Now *that's* interesting."

Not all briefings went so well. One PDB article about the disorder in the Balkans so bewildered Tenet that he vented about it as they drove to the headquarters building, saying, "This piece doesn't make any sense." He put it down, stared off into space for a minute, and picked it up again. Shaking his head, he vigorously repeated himself: "This *doesn't make any sense!*"

CIA director George Tenet looks over his PDB with one of his daily briefers, Rodney Faraon. *Courtesy Rodney Faraon*

Faraon walked through the logic and evidence in the article, pushing back a bit harder than usual to defend the officers who had written it.

Kilauea became Mount St. Helens. "Do you know how bad this is? I'll *tell* you how bad it is!" Tenet snatched his briefer's pen and scribbled profanities across the page just as the car pulled into the CIA headquarters building's underground garage. Ripping the piece right out of the book, he muttered something about shoving it in the face of DDI Winston Wiley as soon as he ran into him upstairs. Tenet threw the rest of the bound pages back at Faraon, who raced upstairs to warn Wiley.

"So, how did it go?" asked the DDI when they met in the hallway.

"Pretty well overall. But there was one piece here the director didn't like. I mean, he *really* didn't like it. He didn't want me to tell you—he said he's going to tell you himself."

Wiley grabbed the mangled PDB. "Which piece is it?"

"Well . . . it's not actually *in* the book anymore. He ripped it out."

Sure enough, Wiley found only a jagged edge where the article used to be. On the page *under* where it once sat, however, a string of curses jumped off the page—etched through onto the next piece by Tenet's anger-driven scrawl.

"Yup," Wiley said as he moved slowly down the hall toward his inevitable verbal beating from the director. "This *is* bad."

"On many days the book is very good," Tenet reflects, "but on some days, it's just not—there isn't as much value for the president as we would hope."

CIA ANALYSTS HAD BEEN informing policy makers for decades about international terrorism. Back in 1968, for example, a request from deputy secretary of defense Paul Nitze prompted a Special National Intelligence Estimate on terrorism and internal security in Israel and Jordan. Palestinian terrorists' attacks at the Munich Olympics in September 1972 led President Nixon to create a Cabinet Committee on Terrorism—giving the Agency an audience for additional products, including a weekly terrorism situation report starting in November 1972.

But the 1990s brought a new dynamic. During the Clinton administration, the al Qaida network of Sunni Islamic extremists combined lessons learned from fighting Soviet troops in Afghanistan during the 1980s with financing from Usama Bin Ladin, a wealthy scion of a Saudi family that had made it big in the construction industry. Various intelligence products, including the President's Daily Brief, highlighted the growing threat from al Qaida.

A prominent example came on Friday, December 4, 1998, when the following article—the only PDB piece yet declassified from the entire decade—appeared in Clinton's book:

SUBJECT: BIN LADIN PREPARING TO HIJACK
US AIRCRAFT AND OTHER ATTACKS
Reporting [text redacted] suggests Bin Ladin and his allies are preparing for attacks in the US, including an aircraft hijacking to obtain the release of Shaykh 'Umar 'Abd al-Rahman, Ramzi Yousef, and Muhammad Sadiq 'Awda. One source quoted a senior member of the Gama'at al-Islamiyya (IG) saying that, as of late October, the IG had completed planning for an operation in the US on behalf of Bin Ladin, but that the operation was on hold. A senior Bin Ladin operative from Saudi Arabia was to visit IG counterparts in the US soon thereafter to discuss options—perhaps including an aircraft hijacking.

IG leader Islambuli in late September was planning to hijack a US airliner during the "next couple of weeks" to free 'Abd al-Rahman and the other prisoners, according to what may be a different source.

The same source late last month said that Bin Ladin might implement plans to hijack US aircraft before the beginning of Ramadan on 20 December and that two members of the operational team had evaded security checks during a recent trial run at an unidentified New York airport. [text redacted]

Some members of the Bin Ladin network have received hijack training, according to various sources, but no group directly tied to Bin Ladin's al-Qa'ida organization has ever carried out an aircraft hijacking. Bin Ladin could be weighing other types of operations against US aircraft.

According to [text redacted] the IG in October obtained SA-7 missiles and intended to move them from Yemen into Saudi Arabia to shoot down an Egyptian plane or, if unsuccessful, a US military or civilian aircraft.

A [text redacted] in October told us that unspecified "extremist elements" in Yemen had acquired SA-7s. [text redacted]

[Text redacted] indicate the Bin Ladin organization or its allies are moving closer to implementing anti-US attacks at unspecified locations, but we do not know whether they are related to attacks on aircraft. A Bin Ladin associate in Sudan late last month told a colleague in Kandahar that he had shipped a group of containers to Afghanistan. Bin Ladin associates also talked about the movement of containers to Afghanistan before the East Africa bombings.

In other [text redacted] Bin Ladin associates last month discussed picking up a package in Malaysia. One told his colleague in Malaysia that "they" were in the "ninth month [of pregnancy]."

An alleged Bin Ladin supporter in Yemen late last month remarked to his mother that he planned to work in "commerce" from abroad and said his impending "marriage," which would take place soon, would be a "surprise." "Commerce" and "marriage" often are codewords for terrorist attacks. [text redacted].

The piece failed to stand out much to either Clinton or Gore, despite its dire tone. When asked the following year about threats to US aviation, Clinton said, "I am not aware of any specific threats against American airlines or airplanes flying out of American airports with large numbers of American passengers. If there have been any such, I don't know about them . . . and as you know, I work on my intelligence information every day." Gore wrote years later that the only major terrorism warnings he remembered reading about during the Clinton administration concerned the Summer Olympic Games in Atlanta in 1996 and the so-called millennium threats centered around the 1999–2000 rollover. A few years later, the 9/11 Commission would conclude that if a wider group of officials had read this PDB item from December 1998, "it might have brought much more attention to the need for permanent changes in domestic airport and airline security procedures."

The fact that the president and vice president didn't remember the "Bin Ladin Preparing to Hijack US Aircraft" article says little about whether they read the book carefully every day or took its contents seriously. Instead, it points to the perishable nature of information and analysis in the PDB, a document superseded by a new edition every twenty-four hours. If one conservatively assumes just six pieces of analysis in the book each day, that means the president and vice president saw some fifteen thousand separate pieces in the PDB alone during their eight years in office. Perhaps that is why Tenet found himself supplementing terrorism analysis in the PDB, VPS, National Intelligence Estimates, and other products with personal letters to the president and his top national security aides laying out his concerns about the terrorist threat to the United States—warnings that Tenet would continue to highlight during the next administration.

PRESIDENT CLINTON SET DOWN the PDB article he had just read.

"From what I am reading here," he said to national security advisor Sandy Berger and Bruce Riedel, the NSC staff's senior South Asia expert, "it appears to me that we know more about both Pakistan's and India's nuclear capacities, intentions, and doctrines of operation than they know about each other."

They replied, in unison, "Yes."

Clinton paused. "Well," he said, "*that* ought to scare the world!"

It was July 4, 1999. The president was preparing to meet with Pakistani prime minister Nawaz Sharif in Washington as the Indian subcontinent teetered on the verge of the world's first nuclear war. The conflict between Pakistan and India had festered for decades; surprise Indian nuclear tests in May 1998 (followed by Pakistani tests within a month) had shown the world that the rivals could unleash unparalleled destruction on each other. By the spring of 1999, Pakistani troops had advanced beyond the Line of Control that divided the disputed Kashmir region. Indian soldiers fought back, and soon Sharif found himself in a tight bind. He could cave to the growing international pressure to withdraw his country's forces, which would bring a backlash, and possibly a coup attempt, from his own powerful military. Or he could continue to support his military's presence in generally recognized Indian territory, in violation of decades-old norms—which would virtually guarantee a wider, potentially calamitous conflict with India.

For several weeks, Sharif had desperately sought a middle ground. He appealed to the United States, Pakistan's traditional superpower patron, for a face-saving way out before the Indian counterattack overwhelmed his troops. Clinton's position remained clear: Pakistani forces had to move back behind the Line of Control before he would help in any way.

Without any guarantee of relief, Sharif came to Washington and eventually found himself sitting down with only Clinton and Riedel (as note taker) at Blair House on July 4. Clinton recalls: "He knew he had messed up by crossing the Line of Control and violating the de facto understanding that had kept a major war from blowing up since 1971." The president had already read his daily intelligence and consulted Berger and Riedel on its content. "I was concerned, in part because of the things I'd read in the PDB. I thought India and Pakistan had less than perfect knowledge about each others' nuclear doctrine and intentions."

Clinton confronted Sharif with his apprehensions. With Sharif's aides out of earshot, Clinton asked if the prime minister knew that his own military was preparing nuclear missiles for action, bringing the dispute closer to a nuclear war. "Sharif seemed taken aback,"

Riedel says, "and said only that India was probably doing the same." The president told Sharif about the Cuban missile crisis, emphasizing how close the superpowers had come to nuclear conflict. He asked if the prime minister realized what would happen if even one bomb went off. An increasingly agitated Sharif acknowledged that it would be a "catastrophe," but he also pushed back, saying he feared for his life if he returned to Pakistan without a way to save face. Clinton stood firm and eventually persuaded him to pull Pakistani troops back. In return, Clinton pledged to encourage India to restart a bilateral dialogue with Pakistan.

This hardline approach helped prevent a nuclear war, but it sealed Sharif's fate. Three months later, the Pakistani military arrested the prime minister and took control of the country. Clinton credits his daily intelligence report for helping him win the day: "I felt particularly well served by the PDB."

AFTER THE MOST CLOSELY contested presidential election in US history in November 2000, a final decision about the President's Daily Brief faced the Clinton team. For decades, tradition had dictated that the current administration would offer the PDB to the president-elect right after election day to prepare him, during the short transition, for the myriad foreign policy threats and opportunities he would inherit come January. Only one thing stopped Clinton from opening up the book right after the election: who had won?

Vice President Gore continued to receive the PDB each morning—no change there. But Texas governor George W. Bush, who appeared to have won the popular vote in Florida and, thus, the Electoral College—stayed out of the loop. Jami Miscik, the DI's number two, stood by the phone day after day, waiting for a call from the White House allowing her to join the analytic and logistics team that the Agency had pre-positioned in Austin in case Bush came out ahead. "While the election results were open," says Podesta, who was chief of staff, "it didn't seem appropriate."

As the days without a formal resolution to the election crisis stretched to weeks, pressure mounted to do *something*, even before the Supreme Court rendered a judgment on the election recount. "No one anticipated how long that would take, so we changed gears," Podesta says. "We decided that the clock was ticking too much; we needed to get him into the system." Clinton authorized the CIA to start giving Bush the same intelligence that the president received each day—the first time in history a presidential candidate started receiving the book *before* being universally acknowledged as the winner.

Miscik heard the news, but not via the call from the West Wing that she had been expecting. "I was standing in my office on the seventh floor with the TV on in the background," she recalls. "All of a sudden I see John Podesta on NBC's *Today* saying President Clinton had offered the intelligence briefings to Governor Bush." She recalls thinking, *They've promised? But I'm still here!* Within hours, she was flying to Texas.

CHAPTER TEN

"THE GOOD STUFF"

GEORGE H. W. BUSH looked Andy Card straight in the eye and said, "Make sure he reads the PDB every day."

It was the week before the November 2000 election, and the former president was speaking to Card about one of his sons, Texas governor and presidential candidate George W. Bush. Card, who had served as Bush 41's deputy chief of staff and secretary of transportation, remembers that the "phenomenally candid and embarrassingly caring" advice from the elder Bush and his wife, Barbara, in that meeting gave him his first hint that their son would appoint him chief of staff if he won the election.

"The President's Daily Brief was literally in the first conversation with the President that I had about his son," Card says. "He told me to make sure he reads it every day, but it went beyond that. He said, 'There's more value in having a briefer there to talk about it than he will recognize before he takes office.' He knew he should get the benefit of not just the document but also the people that would be there to help decipher it."

Although the younger Bush had yet to see the PDB at the time of the conversation, he had received an extensive CIA briefing earlier in the campaign. Back in September, he hosted deputy director John McLaughlin and several other Agency officers for a four-hour session in his living room in Crawford, focusing on China, Russia, North Korea, Iraq, Iran, the Israel-Palestinian conflict, Serbia and

Kosovo, and Latin America. The deputy chief of the CIA's Counterterrorist Center (CTC), renamed the Counterterrorism Center after 9/11, demonstrated terrorists' ability to deploy chemical, biological, or nuclear weapons with a briefcase, like the one that Japan's Aum Shinrikyo cult had used in their sarin gas attack on Tokyo's subway system in March 1995. Bush listened intently, then promptly instructed the officer to get the prop out of the room.

McLaughlin called Bush the most interactive customer he'd dealt with in his thirty-year career. "I remember thinking that whoever would be briefing this President had better be ready for a ride," he says. Indeed, Bush ushered in what some Agency officials have termed the PDB's "golden age," featuring an active and engaged president who not only wanted an in-person intelligence briefing every working day but also started bringing his briefer with him wherever he traveled—including domestic trips such as the one he would take on September 11, 2001.

To PREPARE FOR THE possibility of briefing a new president-elect outside of the Washington area, a program manager back at CIA headquarters in early 2000 had begun developing powerful web-based tools and an iPad-like system that allowed nearly instantaneous recall of intelligence databases and analytic products. His bosses put pressure on him to get these new systems right, telling him that for the incoming commander in chief, "the briefing cannot fail." By election day, a midlevel analyst, a graphic designer, a communications officer, and an information technology expert had set up shop near the governor's mansion in Austin, with the same connectivity they had back at their desks in Langley. Intelligence officers practiced receiving the PDB electronically instead of by fax, as in previous transitions.

The Directorate of Intelligence's top three officials—DDI Winston Wiley and his two deputies, Jami Miscik and Marty Petersen—in November established a weekly rotation for the transition if the Republican candidate won. One would stay at headquarters to run the directorate. The second would travel to Austin to handle the president-elect's daily briefing. The third would work in Washington, briefing Vice President–elect Dick Cheney while assisting at headquarters. Once President Clinton authorized them to give Bush a copy of the PDB, officials quickly settled on a plan for its delivery: the senior

DI officer on duty in Austin would head to the governor's mansion six days a week around 7:30 a.m., wait for Card to escort him or her upstairs, and brief the president-elect at 8:00 for forty-five minutes to an hour. Either Condoleezza Rice or Steve Hadley—the Bush's campaign's top foreign policy aides, both of whom would serve as national security advisor during his two terms—would usually join them.

Despite the long preparation, Bush's first PDB briefing on December 5 almost didn't happen. As the CIA support officers in Austin started printing that day's book a few hours before Wiley's trip to the mansion, the ceiling collapsed. Water poured through, almost drowning their massive high-end printer and sensitive communications equipment. But the team overcame the disruption, and Wiley departed on time for his meeting with the governor. He waited in the mansion's kitchen until 8:00 a.m., when the Secret Service directed him upstairs.

Wiley's memories of the transition extend beyond Bush's keen interest in the book. "I'd give Governor Bush a PDB to hold, and I had a notebook. He was to my right, and I'd drop things on the floor as I flipped through. But Barney kept getting in my briefcase!" This would not be the last time the president's frisky Scottish terrier tested the patience of Bush's CIA briefers.

The PDBs during those Texas briefings covered a wide range of international issues. Wiley, Miscik, and Petersen supplemented Bush's PDB with a background book, provided to both candidates in the still-undecided election, full of insights into the political and personal histories of foreign leaders as well as Agency analysts' speculations about what issues those leaders would raise during congratulatory calls to the eventual winner. Bush's questions about this intelligence material went back to the support team officers in Austin, who researched and answered what they could but often referred issues requiring deeper analytic input back to Langley. The Austin support team struggled less with responding to the governor's taskings than with processing the overwhelming volume of material coming in from CIA headquarters for the briefers to consider showing to Bush. This included a heavy flow of extremely sensitive, hard-copy-only human intelligence reports that kept the classified fax machine humming constantly.

As the Florida recount debacle dragged on into early December, Petersen found himself on duty in Austin. Interruptions to the briefings from sensitive political calls came early and often. "Would you like me to leave the room?" Petersen asked the first time. "No," the governor replied, "I can trust you guys."

Bush explains: "I had great respect for the CIA in large part because of my father's admiration and respect for the CIA. Therefore, when I got elected president, my inclinations towards the CIA were very positive." He would even lean on his briefers for assistance above and beyond typical briefing-related duties. In the middle of one briefing, Petersen recalls, the cat crawled into the Christmas tree. Bush jumped up and called Petersen over to help; the two of them rustled the cat out of the tree before completing their discussion of that day's intelligence.

Finally, on December 12, the Supreme Court upheld Bush's vote count win over Gore in Florida, confirming his victory in the Electoral College and thus his election as president. The next day, Petersen made his way to the governor's mansion and was one of the first to greet Bush with a new term of address: "Good morning, Mr. President-elect." Bush's briefings continued in Texas until he shifted his base of operations to Washington during the two weeks before his inauguration. Wiley found himself pleased with Bush's reaction to the Agency's Austin-based effort: "We went over an hour sometimes," he says. "I knew there was a motorcade waiting, and he would put off the motorcade in order to continue the briefing." Still, Wiley recognized that the biggest challenge remained.

"There was no question we would be in the Oval Office on day one," he says. "I wanted to be in there on day ninety. Our entire mind-set was around that."

NEAR THE END OF the transition, a casual remark from Bush threatened it all.

The DI front office triumvirate had just selected Michael Morell, an analyst and manager with twenty years of Agency experience under his belt, to take over as Bush's briefer, putting trust in his analytic acumen, briefing skills, and sound judgment. On Thursday, January 3, Wiley introduced Morell to the president-elect at the governor's mansion, saying, "Michael is one of our stars and he's going to be here for you." After briefing Bush on most of the PDB, Wiley let Morell lead Bush through one piece about China. That went well, so

Morell handled the next day's entire session for the president while Wiley observed.

At the end of that Friday briefing, Wiley jumped in to tell the president about the changes the DI planned to make to the book after inauguration. "We will make the articles one column only, to give you more white space on the page for notes. We will get rid of *this*," Wiley said, pointing to the spiral binding at the top of Clinton's PDB, "so that we can put items in at the last minute for you."

"Winston, that's all very nice," the president-elect said. "But I don't care about the format. I don't care if you bind it at the top or on the side, if you use staples to hold it together or if you use spit. The one thing I care about is the *content*." He then shook Wiley's hand and complimented the personalized service he had received during the previous few weeks: "It's been a pleasure—you've served me very well. I'm sure that when I become president, you'll start giving me the good stuff."

Oh, shit, Wiley thought. *We've already been giving him the good stuff!*

"I've obviously thought a lot about that phrase," says Wiley, who recalls Bush saying it without irony or harshness. "I think he wanted more spy stories. I had consciously not talked to him specifically about sources. I'd tell him it was a human source close to the king, and so on—but he seemed to be looking for what he'd heard from his father." The DI's leaders quickly concluded that "the good stuff" would thus be the material beyond the core analysis in the President's Daily Brief. "Not the articles themselves," Wiley says, "but the details about sources, substantive depth from the briefer, and the perspective that the director himself can bring." Without altering analytic conclusions, Agency leaders were adjusting the *style* of the presentation for the new occupant of the Oval Office—as they had done regularly since creating John Kennedy's President's Intelligence Checklist forty years earlier.

To get late-arriving raw intelligence reports and other material into the package up to the minute of delivery, they took the PDB's production a step *backward*, in a move they called "breaking the back of the book." The decades of a professionally bound PDB were over. The changes to the physical book, though, only served as a tool to make the entire briefing more source-specific and more interactive. "The conceptual breakthrough for me was that it was an event, not a document," recalls Wiley.

For the idea to work, the DI would need unprecedented input from the Directorate of Operations, the intelligence-collection side of the Agency. "Saying 'a generally reliable source' wasn't going to work in the Oval Office," Petersen says. "We didn't have to give the name, but we needed a lot more granularity about where this was coming from." Wiley went immediately to deputy director for operations Jim Pavitt, who was the right man at the right time.

"I was long an advocate of using sensitive intelligence," says Pavitt. "If you went through the process of spotting, assessing, developing, and recruiting a spy to steal the secret—and you didn't do that if you could get that secret some other way—for whom were you doing it? What were you going to do with that piece of information?" He recalls colleagues of his from the operational side of the CIA occasionally saying, "This is too sensitive to disseminate." Knowing that Bush had trimmed the PDB readership back, Pavitt insisted that they give such information to the briefer to use with the president. "We are *not* going to see this compromised by those who are reading this document," he told the naysayers.

Wiley and Pavitt quickly worked out that the briefing team for the Oval Office customers could get the actual source information. George Tenet, whom Bush would keep on as CIA director, backed this up with a note to the Agency workforce: "I know that we are off to a strong start with President Bush," he wrote. But he added that officers would need to "step up the quality of our support."

To start his term, the president saw Morell and Tenet, usually in the Oval Office, six days a week for thirty to forty-five minutes starting around 8:00 a.m. Morell would go on to serve as the president's sole briefer—only relieved by Wiley, Miscik, or Petersen for occasional days off—throughout Bush's historic first year in office. At first, Morell worried that the PDB's text fell short of the new First Customer's high expectations. "When I started," he says, "the book's quality was poor, it was weak. It took a while for the high bar of the president, and how important this was, to seep down through the organization; direct, daily feedback from the president helped." Morell would usually start each briefing by "teeing up" the first article in the President's Daily Brief, highlighting its provenance or reminding the president about the last article he'd seen on the subject.

Michael Morell, the CIA's PDB briefer to start President George W. Bush's first term, holds the leather binder presented each morning to Bush. *Central Intelligence Agency website photo*

Cheney, Rice, and Card sat in on a regular basis. "The presence of these people made my job even more challenging," Morell notes, "because they were—as they should have been—intensely focused on what I was presenting to their boss." After reading each piece, Bush routinely asked questions of Morell or these others in the room, looking for the story between the lines or his advisors' thoughts about the policy implications of the analysis he'd just read. Tenet jumped in to pull back the curtain on various facets of intelligence collection or add "color commentary" from his experience. With one eye on the clock, Morell would look for a chance to turn to the next piece, repeating the process for all six to eight short analytic articles and additional items.

DURING HIS SECOND WEEK in office, Bush surprised Morell at the end of a briefing in the Oval Office. "I'm going to fly down to Mexico on Friday and come back late in the day," he said. "I want you to come with me."

Morell, thinking that the Agency had never done this before and unsure how it would be done, quickly answered, "Sir, I think that's a long way to go just for a thirty-minute briefing."

He walked out of the room with Tenet, who was shaking his head. "Michael," he said, "I can't believe you just blew off the president of the United States!"

Morell has replayed that tape many times in his head; he understood that he did not handle the question well. In fact, he subsequently joined the president for all of Bush's travel, in the United States or abroad, during the next year. Bush thus took it up a notch from what Gerald Ford and his father had done with *their* CIA briefers. "The president wanted it," recalls Card, "but quite frankly, I recommended it. I found it to be more valuable, particularly on international trips." Whether the briefing occurred on Air Force One, in a hotel, or at a US embassy overseas didn't matter—it was still the PDB. "The setting was different," Bush says, "but the content was thorough in all cases."

During most of Bush's day trips for political events, Morell felt like a fifth wheel. If the stop was scheduled to last only a few hours, he remained on Air Force One instead of tagging along with the president and his party. Morell passed the time by watching movies and catching up on reading, but he also endured some awkward moments. For one, he had to play nice with numerous local dignitaries allowed to walk through the presidential aircraft. Even worse, Morell found himself dealing with Barney. During his first month briefing the president, Morell called Petersen from Air Force One, parked on a runway. Petersen strained to hear him over what sounded like growling and barking in the background. And it was: Barney had picked a fight with a much bigger dog, leaving Morell in the middle trying to make peace.

Briefings during such domestic trips, especially visits to the president's ranch in Crawford, Texas, were more relaxed than the White House sessions. Moving outside the Washington bubble offered at least a healthy chance for more briefing time, letting Morell dig a bit deeper on a few topics. In this way, they paralleled the Saturday PDB briefings, which Bush often held at Camp David. The rustic setting in rural Maryland allowed the president to sit back with Morell (and also, usually, Tenet) after the main PDB session and chat about intelligence and world affairs, sometimes for two full hours.

Whether in the Oval Office or at Camp David, at the president's ranch in Crawford or somewhere overseas, the briefings' interactive nature continued. "I learned best through the Socratic Method," Bush remembers. "I loved to question the briefers. I'd of course read the PDB, but I learned more by trying to get beneath the words, by understanding through the briefer the nuance of some of the information that I had been given." Morell notes: "The president was a guy who raised the bar, constantly. You'd push up the threshold, and he'd push it higher with his questions."

This, in turn, gave analysts back at headquarters more consistent and more specific feedback about the First Customer's reactions to their PDB articles than they had received from any other president across four decades. Morell even began meeting with authors of upcoming pieces in the book *before* they finished writing them. "I challenged analysts to be able to compellingly finish the simple sentence: 'Mr. President, this piece is important because—' If you can't fill in that answer, you don't have a piece. If you can answer it, you do— then you structure the piece to make that point clear, and quickly."

In 2002, Morell left the briefing job, which demanded too much from just one person for so long. Tenet notes that most daily intelligence briefers should move on after a year or so in order to stay sane and, occasionally, to save their marriages. The Agency started a two-briefer system for the president to split the burden. Morell's time as the president's sole briefer laid a solid foundation for eight years of personal, face-to-face intelligence support to the president. "All my PDB briefers were excellent," Bush reflects. "What really impressed me about the briefers was their in-depth knowledge of a variety of subjects. I tried to learn more by understanding through the briefer the nuance of some of the information that I had been given. To a person, they were fully briefed themselves and obviously had spent a lot of time on every subject within the PDB."

Wiley's concern about losing access to the Oval Office within ninety days faded away. "I think the combination of what we did and George's ability to manage the personal relationship meant that we ultimately sailed through that period," he says. "We didn't time out on that."

AS PRESIDENT-ELECT, BUSH HAD been shocked to see that the Clinton administration's PDB dissemination list included dozens of officials. He quickly narrowed the distribution of his book to just six people. Bush initially restricted the PDB readership outside the White House to only the secretaries of state and defense, even scratching the chairman of the Joint Chiefs of Staff off the list before reconsidering.

At the top of the dissemination list sat a man who had wide-ranging experience with intelligence. Vice President Dick Cheney had served as the White House chief of staff, the secretary of defense, and a member of the House Intelligence Committee. His first PDB briefing as part of the Bush 43 administration came on December 5, the same day as Bush's initial PDB session. For the rest of the transition, he received the book from Wiley, Miscik, or Petersen during his short car ride to the transition office, giving the DI's leaders little time for extended discussions with him but a healthy appreciation for his keen interest in the nation's top intelligence product.

The senior DI manager selected as Cheney's first full-time briefer followed his bosses' lead on his first day, handing Cheney the book and sitting silently while he read it. He remembers thinking the whole time, *I'm not sure he's getting the best value out of this.* So he took a chance the next day and started teeing up the pieces, inserting comments about the background behind each item or additional related stories. "It was a calculated risk," he recalls, "and I couldn't tell for a few days if he liked it or not. But he didn't say 'Shut up,' so I kept doing it." From that point on, he gave Cheney at least an oral summary of each PDB article, sometimes mentioning that the piece covered raw intelligence traffic that he had already shown to the VP a day or two earlier. The first few times he suggested that Cheney didn't need to read a piece, the vice president still scanned the piece before flipping the page over. "In fairness to him," the assigned briefer says, "he didn't trust me yet. After a few weeks, though, he came to rely on that."

One day, armed with a thin book and nothing particularly dramatic developing in the world, the briefer struggled as their car got stuck in traffic, nearly doubling the usual thirty-minute drive from Cheney's house in McLean to the White House. The briefer went through all of the PDB, then all of the extra material. The car stayed trapped, so he stretched his oral comments out as long as possible. "That's all we have for you today," he finally admitted. Cheney calmly looked over, cocked his head slightly, and said, "Either there's not much going on in the world or you guys don't know what's going on out there."

From that point on, the vice president had plenty of extra material available in his two-part book. First came the PDB itself, containing the same material that the president would be seeing that morning. "I asked a lot of questions," Cheney remembers. "From a time standpoint, we needed some mechanism where I could get those answers without burdening the president. I wanted to see what he was getting, the product that was going to him." Then came what Cheney and his briefers starting calling "behind-the-tab" intelligence. "The briefers would put material there that had been generated because of the questions I'd ask, or because I'd expressed an interest in a particular subject," says Cheney. "They'd pull something out they thought was useful, whether finished intelligence or raw reports. That was at least double the size of my daily brief." He asked plenty of questions about PDB articles and behind-the-tab products, often tying their content to material he'd seen months or even years earlier. "His memory was phenomenal," the briefer says. "Several times he would say something like, 'When I was secretary of defense, you did a paper on this topic in Russia, back in the summer of 1992.' And every time he said that, sure enough, they went back—and the paper was what and when he said it was. It was scary."

As renovations to the vice presidential residence on the grounds of the US Naval Observatory in Washington wrapped up about a month after inauguration, Cheney's PDB sessions more often than not took place in the mansion's library. They soon settled into a regular forty-minute window, six days a week, often joined by I. Lewis "Scooter" Libby, Cheney's chief of staff and top national security aide. On days with much to discuss, the briefer would hop in the limo with the vice president after the briefing and use the ten-minute ride to the White House to finish up.

Adding in his time with the president each day during Bush's PDB briefing, Cheney some days ended up spending more than an hour and a half on intelligence. As he coolly explains: "I was vice president now, which meant I didn't have as much to do. And the president had asked me specifically to focus on national security and intelligence. It's one of the reasons he'd asked me to be his running mate." Cheney's fascination with intelligence also drove an innovation echoing Michael Morell's travel with the president, as the vice president, too, began taking his PDB briefer on the road.

CIA leaders ensured that briefers carried a copy of the PDB to each customer *before* Bush's briefing, keeping them from being blindsided by his potential calls about items in the book. "When the president asks them what they are doing about this," Miscik says, "they have an answer and they are not hearing it for the first time on the spot. I totally understand it if you're in their position."

Neither Colin Powell at State nor Donald Rumsfeld at Defense was new to the PDB. Powell had seen it for years as President Reagan's deputy national security advisor and then his national security advisor, and again while spanning both the Bush 41 and Clinton administrations as chairman of the Joint Chiefs of Staff. Rumsfeld's experience with the book went back to the 1970s, when he was Gerald Ford's chief of staff and secretary of defense. He proved far more interactive with the document this second time around at the Pentagon, mostly due to George W. Bush's keen interest in his PDB. "It's helpful," Rumsfeld says, "because when he asks you something about it, you will not be unaware of it—you will know what he saw. It's probably helpful to have the senior policy makers and the vice president see the same material the president sees."

These key customers only rarely reached out to senior Agency officers with comments or complaints about the PDB. And when they did, the fact that it was the president's book kept their feedback in its proper perspective. "It's like publishing a newspaper every day," Tenet says. "There are things that are not perfect about every part of what you're doing. I think sometimes what is lost on the recipients is the care, the diligence, the hard work—the hundreds of people who are involved in the process and the editing. They are seeing thousands of pieces a year. They have a right to comment, but not to tell us what to say. If you get five negative phone calls, that's a pretty good track record."

A TERRORISM-FOCUSED PDB ARTICLE from Bush's first year as president, just one and a quarter pages long, stands out more than any other in his eight years in office. In fact, because of al Qaida's attacks on America the following month—and the resulting scrutiny that prompted its unprecedented declassification and public release—the August 6, 2001, piece titled "Bin Ladin Determined to Strike in US" is the most famous item in the entire history of the President's Daily Brief.

During the summer of 2001, George Tenet was telling everyone who would listen that "the system was blinking red." Analysts in the CIA's CTC, mostly Agency officers but including representatives from the wider intelligence community, had been warning in intelligence publications throughout the year that the al Qaida terrorist network seemed primed for a major attack, with titles like "Bin Ladin Threats Are Real." From January 20 to September 10, more than forty pieces in the PDB alone related to Bin Ladin. In response to such analysis, the president several times asked Morell in their daily PDB sessions about the prospects for an attack in the United States itself.

Memories differ on the actual genesis of the August 6 article. Bush wrote in his memoirs that he requested the item: "I had asked the CIA to reexamine al Qaeda's capabilities to attack inside the United States." Condoleezza Rice similarly testified that the article came "in response to questions of the president—and that since he asked that this be done, it was not a particular threat report." Tenet, however, implies that Morell wanted the piece to fill a perceived presidential need for analysis about a potential attack in the United States, not necessarily to answer a specific tasking from Bush: "Mike asked our analysts to prepare a piece that would try to address that question." Morell recalls it similarly.

The now-retired CTC officer who took the lead on the article recalls little clarity on the issue of the memo's actual origins. "When it was first presented to me," she says, "my manager came over, and he implied the White House was asking for it. Maybe the managers decided to do it. Maybe Michael decided he needed it; he really took a firm hand on things." Sources later told the *New York Times* that CIA officials had developed the August 6 article in order to get officials at the White House to pay more attention to the sustained high threat. Richard Ben-Veniste, a member of the 9/11 Commission, wrote that CTC supervisors did not mention to analysts a specific presidential request for this particular PDB piece. Instead, he says, they were eager to put a piece into the book that would prompt Bush to consider the United States as a potential target for the major attack attempt they were anticipating.

Whatever its spark, the article conveys al Qaida's steady historical interest in attacking the United States. The title and lead sentence clearly present the Saudi terrorist financier's intent: "Bin Ladin Determined to Strike in the US: Clandestine, foreign government, and media reports indicate Bin Ladin since 1997 has wanted to conduct terrorist attacks in the US." To support this conclusion, the text that immediately follows relates three different data points from 1997 and 1998, when Bin Ladin talked about hitting the United States on its own turf. And then, as if anticipating a follow-up question on why al Qaida hadn't attacked the homeland already, the article states that the thwarted millennium plotting in 1999 "may have been part of Bin Ladin's first serious attempt to implement a terrorist strike in the US."

Did the absence of such an attempt since the millennium plots mean that Bin Ladin had given up? No, the text said, because al Qaida's 1998 bombings of US embassies in East Africa showed that "he prepares operations years in advance and is not deterred by set-backs." There is even a reference to a "more sensational," uncorroborated report that Bin Ladin wanted to hijack a US aircraft—but, the report said, to secure the release of extremists in US prisons, not to use as a flying bomb.

Up to that point, the piece presented a concise but cogent argument for al Qaida's *intent* to attack within the United States. But what about the other half of any threat calculation: its *capability* for such a strike? Here the piece falls short. The only data points presented were as vague as they were brief: (1) al Qaida members, including some US citizens, for years had lived in or traveled to the United States; (2) FBI information described recent surveillance of federal buildings in New York and other "patterns of suspicious activity"; and (3) the FBI had seventy Bin Ladin–related full-field investigations throughout the country, including one looking into a call-in to the US embassy in Abu Dhabi, United Arab Emirates, that claimed Bin Ladin supporters planned to use explosives in the United States. A strong case was made for Bin Ladin historically wanting to hurt Americans within their own borders, but the analytic case for his actual ability to do so got less attention.

The fault lies, in large part, with the pre-9/11 process for getting FBI information to the PDB, a function of the CIA's tight control of the book. Without any FBI al Qaida experts sitting in the CTC (just Bureau representatives who served a liaison function more than a substantive analytic one), the main author of the piece simply called a contact of hers at the Bureau to ask for input. After adding the line about seventy FBI full-field investigations, she read the piece aloud over a secure telephone line to the Bureau officer, who said the text was fine, but she didn't send it back over after editors had reworked it. Perhaps if FBI analysts had seen the article—or if more people at the Bureau had been involved—the report would have included other relevant information about al Qaida activity in the United States, such as Special Agent Ken Williams's July 10 memo from the Phoenix field office raising concerns about al Qaida flight trainees or even the FBI's 1995 memo addressing a plot by al Qaida affiliates to fly a plane into CIA headquarters. As it turns out, the senior FBI manager with the most experience watching al Qaida in the United States, Thomas Pickard, didn't see the PDB article at all. In fact, he didn't see *any* PDB until after September 11.

The FBI information in the PDB article did not carry through to the version in the Senior Executive Intelligence Brief (SEIB)—the direct descendant of the Central Intelligence Bulletin and National Intelligence Daily—which went to the second tier of national security officials the next day. The SEIB article retained its PDB cousin's title and early paragraphs but dropped its references to hijackings, the apparent surveillance of buildings in New York, the threat phoned in to the embassy in Abu Dhabi, and the FBI's ongoing Bin Ladin–related investigations. Deputy director John McLaughlin told the 9/11 Commission that concerns about protecting ongoing investigations, the fact that the Bureau information had come to the CTC only orally, and the absence of established ground rules for nontraditional content in the SEIB led the Agency's editors to omit the FBI information that had been in the PDB version.

The lead author of the piece gives her editors credit for cutting extraneous text from her original PDB draft and improving her original title, which she recalls as something like "Attacks in US a Goal for al Qaida." But she regrets not hitting the main point harder. "I've thought a lot about how the article reads. It would have been better to say, 'All these threats we have seen all summer could be in the United States.'"

MORELL WENT TO BED early on the night of September 10, as he had done most nights during his tour as the president's briefer. One difference on this Monday evening: instead of settling into his own bed, he found himself trying to fall asleep in a hotel room along Florida's Gulf Coast, listening to the waves roll in, so he could wake up in a few hours to prepare his 8:00 a.m. delivery of the President's Daily

Brief. His travels with the First Customer had brought him to southwest Florida, where the president and his entourage had overnighted ahead of an event to promote Bush's education agenda at a school in Sarasota.

The work for the next morning's session had begun well before he laid down his head that night. He briefed the president, as usual, on Monday morning, telling him about the assassination on September 9 of Ahmad Masood, the central military and political figure in Afghanistan's anti-Taliban Northern Alliance. He informed senior officials at Agency headquarters how the session had gone before boarding Air Force One to travel with the president to a stop in Jacksonville.

After the plane had taken off again for Sarasota, Morell touched base with White House Situation Room director Deborah Loewer, a US Navy captain who was the national security advisor's top-ranking representative on the trip. (Although her duties back at the White House didn't include sitting in on the regular morning PDB sessions, on this trip Loewer served as the replacement for Rice or Hadley, one of whom almost always *did* attend, so that she could relate the substance and tenor of that morning's briefing back to the White House.) Morell arranged to meet her at 7:30 a.m. on Tuesday, a full half hour before his scheduled briefing time, to compare the information that he planned to highlight in the PDB with what she intended to show from Situation Room and NSC materials.

Loewer had graduated at the top of her Surface Warfare Officer Basic Course, commanded two different ships, completed a doctorate in international law, and served as a military assistant to the secretary of defense in the late 1990s. Morell was not about to underestimate her. He had gotten to know her over the Fourth of July holiday, when they both supported Bush at the family compound in Kennebunkport, Maine.

Morell didn't rise with his alarm at 3:30 a.m. on September 11, as he had planned, because he was already up. The anticipation of looking over fresh intelligence reports, reviewing that morning's PDB, and preparing for the president's likely questions often woke him early. He was going to get the PDB that day from CIA headquarters via the White House Communications Agency (WHCA) control room at the Colony Beach and Tennis Resort in Longboat Key—where, just upstairs, the president was still sleeping. This morning had an unusual delay: WHCA didn't get him the book until after 4:30 a.m., leaving him less than three hours to master its content and select supplementary material for the president from the many documents that officers at CIA headquarters had sent for Morell to consider.

He met Loewer at 7:30 for their pre-brief discussion, where they showed each other their intended topics. Just before 8:00, they made their way up to the hallway outside Bush's suite, waiting only a few minutes there before Card opened the door, greeted the pair, and invited them in. The president had just sat down to a table full of breakfast foods and coffee after taking a morning run, showering, and getting dressed. He got down to business quickly, as usual.

Loewer went first. Her material came from the Situation Room's morning report, and she had called the national security advisor to ensure that she would relate to the president exactly the points Rice wanted him to know. Bush started eating a bowl of Raisin Bran as she updated him on the Middle East peace process for a couple of minutes. Her news prompted him to ask to speak with Rice directly. When Loewer stepped over to the secure phone to set up the call, Morell started walking the president through the PDB itself. The material that day focused on Russia, China, and the Palestinian uprising in the Israeli-occupied West Bank and Gaza Strip, a compilation that Morell describes as "uneventful." Less than ten minutes later, Morell had wrapped up, and Bush turned back to Loewer to begin his call with Rice.

"When I hung up the phone for the president," Loewer recalls, "Michael and I looked at each other and realized it was close to 8:30, almost the time when the motorcade was to leave for the school. We hurried out of there, hauling butt to get to the cars, because when the Secret Service grabs the president and takes him to his vehicle, he and the motorcade are *gone*. We didn't want to be left behind." Sure enough, by 8:35, the motorcade was speeding away from the resort, with Loewer in the NSC vehicle. Morell jumped into the staff minivan, where he engaged in light banter with presidential advisors Ari Fleischer, Karl Rove, and Dan Bartlett and Bush's omnipresent photographer.

As Bush and his entourage raced to Emma E. Booker Elementary School in central Sarasota, the senior duty officer (SDO) in the

White House Situation Room called Loewer to inform her a plane had just crashed into the World Trade Center. Around the same time, Fleischer's cell phone rang in the minivan, with a call alerting him to the incident. It prompted him to ask Morell what he knew. Having nothing, the briefer told Fleischer that he'd look into it and started a call of his own to the CIA's Operations Center.

The motorcade arrived at the school at about 8:55, and Loewer took action. "I ran up to the president's car, thinking I was going to brief Andy Card, but then I notice it's the president standing there in front of me. I'm five feet, and Secretary Card is maybe five foot eight, but the president is around six feet—a full foot taller than me!"

She looked up and kept it simple: "Mr. President, the Situation Room is reporting that one of the World Trade Center towers has been hit by a plane," adding only that her experience had taught her first reports were often wrong.

"Thank you, Captain," the president replied as he started toward the school door. "Keep me informed."

She walked briskly to the staff and communications control room, adjacent to the second-grade classroom where Bush would soon sit with a group of children for their reading lesson. Loewer spoke on the phone again with the Situation Room, putting her hand over the phone briefly to request that someone get a television into the school's control room.

Next door, Bush received a brief introduction from the principal and then shook hands with some of the awed students—who were "quiet and just struck by the sight of the President," according to Sandra Kay Daniels, in whose classroom the events took place. He got started by reading from *The Pet Goat*, a book in the class's reading series.

Morell finished up his call to CIA headquarters while entering the school. The officer in the Operations Center had just told him for the first time that the aircraft in question was, in fact, a large commercial jet. *This isn't an accident*, Morell thought as he settled against a wall in the control room, still clutching his briefcase with the PDB. Looking at the TV that Loewer had ordered brought in, he watched the searing live shot of United Airlines Flight 175 hitting the World Trade Center's South Tower. Loewer, looking at the same TV while continuing to talk to her SDO back in the White House, also saw it. Simultaneously, she heard shouts of "Holy shit!" in both ears, coming from the folks in the control room as well as from the Situation Room personnel through her phone.

Protocol dictated that the president's staff should avoid distracting his on-camera activities except for emergencies. Loewer had no doubt this justified an interruption. She just hoped she could slip into the classroom without drawing too much attention from the assembled media. "I had to get past the Secret Service agent, who was guarding the door to the classroom, to get to Andy Card—who, thank God, was sitting stage left." To convey the seriousness of the situation without causing a scene, she whispered a simple message in Card's ear: "A second aircraft has impacted the World Trade Center. The nation is under attack."

"He believed me," she says. "He saw it in my face." Immediately, yet projecting calm, Card walked up to the president, who remained engaged in the student lesson. Daniels, the teacher, noticed Card's motion, which clashed with the instructions to remain still that she and the other school staff had been given. Bush recalls sensing a presence behind him, followed quickly by Card's voice echoing the words he'd just heard from Loewer: "A second plane hit the second tower. America is under attack."

The chief of staff remembers being grateful that the president stayed seated to collect his thoughts. "There's not a doubt in my mind he was reflecting on his responsibilities," Card said. "I was pleased he did nothing to introduce fear to those kids. He did nothing to demonstrate fear to the media, which would have been translated to the satisfaction of terrorists all around the world." Years later, kids who had been in the classroom that day agreed. One says, "I was just 7. I'm just glad he didn't get up and leave, because then I would have been more scared and confused."

After a few minutes, Bush excused himself and headed to the control room, where the assembled White House staff and Morell continued to watch the events in New York City. The president, for the first time, saw the iconic images of the Twin Towers aflame. Loewer proceeded to tell him the limited information they had at that point. After a pregnant pause all around, she asked, "With whom would you like to speak first?" As the president walked to the table with the secure phone, she suggested the vice president. Bush agreed, and the staff put the call through to Cheney, who was already in the White

House bunker. The president found himself sitting uncomfortably in an elementary school chair with only Loewer, Card, Fleischer, and Bartlett around him. Morell and everyone else stayed well back in the room, both to give the president space and to keep their eyes on the screen. Loewer called Rice on her cell phone, which she handed to Bush as he wrapped up with Cheney.

Bush finished the calls, worked on a statement, and returned to the classroom just before 9:30 to speak to the American people. Then the presidential motorcade sped away to get him to Air Force One for a hasty takeoff. Morell stayed with the entourage, facing bomb-sniffing dogs and an inspection of his PDB-laden briefcase before he could get back on the plane. To keep all communication lines open for the president, Loewer gave an order to the communicators on Air Force One comm deck that no one was to make a call off the air-craft without her permission. She learned later that while her order ensured that the president had complete control of the communi-cation lines, it delayed Morell's efforts to call CIA headquarters for updates. Upon learning of his need, she escorted Morell personally to the comm deck and directed the communicators to connect him with whomever he needed to reach at the CIA.

President Bush at Emma E. Booker Elementary School in Sarasota, Florida, on September 11, 2001; Situation Room director Deborah Loewer stands directly behind him, while CIA briefer Michael Morell appears on the left holding his briefcase containing that day's PDB. *White House photo*

Morell was on hand to the president throughout the day as Air Force One flew across the country. First, between Sarasota and Barksdale Air Force Base in Louisiana, Bush asked him about an unconfirmed, and later disavowed, claim that the Democratic Front for the Liberation of Palestine (DFLP) had conducted the attacks. Morell said it was unlikely. Second, between Barksdale and Offut Air Force Base in Nebraska, Bush asked Morell about the most likely culprit. Morell replied that he had no doubt that the attack came from Usama Bin Ladin and al Qaida, but he emphasized that this assessment reflected his personal views, not new intelligence reports. Third, between Offut and Andrews Air Force Base outside Washington, Morell gave the president a six-page fax from Langley, with everything the Agency had at that point—including a French intelligence service's information about "sleeper cells" preparing for a second wave of attacks in the United States. Throughout, Morell's work aboard the president's plane went above and beyond the typical duties of a PDB briefer. As Card says, he "played a big role on 9/11 helping the president as he was making his way back to Washington."

Morell's biggest frustration that day came when he failed to prevent a presidential surprise during an NSC video teleconference at Offut Air Force Base. CIA director Tenet told Bush over the video link that three of the hijackers had ties to al Qaida—information that Tenet's acting executive assistant had *not* told Morell when they spoke by phone just minutes earlier. "The president turned to me and glared," Morell says. Without uttering a word, the president's message was clear: *Why didn't I hear this from you?*

DEFENSE SECRETARY DONALD RUMSFELD had emerged as one of the most interactive and inquisitive customers anyone in the DI could remember. "I had at least half an hour every morning, including Saturdays at his house," says Denny Watson, his first PDB briefer. "He'd read it, challenge it, talk about it, push it, prod it. But once he fought with it, he *owned* it." She remembers hearing some of the precise analytic language in the PDB popping out of his mouth in some of his news conferences days or even weeks later. Rumsfeld, realizing quickly that CIA analysts' answers to his queries ended up in the PDB package, began asking his briefer about topics that he wanted put before the president and other NSC principals.

On Tuesday, September 11, Watson woke in the middle of the night, as usual, to drive to CIA headquarters and prepare for the daily briefing. A few hours later, when the sun finally came up, she went downstairs to meet her driver. The trip to the Pentagon was uneventful. Watson got out at the River Entrance, closest to the secretary's office, leaving her driver to find a place to park as she entered the building. Walking through the metal detector before being allowed up to the fifth floor, she noticed something odd: people staring at a nearby television, which showed the World Trade Center's North Tower smoking after the impact of an airplane.

She arrived in the anteroom of the secretary's office just in time to see the second plane's impact in real time. Instantly she called the Agency's Operations Center. "What do you know—something that you can tell me on an open line, that's not out there in the media right now?" They could only say that there were fifty planes aloft still unaccounted for, with frantic calls being made to each of the pilots. She declined to even open her briefcase to pull out the PDB, figuring it had been overtaken by events.

Rumsfeld didn't wait long before calling Watson in. He had just arrived at his office after meeting nine House Armed Services Committee members for breakfast, at the end of which his senior military assistant had informed him about the first plane's crash in New York City.

"Sir, you just need to cancel this," Watson said as she entered his office. "You've got more important things to do."

"No, no. We're going to do this."

So she proceeded to sit down and tell the secretary—who had not yet seen the second plane's impact—what she had learned from the Operations Center. He nodded and started flipping through the PDB. Within minutes, two of his aides entered and advised him to cancel his appointments for the rest of the day. Watson recalls his reply: "No! If I cancel my day, the terrorists have won." The aides didn't give up, pulling out a copy of the day's agenda and taking him through every item to point out why each one could be canceled. Only then did Rumsfeld turn to the television on his desk and see with his own eyes the video of what had happened just minutes earlier.

The aides left just long enough for him to skim the rest of that day's book. Then the whirring of a blue-and-white helicopter outside the Pentagon stopped him short. "That damn helicopter was hovering

Secretary of defense Donald Rumsfeld with CIA officer Denny Watson, who briefed the book to both Rumsfeld and Vice President Al Gore. *Courtesy Denny Watson*

so close to the window," Watson recalls, "that I could see what one of the men in it looked like: dark hair, a beard and a mustache, and reflector sunglasses. He was *right there*." Rumsfeld and his briefer found themselves commenting on how easy it would have been for the pilot to turn and crash into his office.

As it pulled away, the building suddenly shook. Thinking it was the helicopter, Rumsfeld pressed his nose to his glass window and looked around. Still sitting, Watson said, "Sir, everything in my training says you need to be back, away from those windows."

In fact, American Airlines Flight 77 had crashed into the *other* side of the Pentagon with enough force to rock the entire structure. Within seconds, the secretary's security detail barged in and took him out of his office. He made his way to the crash site to see what happened and briefly treat survivors before returning to the National Military Command Center in the Pentagon's basement to communicate with other national leaders. Despite the unprecedented attack on the US military's headquarters, Rumsfeld would keep the Pentagon open. "Everything went on, even though the building was smoking and they were still pulling body parts out. I just said, 'We're *not* going to shut it down.'"

Watson quickly gathered the PDB and the other briefing materials on her own way out the door. Out of the corner of her eye, she saw Rumsfeld's personal secretary, who had recently moved to the area from Chicago, standing alone with a blank look on her face.

"Come with me," Watson said. "We'll figure it out later!"

The two women ran downstairs toward the River Entrance and Watson scanned the scene for her driver, who had been waiting quietly when the plane's impact—from across the massive building—bounced his car off the ground. Black smoke rose from the building and people ran by him to get away, but he stayed put, knowing his briefer relied on him. Within minutes, Watson jumped into the car and they got moving.

"I had with me the most classified document in the US government, which says 'For the President's Eyes Only,'" she says. "I simply *had* to go back and get it into the office." So the driver left Rumsfeld's secretary at the CIA's Visitor Control Center while Watson tried to get into the compound. "The buildings were being evacuated," she recalls. "I had to argue my way back in." Once upstairs, she threw her briefcase in the office and, to her colleagues still working, shouted a quick, "Get the hell out of here!" Watson drove home, hosting Rumsfeld's secretary for much of the day until area roads opened up so she could get to her own house. Finally back home to stay, Watson collapsed into a restless sleep after the worst briefing day she could remember.

ANALYSTS IN THE CTC who had been writing pieces for the PDB about Bin Ladin and his network sensed as soon as the second plane hit that al Qaida operatives were responsible. Unlike most workers in the Washington area that day, including the vast majority of employees at CIA headquarters itself, CTC officers stayed at their desks to deal with the calamity that they had anticipated. "Everyone just swung into crisis-handling mode," says senior counterterrorism analyst Cindy Storer. In the days that followed, as some of her colleagues who were experts on al Qaida handled overwhelming daytime writing and briefing duties, she came in each night to update PDB articles that had been drafted during the day with late-breaking information and to give the PDB briefers background information on al Qaida early each morning that might prove useful during the forthcoming sessions.

CTC analysts recall an insatiable appetite for al Qaida information in the PDB after the attacks—leading many officers to work around the clock, using their desktops as pillows for brief naps. One senior analyst says the work got harder not only because of the hundreds of taskings but also due to immediate changes in the number of eyes put on outgoing PDB articles. "Everything had to be coordinated with everyone," she notes. "Somebody at every agency would have to look at it."

The workload and its associated stress took a toll. Officers broke down in the hallways, cried during exhausted drives home in the middle of the night, and slept fitfully. "We didn't stop the plot," Storer says. "No matter how much you tell yourself that it's not your fault, that you did everything you possibly could have done, and other people tell you the same thing, you still have this guilt for not having been able to stop it." Not only that; the experts also thought that new attacks loomed, and they could not escape the fact that CIA headquarters itself made an attractive target. "Everybody in the Counterterrorism Center was issued a little plastic whistle/flashlight combination," Storer remembers. "This particular whistle was so loud—it was the most unbelievably loud thing I'd ever heard. The theory was you could be heard if you were buried under a bunch of rubble; somebody would come and save you if you were stuck under there."

Agency leaders recognized the burden. Within a few weeks, Tenet and CTC director Cofer Black delivered a pep talk to the center's officers. Black, after acknowledging the unprecedented workload, cautioned his troops to raise not only their operational and analytic efforts but also each other's spirits. He borrowed a line from the 1989 film *Bill and Ted's Excellent Adventure*: "Be excellent to each other." Tenet, telling the gathered workers about his friend and neighbor who died in the Pentagon attacks, started to choke up and felt his head throb. He reached over to a table for some aspirin, but his hands were shaking so badly that an officer had to come up and help him get the lid off the bottle. "There wasn't a dry eye in the room," Storer recalls. Then, without any wallowing in their emotions, everyone got back to work: Tenet to follow up on that morning's briefing with the president, many of the CTC officers to prepare material for the next day's PDB.

THE ATTACKS ON SEPTEMBER 11 spurred the most dramatic reforms to the national security and intelligence establishment since 1947. Most of the modifications—such as the creation of new entities like the United States Northern Command, the Department of Homeland Security, the National Counterterrorism Center, and the Office of the Director of National Intelligence—took months, even years, to come about. Changes in the daily President's Daily Brief session, however, occurred virtually overnight at Bush's command.

The president expanded his daily briefings the week of 9/11, sometimes doubling the time he spent on intelligence issues to start each day, to cover both traditional international issues and the increasingly complex terrorism information. He had always received raw reports from clandestine sources as part of his PDB package. After 9/11, though, Morell and Tenet brought to the briefing even *more* raw intelligence, with street-level information about al Qaida members and plots, updates on the CIA's efforts to take down terrorists before they could act, and details about the CIA's cooperation with friendly intelligence services worldwide in the hunt for al Qaida members and finances. Additionally, terrorism-related PDB articles started incorporating FBI information more regularly. Morell says he briefed the president on these varying sources in the same way, to try to make it seamless for the chief executive. "We were a nation that had been attacked," Bush says, "and the raw intelligence was a constant reminder that the most important job of the President was to protect the country."

On Friday, September 14, FBI director Robert Mueller got a taste of Bush's singular focus on preventing another al Qaida attack. Early in the morning, Andrew Card called him to say Bush wanted him and attorney general John Ashcroft to come up Pennsylvania Avenue to brief the president after his daily PDB session. Mueller brought a counterterrorism briefer along with him, but the director started the session himself by describing what had happened on 9/11 and the Bureau's investigation into the hijackers. The president didn't let him get far.

"Bob," Bush said, "I expect the FBI to determine who was responsible for the attacks and to help bring them to justice. That is what the Bureau has been doing since its beginning. What I want to know from you—today—is what the FBI is doing to prevent the *next* attack."

Card remembers Mueller looking over to Ashcroft, who glanced back at the Bureau's briefer, who in turn looked at his boss. The FBI director finally spoke. "Mr. President, we'll have to get back to you on that one."

Mueller admits to feeling like a "chastened schoolboy who had turned in the wrong homework assignment." As everybody filed by the Oval Office's grandfather clock to get out of the meeting, Card heard Mueller say to the FBI briefer, "As soon as we get back to the Bureau, we are changing the mission of the FBI." And he did, immediately shifting some two thousand agents from criminal programs into terrorism-related work and expanding Joint Terrorism Task Forces around the nation in order to focus the FBI on thwarting terrorist attacks before they happened.

From that point forward, Ashcroft and Mueller—joined in October by White House homeland security advisor Tom Ridge, soon to become the nation's first Secretary of Homeland Security—met with the president and Tenet in the Oval Office every working day for a US-focused session right as the PDB briefing ended. Fully briefed by CIA officers earlier each morning on relevant PDB material, this new "homeland" audience used the additional daily meeting to discuss intelligence reporting on terrorist threats as well as investigatory leads on the 9/11 attacks. This expansion of the PDB's distribution, echoing that of several administrations, eventually brought the book's recipient list back up to twenty officials.

THE NEW MATERIAL AND wider customer set intersected with a new document called the Threat Matrix, often more than twenty pages long. This spreadsheet, delivered to the president every morning before the PDB briefing, listed every terrorist plot discovered by any means during the previous twenty-four hours as well as prominent ongoing plots and various US government agencies' actions taken against each threat. Mueller told the Senate Committee on Governmental Affairs in June 2002 that the Threat Matrix was the "joint product of the two agencies and seven days a week, we exchange briefing material, all to ensure we are working off a common knowledge base."

Tenet says that although they got better over time at refining the items shown to the president, Agency officers tended to brief too much rather than too little. It is easy in retrospect to forget the pervasive expectation in late 2001 and 2002 of additional strikes in the homeland. "You never knew which attack was going to be the one that panned out," says Miscik, who became DDI in May 2002. "People had been following these hijackers, but we didn't know *that* was the attack that was going to pan out. So how could it be that somewhere in the intelligence take there would be the sign of the next terrorist attack— and you, as president, were going to say, 'I didn't want to see that'?"

One former senior counterterrorism manager at the CIA expresses the view of many that Bush nevertheless lingered too long on the Threat Matrix: "You knew 95 percent of it included things that are not going to happen, but he wanted to read it every day. What was not clear to me was *why*. Was it the daily reminder of the threat? Okay, then it served a worthy purpose. Was it, instead, him thinking, 'What should I do about this?' If so, it should not be taking up his time."

Presidential briefer Michael Morell hated the Threat Matrix. "It was a real challenge," he says. Because Bush received it every morning before the briefing, Morell often would walk in the door and hear, before anything else, "Michael, tell me about number five," or "Whatcha got on number thirty-three?" To ensure he could offer Bush some kind of insight, he drafted a Directorate of Operations officer to help him prepare each morning for inevitable questions about Matrix items by pulling all of the reports and accompanying operational cables. That way, he would have *something* to tell the president, even if only "We think this is unreliable" or "The clandestine sourcing on this one is solid." He tried to add similar value to threats coming from intercepted communications, via enhanced early morning cooperation with NSA.

Some days the daily intelligence briefing seemed particularly threatening. Barely a month after the al Qaida attacks, as letters tainted with anthrax targeted prominent Americans, Cheney flew to New York City to address the annual Al Smith charity dinner. "As our plane landed at LaGuardia," he recalls, "we got a call from the White House saying that one of the detectors indicated there had been a botulinum toxin hit." A few hours later in a Ritz-Carlton hotel room in China, the president joined Rice, Card, Powell, and Morell for his PDB briefing inside a large blue tent, which WHCA had installed to prevent any covert listening devices from picking up their highly classified discussions. Cheney, wearing white tie and tails for his ritzy event, hooked up to the briefing via secure video and told Bush and those joining him in the tent that most of them had probably been exposed to deadly botulinum toxin. Although tests soon confirmed they were all safe, the episode starkly reminded everyone of the twin dangers inherent in briefing the Threat Matrix. The event made it feel as though even out-landish threats could come to fruition—justifying leaders' continued attention to the document. But focusing so much senior-level time on every plot risks losing sight of the forest for the trees.

The stressful times around the expanded PDB briefings and the Threat Matrix solidified the relationship between Tenet and Mueller. Their close communication both led and reflected their historically rival organizations' attempts to build bridges. "One of the things I worked hard at: I never wanted Bob Mueller surprised," Tenet recalls. "So we would do our best the night before to let Bob know what we were going to write. One, he was a friend. Two, he was a good guy. Three, he had a hard job. You don't want to just roll one in and have the director of the FBI not know what we are writing. It doesn't make for a good working session with the president to see a principal sur-prised and not know what we're talking about."

CHAPTER ELEVEN

UNDER INVESTIGATION

CONGRESS, WITH BUSH'S AGREEMENT, in November 2002 established the National Commission on Terrorist Attacks upon the United States. What became known simply as the 9/11 Commission carried a wide mandate to "make a full and complete accounting of the circumstances surrounding the attacks, and the extent of the United States' preparedness for, and immediate response to, the attacks," as well as provide recommendations for preventing future terrorist acts. Bush turned to former New Jersey governor (and former Drew University president) Thomas Kean as chairman, supported by former US representative from Indiana Lee Hamilton as vice-chairman and nine other commissioners.

The commission's staff soon began a massive document review and a wide-ranging slate of interviews. One of the biggest anticipated obstacles was executive privilege, the separation-of-powers-based principle by which presidents withhold certain information from the judicial and legislative branches. Bush had already invoked the doctrine in December 2001, denying documents to congressional committees investigating, among other things, Bill Clinton's fund-raising tactics. Although a creation of Congress, too, the 9/11 Commission nonetheless managed to get White House consent to view National Security Council staff emails and many other closely guarded internal executive branch files.

A more resolute roadblock awaited their unprecedented request to see copies of the President's Daily Brief. To discover what finished intelligence for the president had said about al Qaida's plotting for homeland attacks, the commissioners felt obliged to examine these highly sensitive publications, especially after CBS News had reported in May 2002 on the "Bin Ladin Determined to Strike in US" PDB article from August 2001. This revelation prompted Vice President Cheney to go on the Sunday talk shows and defend the sanctity of the book. "That Presidential Daily Brief is developed from some of our most secret operations and it has to be treated that way," he told Tim Russert on NBC's *Meet the Press*. "It's never been provided to Congress before, to my knowledge." On *Fox News Sunday*, he responded to Tony Snow's question about turning over the PDBs: "My strong feeling is that we should not. Because it comes from the most sensitive sources and methods that we have as a government. It's the family jewels, from that perspective."

The commission requested PDB articles only from January 1, 1998, through September 20, 2001, that addressed Usama Bin Ladin, al Qaida, homeland terrorist threats, the possible weaponization of aircraft, or terrorism-related issues in Afghanistan and five other countries. The White House, however, refused to show them on both legal and policy grounds. John Bellinger, then serving jointly as the legal advisor to the National Security Council and as an associate counsel to the president, says, "When the PDB request came in, the initial response from [White House counsel] Judge [Alberto] Gonzales was as a legal matter: 'No. These are privileged documents. These enjoy executive privilege.' Executive branch officials refer to executive privilege all the time, but these had actually been seen by the president." That wasn't all. The national security advisor, Condoleezza Rice, was adamant as well. "We made this decision with the PDBs essentially sight unseen, to protect the PDB process in general," says Bellinger. "It had nothing to do with protecting any particular PDB."

Cheney described to *Fox News Sunday* the likely detrimental effects of publicizing PDBs: "If we're going to take the PDB that goes to the President and now it's going to be made available to Congress . . . [and] end up in the press, it will have a chilling effect on the people who prepare the PDB. They'll spend more time worried about how the report's going to look on the front page of the *Washington Post* or on Fox News than they will making their best judgment and taking risk and giving us the best advice they can, in terms of what they think's going on." Reflecting on this years later, he expressed a related concern: "You can quickly get to the point where a president, or people around the president, will say, 'Are you sure you want to ask that question, Mr. President?' That worries me. It can do serious damage."

White House officials thus rejected commissioners' access to PDBs from both the Bush administration and the Clinton era. The president's advisors felt they had strong precedent. They had, for example, already denied PDB access to an earlier congressional joint inquiry into the 9/11 attacks. And in the more than thirty years of the PDB's history, no chief executive had seen his own book's content exposed while he held office. Kean and Hamilton understood this logic and recognized that the Bush White House was guarding more Clinton-era PDBs than its own—but they still wanted to appraise the quality of the highest level of intelligence analysis getting to the Oval Office.

The commissioners developed a three-pronged strategy to break the anticipated logjam. First, they took a stepping-stone approach, requesting progressively more sensitive documents to establish momentum. For example, the commissioners asked the CIA for, and received, *every* article related to al Qaida, Bin Ladin, and other requested subjects that had appeared in the SEIB—the daily publication that went to the tier of senior national security officials just below the PDB readership—between January 1998 and September 20, 2001.

Second, they appealed to the court of public opinion, raising concerns about ultimate perceptions of the commission's credibility if it lacked access to the PDBs and allowing pressure from the 9/11 victims' families to grow. "In the minds of the families, the press, and some commissioners," Kean and Hamilton note, "the PDB issue became a litmus test: anything less than direct access to the PDBs would seriously diminish the public's confidence in our report, because people could say, 'Well, you didn't look at the PDBs.' Our commission could be doubted as the Warren Commission was doubted."

Third, because legislation granted the commission subpoena rights, the commissioners held out the possibility of going to court to force the executive branch to show the PDBs. In fact, suspecting that the CIA's physical and bureaucratic distance from the Oval Office would improve their chances of success if they eventually sued for access, the commissioners filed their first request for the PDBs via the CIA instead of through the Office of the President.

Officials in the White House worked with CIA leaders and lawyers to address the commission's appeal for the PDBs. They first proposed a compromise briefing in the New Executive Office Building to cover the PDBs deemed responsive to the commission's request. Although the commissioners were skeptical that this would meet their needs, they decided to see what the administration was willing to show. On October 16, 2003, a team of White House and NSC lawyers walked them and a few of the commission's senior staff through a PowerPoint presentation summarizing the history and process of the President's Daily Brief and showing how many PDBs had mentioned each of the areas that the commission had inquired about. And then it was over, without a word on what was actually *in* the relevant PDB pieces.

"I remember the discussion afterwards, when there was a unified chorus coming up saying this briefing was an outrage because it was so unresponsive," Hamilton says. "We reacted quite strenuously to it." The commissioners prepared for an unprecedented lawsuit, whereby a congressionally mandated commission would sue the executive branch for access to the most tightly controlled document in the world.

BUSH ANNOUNCED IN HIS State of the Union address on January 28, 2003, that he'd ordered the leaders of the FBI, the CIA, the Defense Department, and the brand-new Department of Homeland Security to develop the Terrorist Threat Integration Center. The TTIC, as the center was soon known, began operations on May 1 to "merge and analyze all threat information in a single location." Serving as a clearinghouse for information from all foreign *and* domestic intelligence sources, the TTIC was intended to bring together data points such as those that could have better anticipated the 9/11 attacks—without the bureaucratic obstacles that had stymied previous attempts at coordination. To help the new center accomplish its goal, the president had ordered the FBI to give TTIC officers unfettered access to Bureau systems. As the TTIC's first director, John Brennan, put it, "Anything that's committed to an electron in the FBI system or the CIA system, we have real-time access to it."

But where would its analysts come from? Brennan admitted a few months after the TTIC's creation that he had only a couple dozen of them doing intelligence analysis based on the full array of classified and unclassified sources. This skeleton crew, led by Brennan and a handful of analytic managers sent over from the CIA, began producing every day the President's Terrorism Threat Report, a short publication containing assessments of terrorist threats anywhere in the world for Bush and senior national security officials throughout the US government. By early 2004, detailees from the CIA, DIA, FBI, and, to a lesser extent, other elements of the intelligence community expanded the TTIC's cadre of analysts to several dozen, bolstering the workforce behind the PTTR (widely pronounced as "Putter").

The provision of terrorism analysis to the president via two separate daily publications, the President's Daily Brief and now the PTTR, spurred tensions among counterterrorism analysts. Although the PDB tended to carry more strategic, analytic pieces than the tactical new daily report did, conflicts arose quickly over who had pride of place in assessing terrorist activities and trends and how many analysts should go from the CTC to the new terrorism center. The CIA's officials argued for keeping most analysts in place, where they not only empowered the Agency's wide-ranging actions against al Qaida—a high priority for the Bush administration—but also improved the quality of articles reaching the president. The leaders of the Terrorist Threat Integration Center cited their mandate from Bush to create a central node for threat assessments as ammunition for its growing analytic unit to take the lead on terrorism analysis.

Voices of moderation and compromise strained to be heard. One former senior CIA official says he used to tell Agency analysts who complained about the TTIC's encroachment on the CTC's turf that they should take a step back and look at the bigger picture. After all, analysts at the Defense Intelligence Agency and the military commands looked at the same foreign military issues that CIA military analysts did, without daily screaming matches. He asked them, "Isn't the War on Terror important enough to have two analysts with the exact same account?" But as the TTIC grew, morphing in 2004 into the National Counterterrorism Center (NCTC), these battles only got worse.

OFFICIALS IN THE WHITE House had sought advice from the Office of Legal Counsel, the Justice Department office directly supporting the president and his advisors, about their chances of winning in court if they just said no to the 9/11 Commission's request for access to PDBs. Its legal response, Bellinger recalls, came back as a resounding "We don't know," leaving no one satisfied. The courts, it seemed, had traditionally tried to stay out of big executive privilege issues, emphasizing that the legislative and executive branches should negotiate these things themselves. "That's why we would come out with these compromises," Bellinger says, "At the very minimum, the courts would be expecting to be shown that there had been a process of accommodation."

The legal pressure to accommodate the commission's request paled in comparison to the public relations momentum pushing the administration to show the PDBs. The victims' families kept the issue alive, as did the commissioners themselves both in private meetings at the White House and via appeals to the public. Kean told the *New York Times* in late October 2003 that the commission stood ready to subpoena the PDBs unless the White House budged. "Any document that has to do with this investigation cannot be beyond our reach," he said. "Within the legal constraints that they seem to have, they've been fully cooperative. But we're not going to be satisfied until we get every document that we need." Bellinger saw the writing on the wall: "I absolutely sympathized with and understood the need to be firm on executive privilege for the PDBs in particular. I also tend to be a pragmatist—and I could tell we were going to get overrun."

White House officials first offered to let Kean, Hamilton, and two staff members read a core group of twenty PDB articles that had been judged most directly relevant to the commission's needs; either Kean or Hamilton, along with one staffer, could review a larger set of more than three hundred PDB articles to see if any of them were demonstrably critical to the inquiry. They could use limited notes to report back to the rest of the commission on their overall impression from these documents. The commission pushed back. Eventually, the parties agreed to a hybrid plan by which three commissioners (Kean, Hamilton, and former deputy attorney general Jamie Gorelick) plus Philip Zelikow, the commission's staff director, would look at the core group; they would then select two of their small group to look at the

wider PDB collection. In writing an outline of the full set of conditions on November 11, Gonzales added two key points to the deal:
this compromise set no precedent for future investigations, and any
leaks of information from the unprecedented review would halt the
commission's access to the PDBs.

"The 9/11 Commission report was the first time, to my knowledge, that people outside the small number of policy makers determined by the president got access to PDBs," Hamilton says. "I know
that the precedent of releasing the PDB to non-policy-makers, even
though they were *past* PDBs, was a major concern of the White House.
And it should be. So we went through this elaborate kabuki dance
to work out a system that didn't please our commissioners totally."
Indeed, two members stridently opposed the deal, insisting that *all*
commissioners needed to see the PDBs. Under the negotiated guidelines, the PDB review began on December 2.

Difficulties emerged almost immediately, around two questions:
Could roughly fifty additional PDB articles from the wider group be
added to the core group? And how much detail would be allowed
in notes taken out of the reading room? Gorelick and Zelikow, who
reviewed the larger group of PDBs, resolved the first issue by simply reporting on almost one hundred items in their notes instead of
arguing incessantly over which ones should be moved into the core
group. That only exacerbated the second issue, about the amount of
information in the notes. After several thrusts and parries, everyone
finally agreed that Gorelick and Zelikow could brief the commission
using (1) notes that contained the overall intelligence picture from
the PDBs, (2) brief summaries of nearly a hundred pieces, and (3) a
word-for-word reproduction of the article from August 6, 2001. "This
was less than we wanted, and more than the White House wanted us
to reveal," Kean and Hamilton say. But it worked.

The commission released its final report on July 22, 2004, to
a wide readership and rave reviews; the book version of the report
spent weeks on bestseller lists and garnered a National Book Award
nomination. Despite the great controversy about access to the PDBs,
the text devoted surprisingly little attention to them, with the exception of including the text of two al Qaida–focused articles from
December 4, 1998, and August 6, 2001. Only in footnotes do details
about the PDB's composition and distribution show up. The report's

pages barely touch on the overall intelligence picture that the body of PDBs from this era provided.

Still, the commission broke new ground by publishing nearly verbatim the text from those two PDB articles. Some, like Bellinger, worried that the episode put up a barrier between all future presidents and the intelligence community. "As a result of the 9/11 Commission's insistence on exposure of the PDBs," he says, "the PDB briefing process—I think for the first time in history—has become a political process in and of itself. Any president has got to realize, and even other cabinet secretaries have got to realize, that their reaction to their intelligence briefing is a political act."

Despite signed letters from the White House and CIA saying that this unique case set no precedent, it would become easier for the next commission to request, and obtain, access to the president's book. That would come sooner, in fact, than anyone could have expected.

GEORGE W. BUSH DIDN'T use his PDB briefing sessions only to hear secret intelligence reports and gain insight into the dynamics influencing global developments. He also used the sessions to deepen select relationships. Senior US officials who did not routinely see the book, such as US ambassadors and assistant secretaries, had the chance on occasion to sit in with Bush when they accompanied the president on overseas delegations. Second-term chief of staff Josh Bolten recalls, "It was a way to make them feel part of the team."

The practice became an instrument of statecraft, too, during special mornings with a select few foreign attendees. The specific content in the book on such days, of course, remains classified. "It was a personal diplomacy tool," says national security advisor Steve Hadley. "It was to be seen as taking the foreign leader into his confidence, to strengthen the personal bond of trust. I think he also did it because he wanted the foreign leader to see the kind of things he got—what the big leagues looked like."

British prime minster Tony Blair was an obvious case due to his close support of the United States, which got him an invitation to Bush's briefing in Crawford in April 2002. "The president wanted to show it," recalls Card. "He didn't say to do it—he *asked* if he could do it. So we gave a heads-up to the CIA, the briefer." The Agency stepped up without hesitation. Tenet notes that letting Blair in on the PDB fit into a larger context of cooperation between the allies. "That wasn't unusual," he says, "because we shared a ton of things with the Brits that were enormously sensitive. This is the most unique intelligence relationship in the world." Winston Wiley, the DDI at that time, recalls treating it virtually like regular business, while Miscik, his deputy, recalls, "With Tony Blair, it was easy because we share so much with the British. It's a credit to the community that we just dealt with it." They also adjusted quickly when a few others, including Japanese prime minster Junichiro Koizumi and Spanish prime minister José María Aznar, received similar treatment from Bush.

One such special edition stands out in everyone's mind: when Russian leader Vladimir Putin came to a PDB session in Crawford. "We heard it from the president," says Morell. "He wanted to be able to invite Putin to the session. It was a scramble to find material we could release to the Russians, but we did it." Clearly, it was a different kind of book that day. Card says that early discussions, proper precautions, and extensive preparation made possible what Wiley called "a work of art." The Russian president couldn't resist putting his mark on PDB history, signing his copy of the book, which US officials naturally did *not* let him keep. The most memorable part of the session had nothing to do with the sensitive content of the PDB itself. After what participants describe as a "very serious" working session, Putin walked up to Tenet and said, "You know, we have a book like this, too," to which Tenet quickly replied, "Well, we'd love to see it!"

A historically unique visitor to the PDB briefings sat in more often, starting even before inauguration. Miscik back in December 2000 delivered the PDB to a president-elect and a former president at the same time: George W. Bush and his father, George H. W. Bush. Hadley recalls occasions during the following eight years with both Bushes in the room as fun and lively, though 41 only rarely asked questions, seemingly "respectful of the fact that his son was president and he wasn't." John Negroponte, who would attend PDB briefings in 43's second term, remembers the president's father listening very politely during the joint sessions he witnessed but taking care not to get in the way. "He would politely excuse himself while we continued our discussions after he'd heard the brief," Negroponte says. "He didn't want to interfere."

GEORGE TENET ANNOUNCED IN June 2004 he would step down as CIA director the following month to spend more time with his wife and teenage son. He had served seven years, longer than any of his predecessors except Allen Dulles.

Tenet's replacement, Republican congressman Porter Goss, came to the job with extensive relevant experience. He had spent about a decade after college as a CIA operations officer, and he accepted the director's job while serving his seventh year as chairman of the House Permanent Select Committee on Intelligence. He also brought with him a team of congressional aides who irritated the Agency bureaucracy with personnel changes and a heavy-handed style, repeating some of the early missteps that Stansfield Turner and his staff had made more than twenty-five years earlier.

By any measure, Goss had a rough start, as he acknowledges. "There was huge mistrust when I went into the Agency because I'm from the Hill," he says. "I tried to win over those people—some of whom I did, some of whom I did not." Within five months, all but one of the Agency's seventh-floor leadership cadre left or had been replaced. And Goss sent a poorly received message to the workforce directing them all to "support the administration and its policies." Although the note merely reinforced the traditional intelligence ethos of serving the current president, regardless of political beliefs, one former intelligence official says it came across as "asking people to color their views."

The new director saw hands-on time with the President's Daily Brief as a top priority, but his first impressions of the book left him wanting something better. "More often than not, I was pretty disappointed. I didn't see anything in there that was turning me on. In terms of rebuilding the intelligence community, the only thing that's going to save it is its product, and its principal product is the PDB. That was my message every single day to [new DDI] John Kringen: this is what we live or die on."

To ensure that the book was worth the president's time each day, Goss made it *his* biggest focus, spending five hours every day with the PDB. He says he went through the draft articles and background material for a couple of hours every night before bed, and then woke up early to go through it again during his car ride downtown. During the short drive, he asked his briefer to highlight overnight changes in or additions to what the president would see. In the director's office at the Old Executive Office Building, he sat down with his briefer and then with the president's briefer before heading over to the White House to meet with Bush.

Before he finally went to CIA headquarters, some three or four hours after waking up, Goss would chat with the briefer to ensure they agreed on what follow-up the president needed. Once there, he'd often bring DI leaders into his office to again talk about the briefing. "Then," he says, "it was on to the rest of the world," as he turned his attention to running the Agency, managing the intelligence community, preparing for congressional testimony, meeting with visiting officials from cooperative foreign intelligence services, and handling myriad other tasks.

Goss aired his frustration with the workload during a public speech at the Ronald Reagan Presidential Library in March 2005. Responding to a question, he declared that his job required him to wear five hats—and that participating in the daily PDB briefing stood out as the toughest of them by far. Years later, Goss explained why he, as director, felt the need to take the book so seriously. "It's a dangerous weapon and you've got to get it right," he says. "That was my first responsibility. If I said something to mislead the president that caused somebody to die, or caused them to put the United States on a course that was not the appropriate one, I would never get over it."

By early 2005, however, winds of change were beginning to blow some of those responsibilities off his shoulders. Within weeks, Goss wouldn't have to worry about the PDB anymore.

GEORGE H. W. BUSH, back in 1991, had led an international coalition to liberate Kuwait from Iraqi occupation. Afterward, the world learned that Iraq's weapons of mass destruction (WMD) programs had progressed much farther than the world's intelligence agencies and academic experts had assessed. Twelve years later, his son led an international coalition to remove Saddam Hussein, who had continued to defy United Nations sanctions intended to prevent him from redeveloping WMD or attacking his neighbors for a third time in three decades. Afterward, the world learned that Iraq's WMD programs had progressed much less than the world's intelligence agencies and academic experts had assessed and, in fact, were almost entirely absent.

General Peter Pace, the vice-chairman of the Joint Chiefs of Staff as the war started, states why he and many others believed Hussein was hiding WMD: "He had used them on his own people. He had used them on his neighbors in Iran. He said he had them. Allies were reporting to us that their intel services were reporting to them that he had them. So the fact that our intel folks were reporting all that was one very important piece, but it fed into a mosaic of things that, in my mind, supported the fact that he's got these things." Tenet admits that "getting some forecasts wrong is an unavoidable part of the intelligence business—a business built on uncertainty."

To investigate why the pre-war intelligence assessments on Iraqi WMD missed the mark so widely, Bush created a new investigatory group in February 2004: the Commission on the Intelligence Capabilities of the United States Regarding Weapons of Mass Destruction. Co-chaired by Senator Charles Robb and Judge Laurence Silberman of the US Court of Appeals for the D.C. Circuit, its name commonly was shortened to the Robb-Silberman Commission, the Iraq Intelligence Commission, or—most often—the WMD Commission. This panel had a relatively easier time getting the White House to agree to show copies of the PDB. First, the new group's mandate focused primarily on intelligence, as opposed to the much wider scope of the inquiry into the al Qaida attacks. Second, whereas Congress had created the 9/11 Commission, inherently raising issues of executive privilege for documents such as the PDB, the president used an executive order to create the WMD Commission. The staff's two deputy general counsels received a notebook with *all* of the PDB articles from the previous two years that had mentioned Iraq and WMD. "That had to be well over two hundred articles," remembers Mike Leiter, one of those two notebook recipients.

The easier access to the PDB, and their clarity, didn't soften the new commissioners' assessment of the analytic shortcomings in the president's book. "We conclude that the Intelligence Community was dead wrong in almost all of its pre-war judgments about Iraq's weapons of mass destruction," their report stated. "This was a major intelligence failure. Its principal causes were the Intelligence Community's inability to collect good information about Iraq's WMD programs, serious errors in analyzing what information it could gather, and a failure to make clear just how much of its analysis was based on assumptions, rather than good evidence." The commissioners looked carefully at the PDB, even highlighting it in the brief cover letter that emphasized a select few of the 500-plus-page report's main findings: "The daily intelligence briefings given to you before the Iraq war were flawed. Through attention-grabbing headlines and repetition of questionable data, these briefings overstated the case that Iraq was rebuilding its WMD programs."

The exhaustive WMD Commission explored, and rejected, some pundits' claims that intelligence officers either lied about Iraq's unconventional weapons or told policy makers what they wanted to hear. They found that analysts simply erred, inadvertently misleading policy makers in both the daily intelligence and in longer-form products such as the National Intelligence Estimate (NIE) with well-intentioned but incorrect analysis. As Tenet says, "Even though the daily reports the president saw in the run-up to the production of the NIE were uneven and assertive in tone, and at times more assertive on some issues than the NIE, they were a reflection of honest analysis." The WMD Commission wrote to Bush that they found "no indication that the Intelligence Community distorted the evidence regarding Iraq's weapons of mass destruction. What the intelligence professionals told you about Saddam Hussein's programs was what they believed. They were simply wrong."

So how did well-meaning analysts, managers, and editors go so far off course? The commissioners assessed that errors plagued their work from the start of the analytic process through to the end. Analysts relied on "old assumptions and inferences" about Iraqi intentions and behavior when high-quality intelligence proved lacking, and these solidified over time into firm conclusions. They found confirmation in evidence that "should have been recognized at the time to be of dubious reliability." They "explained away or disregarded" evidence that pointed to different conclusions. Analysts and managers neglected to pass on to policy makers their doubts about "Curveball," a key human intelligence source on Iraq's biological weapons program—an oversight that the commissioners called "a serious failure of management and leadership." Although analysts interviewed by the WMD Commission said they had felt no political pressure to change their analytic judgments, the momentum toward war "did not encourage skepticism about the conventional wisdom." All these factors combined with suboptimal management to produce "loosely reasoned, ill-supported, and poorly communicated" intelligence.

No one associated with the WMD Commission examined the PDBs more closely than Leiter. He says they did a poor job conveying "nuance and uncertainty," with the result that judgments presented in the PDB appeared to be of much greater certainty. "The PDBs made you come away with a stronger view of the presence of WMD than you did had you simply sat down and read the NIE." Leiter also recalls the titles of PDBs on Iraq standing out as "always more alarmist than the actual articles were," echoing what Rice had routinely pointed out to Morell back when he had briefed the president every day during his first year in office. Along with the articles' repetition of judgments about Iraqi WMD programs and intentions, "attention-getting" PDB titles gave the commissioners the impression that CIA analysts and editors were selling intelligence to maintain interest from "at least the First Customer."

These declarations of the PDB's flaws didn't surprise DI leaders, who had already gone through a round of introspection that reached many of the same conclusions. "We found things that were disturbing in our tradecraft," says Miscik, who ran the directorate during the Iraq invasion and throughout most of the commission's investigation. "They weren't up to the standards we should have had for ourselves— the inherited assumptions being critical, but also what I would call 'word creep,' where the judgment just gets a little bit stronger than it really was six months ago."

Indeed, by the time the WMD Commission released its final report on March 31, 2005, reforms related to its recommendations for the PDB had already been put into place or soon would be. The report suggested removing misleading headlines while adding competitive analysis and transparent analytic reasoning—and it urged the newly created director of national intelligence (DNI) to oversee production of the PDB. Card had announced more than a month earlier that the DNI would run the PDB process. A senior intelligence official said days later that headlines on the book's articles had already become less sensational, and alternative views from other agencies had started appearing in the PDB more often, with their frequency soon to increase. General Richard Myers, chairman of the Joint Chiefs of Staff for half of Bush's years in office, recalls: "The confidence levels of what they were saying in the PDB became very clear, that was a big difference. 'We're very confident of this piece, and we're not so confident of this piece, and this is why we're not so confident.' I think breaking that out was a fallout of Curveball."

The WMD Commissioners recommended more generally that policy makers "actively probe and question analysts." Bush, of course, had been doing that for years. And he wasn't stopping, despite heightened tensions after the 9/11 Commission, the Iraqi WMD intelligence debacle, and frequent reports in his PDB every week about the deterioration inside Iraq as the anti-US insurgency expanded. Hadley says, "Most of what the intelligence community was writing was very critical of the policy—not explicitly, but indirectly—but I don't think anybody pulled any punches with the president of the United States, and I don't think anybody was pressured to. It was a very healthy exchange."

BEFORE THE WMD COMMISSION released its report, Congress had moved forward in December 2004 with dramatic changes to the intelligence establishment with the Intelligence Reform and Terrorism Prevention Act. It ushered in a new intelligence super-bureaucracy, the Office of the Director of National Intelligence (ODNI), which came into force in April 2005. The most profound changes to the PDB's management in its forty years of production and delivery would follow.

The legislation directed the new DNI to serve as head of the intelligence community without concurrently leading the CIA or any other intelligence element and to act as the principal intelligence advisor to the president and NSC. The title of director of central intelligence went away, along with its dual responsibilities for managing the intelligence community *and* the CIA. Soon the White House declared that the first DNI, career diplomat and former deputy national security advisor John Negroponte, would personally attend the daily PDB sessions. Andy Card made it clear: "He'll be responsible for producing the President's Daily Brief."

On behalf of the president, Card asked Negroponte to keep bringing Porter Goss, who found himself suddenly running just the CIA instead of the whole community. "I did it for the signal to the rest of the world, that the CIA is not going to be excluded," Card says. "I also did it because the DNI, almost by definition, has no tactical knowledge. I liked the dynamic of having the CIA director there in case the president said, 'How are your spies doing today? Got any good operations going on?'" Less than two months later, Goss stopped coming, while Negroponte continued to escort Bush's briefer. The CIA director felt fine with that, especially because the president still saw him every Thursday morning for regular discussions of clandestine operations.

The PDB became a community product. Seeing the writing on the wall, CIA analytic chief John Kringen had already been reaching out to counterparts at other agencies within the intelligence community to seek their officers' contributions to the PDB, but they weren't exactly clamoring to write for the book. "I'm not interested in spending any time on something I can't read," responded Thomas Fingar, who ran the State Department's INR at the time. "There's no way I'm going to make my people write to a format they can't see and don't understand."

So the book's content and production remained largely an Agency process—even run out of the same office at CIA headquarters, just with a different organization's name over the door into the Top Secret vault. "How did the PDB become mine? I'll be damned if I know," Negroponte says. "I'll be damned if I can tell you that it's really that different. We left it all over at the CIA building. We were under no illusions that there was going to be some kind of revolution in the way things were done." The president's briefers remained CIA careerists; they simply were seconded to the ODNI for the duration of their briefing tour. Fingar, whom Negroponte brought in to oversee the PDB as the first deputy DNI for analysis, says that Agency authors still contributed by far the most to the book.

Because some senior officials had told Fingar that they had lost confidence in the daily book, he feared the PDB could become what he calls a "hugely expensive irrelevance." He directed analysts to explore alternative hypotheses more often and to be clear about differing interpretations among analysts. Quickly, however, he realized that the president himself largely liked the product, so he avoided revolutionary changes. Fingar told a colleague, "I'm going to leave it where it is. The one thing we can't do is break it."

Most had no illusions, realizing that it was still de facto a product of Agency analysts, just under new management. A senior DI manager during Bush's second term says, "I don't think anybody else, like the head of INR, went to bed at night and got up in the morning, thinking his responsibility was the PDB. We were still the only ones who felt ownership and responsibility for the PDB." Michael Hayden agrees, recalling that when he took Goss's place as CIA director in May 2006, it was even more clear to him than when he had been deputy DNI that the Agency dominated the PDB: "Because most of the book was still written by CIA authors, I felt total ownership." The book's format, general writing style, and briefing patterns stayed almost unchanged.

Predictably, the topic with the most input from outside the CIA was terrorism. Key articles came from the National Counterterrorism Center (the successor to the Terrorist Threat Integration Center). The NCTC had taken many analysts and managers from the Agency, but its competition with the Counterterrorism Center for space in the President's Daily Brief continued unabated. CTC analysts felt that all others suffered due to their distance from on-the-ground intelligence collection and covert action (run out of the CIA); NCTC analysts—even those seconded from the Agency—began to see their unique access to the entire government's sources of counterterrorism information as providing them a better angle on terrorism analysis. A senior CTC official of the time says that he and his NCTC managerial counterparts regularly had to get directly involved in analytic firefights about individual pieces for the president. The WMD Commission lambasted the turf battle between the two groups and encouraged the new director of national intelligence to impose order on the chaos. Tensions remained high for years.

All of the friction behind the scenes, though, failed to register as anything beyond background noise for the man who mattered most. After all, Bush remained intensely interested in the nuts and bolts of counterterrorism information and analysis. As Leiter, who became the NCTC's director in November 2007, says: "Bush was *so* focused. We'd go through the PDB, all the counterterrorism articles, and he would dig in at a serious level of detail. We used to joke that he knew the names of more British Muslims than the prime minister did." In his second term, the president shifted his discussions about homeland terrorist threats from daily meetings after the PDB briefing into longer weekly sessions known colloquially as "Terrorism Tuesdays."

When asked almost four years after leaving office what issues he had noticed when the PDB shifted to the DNI's management, Bush said, "None. I don't remember seeing any changes because the CIA analysts were still the briefers."

SOON AFTER BOLTEN SUCCEEDED Card as chief of staff, he accompanied the president to St. Petersburg, Russia, for a summit of G8 leaders. Concerned that the hosts had wired the guest villas, Bolten insisted that Bush, Hadley, and the PDB briefer trudge out to the presidential limousine with him for the daily session. "One thing that I was confident in: the Secret Service would *not* have allowed the limo to be compromised," he says. "The president thought we were jackasses. But he just sighed and went along with it."

Over the next several months, Bolten became increasingly worried that the president's daily dialogue with the briefer, "who was very well informed but was not the expert," he says, wasn't giving Bush all that he needed. "The president often disagreed with the perspective that he thought a piece reflected. Then he would have an exchange with the briefer, which wasn't fair to the briefer—or to the piece's author. And it wasn't satisfying the president." So in early 2007, he suggested to a receptive Hadley that they add regular subject-matter expert briefings to the president's schedule. Bolten then chatted with Michael McConnell, who had moved into the DNI's office in February (when Negroponte became Condoleezza Rice's deputy at the State Department) and who worked out the details with Hadley. McConnell put a label on the proposed sessions that stuck, calling them "deep dive" briefings.

Bush liked the plan. "I wanted some of the analysts to come in the Oval Office so I could question them," he says. "One, I wanted to learn more, but I also wanted to send word through the building that the PDB and its different articles meant a lot to me. It was a chance to, in essence, give the entire building a pat on the back." The first deep dive, on a Saturday morning soon thereafter, was a hit; the president extended his intelligence time that day to more than ninety minutes. "I like this," Bush said. "As long as I'm president, we're going to keep doing this." Soon there were two deep dives a week. Within eighteen months, he'd seen more than two hundred analysts.

Bush's policy and intelligence advisors put plenty of thought into which topics to address in the new forum. "Mike McConnell and

I would go over the agenda for PDB pieces," Hadley says, "particularly the major analytical pieces. And the ones that we knew were going to lead to a policy discussion we would try to do on Wednesday or Saturday for a deep dive session." The vast majority of deep dive analysts—just like most PDB authors—came from the CIA. Hayden would prepare his officers to go into the Oval Office, most often for the first time, with a clear preview of what to expect: "You've got two chairs by the fireplace, for the president and the vice president—don't sit there. Sit on the couch, nearest the vice president. The president will have read your piece overnight. He is interactive; you'll start to talk and he'll interrupt. So you've got about three sentences of free fire to get your point out. After that, it's game on." The president so regularly asked the briefers about their educations, their time covering the issue at hand, and their experiences overseas that CIA managers started including briefers' biographies with the written products they sent to Bush the day before each deep dive.

Hadley regularly invited the secretaries of state and defense, the chairman of the Joint Chiefs, a representative of the Treasury Department, and occasional others. "They would all read the analytic piece in advance, hear the intelligence briefing, and then participate in the policy discussion," he says. After probing the analysts' credibility, Bush would proceed to grill them on their information and analysis. "They were tough questions, forcefully expressed," Bob Gates remembers, "and I can see how some might have seen the experience as intimidating. Others found the give-and-take with the president exhilarating." Hayden compared the average PDB article to something on CNN Headline News, while deep dives, to him, felt more like in-depth BBC news analysis. "The analysts loved it," says one senior intelligence official who sent several of his officers to these sessions. "Everyone came back and said it was the highlight of their career."

Bolten remembers most of the deep dive briefers doing well, despite often seeming surprised at just how "sharp and engaged" the president was. He judges that the sessions improved leaders' perception of and confidence in the intelligence community. Cheney agrees: "We got more in-depth stuff by actually bringing in the folks who had done the work, the analysts who had written the pieces. I was pleased because I thought in our Administration, we used it about as well as it could be." Treasury secretary Hank Paulson attended the deep dives when he could but, especially during the worst of the financial crisis, often sent in his stead his deputy secretary, Bob Kimmitt, who briefed him on any important items relevant to Treasury. Kimmit recalls thinking: "How great is this for these analysts, to have that access to the president of the United States? Not only is it fun to be in the Oval Office, but it makes them such better analysts—because they know how to take all that brainpower and put it into a form that is useful for strategic decision makers, starting with the president." Bush clearly enjoyed the innovative briefings, saying years later that he found them "very intellectually stimulating."

CHAPTER TWELVE

THE PDB, TODAY AND TOMORROW

THE UNPRECEDENTED PUBLICITY SURROUNDING the President's Daily Brief during the George W. Bush administration set up his predecessor for increased scrutiny of his own daily intelligence habits. From the 1960s through the 1990s, the book had been largely an inside secret, its existence widely known within Washington circles but remaining a mystery to most others. Not so for Barack Obama's PDB, which became the subject of media scrutiny because of his preference for reading the book and taking frequent but irregular briefings instead of insisting on in-person discussions with intelligence officers every day. Even a shift in the format of his briefing, from text on a page to electrons on a screen, hit the spotlight—in that case because the White House itself publicized the change. Such politicking over the process and content of the PDB, unheard of for decades, seems here to stay, adding to the list of inherent tensions involved in producing and delivering the book.

AFTER STARTING WITH GREETINGS and smiles all around, President-elect Obama's first PDB session, on November 6, 2009, took a turn for the worse.

DNI Michael McConnell had asked Michael Morell, then the head of the CIA's Directorate of Intelligence, to go to Chicago for a couple of months. Morell would not brief Obama directly, for he had already picked two CIA officers to split that duty. First, however, he would arrange a series of non-PDB intelligence presentations for the incoming president, ranging from an overview of existing covert action programs to briefings responding to Obama's specific requests. Then he would serve as a steady presence in what officials expected to be a series of regular PDB briefings, performing the same "color commentator" function for Obama and his briefers that George Tenet had performed for Bush and Morell back in 2001. The pattern for the next several weeks would hinge on this first post-election meeting.

Before the book even came out of the briefer's hands, a misunderstanding surfaced. The president-elect thought all of his senior advisors would be able to attend this meeting. The DNI, however, had firm guidance from the White House that none of them should join the session, or see the book at all, unless their security clearances had come through. The earlier smiles vanished as Obama's aides huddled. Eventually he acquiesced to taking the day's briefing alone—but he decreed that starting the next day, until his people were cleared, he would read the PDB by himself instead of taking a briefing. McConnell's well-laid plans for daily, in-person support featuring color commentary from the former presidential briefer faded away. "We should have just done it," Morell says.

John Podesta, who managed the transition for Obama, recalls discussing the issue with the sitting chief of staff, Josh Bolten. The outgoing administration's position remained firm: the world's most sensitive daily document had to be kept secure, even if that meant that only the recently elected Obama and his vice president–elect, Joe Biden, would have access to the book for a matter of days or weeks. "I was very adamant that this does the president no justice," Podesta says. "If you can't talk to anybody about what's in the PDB, then why bother reading it?" Eventually the parties settled on a protocol in which people could begin to receive the book as they were announced for jobs that would entail seeing it once in office.

Although CIA authors continued to take the lead on most PDB pieces, Hayden didn't even mention the book in his briefing with Obama on December 9; the discussion instead covered the gamut of extant covert actions. However, a briefing a few weeks earlier by FBI director Mueller and NCTC director Leiter, joined by Morell, had revealed much about how the president-elect would approach

THE PDB, TODAY AND TOMORROW – 275

intelligence assessments. As he received a set presentation on threats
to the homeland, featuring a big map showing what was being done
on the counterterrorism front, Obama paid close attention but barely
spoke. Leiter wishes he had figured out Obama's style right away. "I
didn't realize, and I should have, that he didn't want to sit there and
track every plot," he says. "He was viewing this as a broader strategic
issue. In subsequent PDBs and all our sessions with him, those are
the sorts of issues that captured his attention—much more so than
the details."

Leiter applied this lesson quickly. After the briefers wrapped up,
Obama asked them what their agencies needed in order to do better.
Mueller and Morell mentioned additional resources; Leiter ventured,
"We are losing the war of ideas. Even if we're doing really well on
all of *this*," he said while pointing to the map, "we've got to change
the tone." Obama leaned forward, newly animated, and exclaimed,
"That's what we're going to do."

As OBAMA MADE HIS way to the nation's capital to take office, McConnell stayed on as DNI while his replacement awaited confirmation.
"They didn't want to be without a DNI if something happened,"
he says. His attendance at the president's PDB sessions, however,
remained uncertain.

An assistant popped into McConnell's office on inauguration
day. "Sir, the White House called," she said. "They don't need you for
the briefing."

McConnell had been inside the Beltway long enough to ask,
"*Who* called?"

"Some staffer."

"You call them back," McConnell said. "I'll be there."

So he showed up, as he'd been doing to close out the previous
administration. The briefer and the DNI jointly entered the Oval
Office precisely at the scheduled time, in contrast to the first PDB
briefing sixteen years earlier for the last Democratic president, Bill
Clinton.

During Obama's first week, attendees of the PDB session noticed
a few differences from the Bush sessions that would become custom-
ary early in this administration. First, the PDB session no longer religiously came early in the morning but instead started at 9:30 a.m.

(or, often, later), after a new daily economic briefing and sometimes delayed by other presidential priorities. Second, as the briefer and DNI leaned forward to talk, Obama said, "Let me read." The ping-pong-style interaction of the previous eight years had given way to a new, more reserved style. Third, although others from the White House—notably Biden, national security advisor Jim Jones, deputy national security advisor Tom Donilon, top homeland/counterterrorism advisor John Brennan, and chief of staff Rahm Emanuel—would usually attend, Obama directed the intelligence officers to leave right after the core PDB briefing and stay out of the follow-on policy discussions.

Admiral Dennis Blair took over for McConnell nine days after inauguration to become the country's third DNI in less than four years. His delay in taking the position symbolized the distance between Blair, who had served as commander in chief of the US Pacific Command and associate director of central intelligence for military support, and the inner circle of White House aides surrounding the president. Admitting that his ideas for modifying the PDB were "completely uninformed by dialogue with the president or anyone else," he came in determined to take the PDB from its tactical detail to a more strategic level, where he believed the president belonged, and increase the number of PDB pieces about longer-term trends.

When he started attending the Oval Office PDB sessions, Blair was surprised to find them short, sometimes cut down to ten minutes. It became clear that the president was reading the book before his intelligence team arrived. The DNI worked with the briefers to make the best use of their limited time slot. "In our pre-briefs before walking in to see him," Blair says, "we would try to find some angle to attack that had not appeared explicitly in the text but would stimulate a discussion. We picked out, in any PDB, one or two articles that seemed to us to be most important and would come up with some point, like 'The Europeans have a different opinion about this.'"

Two months into the job, Blair told reporters that he was working hard to ensure that these morning sessions focused on intelligence linked to policies on the president's plate. He also bucked tradition, changing the timing of pieces' publication in the PDB to better get information to next-tier officials as they were forming policy. For decades, key intelligence assessments usually appeared in the

PDB first—or, at least, no later than they went into lower-level publications—so that the president would not be seeing sensitive analysis after assistant secretaries did. The new DNI saw things differently. Having the PDB out of rhythm with the progressive pattern of national security decision making, he assessed, increased the chances that the book would insert "gotchas" late in the policy process (as many military officers had perceived the book did in 1991, before the initiation of the ground war against Iraq). Blair declared that he was generally in favor of delaying some articles to give a heads-up to the policy makers most likely to act on it.

Blair's various tweaks to the PDB process, however, failed to create a bond with the president. Within a few months, Obama began holding the briefing sessions less regularly, while continuing to read the book every day.

OBAMA TOOK OFFICE DURING the biggest global economic downturn since World War II, what economists have called the Great Recession. Naturally, he devoted great attention to domestic and international financial markets and related issues, prompting innovation from his intelligence leaders. After just over a month in office, he started receiving a new CIA product on his desk each morning to supplement the PDB: the Economic Intelligence Brief, or EIB. A typical issue carried two or three PDB-style articles with classified reporting and analysis on issues such as the economic implications of international political developments, global oil market dynamics, or how US allies' budgetary difficulties could reduce security cooperation. The EIB also included a monthly review of countries most vulnerable to economic crisis. New CIA director Leon Panetta described the new product's value: "We have to know whether or not the economic impacts in China or Russia or any place else are influencing the policies of those countries when it comes to foreign affairs and when it comes to the issues that we care about."

The PDB also continued to carry articles analyzing counterterrorism issues, and the Obama administration kept its predecessor's "Terrorism Tuesdays" on the schedule so that holdover officials such as Mueller, Leiter, and NSA chief Keith Alexander, along with Panetta, could brief the president. Policy-making attendees for this one-hour meeting included much of the same White House crowd as for Obama's daily national security sessions, plus PDB principals such as defense secretary Robert Gates, secretary of state Hillary Clinton, homeland security secretary Janet Napolitano, and attorney general Eric Holder. During one of these Tuesday briefings, Mueller focused Obama's attention on al Qaida's bomb-making capabilities; other sessions addressed specific al Qaida operatives, airport screening measures, and related issues. Like Eisenhower's stately procession of fixed-subject NSC meetings more than fifty years earlier, Obama's "Terrorism Tuesdays" explored topics typically placed on the agenda a week or two earlier.

The approach to counterterrorism intelligence came under more scrutiny after Umar Farouk Abdulmutallab tried to take down Northwest Airlines flight 253 from Amsterdam to Detroit on Christmas Day 2009. His underwear bomb failed to detonate properly, sparing the plane and its nearly three hundred passengers and crew. Yet it still set off an intense US government effort to determine how to fill the gaps in intelligence and homeland security that let Abdulmutallab get as close as he did to pulling off the dramatic attack. Leiter at the NCTC says the event changed the mood at the weekly terrorism briefings for the president. "The session became very different. Before 12/25, no detail whatsoever. After 12/25, more so." Another participant agrees, noting how "much more focused on the specific details of counterterrorism operations" those meetings became after the botched attack.

The PDB itself, however, went forward largely the same. Bigger-picture analysis of ongoing threat streams continued in the "Terrorism Tuesday" sessions, with Leiter briefing the president from a single sheet of paper that showed high-priority issues, obviating the need for duplication in the book. Because the White House's internal review of the circumstances leading up to the attack highlighted human errors and systematic breakdowns in the watchlisting process and in analysis of threat streams, intelligence officers expanded their efforts to cite in the PDB and other finished intelligence products "actions taken": what various government agencies and foreign intelligence partners were doing to follow up on threats.

The Christmas Day attack had a side effect with another implication for the President's Daily Brief: reduced tension in the testy relationship between the NCTC and the Counterterrorism Center at the CIA. Andy Liepman, a veteran Agency analyst and manager who was running the analysis shop at the NCTC, says leaders of both organizations realized that the tension and competition between them "was 80 percent about the PDB." So after the underwear bombing incident, Liepman deemphasized the president's book, shifting his center's analytic focus toward more tactical intelligence. "Pre-12/25, we thought we needed to get into the PDB regularly. But post-12/25, while agreeing we had to do some PDBs—we sometimes had a different view from CTC—we valued more our weekly threat briefing face time with the president. It became silly to fight CTC when we had that access."

The NCTC by then had built a second product on the foundation of the earlier President's Terrorism Threat Report to get high-level counterterrorism-related analysis to those who needed it most. The National Terrorism Bulletin (NTB), which began in the Bush years and got its legs fully under it during the Obama administration, went to a few dozen top-tier customers, including cabinet secretaries, the FBI director, and the president's top counterterrorism and homeland security aides. "I've always thought that the NTB was, in many ways, more important than the PDB," Leiter says. "The PDB told a perfectly good story, but everybody I cared about was going to see the NTB. The most important customer was John Brennan: as soon as he thought something in it was important, the rest of the community would take note. And if there was a good NTB piece, we just made it into a PDB piece."

"WHAT ARE YOU TRYING to do with this?" chief of staff Rahm Emanuel barked at Dennis Blair in May 2009.

"I'm trying to tell the president what the greatest threat to the United States is," the DNI replied.

"No, you're not," Emanuel replied. "You're trying to cover your ass so that if something happens—"

Blair cut in. "Rahm, I'm the president's top intelligence officer. I'm doing my job."

Emanuel had called Blair in because the night before, Blair had approved a PDB article about the threat from Americans who had trained with terrorists overseas and come back to the homeland. After their testy chat, Emanuel settled down, and the president quickly called a meeting to address the issue. Everybody agreed that it was a significant threat—and that there was little the president himself could do about it.

Intelligence officials often feel a strong duty to warn, even when little can be done immediately, lest the president lack the information he needs to manage the US government's operations against high-priority threats. White House staffers, however, can find it irresponsible to take difficult issues to the president when there is little he can do about it; it smells like his intelligence officers are seeking political cover in case something goes wrong.

Blair stands by his choices. "The PDB should give more on warning; it should spark the kinds of policy discussions that the president ought to be thinking about and help him see around the corner," he says. "I was frustrated that I wasn't able to have it valued for that function. The attention in the White House was very much on current concerns." This dynamic played out at the end of 2010—and beyond, in a prolonged episode with lingering reverberations. A street vendor in Tunisia set himself on fire in mid-December, setting off a series of protests there and, soon, throughout the region. Many Arab governments would be challenged, and a few would topple, in what became known as the brief "Arab Spring." Policy makers felt blindsided by the events across the Arab world; rebuttals that social dynamics in Tunisia had not been a top priority did little to make the lack of a warning feel better.

Blair's successor, Jim Clapper, had come to the job by then, bringing with him a more solid background of managing intelligence organizations than his three predecessors combined. After retiring in 1995 from more than thirty years of service in the Air Force, where he rose to the rank of lieutenant general, he had led the Defense Intelligence Agency, the National Geospatial-Intelligence Agency, and then the Defense Department's entire intelligence operations as undersecretary of defense for intelligence. Perhaps this experience proved the key element in helping him find his niche in the policy process better than Blair had done. He focused less on what remained of the PDB briefings than on managing the intelligence community—heeding signals from White House officials that he wouldn't need to attend the president's briefings personally.

Instead, Clapper often delegated presidential briefing duty to Robert Cardillo, the former head of analysis at the Defense Intelligence Agency, who took office as the first deputy director of national intelligence for intelligence integration in fall 2010. During these briefings, Clapper or Cardillo answered any questions Obama had about items in the PDB, updated its articles with late-breaking traffic or additional analytic insights, or walked something new into the Oval Office that had not appeared in the book itself. Then, as he had done since the start of his term, the president turned to policy discussions with his aides, when the visiting intelligence officials would still generally leave the room.

Obama seemed pleased with the arrangement, singling out Cardillo for praise in October 2014: "I've gotten to know Robert really well; he's often delivered my daily briefings. He's smart. He's unflappable. He's earned my complete confidence."

THE VERY FACT THAT Obama eschewed daily briefings while still reading the book every day created a media controversy about the PDB that would have been unimaginable decades earlier. It started with a September 2012 claim from the Government Accountability Institute—which describes its mission as seeking to "investigate and expose crony capitalism, misuse of taxpayer monies, and other governmental corruption or malfeasance"—that the president to that point had attended his intelligence briefings on only 43.8 percent of his days in office. An opinion piece in the *Washington Post* publicized the findings, noting that the briefing attendance rates decreased after the first two years to less than 40 percent of all days. Although an NSC spokesman called the numbers "not particularly interesting or useful," national media outlets gave the story legs.

These numbers reveal less than they seem to. For example, the calculation appears to include Sundays as days that Obama missed his briefings, ignoring the fact that, as a general rule, *no* president has scheduled in-person briefings (or even had PDBs printed) on Sundays. This attention to the president's schedule nonetheless highlights a fundamental truth: Obama has preferred to read the PDB alone and then hold a national security meeting with White House aides rather than sit through a briefing of the PDB every day.

"With Obama," says Michael Morell, who remained involved in the machinery supporting these briefings while serving as CIA's deputy director from May 2010 to August 2013, "it was clear that he absorbs information best by reading, and he did so on his own—not with others in the room, not at the daily intelligence briefing."

This led some to question whether Obama focused on the PDB at all. Morell says it remained evident to him that Obama read the book. "I was impressed in NSC meetings that the PDB was informing him. He didn't refer to it explicitly, but you could see that he had internalized the analysis. The idea that he doesn't read the PDB is total crap."

Other intelligence officers perceive the lack of daily, direct interaction with the current First Customer as a failure. "It was clear to everyone that the less attention President Obama gave the PDB, the harder we tried," says one recently retired senior Agency officer. "The value of the product was going down, but the amount of time we spent on it was going up. We spend more time on the PDB now than we've ever spent on it." This is nothing new; CIA officers for generations have used presidential disengagement with daily intelligence products as an excuse to replace or at least reengineer premier publications, from the Daily Summary and Current Intelligence Bulletin to the President's Intelligence Checklist and the President's Daily Brief itself.

Some analysts and managers, especially at the CIA, find it difficult to avoid feeling rejected when a president gives the impression that he just isn't that into the PDB. ODNI and CIA leaders who put heavy emphasis on the PDB magnify the effect. One officer says, "The impression that a lot of the analysts had from their bosses was, 'You just have to try harder. If only you produced better stuff, the president would read it.'" As Morell observes from his more than three decades working with the book, "A long-time sine wave is associated with the PDB. When negative feedback gets too much, senior DI leaders paid close attention to it—and the quality goes up. When the quality went up, the customers stopped complaining about it. With less feedback, DI leaders focus elsewhere, the DI lets its guard down, the quality goes down, and eventually critiques start coming in again."

Another tendency over the decades has been for the distribution of the book to expand as top-level interest in briefings fades. Requests for additions to the PDB's dissemination list received by the DNI early in the Obama years were forwarded to the national security advisor for approval, which Blair says always came. By 2013, the PDB was making its way to more than thirty recipients, exceeding even the Clinton-era distribution list. The book went to customers like Ben Rhodes, the president's top strategic communications aide and speechwriter, as well as to deputy secretaries of national security departments. This allowed specific items from the PDB to be discussed at both Principals Committee *and* Deputies Committee meetings, because everybody in both rooms would have read it.

MORE THAN FORTY YEARS after Henry Kissinger passed up the chance to take Richard Nixon's PDB electronic, Barack Obama started reading his daily intelligence report on an iPad.

The idea of a paperless PDB hadn't gone away completely since the early 1970s. A few months after Jimmy Carter took office in 1977, CIA director Stansfield Turner considered options for delivering the president's book via a cathode-ray tube in Carter's office, encrypted television transmission, or videocassette. Internal CIA memos reveal that Turner continued to explore PDB delivery innovations into the last year of Carter's term, though he stopped short of putting any such system in front of the president. More than a decade after leaving office, Carter said, "If I was in the White House now I would welcome it . . . not as a substitute for the other support, the PDB and the briefings, but in addition to it."

Obama's White House was happy to publicize the president's turn to modernity. On January 31, 2012, the White House website's "Photo of the Day" featured Obama, head bent down over an iPad, as Cardillo reviewed key items from the PDB on it. Observers called it "proof positive that the megatrend towards a consumerization of IT is not only unstoppable, but is changing enterprises everywhere in very positive ways." If nothing else, the use of a tablet platform for the PDB eases the incorporation of media such as interactive graphics and video. It enables customers, with a simple touch on the screen, to drill down into raw intelligence reports or published intelligence assessments.

Two members of a panel of information technology experts that the intelligence community formed to explore the implications of new technologies on the PDB looked at the iPad as a springboard toward a more dynamic briefing process, noting, "A more radical future vision is thus eminently plausible: a shift in the *PDB* from a once-a-day production-and-brief-engagement model, to continuous, near real-time, virtual support, punctuated by periodic physical interactions, some regularly scheduled and some when called for by urgent situations."

President Barack Obama has shifted from reading the PDB on paper to viewing it on an iPad, in this case with deputy director of national intelligence for intelligence integration Robert Cardillo in the Oval Office on January 31, 2012. *White House photo*

PDB recipients have more limited expectations. Several simply want their tablets to provide direct access to reference documents, from unclassified material such as the CIA's *World Factbook* and media highlights to Top Secret products such as raw intelligence reporting and the CIA's World Intelligence Review, or WIRe (which evolved from the SEIB). Others hope for options such as an electronic PDB linked to secure email, video news feeds on the tablet, and even secure docking stations in their offices to allow updating throughout the day. A senior leader of the DNI's PDB staff says, "Access to original source intelligence is the most frequently asked question by principals who receive the PDB."

Daily briefers in the Obama administration who show the PDB to their customers each morning on classified iPads have expressed concerns that today's analysts need to enhance their skills to take better advantage of the iPad's capabilities. They also raise concerns about some potential problems with this method of PDB delivery, such as non-authoritative or inadequately vetted information on a tablet leading to flawed policy decisions; customer frustrations about receiving overwhelming amounts of data in a limited window of time; or recipients' eventual judgment that the iPad's enhanced capability renders briefers obsolete.

At least for this president, the debate over the value of the iPad PDB compared to its traditional paper version is over. On February 15, 2014, just under ten months shy of the President's Daily Brief's fiftieth anniversary, CIA presses printed the final hard-copy edition of the PDB.

Managing the PDB, whether disseminated on paper or on a touchscreen, presents unique challenges to CIA (and now ODNI) leaders as well as line managers responsible for reviewing the assessments that working-level analysts produce for the book every day. Focusing too little managerial and analytic attention on the PDB does a disservice to the president, who might make vital national security decisions based on words put in front of him without proper vetting. Quality control matters. But concentrating too much on the book brings diminishing returns. The report only marginally improves with each additional layer of review—and every senior manager who chooses to spend more time on the daily content of the PDB effectively chooses not to attend to other organizational needs.

"Because of its importance, the PDB has started to define us," one former senior CIA official laments. "Not only is it the most expensive periodical in the world, but it has gotten *too* expensive. We can't afford to obsess about it the way we do. It is eating management time, way more than analyst time. A bunch of senior managers spend a *lot* of time on the book. That's what makes the PDB so expensive, more expensive than we can afford—because we produce routinely better quality than we let ourselves believe."

The more that analysts worry about a manager, an editor, or even the president chastising them for "missing the call," the less likely they become to offer creative insights that actually inform policy making beyond just predicting the obvious. It's the difference between swinging a bat to make contact, *any* contact, with the ball—which fosters a mentality of swinging not to miss—and trying for a game-changing home run. Sure, the latter will result in missing the ball more often, but when you *do* hit it, your contribution to the president's decision making justifies the PDB's vast expense more than dozens of bland assessments that are difficult to disprove. This tension goes back to the early days of presidential intelligence. Recall that analysts in June

1962, writing about a Chinese communist military buildup in the President's Intelligence Checklist for John Kennedy, offered only that "the possibility of some offensive action (perhaps against the offshore islands) cannot be dismissed." It's hard to imagine the president felt particularly well served by such lackluster prose.

The need for inspired analysis seems especially acute for the hardest problems of intelligence analysis, where open sources reveal little and even classified information is hard to come by. "The key question is, where does intelligence add value?" Bob Gates asks. "In some areas—like what's going on politically in Israel or Germany—the *Financial Times* may be better informed than the PDB. But when it comes to Iran or North Korea, the media can't hold a candle to it. The focus should be on the areas where intelligence genuinely adds value, rather than chasing what's on the daily news—or, even more significantly, what the president just learned in a telephone call with the Israeli prime minister or the German chancellor."

IT IS EASY TO forget that presidents before John Kennedy tackled momentous national security decisions without a daily book of intelligence analysis tailored to their needs and personal style—and that, before Harry Truman, they conducted foreign policy without the benefit of any institutionalized intelligence assessments at all. Historians can speculate about how much personalized intelligence analysis would have helped James Madison before and during the War of 1812, James Polk before and during the Mexican-American War, or William McKinley before and during the Spanish-American War. John Kennedy certainly found himself better prepared to react to international threats and opportunities after the genesis of the President's Intelligence Checklist, and his successors have had access to the more robust President's Daily Brief each day.

But how much difference has the PDB really made? After all, the book left Richard Nixon unprepared for the 1973 October War, failed to predict for Jimmy Carter the Iranian Revolution in 1978–79, and missed the al Qaida plot that led to the attacks on September 11, 2001, during George W. Bush's administration. If the intelligence community's billions of dollars for gathering secrets and assessing world events leave the president uninformed on such critical developments, the PDB can look wasteful.

When intelligence collection and analysis meet their potential, however, the PDB enlightens presidents as they prepare to resolve some of the most difficult dilemmas of their lives. Its insights into what counterparts around the globe are doing, not doing, or considering doing afford the commander in chief a decisive advantage in getting ahead of crises before they develop or reacting to them more confidently if they do erupt. Bill Clinton, for example, says there were few days when he felt he got *nothing* out of the PDB.

And yet most presidents have missed opportunities to make more of the PDB. Richard Nixon stands out the most. His distrust of the Central Intelligence Agency, reinforced by Henry Kissinger's rigorous control of all national security paperwork entering the Oval Office, prompted him to undervalue much of the analysis in the book, if he read it at all. Nixon and Kissinger's shared perception of an inherent CIA liberal bias pushed them to discount potentially insightful inputs from the PDB that might have helped them take their generally successful foreign policy to even greater heights.

On the other end of the spectrum, George W. Bush's deep engagement set a high bar for First Customer interactions with the PDB and intelligence briefers. Indeed, his understanding of the ground truth around the world on any given day may never be surpassed. However, did his fascination with the nuggets of day-to-day intelligence collection and his consistent interest in analysts' assessments of what was going on *right now* spur an unfortunate side effect: diverting attention from longer-term impacts of foreign policy decisions?

The PDB's effectiveness will vary depending on each president's personality, the international environment at the time, and that administration's particular national security decision-making process. One size does not fit all; different people simply process information and use their time differently. Thus it is folly to think that what works best for one president, or even most presidents, will work best for any other. As John Negroponte, who served as deputy national security advisor to one commander in chief and DNI to another, asserts, "No one's going to tell me that a president doesn't understand what he needs after he's been in office for a year or two. They know what they need, and what they are comfortable with."

A president who dismisses the PDB outright, however, does so at great peril. If nothing else, declining an important input into vital national security issues would provide fodder for political opponents. But it goes deeper than that. As each president learns that the PDB really is *his* book, he discovers that his engagement motivates analysts to deliver deeper insights. Having customized the book for diverse customers across five decades, the intelligence community has a healthy amount of institutional experience in altering the PDB to bring value to the Oval Office regardless of its occupant. Barack Obama's shift to the iPad is just the latest example.

Should the president read the PDB or be briefed on it? Few things, after all, are as scarce as time on the daily schedule of the president of United States. Some observers contend that presidents who fail to schedule in-person briefings with intelligence officers every day— as Gerald Ford did during his first year, and as George H. W. Bush and George W. Bush insisted on throughout their administrations— neglect their duty, as if an accomplished adult cannot absorb clearly written assessments on his or her own. Others flip this logic, claiming that commanders in chief who receive daily briefings instead of reading the book alone "only" get oral summaries of the PDB (and, by implication, take the intelligence product less seriously than those, like Obama, who read it intently each day *without* a briefer in the room). A significant cost certainly accrues to the intelligence community when it moves some of its most experienced officers offline to serve as briefers who take *other* experts' analysis downtown every morning. "That's a hell of an investment we made," says former DNI Dennis Blair, "taking ten or twelve of our top analysts, who aren't thinking and analyzing anymore—they are just briefing."

The advantages of in-person briefings, on balance, outweigh the downsides. The interaction allows presidents to ask questions about assumptions underlying the substantive arguments, probe briefers about the confidence in various analytic conclusions, discuss alternative assessments, and hear supplementary data points or higher-order implications that might not come out without spontaneous discussion. Even if rich dialogue doesn't fit a particular chief executive's style, giving an intelligence officer time somewhere on the president's schedule—just to highlight the book's most crucial content and answer immediate questions—helps prevent the PDB from becoming a very expensive paperweight. Bob Gates has had insight into virtually every president's use of the PDB since Lyndon Johnson. "One of the greatest values of the PDB," he says, "is the interaction with the president, which allows the leadership of CIA and the community to have a better idea of what's on the president's mind, where he is coming from on issues, what's on his agenda, and what he needs to know."

DECEMBER 1, 2064: THE president enters the Oval Office at 8:30 a.m., as she has done virtually every day since entering office almost four years ago, and sits down behind the desk. She briefly but intensely focuses her mind on her daily intelligence report. The thought alone brings up, as usual, an interactive virtual screen that only she and her national security advisor can see, showing them this morning's menu of 4-D analytic assessments, interactive and continually updated graphs and charts, up-to-the-minute satellite and cyber imagery, and even old-fashioned text stories.

THE PDB MAY NOT feature holograms anytime soon, but three things seem certain. First, the President's Daily Brief will continue. While its First Customers have varied quite widely in how they receive the book and how much attention they give it, future presidents are unlikely to forgo departmentally independent, personally tailored assessments of crucial national security threats and opportunities. Bill Clinton, one of those who wavered between reading the PDB alone and receiving in-person briefings, says, "I can't imagine any president not taking it seriously, not reading it carefully, and not using it as a learning tool and an information leader to follow up on things that you need more on."

Second, the PDB surely will incorporate technologies yet to be invented—making it look far different from its very first issue, a black-and-white booklet Lyndon Johnson received in 1964. Officers back then in the CIA's Office of Current Intelligence would have been shocked at the prospect of a handheld tablet computer displaying full-color, touch-activated interactive visuals; we should be wary of overly confident predictions of how the PDB will evolve over the next fifty years.

Third, the PDB will remain a tightly controlled product, guarded like no other. The book that has consistently failed to align with its "For the President's Eyes Only" tagline still has a smaller distribution than any other such publication. Even if the book's circulation continues to widen, some compilation of presidentially focused analysis will be provided to the Oval Office—and will be protected accordingly.

Whatever the President's Daily Brief looks or feels like in the coming decades, its primary goal will remain the same as that of intelligence analysis more generally, from Dick Lehman's day to our own: truth to power. That has been, and will remain, the guiding philosophy of the president's daily book of secrets.

ACKNOWLEDGMENTS

THE BULK OF THE raw material for this book came from interviews with more than one hundred former senior US policy makers and intelligence officials. I thank all of them for sharing with me their stories about the President's Daily Brief and the other finished intelligence products that they wrote, edited, briefed, delivered, or received—in some cases more than fifty years ago.

On the policy-making side, the vast majority of the PDB's living recipients across five decades, including all of the living former presidents and vice presidents, provided input specifically for this book. Many others added great value by educating me about the logistical and political context of the book's delivery. On the intelligence side, a veritable who's who of retired executives, managers, analysts, and briefers from the Central Intelligence Agency and elsewhere offered recollections of both personalities and publications. Even where policy makers' or intelligence officers' input did not make the final cut, or in the few cases where they asked to remain unidentified, this truly is *their* story.

George H. W. Bush, the only person to serve as director of central intelligence, vice president, *and* president, has my particularly warm gratitude for not only contributing to this book's content but also agreeing to write its foreword. Jean Becker in his office assisted me on that front and also catalyzed my contacts with other presidents and vice presidents—all the while making me feel like I was doing *her* a favor by accepting her kindness. She and Nancy Lisenby have earned my deep appreciation.

Bruce Pease, by chance the first intelligence manager I met when entering the CIA almost twenty years ago, has been a steady source of ideas and reinforcement since the genesis of this project. (Bruce: I can't possibly buy you enough burritos to repay your support—but I'm confident that you'll let me try.) Former deputy director of central intelligence John McLaughlin, a role model for generations of intelligence officers, helped me obtain early interviews and gave me counsel to keep me in safe ethical territory during this potentially tricky project. John Hedley offered wise advice about both digging into the PDB's history and navigating the CIA's prepublication review process. David Lehman generously pulled from his memories as well as his late father's papers to educate me about Dick Lehman. Others who opened doors above and beyond what simple courtesy demanded include James Baker, Tom Fingar, John Gannon, Bill Harlow, Michael Hayden, Dick Kerr, John Kringen, Bud McFarlane, Jami Miscik, Richard Myers, John Negroponte, Al Pierce, Donald Rumsfeld, Denny Watson, Winston Wiley, and James Woolsey. I thank you all.

Several intelligence professionals warrant recognition for thoughtfully documenting the history of top-tier intelligence. Paul Corscadden, David Peterson, Dick Kerr, Dix Davis, Chuck Peters, and Michael Morell all wrote articles for the CIA's classified in-house journal, *Studies in Intelligence*, about their experiences briefing various presidents. Dick Lehman unveiled details of his intelligence support to seven administrations in an extensive interview also appearing in *Studies in Intelligence*. The recent declassification of these writings adds much to the tales told here. Douglas Garthoff's book on the directors of central intelligence and John Helgerson's recently expanded seminal work on intelligence briefings during presidential transitions—each produced at the behest of the CIA's Center for the Study of Intelligence and available for all to see on the CIA's website—proved invaluable. Mark McLaughlin and Heather Anderson provided careful research assistance and have earned my lasting appreciation.

For their expert help, I acknowledge the undervalued employees of our presidential libraries, most of all Steve Plotkin and Stacey Chandler (Kennedy), Regina Greenwell (Johnson), Meghan Lee-Parker and Jon Fletcher (Nixon), Jeremy Schmidt (Ford), Keith Shuler and Polly Nodine (Carter), Ray Wilson and Michael Pinckney (Reagan), Bob Holzweiss and Mary Finch (George H. W. Bush), and Herbert Ragan (Clinton). Members of the CIA's History Staff, too, kindly pointed me in the right direction on a few topics after determining that my goal in this project was serious, not sensationalist. And the CIA's overworked Publications Review Board examined the stories in this book to ensure they did not disclose still-classified information. Its review, of course, does not constitute an official release of CIA information. All statements of fact, opinion, or analysis expressed here are mine and do not reflect the official positions or views of the CIA or any other US government agency. Nothing in the contents should be construed as asserting or implying US government authentication of information or CIA endorsement of the views herein. This material has been reviewed solely for classification.

Most recently, the efforts of a talented team molded raw text into a complete package. My agent, the indomitable Andrew Wylie, has earned my respect and gratitude. PublicAffairs publisher Clive Priddle's gift for polishing prose is matched only by his patience with me. Collin Tracy, Sue Warga, Jack Lenzo, and Melissa Raymond all helped to turn my words into something worth looking at. You might not even know about this book if not for the efforts of Lindsay Fradkoff, Nicole Counts, Jaime Leifer, and Kristina Fazzalaro. Thank you all.

Finally, my family and friends fueled my efforts when my own stores of energy were running low. For Dianne, Carter, Cheryl, Maria, and Dave, as well as for Dean, Ashu, David, Ethan, and Jeff: I appreciate your steadfast support on this book and so much else.

I dedicate this book to Renee and Griffin, who encouraged me in ways small and large. I love you both, more than words can say.

NOTES

ONE: BEFORE THE BOOK

1 **"It is by comparing":** "Our First Line of Defense: Presidential Reflections on US Intelligence: George Washington, 1789–97," March 19, 2007, Center for the Study of Intelligence, CIA, available at https://www.cia.gov /library/center-for-the-study-of-intelligence/csi-publications/books-and -monographs/our-first-line-of-defense-presidential-reflections-on-us -intelligence/washington.html.

2 **The duties and the operations:** Christopher Andrew, *For the President's Eyes Only: Secret Intelligence and the American Presidency from Washington Through Bush* (New York: Harper Collins, 1995), 21–24.

2 **the US intelligence system:** Ibid., 29.

2 **Woodrow Wilson allowed:** "Our First Line of Defense: Presidential Reflections on US Intelligence: Woodrow Wilson, 1913–21," March 19, 2007, Center for the Study of Intelligence, CIA, available at https:// www.cia.gov/library/center-for-the-study-of-intelligence/csi-publications /books-and-monographs/our-first-line-of-defense-presidential-reflections -on-us-intelligence/wilson.html.

2 **largely ignoring the small intelligence division:** Andrew, *For the President's Eyes Only*, 60.

2 **The analysis he did receive:** See ibid., 65.

3 **A lesser-known OSS component:** John Hollister Hedley, "The DI: A History of Service," in *The Directorate of Intelligence: Fifty Years of Informing Policy, 1952–2002*, expanded ed. (Washington, DC: CIA, 2002), 2.

3 **The initial division of R&A officers:** John D. Wilson, "One Man's History in OSS: At Work with Donovan," *Studies in Intelligence* 37, no. 5 (1994): 72, available at https://www.cia.gov/library/center-for-the-study -of-intelligence/kent-csi/vol37no3/pdf/v37i3a09p.pdf.

3 **many of them prominent scholars:** Ibid.

3 **nearly a thousand:** Ibid.

3 **He worked hard to get them:** Ray S. Cline, *The CIA Under Reagan, Bush and Casey: The Evolution of the Agency from Roosevelt to Reagan* (Washington, DC: Acropolis Books, 1981), 76.

3 **With scant feedback from Roosevelt:** Russell Jack Smith, *The Unknown CIA: My Three Decades with the Agency* (New York: Berkley Books, 1992), 37–38.

3 **Donovan sent FDR:** "Memoranda for the President: Sunrise," *Studies in Intelligence* 7, no. 2 (Spring 1963), available at https://www.cia.gov/library/ center-for-the-study-of-intelligence/kent-csi/vol37no3/pdf/v37i3a09p. pdf, 73.

3 **Roosevelt appeared to like:** William R. Johnson, "Clandestinity and Current Intelligence," *Studies in Intelligence* 20, no. 3 (Fall 1976), reprinted in H. Bradford Westerfield, ed., *Inside CIA's Private World: Declassified Articles from the Agency's Internal Journal, 1955–1992* (New Haven: Yale University Press, 1995), 123.

3 **decidedly nonacademic phrases:** Ibid., 124.

3 **"one of the few original contributions":** Woodrow Kuhns, "The Beginning of Intelligence Analysis in CIA," *Studies in Intelligence* 51, no. 2 (2007), available at https://www.cia.gov/library/center-for-the-study- of-intelligence/csi-publications/csi-studies/studies/vol51no2/the-begin- ning-of-intelligence-analysis-in-cia.html.

4 **Not only did wartime analysts:** Cline, *The CIA Under Reagan, Bush and Casey*, 81.

4 **R&A officers in 1945 produced:** Wilson, "One Man's History in OSS," 74.

4 **Hopes faded for a rigorous system:** Cline, *The CIA Under Reagan, Bush and Casey*, 81.

4 **The ailing leader had spent:** David McCullough, *Truman* (New York: Simon and Schuster, 1992), 339.

4 **neglected to tell Truman:** Harry S. Truman, *Memoirs*, vol. 1, *Year of Decisions* (Garden City, NY: Doubleday, 1955), 10.

4 **a suggestion from his budget director:** Wilson, "One Man's History in OSS," 78.

4 **R&A officers who had neither:** Ibid.

4 **"an intelligent and understandable form":** Harry S. Truman, *Memoirs*, vol. 2: *Years of Trial and Hope* (Garden City, NY: Doubleday, 1956), 56.

4 **The president lightened the mood:** "Cloak and Dagger: The Unexpected Beginnings of CIA," CIA website Featured Story Archive, posted January 23, 2015, available at https://www.cia.gov/news-information /featured-story-archive/2015-featured-story-archive/cloak-and-dagger -the-unexpected-beginnings-of-cia.html.

5 **"the correlation and evaluation of intelligence":** Letter from President Truman to the Secretaries of State, War, and Navy, January 22, 1946, Doc. 7 in Michael Warner, ed., *The CIA Under Harry Truman: CIA Cold War Records* (Washington, DC: Center for the Study of Intelligence, CIA, 1994), 29–30.

5 **complaining when conflicting reports:** Truman, *Years of Trial and Hope*, 56.

5 **The first issue:** Kuhns, "The Beginning of Intelligence Analysis in CIA."

5 **his new product initially lacked SIGINT:** "A Look Back . . . The President's First Daily Brief," CIA website Featured Story Archive, posted February 6, 2008, available at https://www.cia.gov/news-information /featured-story-archive/2008-featured-story-archive/the-presidents -first-daily-brief.html.

5 **Byrnes asserted:** Kuhns, "The Beginning of Intelligence Analysis in CIA."

5 **"Department of State prepared its own digest":** Ibid.

5 **"probably did little but confuse":** Ibid.

5 **He noted the Daily Summary:** Truman, *Years of Trial and Hope*, 58.

6 **Truman began asking for it:** Smith, *The Unknown CIA*, 37–38.

6 **CIG's personnel expanded:** "Preface," in Warner, ed., *The CIA Under Harry Truman*, xiv.

6 **they kept doing it:** Kuhns, "The Beginning of Intelligence Analysis in CIA."

6 **White House officials simply never informed:** Smith, *The Unknown CIA*, 39.

7 **"he personally originated the *Daily*":** Kuhns, "The Beginning of Intelligence Analysis in CIA."

7 **also went to about fifteen:** Ibid.

7 **"valuable" but not "indispensable":** Ibid.

7 **"avidly and regularly":** Ibid.

7 **"to correlate and evaluate intelligence":** National Security Act of 1947, available at http://www.intelligence.senate.gov/nsact1947.pdf.

7 **the Agency thus kept producing:** Truman, *Years of Trial and Hope*, 58.

8 **"CIA does not believe":** Kuhns, "The Beginning of Intelligence Analysis in CIA."

8 **"The Soviet action":** Ibid.

8 **"In sponsoring the aggression":** Ibid.

8 **"approximately ninety per cent":** Ibid.

8 **laid the blame at the feet:** "Contents of the CIA Daily Summary," memorandum from Chief, D/Pub R. Jack Smith to AD/ORE Theodore Babbitt, September 21, 1950, Doc. 62 in Warner, ed., *The CIA Under Harry Truman*, 337–38.

9 **his legendary temper:** Cline, *The CIA Under Reagan, Bush and Casey*, 131–32.

9 **took shape and began revamping:** "The Office of Current Intelligence: A Study of Its Functions and Organization," CIA Office of Training (CIA-RDP80-00317 A000100030001-4), 3, CREST.

9 **with an issue covering:** Daily Summary, February 20, 1951, in "CIA's Early Days: Historical Intelligence Documents," *Studies in Intelligence* 38, no. 5 (Spring 1995): 93–95, available at http://www.foia.cia.gov/sites /default/files/DOC_0000622799.pdf.

9 **the all-source Current Intelligence Bulletin debuted:** G. Fred Albrecht, "A History of the Central Intelligence Bulletin," CIA internal paper, May 12, 1967, 16, available at http://www2.gwu.edu/~nsarchiv /NSAEBB/NSAEBB116/albrecht.pdf.

9 **initially went only to a select few:** "The Office of Current Intelligence: A Study of Its Functions and Organization," 4; Albrecht, "A History of the Central Intelligence Bulletin," 18.

9 **one piece in March indicated:** Albrecht, "A History of the Central Intelligence Bulletin," 23.

9 **"I have been reading":** Letter from Harry Truman to Walter B. Smith, March 6, 1951, in "CIA's Early Days: Historical Intelligence Documents," 96.

10 **OCI officers knew little:** Kuhns, "The Beginning of Intelligence Analysis in CIA."

10 **"This agency puts the information":** "Remarks of the President to the Final Session of the C.I.A.'s Eighth Training Orientation Course for Representatives of Various Government Agencies," Department of Agriculture Auditorium, Washington, DC, November 21, 1952, Doc. 81 in Warner, ed., *The CIA Under Harry Truman*, 337–38.

10 **more international experience than Harry Truman:** See Stephen E. Ambrose, *Ike's Spies: Eisenhower and the Espionage Establishment* (New York: Random House, 1981), 156–57.

10 **he joined the small (at that point) circle:** Albrecht, "A History of the Central Intelligence Bulletin."

10 **"I would much rather have it":** Former senior CIA official, CIA internal history interview, September 24, 1973 (CIA-RDP79T01762 A001200050001-0), CREST.

10 **Eisenhower chaired virtually every Thursday:** Gordon Gray, interview by Maclyn P. Burg, June 25, 1975, Oral History Program, DDEL, available at http://www.eisenhower.archives.gov/research/oral_histories /oral_history_transcripts/Gray_Gordon_342.pdf, 16.

11 **his boss made the vast majority:** Robert Cutler, "Intelligence as Foundation for Policy," *Studies in Intelligence* 3, no. 4 (Fall 1959): 61, available at https://www.cia.gov/library/center-for-the-study-of-intelligence/kent-csi /vol3no4/pdf/v03i4a05p.pdf.

11 **situation that continued under Allen Dulles:** Former senior CIA official, CIA internal history interview, September 24, 1973 (CIA-RDP 79T01762 A001200050001-0), CREST.

11 **"Every President has his own system":** Allen W. Dulles, interview by Thomas Braden, December 5 and 6, 1964, Oral History Program, JFKPL, available at http://www.jfklibrary.org/Asset-Viewer/Archives/JFKOH-AWD-01.aspx.

11 **The director started each meeting:** Andrew Goodpaster, interviewed by John Helgerson, cited in John L. Helgerson, *Getting to Know the President: Intelligence Briefings of Presidential Candidates, 1952–2004*, 2nd ed. (Washington, DC: CIA, Center for the Study of Intelligence, 2012), 21; senior former CIA official, CIA internal history interview, September 24, 1973 (CIA-RDP79T01762 A001200050001-0), CREST.

11 **schedule of topics for forthcoming NSC sessions:** Richard Lehman, interview by Richard Kovar, undated, in "Mr. Current Intelligence: An Interview with Richard Lehman," *Studies in Intelligence*, Summer 2000, available at https://www.cia.gov/library/center-for-the-study-of-intelligence/kent-csi/vol44no3/html/v44i3a05p.htm.

11 **"set months in advance":** Ibid.

11 **"Just small stuff":** Ibid.

12 **his boss avoided reading:** Richard M. Bissell Jr., *Reflections of a Cold Warrior: From Yalta to the Bay of Pigs* (New York: Oxford University Press, 2004), 115; Helgerson, *Getting to Know the President*, 23.

12 **distribution outside the Agency had expanded:** Albrecht, "A History of the Central Intelligence Bulletin," 29–30.

12 **Eisenhower grumbled in early 1954:** Ambrose, *Ike's Spies*, 253.

12 **tasked this group of experts:** Andrew Goodpaster, interview by Thomas Soapes, January 16, 1978, Oral History Program, DDEL, available at http://www.eisenhower.archives.gov/research/oral_histories/oral_history_transcripts/Goodpaster_Andrew_378.pdf, 96–97.

12 **new focus was placed:** Douglas F. Garthoff, *Directors of Central Intelligence as Leaders of the U.S. Intelligence Community, 1946–2005* (Washington, DC: Potomac Books, 2007), 20.

13 **Dulles took time to write:** Albrecht, "A History of the Central Intelligence Bulletin," 32–33.

13 **"The present publication":** Ibid., 40.

13 **they replaced the Current Intelligence Bulletin:** "The Office of Current Intelligence: A Study of Its Functions and Organization," 2.

13 **The first issue featured:** Albrecht, "A History of the Central Intelligence Bulletin," 45–47.

13 **the new CIB successfully forecasted:** Ibid., 51.

13 **the dissemination quickly rose:** Ibid., 45–47.

TWO: FOR THE PRESIDENT'S EYES ONLY

15 **"pickup touch football game":** Russell Jack Smith, *The Unknown CIA: My Three Decades with the Agency* (New York: Berkley Books, 1992), 130.

15 **"wasn't going to fool around":** Robert Amory Jr., interview by Joseph E. O'Connor, February 9, 1966, Oral History Program, JFKPL.

15 **"their own damned government":** Quoted in Peter Collier and David Horowitz, *The Kennedys: An American Drama* (New York: Encounter Books, 2002), 234.

16 **"CIA is the place I have to go":** Amory, interview by O'Connor.

16 **"He consumed five or six papers":** Cecil Stoughton and Chester V. Clifton, narrated by Hugh Sidey, *The Memories: JFK, 1961–1963* (New York: W. W. Norton, 1973), 3.

16 **everyone read the newspapers:** Ibid.

16 **month-long speed reading course:** Collier and Horowitz, *The Kennedys*, 223.

16 **he preferred a text:** Stoughton and Clifton, *The Memories*, 3.

16 **"I've only got a half hour":** Richard Reeves, *President Kennedy: Profile of Power* (New York: Touchstone, 1993), 45.

16 **memoranda and reports for Kennedy:** Untitled internal CIA note to Director of Central Intelligence Allen Dulles, February 10, 1961 (CIA-RDP80B01676 R002700080049-4), CREST.

17 **"some secret skill":** Arthur M. Schlesinger, *A Thousand Days: John F. Kennedy in the White House* (New York: Houghton Mifflin, 1965), 258.

17 **His takeaway from the Bay of Pigs:** Clark Clifford with Richard Holbrooke, *Counsel to the President: A Memoir* (New York: Random House, 1991), 350.

17 **changed the president's whole method:** Theodore C. Sorensen, *Kennedy* (New York: Harper & Row, 1965), 630.

17 **"He might make mistakes":** Clifford, *Counsel to the President*, 349.

17 **Kennedy had balked:** John L. Helgerson, *Getting to Know the President: Intelligence Briefings of Presidential Candidates, 1952–2004*, 2nd ed. (Washington, DC: CIA, Center for the Study of Intelligence, 2012), 48.

17 **Dick Lehman never intended:** Richard Lehman, interview by Richard Kovar, undated, in "Mr. Current Intelligence: An Interview with Richard Lehman," *Studies in Intelligence*, Summer 2000, available at https://www.cia.gov/library/center-for-the-study-of-intelligence/kent-csi/vol44no3/html/v44i3a05p.htm; "Comments by Dick Lehman on the Occasion of His Retirement," excerpt from a bulletin of the Central Intelligence Retirees Association, undated (courtesy of David Lehman).

17 **"just remember one thing":** "Comments by Dick Lehman."

17 **Starting as a P-1 analyst:** Lehman, interview by Kovar.

18 **"Good pitcher—can't hit":** Ibid.

18 **"There is no experience":** John F. Kennedy, "Television and Radio Interview: After Two Years—a Conversation with the President," December 17, 1962, *American Presidency Project*, http://www.presidency.ucsb.edu/ws/?pid=9060.

18 **"foreign policy can kill us":** Schlesinger, *A Thousand Days*, 329.

19 **"when the President is your desk officer":** Quoted in ibid., 330. Some

ten years later, the CIA's Office of Current Intelligence continued to tell this story to cite Kennedy's detailed attention to foreign policy areas of particular interest; see "The Office of Current Intelligence: A Study of Its Functions and Organization," CIA Office of Training paper (CIA-RDP80 -00317 A000100030001-4), 34, CREST.

19 **"We couldn't say to President Kennedy":** Bromley Smith, interview by Paige E. Mulhollan, July 29, 1969, Oral History interview I, Internet Copy, LBJL.

19 **Bundy finally vented to Kennedy:** "Memorandum from the President's Special Assistant for National Security Affairs (Bundy) to President Kennedy," May 16, 1961, *FRUS, 1961–1963*, vol. XXV, Document 13, 28–31.

20 **"All this, if it is done right":** Ibid., 31.

20 **the military assistant had been assembling:** Helgerson, *Getting to Know the President*, 48.

20 **he felt increasingly uncomfortable:** Lehman, interview by Kovar.

20 **Kennedy found himself blindsided:** Richard Lehman, "History of the CIA Years," unpublished draft, 2001 (courtesy of David Lehman); Lehman, interview by Kovar.

20 **"Bring one of your writers over":** Lehman, "History of the CIA Years."

21 **"What I need":** Lehman, interview by Kovar; Lehman, "History of the CIA Years."

21 **Clifton painted a picture:** Lehman, interview by Kovar.

21 **Clifton wanted a document:** Lehman, "History of the CIA Years."

21 **"What he asked us to do":** Lehman, interview by Kovar; Lehman, "History of the CIA Years."

21 **Less than twenty-four hours later:** Ibid.

21 **the three officials above Sheldon:** Ibid.

21 **Clifton liked what he saw:** Lehman, "History of the CIA Years."

22 **Only twenty-five minutes:** Steven L. Brawley's Jackie Kennedy tribute site, pinkpillbox.com/glenora.htm (accessed June 2011; no longer active).

22 **called on owner Gladys Tartiere three times:** Clifford, *Counsel to the President*, 362.

22 **Army Signal Corps set up a trailer:** Brawley, pinkpillbox.com/glenora .htm.

22 **he made a point to head there:** Schlesinger, *A Thousand Days*, 272; Collier and Horowitz, *The Kennedys*, 238.

22 **he swam as often as twice a day:** Sorensen, *Kennedy*, 373; Michael Dobbs, *One Minute to Midnight: Kennedy, Khrushchev, and Castro on the Brink of Nuclear War* (New York: Vintage Books, 2008), 269.

22 **sitting on the diving board:** Lehman, "History of the CIA Years."

22 **8½-by-8-inch booklet:** Helgerson, *Getting to Know the President*, 49.

22 **he approved the continued production:** Lehman, "History of the CIA Years."

23 **Sheldon finally reported:** Lehman, interview by Kovar.

23 **"go ahead—so far, so good":** Helgerson, *Getting to Know the President*, 49.

23 **wherever his boss went:** Sorensen, *Kennedy*, 376.

23 **the only other copies of the Checklist:** Lehman, interview by Kovar.

24 **"Thoreau-like style":** Smith, *The Unknown CIA*, 175–176.

24 **Lehman credited his Harvard introductory writing course:** David Lehman (son of Richard Lehman), interview by the author, December 2012.

24 **The production of each day's issue:** Lehman, interview by Kovar.

24 **Lehman or others might roll:** Lehman, interview by Kovar; Smith, *The Unknown CIA*, 175–76.

24 **in the presence of the OCI officer:** "Memorandum for the Director" from Deputy Director of Central Intelligence Marshall Carter, April 7, 1962 (CIA-RDP80B01676 R001300050097-9), CREST; see also Carl Kaysen, interview by Joseph E. O'Connor, July 11, 1966, Oral History Program, JFKPL.

24 **Kennedy usually awoke:** Sorensen, *Kennedy*, 371; see also Reeves, *President Kennedy*, 66.

25 **The Checklist's authors and editors occasionally waited:** "Memorandum for the Director" from Cabell, April 7, 1962; Kaysen, interview by O'Connor.

25 **"Almost all requests for memos":** "Memorandum for General Carter," September 21, 1962 (CIA-RDP80B01676 R000200140040-3), CREST.

25 **"snappy, short":** Allen W. Dulles, interview by Thomas Braden, December 5 and 6, 1964, Oral History Program, JFKPL.

25 **one issue from February 1962:** President's Intelligence Checklist, February 15, 1962, in Chester V. Clifton Files, President's Intelligence Checklist, Box 353, National Security Files, JFKPL.

26 **After these nine short items:** Ibid.

26 **Successive Checklists often contained:** From a survey of available Checklists in the Chester V. Clifton Files, President's Intelligence Checklist, National Security Files, JFKPL.

26 **"These incidents have given Havana the jitters":** President's Intelligence Checklist, August 31, 1962, Clifton Files, Box 356, JFKPL.

26 **"The [Chinese] Nationalists are dropping hints":** President's Intelligence Checklist, July 12, 1962, Clifton Files, Box 356, JFKPL.

27 **"Nehru's daughter has admitted":** President's Intelligence Checklist, June 20, 1962, Doc. No./ESDN 0000415958, CIA FOIA Electronic Reading Room at www.foia.coa.gov.

27 **"As time goes on":** President's Intelligence Checklist, June 19, 1962, Doc. No./ESDN 0000416213, www.foia.coa.gov.

27 **"President Goulart [of Brazil]":** President's Intelligence Checklist, June 20, 1962, Doc No/ESDN: 0000415958, www.foia.cia.gov.

27 **"The Soviet airlift into Laos":** President's Intelligence Checklist, August 28, 1962, Clifton Files, Box 356, JFKPL.

27 **"The stuff for Kennedy":** Lehman, interview by Kovar.

28 **"The King of Thailand":** President's Intelligence Checklist, June 20, 1962.

28 **"Diem's brother Nhu"**: President's Intelligence Checklist, July 14, 1962, Clifton Files, Box 356, JFKPL.

28 **"the government is neither fish nor fowl"**: President's Intelligence Checklist, July 17, 1962, Clifton Files, Box 356, JFKPL.

28 **"The Saudis, fed up"**: President's Intelligence Checklist, October 15, 1962, Clifton Files, Box 357, JFKPL.

28 **surface-to-surface missile equipment:** David M. Barrett and Max Holland, *Blind over Cuba: The Photo Gap and the Missile Crisis* (College Station, TX: Texas A&M University Press, 2012), 10.

28 **elaborate campaign to deny intelligence collection:** See the compelling accounts in Dobbs, *One Minute to Midnight*, and Anatoli I. Gribkov and William Y. Smith, *Operation ANADYR: U.S. and Soviet Generals Recount the Cuban Missile Crisis*, ed. Andrew Friendly (Chicago: Edition Q, 1993).

28 **standing down surveillance overflights:** Barrett and Holland, *Blind over Cuba*.

28 **"Eleven Soviet merchant ships"**: President's Intelligence Checklist, August 4, 1962, Clifton Files, Box 356, JFKPL.

28 **"Soviet shipments to Cuba have been arriving"**: President's Intelligence Checklist, August 9, 1962, Clifton Files, Box 356, JFKPL.

29 **some forty thousand Soviet troops:** Gribkov and Smith, *Operation ANADYR*, 28.

29 **"Most of our information from within Cuba"**: President's Intelligence Checklist, August 23, 1962, Clifton Files, Box 356, JFKPL.

29 **increasing budget:** President's Intelligence Checklist, August 28, 1962, Clifton Files, Box 356, JFKPL.

29 **"We are not able"**: President's Intelligence Checklist, August 30, 1962, Clifton Files, Box 356, JFKPL.

29 **The earliest indication about missiles:** "New Draft of Cuban Study," Memorandum from Richard Lehman to the CIA Executive Director, November 15, 1962 (CIA-RDP80B01676 R001700180076-4), CREST; "Inspector General's Survey of Handling of Intelligence Information During the Cuban Arms Build-Up, August to Mid-October 1962," report to Director of Central Intelligence John McCone, November 20, 1962 (CIA-RDP80B01676 R001800060005-4), CREST.

30 **"We are under a White House injunction"**: "Inspector General's Survey of Handling of Intelligence Information."

30 **"[cut] the *Checklist* off"**: "New Draft of Cuban Study."

30 **"at most the President might have learned"**: Ibid. Lehman's study fed into the inspector general's study cited above.

30 **"Our latest photography has turned up"**: President's Intelligence Checklist, October 18, 1961, Clifton Files, Box 357, JFKPL.

31 **"Why summarize what the President already knew?"**: Lehman, interview by Kovar.

31 **hearing the voice of President Kennedy:** Dick Kerr (then OCI analyst and later deputy director of central intelligence), telephone interviews by the author, October and November 2011.

31 **Bromley Smith showed him the text:** Lehman, interview by Kovar.

32 **"The President read the checklist":** "Memorandum for the Record," November 1, 1962, Clifton Files, Box 358, JFKPL.

32 **the use of the Azores:** "Memorandum for the Record," February 5, 1962, Clifton Files, Box 353, JFKPL.

32 **a more complete briefing on Berlin:** "Memorandum for the Record," March 9, 1962, Clifton Files, Box 354, JFKPL.

32 **Chinese Communist activity in northern India:** "Memorandum for the Record," May 16, 1962, Clifton Files, Box 355, JFKPL.

32 **Dutch lower house's rejection:** "Memorandum for the Record," May 26, 1962, Clifton Files, Box 355, JFKPL.

32 **prepare a story on US nuclear-powered aircraft:** "Memorandum for the Record," July 6, 1962, Clifton Files, Box 356, JFKPL.

32 **the woman who interpreted:** "Memorandum for the Record," December 1, 1962, Clifton Files, Box 358, JFKPL.

32 **Ethiopian leader Haile Selassie:** "Memorandum for the Record," November 21, 1963, Clifton Files, Box 359, JFKPL.

33 **"quite a barrage of questions":** Dulles, interview by Braden.

33 **"The Director and I must be protected":** Memorandum from Acting Director Marshall S. Carter to the Deputy Director (Intelligence), February 13, 1963 (CIA-RDP80B01676 R003100100014-4), CREST.

33 **"We tried very hard":** Amory, interview by O'Connor.

33 **Kennedy engaged "enthusiastically":** Smith, *The Unknown CIA*, 176.

33 **didn't always appreciate Kennedy's attention:** Ray S. Cline, *The CIA Under Reagan, Bush, and Casey* (Washington, DC: Acropolis Books, 1981), 225.

33 **intimate details about foreign leaders:** Michael R. Beschloss, *Kennedy v. Khrushchev: The Crisis Years, 1960–63* (London: Faber and Faber, 1991), 3.

34 **Morale among OCI analysts:** Helgerson, *Getting to Know the President*, 50.

34 **"the *Checklist* was all he needed":** "Memorandum for the Record" from Deputy Director of Central Intelligence Marshall Carter, November 23, 1962 (CIA-RDP80B01676 R001300040033-0), CREST.

34 **bread-and-butter activity:** Smith, *The Unknown CIA*, 175.

34 **directed the CIA to provide copies:** "Memorandum for the Secretary of State, Secretary of Defense, and Director of Central Intelligence" from C. V. Clifton, December 1, 1961 (CIA-RDP80B01676 R00400180001-0), CREST.

34 **OCI officers dutifully delivered the Checklist:** Richard Helms with William Hood, *A Look over My Shoulder: A Life in the Central Intelligence Agency* (New York: Ballantine Books, 2003), 379.

34 **chairman of the Joint Chiefs of Staff:** Helgerson, *Getting to Know the President*, 51.

34 **"includes more than intelligence items":** "Memorandum for the Secretary of State, Secretary of Defense, and Director of Central Intelligence" from C. V. Clifton, December 1, 1961 (CIA-RDP80B01676 R00400180001-0), CREST.

35 **"I believe it is of definite value":** Letter from Deputy Secretary of

Defense Roswell Gilpatric to Director of Central Intelligence John McCone, December 29, 1961 (CIA-RDP80B01676 R000800040001-1), CREST.

35 **informed him of "developments":** Letter from Secretary of State Dean Rusk to Director of Central Intelligence John McCone, January 2, 1962 (CIA-RDP80B01676 R002900220021-6), CREST.

35 **"a damned useful document":** Helgerson, *Getting to Know the President*, 50.

35 **Cabell, the deputy director, told McNamara's assistant:** "Memorandum for the Deputy Director for Intelligence" from the Deputy Director of Central Intelligence, April 26, 1962 (CIA-RDP80B01676 R001300050009-6), CREST.

36 **a handwritten note from Jackie Kennedy:** See note in Clifton Files, Box 359, JFKPL.

THREE: THE BIRTH OF THE BOOK

37 **the depth of the animosity:** See Robert A. Caro, *The Years of Lyndon Johnson: The Passage of Power* (New York: Vintage Books, 2012), Chapter 7.

37 **Schlesinger claimed:** Arthur M. Schlesinger, *A Thousand Days: John F. Kennedy in the White House* (New York: Houghton Mifflin, 1965), 704.

37 **he would happily see three men:** Charles Bartlett, interview by Fred Holborn, February 20, 1965, Oral History Program, JFKPL.

38 **"When you get into these problems":** Ibid.

38 **"One of the assignments we picked up":** Bromley Smith, interview by Paige E. Mulhollan, July 29, 1969, Oral History interview I, Internet Copy, LBJL.

38 **Neither Allen Dulles nor John McCone:** John L. Helgerson, *Getting to Know the President: Intelligence Briefings of Presidential Candidates, 1952–2004*, 2nd ed. (Washington, DC: CIA, 2012), 50.

38 **Johnson had lacked any real contact:** Richard Helms with William Hood, *A Look over My Shoulder: A Life in the Central Intelligence Agency* (New York: Ballantine Books, 2003), 292.

39 **"What about the Vice President?":** Richard Lehman, interview by Richard Kovar, undated, in "Mr. Current Intelligence: An Interview with Richard Lehman," *Studies in Intelligence*, Summer 2000, available at https://www.cia.gov/library/center-for-the-study-of-intelligence/kent-csi/vol44no3/html/v44i3a05p.htm.

39 **Cline called him into his office:** Ibid.

39 **The CIA director maneuvered his way:** Helgerson, *Getting to Know the President*, 51–52.

40 **a "very, very frequent visitor":** Carl Kaysen, interview by Joseph E. O'Connor, July 11, 1966, Oral History Program, JFKPL.

40 **focused that morning on practical issues:** For the context of Johnson's morning, see Caro, *The Years of Lyndon Johnson: The Passage of Power*, 374–75.

40 **The president told McCone:** "Memorandum for the Record" by John McCone, November 25, 1963, McCone Memoranda, Meetings with the President, Box 1, LBJL.

40 **he recalled being relieved:** Lyndon Baines Johnson, *The Vantage Point: Perspectives of the Presidency, 1963–1969* (New York: Holt, Rinehart and Winston, 1971), 22.

40 **The director reported back:** "Memorandum for the Record" by John McCone, November 25, 1963.

40 **a global *tour d'horizon*:** Johnson, *The Vantage Point*, 22. Johnson does not mention the Checklist by name. He only writes, disingenuously, that "President Kennedy had kept me well informed on world events, so I was not expecting any major surprises in that first intelligence briefing." Ibid.

40 **That first day, the Checklist led with:** President's Intelligence Checklist, November 23, 1962, Intelligence Briefings, President's Intelligence Checklist, 11/23/63–12/5/63, Box 1, National Security File, LBJL.

41 **Johnson asked a few questions:** Johnson, *The Vantage Point*, 22.

41 **Lehman began writing "at great length":** Lehman, interview by Kovar.

41 **Bromley Smith at the NSC signed off:** Helgerson, *Getting to Know the President*, 52.

41 **"The North Vietnamese have told the French":** President's Intelligence Checklist, November 24, 1962, Box 1, LBJL.

41 **the other topics that day:** Ibid.

41 **During his first week as president:** From a survey of the article and note headlines in the President's Intelligence Checklists, November 23–29, 1962, Box 1, LBJL.

42 **"Oswald":** President's Intelligence Checklist, November 25, 1962, Box 1, LBJL.

42 **"very brief":** "Meeting with the President—10:15—9 December 1963," McCone Memoranda, Box 1, LBJL.

42 **"One day I'd worked hard":** Robert Gates, telephone interview with the author, August 2012.

43 **Johnson failed to engage Colby:** William Colby and Peter Forbath, *Honorable Men: My Life in the CIA* (New York: Simon and Schuster, 1978), 241.

43 **national security advisor, Bundy, quickly adjusted:** Ivo H. Daalder and I. M. Destler, *In the Shadow of the Oval Office: Profiles of the National Security Advisers and the Presidents They Served—from JFK to George W. Bush* (New York: Simon and Schuster, 2009), 41.

43 **Lehman kicked an idea around:** Richard Lehman, "History of the CIA Years," unpublished draft, 2001 (courtesy of David Lehman).

43 **five copies of a memorial Checklist:** Letter from R. J. Smith to Ted Clifton, December 4, 1963, C. V. Clifton Files, President's Intelligence Checklist, Box 1, National Security File, LBJL.

43 **"In honor of President Kennedy":** For years, the backdating of this tribute Checklist led historians to imply that this special edition was the actual Checklist that McCone delivered to President Johnson on Saturday, November 23, 1963. See Christopher Andrew, *For the President's Eyes Only: Secret Intelligence and the American Presidency from Washington through*

Bush (New York: Harper Collins, 1995), 309. But like the Checklist itself during Kennedy's years in office, this memorial Checklist was kept from Johnson. The NSC's Bromley Smith recognized that reminding the new president of the Checklist's personal link to Kennedy would only make his job of keeping Johnson interested in the daily intelligence product harder. Letter from R. J. Smith to Ted Clifton, December 4, 1963, Clifton Files, Box 1, LBJL. See also Helgerson, *Getting to Know the President*, 57.

43 **"some regularity":** "Memorandum for the Record," January 6, 1964, cited in *FRUS, 1964–1968*, vol. XXXIII, Document 187.

43 **"not getting a steady feed of intelligence":** Editorial note, *FRUS, 1964–1968*, vol. XXXIII, Item 187, 416.

43 **had not looked at any finished intelligence:** "Memorandum for Mr. Jenkins" by C. V. Clifton, January 9, 1964, LBJL.

43 **"shortest possible review of highlights":** Ibid.

44 **new Current Intelligence Review:** Editorial note, *FRUS, 1964–1968*, vol. XXXIII, Item 187, 416.

44 **"worked like a charm":** Helgerson, *Getting to Know the President*, 56–57.

44 **"The first day you stop":** Editorial note, *FRUS, 1964–1968*, vol. XXXIII, Item 187, 416.

44 **Carroll had begun to see a copy:** Memorandum for the DD/I from H. Knoche, December 5, 1963 (CIA-RDP80B01676 R003100100005-4), CREST.

44 **copies also started going to:** "The President's Intelligence Checklist," memorandum from CIA Deputy Director (Intelligence) Ray Cline to Bundy, February 21, 1964, LBJL.

44 **"just another intelligence paper":** "Draft Memorandum from the Executive Director of the National Security Council (Smith) to the President's Special Assistant for National Security Affairs (Bundy)," undated (but its filing location suggests it was prepared between February 21 and 24, 1964), *FRUS, 1964–1968*, vol. XXXIII, Item 192, 426.

45 **"serious reservations":** "Intelligence Support to Ambassador Stevenson," memorandum from Jack Smith to Bundy, February 21, 1964, LBJL.

45 **"one effort to tighten the crucial relationship":** "Memorandum from Director of Central Intelligence McCone to the President's Special Assistant for National Security Affairs (Bundy)," April 6, 1964, *FRUS, 1964–1968*, vol. XXXIII, Item 198, 439.

45 **he was "highly dissatisfied":** "Breakfast Meeting at the White House—22 April 1964," McCone Memoranda, Box 1, LBJL.

45 **"I was concerned":** "Discussion with President Johnson—Wednesday Afternoon—29 Apr. 4:45 in His Office," McCone Memoranda, Box 1, LBJL.

45 **catching up on the Review upon returning:** Helgerson, *Getting to Know the President*, 57.

45 **McCone himself began to doubt:** Ibid.

46 **the president's lack of interest:** Lehman, interview by Kovar.

46 **Cline had worked just about every angle:** Ray S. Cline, *The CIA Under Reagan, Bush and Casey: The Evolution of the Agency from Roosevelt to Reagan* (Washington, DC: Acropolis Books, 1981), 74–76.

46 **called Bundy on the night of October 15, 1962:** Ibid., 220.

46 **create a new publication:** Editorial note, *FRUS, 1964–1968,* vol. XXXIII, Item 187, 416.

46 **now a full-sized document:** Editorial note, *FRUS, 1964–1968,* vol. XXXIII, Item 214, 473.

47 **Each day's edition had a simple cover:** President's Daily Brief, August 7, 1965, President's Daily [Intelligence] Brief (PDB) Reference File, LBJL.

47 **"this new form of a daily intelligence briefing":** Memorandum from McGeorge Bundy to President Johnson, December 1, 1964, RAC Project File, Box 3, Documents from the National Security File, Intelligence Briefings File, LBJL.

47 **"Mac, the President likes this very much":** Ibid. (notation on the memo).

47 **Moyers passed word:** Editorial note, *FRUS, 1964–1968,* vol. XXXIII, Item 214, 474.

47 **OCI replaced:** Ibid., 473.

47 **"he has seemed quite chipper lately":** President's Daily Brief, August 7, 1965.

47 **a map of Communist China:** Ibid.

47 **"the most helpful document":** Memorandum for the Deputy Director (Intelligence) from Deputy Director Marshall S. Carter, February 23, 1965 (CIA-RDP80B01676 R001300060004-0), CREST.

48 **Johnson named him special assistant:** See W. Marvin Watson with Sherwin Markman, *Chief of Staff: Lyndon Johnson and His Presidency* (New York: Thomas Dunne Books/St. Martin's Press, 2004), 76.

48 **Watson, who had arrived at dawn:** Marvin Watson, interview by the author, May 2012.

48 **filled with his "night reading":** Ibid. See also Watson, *Chief of Staff,* 90, and Hugh Sidey, *A Very Personal Presidency: Lyndon Johnson in the White House* (New York: Atheneum, 1968), 249.

49 **"I don't think he was ever wrong":** Watson, *Chief of Staff,* 91.

49 **candidate items for the president's night reading:** Watson, interview by the author.

49 **Johnson even liked the PDB enough:** "Editorial Note," *FRUS, 1964–1968,* vol. XXXIII, Item 214, 473; Watson, interview by the author.

49 **he intended to resign:** Helgerson, *Getting to Know the President,* 56.

49 **"McCone had one view of the CIA":** Watson, interview by the author.

49 **McCone showed up at the White House:** Ibid.

49 **little choice but to leave the Agency:** Richard M. Helms, interview by Mary S. McAuliffe, June 19, 1989, available at http://www.foia.cia.gov /sites/default/files/ document_conversions/45/6_19_oral.pdf.

50 **Johnson cajoled Raborn:** "Telephone Conversation Between President Johnson and Admiral Raborn," April 6, 1965, *FRUS, 1964–1968,* vol. XXXIII, Document 223.

50 **choice of Raborn baffling:** Cline, *The CIA under Reagan, Bush and Casey,* 235.

50 **"Which tribe in Liberia are the oligarchs?":** Thomas Powers, *The Man Who Kept the Secrets: Richard Helms and the CIA* (New York: Washington Square Press, 1979), 214.

50 **"If I want to see you":** Helms, *A Look over My Shoulder*, 294.

50 **he frequently told the OCI what to include:** For examples, see Memoranda for the Record from the DCI's Morning Meetings on November 30, 1965 (CIA-RDP80B01676 R001500060163-8), December 7, 1965 (CIA-RDP 80B01676 R001500100037-3), CREST; December 8, 1965 (CIA-RDP80 B01676 R00150010036-4), CREST; January 14, 1966 (CIA-RDP80B01676 R 001500100011-1), CREST; and March 22 1966 (CIA-RDP80B01676 R00 1500090048-3), CREST.

50 **Raborn took Cline's description:** Memorandum for the Record, Morning Meeting of December 15, 1965 (CIA-RDP80B01676 R001500100031-9), CREST.

50 **its distribution remained limited:** "Dissemination of the President's Daily Brief," memorandum from the Assistant for Special Projects in CIA's Office of Current Intelligence to Bromley Smith, September 16, 1965, RAC Project File, Box 3 (Documents from the National Security File, Intelligence Briefings File), LBJL.

50 **Watson . . . also saw the book every day:** Watson, interview by the author.

51 **US involvement in Vietnam:** Douglas F. Garthoff, *Directors of Central Intelligence as Leaders of the U.S. Intelligence Community, 1946–2005* (Washington, DC: Potomac Books, 2007), 53.

51 **a daily Vietnam report:** Helgerson, *Getting to Know the President*, 58.

51 **obviating the need for the PDB:** Jim Jones (Marvin Watson's successor as de facto White House Chief of staff), interview by the author, January 2012.

51 **The North Vietnamese seem to want:** President's Daily Brief, May 13, 1967.

51 **analysts discounted field reports in early 1968:** David S. Robarge, "Richard Helms: The Intelligence Professional Personified: In Memory and Appreciation," internal CIA retrospective at http://www.foia.cia.gov /sites/default/files/ document_conversions/45/intel_professional.pdf.

51 **despite Johnson's anger:** Helms, *A Look over My Shoulder*, 328.

51 **excluded Vice President Hubert Humphrey:** Vice President Humphrey took this as just one manifestation of his exclusion from foreign policy overall. See Carl Solberg, *Hubert Humphrey: A Biography* (New York: W. W. Norton, 1984), 270–75.

51 **a chance to kick policy ideas around:** For his thoughts on the Tuesday lunch, see McGeorge Bundy, interview by Paige E. Mulhollan, January 30, 1969, Oral History Interview I, Internet Copy, LBJL.

52 **"complete confidence and candor":** Dean Rusk, interview by Paige E. Mulhollan, September 26, 1969, Oral History interview, Internet Copy, LBJL.

52 **"The cabinet secretaries knew":** Smith, interview by Mulhollan.

52 **added as regular members:** Walt W. Rostow, interview by Paige E. Mulhollan, March 21, 1969, Oral History interview I, Internet Copy, LBJL.

52 **delivering the PDB before the president woke up:** Editorial note, *FRUS, 1964–1968*, vol. XXXIII, Item 214, 474; Memorandum for the Record, Morning Meeting of 3 March 1966 (CIA-RDP80R01284 A001800010021-4), CREST.

52 **OCI analysts would have to publish:** Paul Corscadden, "DDI/New York: Intelligence During a Presidential Transition," *Studies in Intelligence* 13, no. 4, Fall 1969, 96, CIA-RDP78T03194 A000300010008-4, CREST.

52 **"Johnson had his at 7:00":** Watson, interview by the author.

52 **the change in delivery should affect:** See, for example, the dissemination list attached to "Transmittal of Report [Redacted]," CIA memorandum, December 13, 1967 (CIA-RDP71T00730 R000400260001-0), CREST; and Memorandum from the Military Assistant-Designate (Haig) to the President's Assistant for National Security Affairs-Designate (Kissinger), January 8, 1969, Item 5, *FRUS, 1969–1976*, 2:19.

52 **"going all out to show":** President's Daily Brief, May 16, 1967, President's Daily (Intelligence) Brief (PDB) Reference File, LBJL.

53 **the PDB was delivered for five days:** See President's Daily Brief, May 29, 1967.

53 **analysts rescrubbed the data:** Helms, *A Look over My Shoulder*, 298.

53 **"Although the analysis ran contrary":** Emile A. Nakhleh, "The June 1967 and October 1973 Arab-Israeli Wars," in *The Directorate of Intelligence: Fifty Years of Informing Policy, 1952–2002*, expanded ed. (Washington, DC: CIA, 2002), 203–4.

54 **"President Johnson came to understand":** Richard Helms, interview by Paige Mulhollan, April 4, 1969, oral history interview, available at http://web2.millercenter.org/lbj/oralhistory/helms_richard_1969_0404.pdf.

54 **tactical developments and analysis of breaking events:** Helms, *A Look over My Shoulder*, 298.

54 **"an early and perhaps overwhelming victory":** President's Daily Brief, June 6, 1967, President's Daily (Intelligence) Brief (PDB) Reference File, LBJL.

54 **resonated with Johnson:** Helms, interview by Mulhollan.

54 **"The US Embassy in Benghazi":** President's Daily Brief, June 5, 1967, President's Daily (Intelligence) Brief (PDB) Reference File, LBJL.

55 **"Writing for the PDB":** Gates, interview by the author.

55 **"occasional bag of dirt":** Lehman, "History of the CIA Years."

55 **"the same kinds of dirt":** Gates, interview by the author.

55 **"We doubt that it will amount to much":** President's Daily Brief, April 1, 1968, President's Daily (Intelligence) Brief (PDB) Reference File, LBJL.

55 **"We do not know just what caused the delay":** President's Daily Brief, July 24, 1968, President's Daily (Intelligence) Brief (PDB) Reference File, LBJL.

55 **"Students are still in a defiant mood":** President's Daily Brief, October 1 and October 4, 1968, President's Daily (Intelligence) Brief (PDB) Reference File, LBJL.

55 **"the capital is rife with rumors":** President's Daily Brief, October 5, 1968, President's Daily (Intelligence) Brief (PDB) Reference File, LBJL.

56 **comparing and contrasting student unrest:** President's Daily Brief, October 10, 1968, President's Daily (Intelligence) Brief (PDB) Reference File, LBJL.

56 **presentation of the defense budget:** President's Daily Brief, December 11, 1968, President's Daily (Intelligence) Brief (PDB) Reference File, LBJL.

56 **in six months the USSR:** President's Daily Brief, December 18, 1968, President's Daily (Intelligence) Brief (PDB) Reference File, LBJL.

56 **nuclear attack submarine . . . and helicopter carrier capabilities:** President's Daily Brief, January 18, 1969, President's Daily (Intelligence) Brief (PDB) Reference File, LBJL.

56 **flight of a supersonic aircraft:** President's Daily Brief, January 11, 1969, President's Daily (Intelligence) Brief (PDB) Reference File, LBJL.

56 **"I could tell from the questions":** Helms, interview by Mulhollan.

56 **Rusk at State and McNamara at Defense:** Memorandum for the Record, Morning Meeting of 20 September 1966 (CIA-RDP80B01676 R00150007008-9), CREST.

57 **"exceptionally good":** Dean Rusk with Richard Rusk and Daniel S. Papp, *As I Saw It* (New York: W. W. Norton, 1990), 552–53.

57 **"little incremental value":** Francis Bator, telephone interview by the author, June 2012.

57 **"see what the president was seeing":** Robert Pursley, interview by the author, August 2012.

57 **hard to focus him on anything else:** Ibid.

57 **praised its sophistication:** Cline, *The CIA Under Reagan, Bush and Casey*, 227.

57 **pride that intelligence analysts had:** Russell Jack Smith, *The Unknown CIA: My Three Decades with the Agency* (New York: Berkley Books, 1989), 174.

57 **"remarkably well done":** Memorandum for the Record, Morning Meeting of 28 September 1966 (CIA-RDP80B01676 R001500070003-4), CREST.

FOUR: OUT IN THE COLD

59 **"had it in for the Agency":** "An Interview with Richard Helms," *Studies in Intelligence* 44, no. 4, available at https://www.cia.gov/library/center -for-the-study-of-intelligence/kent-csi/vol44no4/html/v44i4a07p_0005. htm; Henry Kissinger, interview by Richard Norton Smith, April 8, 2009, Gerald R. Ford Oral History project of the Gerald R. Ford Presidential Foundation, available at http://geraldrfordfoundation.org/centennial /oralhistory/henry-kissinger.

59 **believed the CIA's analysts to be part of:** See Robert M. Hathaway and Russell Jack Smith, *Richard Helms as Director of Central Intelligence, 1966–1973* (Washington, DC: Center for the Study of Intelligence, CIA, 1993), 9–10.

59 **"Ivy League liberals":** Henry Kissinger, *White House Years* (New York: Little, Brown, 1979), 11.

59 **"I thought the analytic branch":** Henry Kissinger, interview by the author, October 2011.

60 *Manhattan, mid-November 1968:* Richard Lehman, interview by Richard Kovar, undated, in "Mr. Current Intelligence: An Interview with Richard Lehman," *Studies in Intelligence*, Summer 2000, available at https://www .cia.gov/library/center-for-the-study-of-intelligence/kent-csi/vol44no3 /html/v44i3a05p.htm; Paul Corscadden, "DDI/New York: Intelligence During a Presidential Transition," *Studies in Intelligence* 13, no. 4, Fall 1969, 92–93 (CIA-RDP78T03194 A000300010008-4), CREST.

60 **unprecedented, full-time support hub:** Lehman, interview by Kovar; Corscadden, "DDI/New York: Intelligence During a Presidential Transition," 92–93; see also Hathaway and Smith, *Richard Helms as Director of Central Intelligence*, 8.

60 **the site would stay anonymous:** Corscadden, "DDI/New York," 92–93; see also Hathaway and Smith, *Richard Helms as Director of Central Intelligence*, 8.

60 **On Tuesday, November 19:** John L. Helgerson, *Getting to Know the President: Intelligence Briefings of Presidential Candidates, 1952–2004*, 2nd ed. (Washington, DC: CIA, 2012), 66.

60 **delivered it to Nixon's secretary:** Corscadden, "DDI/New York," 92–93; see also Hathaway and Smith, *Richard Helms as Director of Central Intelligence*, 8.

61 **appropriate clearances and a suitable safe:** Helgerson, *Getting to Know the President*, 66.

61 **the "Nixon Special":** Corscadden, "DDI/New York," 92–94.

61 **Lehman came up to New York:** Lehman, interview by Kovar.

61 **Mitchell ended up meeting with a CIA officer:** Corscadden, "DDI/ New York," 95.

61 **classified reading room:** Ibid., 92–94.

61 **how the PDB might work better:** Richard Allen, telephone interview by the author, March 2012.

61 **expanded transition version of the PDB:** Corscadden, "DDI/New York," 95–96.

61 **They learned on December 18:** Helgerson, *Getting to Know the President*, 72.

62 **"Back in 1968":** Richard Allen, telephone interview by the author.

62 **By the time it closed up shop:** Corscadden, "DDI/New York," 93–94.

62 **"an impressive performance":** Lehman, interview by Kovar.

62 **"I lost track":** Richard Allen, telephone interview by the author.

62 **"against my better judgment":** Ibid.

62 **"We were dealing with Kissinger":** Lehman, interview by Kovar.

63 **several ad hoc briefings:** Corscadden, "DDI/New York," 95.

63 **Kissinger had complained:** Helgerson, *Getting to Know the President*, 68.

63 **add speculative annexes to the PDB:** "Memorandum for the Record," DCI's Morning Meeting, December 23, 1968 (CIA-RDP80R01284 A001800070033-5), CREST.

63 **"Do you have a regional quota":** Smith, *The Unknown CIA*, 237–38.

64 **The PDB's distribution at the White House:** "Handling of Information for President Nixon," Memorandum from Al Haig to Henry Kissinger, January 17, 1969, NSC Institutional ("H") Files: NSC System, Box H-301, Folder 2, RNL.

64 **Johnson had been receiving the PDB:** "Processing of Information and Intelligence for the President-Elect," Memorandum from Al Haig to Henry Kissinger, January 8, 1969, *FRUS, 1969–1976*, vol. II, Document 5, 19–21.

64 **Haig reminded Kissinger:** Ibid.

65 **current intelligence officers could just put:** Corscadden, "DDI/New York," 92–94.

65 **"Henry is brilliant":** David Young, interview by the author, March 2013.

65 **daily Pentagon brief and State Department report:** Robert McFarlane, interview by the author, October 2011.

65 **"On top of it all would be Henry's paper":** Ibid.

65 **"We may have commented on it":** Kissinger, interview by the author.

65 **Nixon "frequently ignored it":** Henry Kissinger, *Years of Renewal* (New York: Simon and Schuster, 1999), 189.

65 **the president let Kissinger summarize:** "The New Espionage, American Style," *Newsweek*, November 22, 1971, 30.

65 **the State Department's Evening Report:** "Memorandum for the President—Evening Report," November 12, 1969, *FRUS, 1969–1976*, vol. XVII, Document 44, 121 n. 1.

65 **"Nobody from the Agency":** John Hedley, interview by the author, July 2011.

66 **"I remember the deep frustration of Dick Lehman":** Charlie Allen, interview by the author, May 2011.

66 **"We had the impression as young analysts":** Former senior CIA officer, interview by the author, June 2011.

66 **"I am sure that Nixon read it":** Kissinger, interview by the author.

66 **"Kissinger must have had two copies":** Young, interview by the author.

66 **Nixon had appreciated the PDB:** "Memorandum for the Record," DCI's Morning Meeting, August 7, 1969 (CIA-RDP80R01284 A001800110066 -4), CREST.

66 **"He was curious":** James Schlesinger, interview by the author, April 2013.

66 **"Nixon, being the devious guy he was":** Former CIA officer, telephone interview with the author, May 2013.

66 **"become their own intelligence analysts":** Memorandum of Conversation, March 18, 1970, NSC Files, Name Files, Box 825: Andrew Marshall, vol. 1, 1969–1971, RNL.

66 **"You have to remember":** Kissinger, interview by the author.

67 **"The burden placed on the Agency":** Dino Brugoni and Urban Linehan, "Lawrence K. White on the Directors," *Studies in Intelligence* 31 (Winter 1987), available at http://www.foia.cia.gov/sites/default/files/DOC_0000620551.pdf.

67 **"Kissinger certainly had a sense":** Hedley, interview by the author.

67 **Nixon and Kissinger restricted senior CIA officials' access:** Hathaway and Smith, *Richard Helms as Director of Central Intelligence*, 38.

67 **"Nobody came in and briefed the president":** Kissinger, interview by the author.

67 **"virtually worthless":** "Board Meeting with the President," Memorandum for the Record, October 24, 1969, 3, RNL, December 9, 2010, materials release, available at http://www.nixonlibrary.gov/virtuallibrary/releases/dec10/20.pdf.

67 **"The policymaker tends to take his intelligence for granted":** "Current Intelligence and Its Audience," internal OCI paper, February 27, 1970 (CIA-RDP79T01762 A000400080007-0), CREST.

67 **less than eighteen months:** "Russell Jack Smith, Giant of CIA Analysis, Dies at 95," CIA News & Information website, Featured Story Archive, June 3, 2009, available at https://www.cia.gov/news-information/featured-story-archive/jack-smith.html.

67 **"flavored by policy considerations":** "Talking Points for PFIAB Meeting, 12:30 p.m., Thursday, December 3, 1970," memo from Al Haig to Henry A. Kissinger, December 2, 1970, 3, RNL, June 26, 2012, materials release, available at http://www.nixonlibrary.gov/virtuallibrary/releases/jun12/declass09.pdf.

68 **just four other men:** "President's Daily Brief," memorandum from Director of Central Intelligence Helms to Secretary of State Rogers, January 22, 1969, *FRUS, 1969–1976*, vol. II, Document 181, 368–69.

68 **Agency couriers would visit their offices:** Ibid.

68 **Vice President Spiro Agnew:** "Intelligence Publications and Their Distribution," Memorandum from Tom Latimer of the National Security Council Staff to Henry Kissinger, December 1, 1970, *FRUS, 1969–1976*, vol. II, Document 217, 467–72; see also "Minutes: DD/S Staff Meeting," October 17, 1972 (CIA-RDP75B00514 R000200300002-0), CREST.

68 **"I would always read it":** Melvin Laird, telephone interview by the author, June 2012.

68 **"I'd like David Packard to have a copy":** Ibid.

68 **"At least we've got *one* good reader":** Charlie Allen, interview by the author.

68 **"I'm not sure whether I asked":** Laird, telephone interview by the author.

68 **"President Nixon said we'd never":** George Shultz, interview by the author, April 2012.

69 **They delivered it to him:** "The Role of CIA's Daily Publications," internal OCI paper, November 12, 1969 (CIA-RDP79T01762 A000400080007-0), CREST.

69 **"I decided I was not reading anything useful":** Shultz, interview by the author.

69 **virtual "Assistant President":** "Support of Attorney-General," memorandum from Deputy Director of Current Intelligence Richard Lehman to the Deputy Director for Intelligence, January 9, 1969 (CIA-RDP80B01086 A000800030003-9), CREST.

69 **"my most trusted friend and adviser":** Richard Nixon, *RN: The Memoirs of Richard Nixon* (New York: Touchstone, 1978), 339.

69 **"the same intelligence Mr. Nixon gets":** "Support of Attorney-General."

69 **"Mitchell was very affable":** Arthur Hulnick, telephone interview with the author, May 2013.

69 **His briefer had no trouble:** Ibid.

69 **"I've never seen you guys call one":** Robert S. Sinclair, "Communication to the Editor," *Studies in Intelligence* 23, no. 1 (Spring 1979), 39.

70 **"I feel there is a real problem here":** "Evaluation of the Process Leading to the President's Morning Intelligence Package," memo from A. W. Marshall to Henry A. Kissinger, March 18, 1970, RNL, November 28, 2007, materials release, available at http://www.nixonlibrary.gov/virtual library/releases/nov07/031870_pdb.pdf.

70 **"probably is the only part of the package":** Ibid.

70 **He warned Kissinger:** Ibid.

70 **This overlap problem:** Ibid.

71 **"Your style of work":** Ibid.

71 **Kissinger wanted to see a sample:** Ibid.

71 **senior Nixon staffers informed CIA officers:** "White House/ NSC Intelligence Requirements," Memorandum for the Record from [redacted], March 23, 1973 (CIA-RDP80M01133 A000900040001-5), CREST.

71 **"flexible on-line reading program":** "Evaluation of the Process Leading to the President's Morning Intelligence Package."

71 **"This would have been totally wasted":** Kissinger, interview by the author.

72 **"The President is a lawyer":** Russell Jack Smith, "Intelligence Production During the Helms Regime," *Studies in Intelligence*, undated, 100, available at http://www.foia.cia.gov/sites/default/files/DOC_0006122498 .pdf.

72 **start separating facts and opinions:** Ibid.

72 **"You started out with a factual lead":** Hedley, interview by the author.

72 **the PDB's text lacked:** The President's Daily Brief, August 19, 1969, National Archives, available at http://www.archives.gov/declassification /iscap/pdf/2005-003-doc1.pdf.

73 **"The Chinese chose the eve":** The President's Daily Brief, August 20, 1969, National Archives, available at http://www.archives.gov /declassification/iscap/pdf/2005-003-doc2.pdf.

73 **"The PDB is something that happened":** Winston Wiley, interview by the author, April 2011.

73 **"prune some articles of excess verbiage":** "Production of the PDB," Memorandum, January 16, 1970, 4, included in Richard M. Nixon Library, November 28, 2007, materials release, available at http://www .nixonlibrary.gov/virtuallibrary/releases/nov07/031870_pdb.pdf.

73 **"I'm standing in line":** Wiley, interview by the author.

74 **Johnson had vouched for Helms:** Richard Helms with William Hood, *A Look over My Shoulder: A Life in the Central Intelligence Agency* (New York: Ballantine Books, 2003), 376.

74 **Laird helped kill Nixon's plan:** Hathaway and Smith, *Richard Helms as Director of Central Intelligence*, 8–9; Douglas F. Garthoff, *Directors of Central Intelligence as Leaders of the U.S. Intelligence Community, 1946–2005* (Washington, DC: Potomac Books, 2007), 64.

74 **"perpetually cranky":** Helms, *A Look over My Shoulder*, 394.

74 **"There was not very much opportunity":** Richard Helms, interview by Paige Mulhollan, April 4, 1969, oral history interview, available at http://web2.millercenter.org/lbj/oralhistory/helms_richard_1969_0404 .pdf.

74 **the CIA director's main point of contact:** Hathaway and Smith, *Richard Helms as Director of Central Intelligence*, 12.

74 **he regularly called Helms:** Kissinger, interview by the author.

74 **"pick on the Agency":** Richard M. Helms, interview by R. J. Smith, April 21, 1982, cited in Hathaway and Smith, *Helms as Director of Central Intelligence*, 208.

74 **"use intelligence to *support* conclusions":** "Memorandum from [name not declassified] of the CIA to Director of Central Intelligence Helms," June 18, 1969, *FRUS, 1969–1976*, vol. II, Document 191, 368–69.

74 **"What the hell do those clowns do":** Richard Nixon, *RN*, 447.

74 **"The CIA tells me nothing":** H. R. Haldeman, *The Haldeman Diaries: Inside the Nixon White House* (New York: G. P. Putnam's Sons, 1994), 330.

74 **"muscle-bound bureaucracy":** "Memorandum from President Nixon to His Assistant (Haldeman)," May 18, 1972, *FRUS, 1969–1976*, vol. II, Document 273, 620–21.

75 **"Helms will play whatever role":** "Memorandum from President Nixon to His Assistant for National Security Affairs (Kissinger)," November 30, 1970, *FRUS, 1969–1976*, vol. II, Document 216, 368–69, 467.

75 **he would back any legal action:** Nixon, *RN*, 640.

75 **nobody could have handled:** Ray S. Cline, *The CIA Under Reagan, Bush and Casey: The Evolution of the Agency from Roosevelt to Reagan* (Washington, DC: Acropolis Books, 1981), 240.

75 **"meticulously fair and discreet"**: Henry Kissinger, *White House Years* (New York: Little, Brown, 1979), 37.

75 **Helms ignored the order**: Helms, interview by Smith, cited in Hathaway and Smith, *Richard Helms as Director of Central Intelligence*, 207.

75 **Helms guessed**: Ibid.

75 **Nixon fired him**: Haldeman, *The Haldeman Diaries*, 540.

75 **on the spur of the moment**: Richard Helms, interview by John Bross, December 14, 1982, cited in Hathaway and Smith, *Richard Helms as Director of Central Intelligence*, 211.

76 **"I flew up to Camp David"**: Schlesinger, interview by the author.

76 **the need for a change in direction**: Haldeman, *The Haldeman Diaries*, 541.

76 **"you work for the United States government"**: Robert M. Gates, interview by Timothy J. Naftali et al., July 24, 2000, George H. W. Bush Oral History Project, Miller Center, University of Virginia.

76 **planned to dismantle the Directorate of Intelligence**: Randall B. Woods, *Shadow Warrior: William Egan Colby and the CIA* (New York: Basic Books, 2013), 355.

76 **"Remember who you are dealing with"**: Schlesinger, interview by the author.

76 **"the PDB consistently fails"**: "White House/NSC Intelligence Requirements," Memorandum for the Record from [redacted], March 23, 1973 (CIA-RDP80M01133 A000900040001-5), CREST.

76 **not from "those DI bastards"**: George Lauder, interview by Harold P. Ford in Washington, DC, March 13, 1987, cited in Harold P. Ford, *William E. Colby as Director of Central Intelligence*, book published by the CIA's Center for the Study of Intelligence (Chapter 3, "The Yom Kippur War of October 1973," declassified text released online at http://www.foia.cia.gov/sites/default/files/document_conversions/1699355/1993-01-01.pdf), 27 n. 9.

77 **"I was only effectively at the CIA"**: James Schlesinger, interview by Timothy Naftali, December 10, 2007, Richard Nixon Oral History Project of RNL, available at http://www.nixonlibrary.gov/virtuallibrary/documents/histories/schlesinger-2007-12-10.pdf.

77 **Colby received *one* call**: William Colby, interview by Loch Johnson, January 22, 1991, in Loch K. Johnson, "A Conversation with William E. Colby," *Intelligence and National Security* 22, no. 2 (April 2007): 250–69.

77 **more inside information for their assessments**: "CIA Support for Middle East Peace Negotiations," Memorandum from William Colby to Assistant to the President for National Security Affairs Henry A. Kissinger, December 28, 1973, National Security Adviser, Kissinger-Scowcroft West Wing Office Files, 1969–1977, Box 2, CIA Communications, 12/13/73–12/31/73 Folder, GRFPL.

77 **"I pointed out"**: "Meeting with Andrew Marshall, 10 October 1972," Memorandum for the Record from Bronson Tweedy, October 13, 1972 (CIA-RDP80M01133 A000900030001-6), CREST.

77 **Scowcroft told Kissinger:** "CIA Support for Middle East Peace Negotiations," Memorandum from William Colby to Assistant to the President for National Security Affairs Henry A. Kissinger, December 28, 1973, National Security Adviser, Kissinger-Scowcroft West Wing Office Files, 1969–1977, Box 2, CIA Communications, 12/13/73–12/31/73 Folder, GRFPL.

77 **excluded from NODIS material again:** William Colby and Peter Forbath, *Honorable Men: My Life in the CIA* (New York: Simon and Schuster, 1978), 355–56.

78 **trifurcated sub-PDB product:** "Current Intelligence and Its Audience," internal OCI paper, February 27, 1970 (CIA-RDP79T01762 A000400080007-0), CREST; "Minutes: DD/S Staff Meeting," October 17, 1972 (CIA-RDP75B00514 R000200300002-0), CREST.

78 **exclusive "Black Book" . . . Top Secret "Red Book":** "Current Intelligence and Its Audience," internal OCI paper, February 27, 1970 (CIA-RDP79T01762 A000400080007-0), CREST; "Minutes: DD/S Staff Meeting," October 17, 1972 (CIA-RDP75B00514 R000200300002-0), CREST.

78 **Secret-level "White Book":** "Minutes: DD/S Staff Meeting," October 17, 1972.

78 **why they bothered to issue:** "Odds and Ends," Note from ADDI Paul V. Walsh to Mr. Colby, June 15, 1973 (CIA-RDP80B01495 R000300050048 -5), CREST.

78 **reformatting the CIB as a fold-out newspaper:** See Colby and Forbath, *Honorable Men*, 353–54.

78 **Kissinger had encouraged Colby to experiment:** Ibid.

78 **he turned against:** "Minutes of a Washington Special Actions Group Meeting," August 9, 1974, *FRUS, 1969–1976*, vol. XXXVIII, Part 1, Document 38, 206.

78 **"I'm going to get that thing abolished!":** "The *National Intelligence Daily*," Memorandum from Director of Current Intelligence Richard Lehman to All Members of OCI, June 11, 1974 (CIA-RDP79B01737 A000700060005-7), CREST.

78 **Fewer than fifty copies of the NID:** "Establishment of the National Intelligence Daily," Office of Current Intelligence Notice N 1-30 from Director of Current Intelligence Richard Lehman, November 26, 1973 (CIA-RDP79B01737 A001000070008-6), CREST; "OCI's Publications: Priorities and Relationships," internal OCI paper, June 3, 1974 (CIA-RDP79B01737 A000700060003-9), CREST.

78 **"It is no hyperbole":** "Establishment of the National Intelligence Daily."

79 **OCI started delivering the PDB:** "OCI's Publications: Priorities and Relationships"; "Establishment of the National Intelligence Daily."

79 **PDB worked fine in that format:** Nicholas Dujmovic, interview by the author, February 2012.

79 **Lehman in late 1973 told:** "Establishment of the National Intelligence Daily."

79 **he still operated under Haldeman's guidance:** "Difference in Content in OCI's Dailies," Memorandum from Director of Current Intelligence

Richard Lehman to Director of Central Intelligence, June 4, 1974 (CIA-RDP79B01737 A000700060004-8), CREST.

79 **more time working on Colby's new NID:** "OCI's Publications: Priorities and Relationships."

79 **moved to the current intelligence production staff:** Charlie Allen, interview by the author.

80 **Egyptian leaders had tasked:** Henry Kissinger, *Years of Upheaval* (New York: Little, Brown, 1982), 461–62.

80 **"the game was over at that point":** "Nixon and the Role of Intelligence in the 1973 Arab-Israeli War" conference, RNL, January 30, 2013, video online at http://www.youtube.com/watch?v=NZfGBguAqX4, comments by Martha Kessler.

80 **"I spent a good deal of the day":** Ibid., comments by Charlie Allen.

80 **Allen remembers finishing his work:** Ibid.

80 **"I was waiting for a final input":** Ibid., comments by Richard Kovar.

81 **"And then I opened the PDB":** Brent Scowcroft, interview by the author, January 2012.

81 **"The exercise and the activities underway":** "Nixon and the Role of Intelligence in the 1973 Arab-Israeli War" conference, comments by Charlie Allen.

81 **news of the attack shocked him:** Nixon, *RN*, 920.

81 **"they were wrong on everything":** Kissinger, interview by the author.

82 **"Logic says it won't happen":** Scowcroft, interview by the author.

82 **his most embarrassing moment as an analyst:** Robert M. Gates, *From the Shadows: The Ultimate Insider's Story of Five Presidents and How They Won the Cold War* (New York: Touchstone, 1996), 40–41.

82 **ringing telephone had awoken:** "Nixon and the Role of Intelligence in the 1973 Arab-Israeli War" conference, comments by Charlie Allen.

82 **"In the years that followed":** Ibid.

82 **"I would always work a lot harder":** Quoted in Justin Rood, "Getting Serious," *Government Executive*, December 14, 2005, available at http://www.govexec.com/excellence/management-matters/2005/12/getting-serious/20808.

82 **Middle East Task Force:** Peter Nyren, "CIA's Middle East Task Force and the 1973 Arab-Israeli War," paper from the CIA Historical Collections Division, undated, CIA FOIA archive, available at http://www.foia.cia.gov/sites/default/files/document_conversions/1699355/2012-12-10F.pdf.

83 **"Have you all seen this?":** Ibid.

83 **"Winston, there's a task force going on":** Wiley, interview by the author.

FIVE: FACE-TO-FACE

85 **"Can you imagine Jerry Ford":** Henry Kissinger, interview by Richard Norton Smith, April 8, 2009, Gerald R. Ford Oral History project of the Gerald R. Ford Presidential Foundation, available at geraldfordfoundation.org/centennial/wp-content/uploads/2013/05/Henry-Kissinger.pdf.

85 **convinced him that only Ford:** Gerald R. Ford, *A Time to Heal: The Autobiography of Gerald R. Ford* (New York: Harper & Row, 1979), 107.

85 **Starting as a young representative:** Ibid., 128–29.

86 **briefed Ford about leading international developments:** Kissinger, interview by Smith.

86 **sitting with Ford for an hour or two:** Brent Scowcroft, interview by the author, January 2012; Brent Scowcroft, interview by Timothy Naftali, June 29, 2007, Richard Nixon Oral History Project of RNL, available at http://www.nixonlibrary.gov/virtuallibrary/documents/histories/scowcroft-2007-06-29.pdf.

86 **Colby visited the vice president:** William Colby, interview by Christopher Andrew, March 14, 1994, cited in Christopher Andrew, *For the President's Eyes Only: Secret Intelligence and the American Presidency from Washington through Bush* (New York: Harper Collins, 1995), 398.

86 **Ford visited CIA headquarters:** "Gerald Ford and the President's Daily Brief," *Studies in Intelligence*, undated, available at http://www.foia.cia.gov/sites/default/files/DOC_0006174167.pdf.

86 **Colby walked the vice president through the building:** John L. Helgerson, *Getting to Know the President: Intelligence Briefings of Presidential Candidates, 1952–2004*, 2nd ed. (Washington, DC: CIA, 2012), 76; John Hedley, interview by the author, July 2011.

86 **visited the Office of Current Intelligence:** Helgerson, *Getting to Know the President*, 76; Hedley, interview by the author.

86 **offer it to the vice president:** John H. Hedley, "The DI: A History of Service," in *The Directorate of Intelligence: Fifty Years of Informing Policy, 1952–2002*, expanded ed. (Washington, DC: CIA, 2002), 13; Helgerson, *Getting to Know the President*, 76.

86 **"innocent" and "inadvertent":** Ibid.

86 **"We should get the PDB to the Vice President":** William Colby, interview by John Helgerson on April 7, 1993, cited in Helgerson, *Getting to Know the President*, 76.

86 **included a brief biography:** Letter from William Colby to Assistant to the Vice President for Defense Affairs John Marsh, June 11, 1974, Ford Vice Presidential Papers, Office of Assistant for Defense and International Affairs, 1973–74, John O. Marsh, Box 59, GRFPL.

87 **the White House added Ford:** Hedley, "The DI," 13.

87 **"Mr. Ford accepted my suggestion":** "Gerald Ford and the President's Daily Brief."

87 **experienced senior current intelligence officer:** Hedley, interview by the author.

87 **"this would be the most secure way":** "Gerald Ford and the President's Daily Brief."

87 **Agency leaders matched Peterson to Ford:** Hedley, interview by the author.

87 **"comfortable relationship":** Richard Lehman, interview by Richard Kovar, undated, in "Mr. Current Intelligence: An Interview with Richard

Lehman," *Studies in Intelligence,* Summer 2000, available at https://www
.cia.gov/library/center-for-the-study-of-intelligence/kent-csi/vol44no3
/html/v44i3a05p.htm; interviews by the author of several former colleagues of Peterson, 2011–13.

87 **get the PDB early each morning:** "Gerald Ford and the President's
Daily Brief."

87 **personalized PDB sessions:** Ibid.; John H. Hedley, "Intelligence and
the Presidency," *SpyCast: The Podcast of the International Spy Museum,* posted
August 1, 2008.

87 **always a gracious host:** Helgerson, *Getting to Know the President,* 77.

87 **enjoy hearing Peterson's stories:** Hedley, interview by the author.

87 **he spent a full hour:** Schedule, July 1, 1974, Ford Vice Presidential
Papers, Deputy Assistant for Scheduling and Appointments, 1973–74,
Warren S. Rustand, Box 179, Vice President's Schedule: June 1–10, 1974,
folder, GRFPL.

87 **Peterson jumped out of Ford's car:** Charlie Allen, interview by the
author, May 2011.

88 **Peterson informed Marsh, not Ford:** Memorandum from Jack Marsh
to the Vice President, July 23, 1974, Ford Vice Presidential Papers, Robert
Hartmann Files, 1948–1973, Staff Memos File, Box 223, Marsh, Jack:
Memos to Others folder, GRFPL.

88 **he was "furious":** "Gerald Ford and the President's Daily Brief."

88 **he was a better listener:** "Meeting in the Cabinet Room," Blind Memorandum, August 9, 1974, courtesy of the Rumsfeld Archive, available as
08-09-1974-2.pdf at http://papers.rumsfeld.com/library.

89 **"Ford was a very diligent president":** Robert McFarlane, interview by
the author, October 2011.

89 **"Mr. Ford seemed as awed as I was":** "Gerald Ford and the President's
Daily Brief."

89 **joking with Haig:** Ibid.

89 **Peterson updated the new president:** Ibid.

89 **Ford declared that he liked this routine:** Helgerson, *Getting to Know
the President,* 77–78.

89 **"The initial session in the Oval Office":** "Gerald Ford and the President's Daily Brief."

89 **"The first time I tried":** Hedley, interview by the author.

89 **During his senior staff meeting:** "Gerald Ford and the President's
Daily Brief"; Helgerson, *Getting to Know the President,* 78; "Memorandum of
Meeting with the President," August 12, 1974, courtesy of the Rumsfeld
Archive, available at http://library.rumsfeld.com/doclib/sp/2374/1974-08
-12.pdf.

90 **Kissinger gave his blessing:** "Executive Council Meeting on 16 August
1974," Memorandum from the Chief, DDI Executive Staff, August 16,
1974 (CIA-RDP80B01495 R000700170033-4), CREST.

90 **"Scowcroft's presence undoubtedly enhanced the value":** "Gerald
Ford and the President's Daily Brief."

90 **his presence minimized the possibility:** Helgerson, *Getting to Know the President*, 78.

90 **"No previous President had derived such prompt benefit":** "Gerald Ford and the President's Daily Brief."

90 **"complete control of his copy":** Ibid.

90 **Agency leaders now included:** Helgerson, *Getting to Know the President*, 79.

90 **"short sentences, short paragraphs, and simple language":** IAS Staff Meeting notes, August 16, 1974 (CIA-RDP82T00285 R000100110035-5), CREST.

90 **the president was reading both:** "Executive Council Meeting on 3 September 1974," Memorandum from the Chief, DDI Executive Staff, September 3, 1974 (CIA-RDP80B01495 R000700170029-9), CREST.

90 **Peterson called the director of OCI:** "Gerald Ford and the President's Daily Brief."

90 **visited the White House Situation Room:** Ibid.

91 **"that usually means you have bad news":** Ibid.

91 **"It cannot be that the president":** Henry Kissinger, interview by the author, October 2011.

91 **reading Scowcroft's copy:** Helgerson, *Getting to Know the President*, 39; Kissinger, interview by the author. The tight control of the PDB remained for a while; the director of current intelligence in the DI suggested to DDI Ed Proctor in March 1976 a PDB "with a circulation *expanded* to include the current Presidential foreign affairs 'team,' which I understand includes the Secretary of State and the Secretary of Defense" (emphasis added). "Review of OCI's Periodical Publications," Memorandum from Director of Current Intelligence William K. Parmenter to the Deputy Director for Intelligence, March 5, 1976 (CIA-RDP91M00696 R000900010005-2), CREST.

91 **would often discuss the PDB:** Henry Kissinger, *Years of Renewal* (New York: Simon and Schuster, 1999), 189.

91 **began delivering to Kissinger his own copy:** "The Vice President and the PDB," Memorandum from Director of Current Intelligence William K. Parmenter to the Director of Central Intelligence, July 10, 1975 (CIA-RDP80B01495 R000600140029-3), CREST.

91 **"You shouldn't see it as we were waiting":** Kissinger, interview by the author.

91 **"That shows what the CIA brief is":** "Memorandum of Conversation," President Ford's meeting with Henry Kissinger and Brent Scowcroft, July 7, 1975. National Security Advisor, Memoranda of Conversations, Box 13, GRFPL.

92 **including a young George H. W. Bush:** Herbert S. Parmet, *George Bush: The Life of a Lone Star Yankee* (New York: Scribner, 1997), 167–71.

92 **Colby informed congressional leaders and President Ford:** Douglas F. Garthoff, *Directors of Central Intelligence as Leaders of the U.S. Intelligence Community, 1946–2005* (Washington, DC: Potomac Books, 2007), 105.

93 **"That blew the roof":** William Colby, interview by the CIA Center for the Study of Intelligence, March 15, 1988, in "Oral History: Reflections of DCI Colby and Helms on the CIA's 'Time of Troubles,'" *Studies in Intelligence* 51, no. 3 (2007), available at https://www.cia.gov/library/center-for-the-study -of-intelligence/csi-publications/csi-studies/studies/vol51no3/reflections -of-dci-colby-and-helms-on-the-cia2019s-201ctime-of-troubles201d.html.

93 **"Time of Troubles":** "Oral History: Reflections of DCI Colby and Helms."

93 **routinely besieged by his staff:** "Current Intelligence Support for the Vice President," Memorandum to the DCI, July 9, 1975 (CIA-RDP80B01495 R000600140029-3), CREST.

93 **Howe told his CIA contact:** Ibid.

93 **the Agency provided a cable version of the PDB:** Ibid.

94 **received it around 7:30 a.m.:** Ibid.

94 **Colby himself approved the plan:** "The Vice President and the PDB."

94 **asking questions or starting discussions:** Jonathan Howe, telephone interview by the author, October 2012.

94 **"a good use of his time":** Ibid.

94 **"what you saw was what you got":** Kissinger, interview by the author.

94 **"He wanted to know about people":** Scowcroft, interview by the author.

94 **"He would sort of listen to people":** Kissinger, interview by Smith.

94 **he asked point-blank what UNESCO did:** James M. Cannon, "Domestic Issues and the Budget," in Kenneth W. Thompson, ed., *The Ford Presidency: Twenty-Two Intimate Perspectives of Gerald R. Ford* (Lanham, MD: University Press of America, 1988), 161.

95 **the president's golden retriever, Liberty:** Helgerson, *Getting to Know the President*, 80 n. 10.

95 **"very few rigid guidelines":** John McLaughlin, interview by the author, February 2011.

96 **"the product lost a lot of its class":** Dick Kerr, telephone interview by the author, November 2011.

96 **"The readers of the PDB probably need":** Letter from DDI Ed Proctor to Director of Current Intelligence Dick Lehman, November 7, 1974 (CIA-RDP80B01495 R000600130016-8), CREST.

96 **he would occasionally add summaries:** "Gerald Ford and the President's Daily Brief," *Studies in Intelligence*, undated, available at http://www.foia.cia.gov/sites/default/files/DOC_0006174167.pdf.

96 **a short film on Soviet leader Leonid Brezhnev:** Donald Rumsfeld, "Meeting with the President," November 13, 1974, courtesy of the Rumsfeld Archive, available at http://library.rumsfeld.com/doclib/sp/153/11 -13-1974.pdf.

96 **suggesting that he discontinue his daily morning meeting:** Donald Rumsfeld and Richard Cheney, Memorandum for the President, October 24, 1975, courtesy of the Rumsfeld Archive, available at http://library .rumsfeld.com/doclib/sp/174/1975-10-24%20To%20Gerald%20Ford%20 re%20Re-election%20and%20Rumsfeld%20and%20Cheney%20 Resignations.pdf.

97 **put distance between himself and the CIA:** Lehman, interview by Kovar.

97 **"He will not need you or Dave Peterson":** Memorandum from Don Rumsfeld to Brent Scowcroft, October 28, 1975, National Security Adviser, Kissinger-Scowcroft West Wing Office Files, 1969–1977, Box 3, Cheney-Rumsfeldgrams (3) File, GRFPL.

97 **Scowcroft's early morning meetings with Ford:** "Gerald Ford and the President's Daily Brief."

97 **handed the book each morning to Scowcroft:** Ibid.

97 **annotations on the book and other material:** McFarlane, interview by the author.

97 **the president's move was merciful:** Brent Scowcroft, quoted in *The Man Nobody Knew*, a film directed by Carl Colby (2011).

97 **Colby said he would resign:** James Cannon, *Gerald R. Ford: An Honorable Life* (Ann Arbor: University of Michigan Press, 2013), 384.

98 **even slinging his leg over the armrest:** Kissinger, interview by Smith.

98 **prompting Schlesinger to snap back:** Kissinger, *Years of Renewal*, 178–79.

98 **Scowcroft advised him:** Brent Scowcroft, interview by Philip Zelikow et al., November 12, 1999, George H. W. Bush Oral History Project, Miller Center, University of Virginia, 16.

98 **"It's a pity":** Kissinger, interview by Smith.

98 **the defense secretary disregarded his orders:** Cannon, *Gerald R. Ford*, 373.

98 **"This is my decision":** Jack Marsh, interview by Richard Norton Smith, October 7, 2008, Gerald R. Ford Oral History project of the Gerald R. Ford Presidential Foundation, available at http://geraldrfordfoundation.org/centennial/oralhistory/jack-marsh.

98 **only made him more certain:** Cannon, *Gerald R. Ford*, 384.

99 **a move that he knew:** Gerald Ford, interview by Douglas Brinkley, March 23, 2003, cited in Douglas Brinkley, *Gerald R. Ford* (New York: Times Books, 2007), 130.

99 **resigning in protest would have been immature:** Henry Kissinger, *Years of Upheaval* (New York: Little, Brown, 1982), 435–37.

99 **appreciated Scowcroft's succinctness and competence:** See Cannon, *Gerald R. Ford*, 382.

99 **"The President asks that you consent":** George Bush, *All the Best, George Bush: My Life in Letters* (New York: Scribner, 1999), 233.

99 **experience he found challenging and rewarding:** George Bush with Victor Gold, *Looking Forward* (New York: Bantam, 1988), 128.

99 **"When President Ford asked me":** George H. W. Bush, correspondence with the author, November 2012.

100 **"When the cable came in":** George H. W. Bush, luncheon remarks at the "US Intelligence and the End of the Cold War" conference at Texas A&M University, College Station Texas, November 19, 1999, available at http://www.foia.cia.gov/sites/default/files/document_conversions/89801/DOC_0001445131.pdf.

100 **"You can't turn a president down":** Parmet, *George Bush*, 158–59.

100 **"My Dad inculcated into his sons":** Bush, *All the Best, George Bush*, 233–34.

100 **a rare classy moment:** Kissinger, *Years of Renewal*, 842.

100 **wrap up preparations in China:** Garthoff, *Directors of Central Intelligence*, 105.

100 **Agency's small office near the White House:** Ibid., 113 n. 7.

100 **settled in at CIA headquarters:** Bush, *Looking Forward*, 164.

100 **his political days were behind him:** Parmet, *George Bush*, 192.

101 **he would leave the room:** George Bush and Brent Scowcroft, *A World Transformed* (New York: Alfred A. Knopf, 1998), 21.

101 **"I depend on you":** Gerald Ford, comments at swearing-in ceremony of George Bush as DCI, January 30, 1976, available at https://www.cia.gov /library/center-for-the-study-of-intelligence/csi-publications/books-and -monographs/our-first-line-of-defense-presidential-reflections-on-us -intelligence/ford.html.

101 **"And when I did":** John McMahon, interviews on December 4, 1997, and February 4, 1998, printed in "An Interview with Former DDCI John N. McMahon: Tough, Unconventional, and Effective," *Studies in Intelligence* 43, no. 1 (1999): 8, available at http://www.foia.cia.gov/sites /default/files/DOC_0001407025.pdf.

102 **read it in the car alone:** Bush, *Looking Forward*, 166.

102 **"I deferred to the intelligence people":** Bush, correspondence with the author.

102 **"a 'band of brothers'":** Lehman, interview by Kovar.

102 **"What are they trying to do to us?":** William Colby, interview by Loch Johnson, January 22, 1991, in Loch K. Johnson, "A Conversation with William E. Colby," *Intelligence and National Security* 22:2 (April 2007), 264.

102 **He wrote to a friend in early 1976:** Letter from George Bush to Jack Mohler, in Bush, *All the Best, George Bush*, 255.

102 **"I was getting a briefing from DIA":** Donald Rumsfeld, interview by the author, April 2012.

103 **Rumsfeld raised the anomaly:** Memorandum from Don Rumsfeld to Staser Holcomb, March 6, 1976, courtesy of the Rumsfeld Archive, available at http://library.rumsfeld.com/doclib/sp/4346/1976-03-06%20 To%20Staser%20Holcomb%20re%20George%20Bush%20Receiving %20a%20Copy%20of%20President%20Fords%20Daily%20Brief%20 .pdf; "Daily CIA Briefings," Memorandum from James E. Connor to the President, March 10, 1976, Presidential Handwriting File, Box 9, GRFPL; and "Daily CIA Briefings," Memorandum from James E. Connor to Director, CIA George E. Bush [*sic*], March 12, 1976, Presidential Handwriting File, Box 9, GRFPL.

103 **Simon received CIA publications:** "Meeting with Secretary Simon," Memorandum from Maurice C. Ernst, Director of Economic Research to the Director of Central Intelligence, April 9, 1976 (CIA-RDP79M 00467A00310003022-1), CREST.

103 **Every Thursday or Friday:** Bush, *Looking Forward*, 167.

103 **"very, very important":** Garthoff, *Directors of Central Intelligence*, 115.

103 **bring along working-level officers:** Bush, *Looking Forward*, 167.

103 **"Ford loved it":** Scowcroft, interview by the author.

103 **predictor of trouble on the foreign policy horizon:** Bush and Scowcroft, *A World Transformed*, 20.

103 **"All these years later":** Bush, correspondence with the author.

SIX: PLAINS AND SIMPLE

105 **Lehman spent the evening:** Richard Lehman, interview by Richard Kovar, undated, in "Mr. Current Intelligence: An Interview with Richard Lehman," *Studies in Intelligence*, Summer 2000, available at https://www.cia.gov/library/center-for-the-study-of-intelligence/kent-csi/vol44no3/html/v44i3a05p.htm.

105 **the Agency's Gulfstream flew Lehman:** Ibid.

105 **Carter had requested an intelligence briefing:** John L. Helgerson, *Getting to Know the President: Intelligence Briefings of Presidential Candidates, 1952–2004*, 2nd ed. (Washington, DC: CIA, 2012), 87.

106 **"terribly interested":** Ibid., 88; Lehman, interview by Kovar.

106 **"very honored" by Bush's personal attendance:** Helgerson, *Getting to Know the President*, 87–88.

106 **first post-convention session:** Lehman interview by Kovar.

106 **absorbed briefings on:** Helgerson, *Getting to Know the President*, 90.

106 **"totally concentrating and taking it all in":** Lehman, interview by Kovar.

106 **grilled the briefers on arms control details:** Helgerson, *Getting to Know the President*, 90–91.

106 **"We all sat around":** Lehman, interview by Kovar.

106 **Carter's wife, Rosalynn, delivered peaches:** Helgerson, *Getting to Know the President*, 90–91.

107 **The CIA team prevented:** Ibid., 92.

107 **"We could see him prowling":** Lehman, interview by Kovar.

107 **"extremely pleased":** Helgerson, *Getting to Know the President*, 90–91.

107 **second six-hour session in Plains:** Ibid., 92–93.

107 **Mondale avoided overly inquisitive lines of questioning:** Ibid., 92.

107 **worried Bush and Lehman enough:** Ibid., 91.

107 **Bush would prefer:** Ibid., 91.

107 **Mondale in this second session:** Ibid., 93.

107 **"I was impressed with Carter":** Wayne Wolfe, interview by John Helgerson, December 12, 1993, cited in Helgerson, *Getting to Know the President*, 93.

107 **"I wanted the long briefing in Plains":** Jimmy Carter, interview by John Helgerson, June 23, 1993, cited in Helgerson, *Getting to Know the President*, 88.

107 **Bush brought a copy of the book:** "Meeting in Plains, Georgia, 19 November 1976, 1:00 to 2:00 p.m.," Memorandum for the Record from George H. W. Bush, November 22, 1976; National Security Adviser collection, Zbigniew Brzezinski's CIA President's Daily Brief files, JCL.

108 **"As I look back on it":** "Meeting in Plains, Georgia, 19 November 1976, 1:00 to 2:00 p.m."

108 **Lehman and a team of Agency briefers:** Helgerson, *Getting to Know the President*, 99; "Briefing of the President-Elect, 19 November 1976," Memorandum for the Record from Richard Lehman (CIA-RDP79M00467 A003100120004-1), November 22, 1976, CREST.

108 **he cornered the president-elect:** "Briefing of the President-Elect, 19 November 1976."

108 **the CIA began daily, on-site support:** Helgerson, *Getting to Know the President*, 102.

108 **A midlevel imagery analyst:** Ibid., 104.

108 **Biddiscomb also gave Carter:** Ibid.

108 **oral and written remarks informed:** Ibid.

108 **formal, detached air:** Ibid., 104–5.

108 **"I went down to the house":** Lehman, interview by Kovar.

108 **"voracious reader of the press":** Helgerson, *Getting to Know the President*, 105.

109 **"he wanted to talk":** Lehman, interview by Kovar.

109 **Lehman introduced Dave Peterson:** David Peterson, interview by John Helgerson, March 4, 1993, cited in Helgerson, *Getting to Know the President*, 106.

109 **Carter seemed more relaxed:** Helgerson, *Getting to Know the President*, 105–6.

109 **Carter settled on a simple PDB format:** Ibid., 107.

109 **"extract the essence of the PDB":** Jimmy Carter, correspondence with the author, August 2013.

109 **"as thorough as possible":** Jimmy Carter, telephone interview by the author, September 2013.

109 **"comprehensive but extremely succinct":** "Session with Dr. Zbigniew Brzezinski," Memorandum for the Record from Richard Lehman (CIA-RDP80M00165 A002200140010-5), January 8, 1977, CREST.

110 **Peterson dutifully hand-carried:** Helgerson, *Getting to Know the President*, 107.

110 **"Long before I ever was elected President":** Jimmy Carter, interview by James Sterling Young et al., November 29, 1982, Miller Center, University of Virginia, available at http://millercenter.org/president/carter /oralhistory/jimmy-carter.

110 **"In private, you have the obligation":** Zbigniew Brzezinski, "A Forum on the Role of the National Security Advisor," cosponsored by the Woodrow Wilson International Center for Scholars and the James A. Baker III Institute For Public Policy of Rice University, April 12, 2001, available at http://bakerinstitute.org/videos/forum-role-national -security-advisor.

110 **Peterson's job defaulted:** "President's Daily Brief (PDB)," Memorandum to Dr. Brzezinski from Rick Inderfurth, January 18, 1977; National Security Adviser collection, Zbigniew Brzezinski's CIA President's Daily Brief files, JCL.

110 **he briefed the national security advisor:** Helgerson, *Getting to Know the President*, 107–9.

111 **"I would come to my office":** Zbigniew Brzezinski, interview by James Sterling Young et al., February 18, 1982, Miller Center, University of Virginia, available at http://millercenter.org/president/carter/oralhistory /zbigniew-brzezinski.

111 **He had scanned:** Zbigniew Brzezinski, comments during "Carter Administration and Middle East Policy" panel, University of Georgia School of Public and International Affairs, January 20, 2007, available at www.c-spanvideo.org.

111 **he jotted down three or four main points:** Brzezinski, interview by James Sterling Young; Robert Gates, telephone interview by the author, August 2012.

111 **"Zbig and I discussed most of the PDB items":** Carter, correspondence with the author.

111 **"We discovered before too long":** Brzezinski, comments during "Carter Administration and Middle East Policy" panel.

112 **Turner does not recall even meeting Carter:** Stansfield Turner, *Secrecy and Democracy: The CIA in Transition* (Boston: Houghton Mifflin, 1985), 14.

112 **Turner had enough talent:** Robert M. Gates, *From the Shadows: The Ultimate Insider's Story of Five Presidents and How They Won the Cold War* (New York: Touchstone, 1996), 141.

112 **he loved the PDB:** "Gleanings from DDI Morning Meeting, 22 February 1977," Memorandum for D/DCI/NI, February 22, 1977 (CIA-RDP78Z02997 A000100030008-8), CREST.

112 **He simply changed Carter's schedule:** Stansfield Turner, interview by the author, April 2014.

112 **"Brzezinski was very domineering":** Ibid.

112 **"Zbig was enough day-to-day":** Carter, interview by Helgerson, cited in Helgerson, *Getting to Know the President*, 108.

112 **"sharpened in focus":** "Transcript of E. H. Knoche Address to Employees on 31 May 1977," undated (CIA-RDP80M00165 A002600110017-7), CREST; Helgerson, *Getting to Know the President*, 107.

112 **"It wasn't necessary":** Carter, correspondence with the author.

113 **put its "very best intelligence in it":** "Transcript of E. H. Knoche Address to Employees on 31 May 1977."

113 **"The most important thing about it":** Harold Brown, telephone interview by the author, July 2012.

113 **Blumenthal's assistants called the NSC staff:** "President's Daily Brief," Memorandum to Zbigniew Brzezinski from Samuel M. Hoskinson, January 21, 1977; National Security Adviser collection, Brzezinski's CIA President's Daily Brief files, JCL.

113 **Brzezinski kept even the acting secretaries:** "Conversation with Dr. Brzezinski, 17 January 1978," Memorandum for the Record from Director Stansfield Turner, January 18, 1978 (CIA-RDP80B01554 R003300010010-8), CREST.

113 **Carter entered the White House:** Jimmy Carter, *Keeping Faith: Memoirs of a President* (New York: Bantam, 1982), 37.

113 **insisted that Walter Mondale attend:** Helgerson, *Getting to Know the President*, 106.

113 **gave Mondale space adjacent to the Oval Office:** Jimmy Carter, *White House Diary* (New York: Farrar, Straus and Giroux, 2010), 89.

113 **three other ways in which Carter followed through:** Richard Moe, interview by James Sterling Young et al., January 15–16, 1982, Miller Center, University of Virginia, available at http://millercenter.org/president/Carter/oralhistory/richard-moe-and-michael-berman.

113 **"The President would read it":** Walter Mondale, correspondence with the author, November 2011.

113 **the president's personal secretary would deliver it:** "President's Daily Brief (PDB)," Memorandum for the Vice President from Denis Clift, October 19, 1977, National Security Adviser collection, Zbigniew Brzezinski's CIA President's Daily Brief files, JCL; A. Denis Clift, interview by the author, December 2011.

114 **Mondale followed a strict regimen:** Ibid.

114 **"judgment, honesty, and frankness":** Carter, *White House Diary*, 89.

114 **The vice president would also see a copy of the PDB:** Mondale, correspondence with the author.

114 **get the PDB to Clift:** Clift, interview by the author.

114 **"I would inevitably be shaving":** Ibid.

114 **After Mondale read the book:** Mondale, correspondence with the author; Clift, interview by the author.

114 **"I read the PDB carefully every day":** Mondale, correspondence with the author.

114 **acknowledging that it added value:** Walter Mondale, "An Evening with Walter Mondale" event, Jimmy Cater Library and Museum, March 14, 2006, available at www.c-spanvideo.org.

114 **"Many of the items appearing in the Brief":** Mondale, correspondence with the author.

115 **Carter's Friday foreign policy breakfasts:** Zbigniew Brzezinski, *Power and Principle: Memoirs of the National Security Adviser, 1977–1981* (New York: Farrar Straus Giroux, 1983), 68–69.

115 **"Most of the most important foreign policy decisions":** Robert M. Gates, interview by Timothy J. Naftali et al., July 23, 2000, George H. W. Bush Oral History Project, Miller Center, University of Virginia.

115 **bungled the president's wishes:** Brzezinski, *Power and Principle*, 68.

115 **Brzezinski repeatedly argued with Carter:** Gates, interview by Naftali.

115 **"The commonly read PDB":** Carter, correspondence with the author.

115 **entering the CIA director's suite:** Douglas F. Garthoff, *Directors of Central Intelligence as Leaders of the U.S. Intelligence Community, 1946–2005* (Washington, DC: Potomac Books, 2007), 133.

116 **two provocative questions:** Ibid.

116 **management advisory group:** "DCI Meeting with the Management Advisory Group for the Intelligence Directorate (MAGID): Agenda," June 8, 1977 (CIA-RDP80M00165 A001200040028-8), CREST.

116 **"I always felt a tremendous responsibility":** Turner, interview by the author.

116 **editing the book every night was proper:** Turner, *Secrecy and Democracy*, 184.

116 **"I was very concerned":** Turner, interview by the author.

116 **in "a far more direct and involved way":** Bruce Clarke, correspondence with the author, February 2012.

116 **"Stan essentially reviewed the PDB":** Robert Gates, telephone interview by the author, August 2012.

117 **"I believe we should get the point across":** "Possible PDB Items," Memorandum for the National Intelligence Officer for China and Chief, Current Intelligence Group, OCO from DCI Stansfield Turner, April 7, 1980 (CIA-RDP80B01554 R003300150020-2), CREST.

117 **"he would tell us around noon":** Mike Barry, interview with the author, June 2011.

117 **"anything requested for analysis":** Garthoff, *Directors of Central Intelligence*, 134.

117 **"happy to have a director that cared":** Gates, telephone interview by the author.

117 **"I tried to make sure the analysts":** Turner, interview by the author.

118 **"a brief outline in the PDB":** Carter, correspondence with the author.

118 **PDB topics that left Carter wanting more:** Carter, interview by Helgerson, cited in Helgerson, *Getting to Know the President*, 109–10.

118 **up to three 30-minute intelligence briefings:** Turner, *Secrecy and Democracy*, 128–29.

118 **studied up to twelve hours:** Turner, interview by the author.

118 **"I just told the president":** Ibid.

118 **"go with me to the White House":** Ibid.

118 **"good for the president to hear":** Ibid.

119 **"If he questioned something today":** Ibid.

119 **oil production and demand curves would cross:** Memorandum to Dr. Sayre Stevens from Admiral Turner, April 19, 1977 (CIA-RDP80M00165 A000300180001-2), CREST.

119 **clear advice for the PDB's preparation:** "Gerald Ford and the President's Daily Brief," *Studies in Intelligence*, undated, available at http://www.foia.cia.gov/sites/default/files/DOC_0006174167.pdf.

119 **"Even with limited distribution of the PDB":** "Conversation with Dr. Brzezinski, 18 October 1978," Memorandum for the Record by Director Stansfield Turner, October 19, 1978 (CIA-RDP80B01554 R003200210011-6), CREST.

119 **down to twice a month:** Brzezinski, *Power and Principle*, 73.

119 **"Stan was outstanding":** Carter, correspondence with the author.

119 **"more thoroughly through verbal exchange":** Carter, telephone interview by the author.

119 **"That was a habit that I maintained":** Ibid.

120 **"with his beautiful, engineer's hand":** Clift, interview by the author.

120 *any* **notation from Carter:** Helgerson, *Getting to Know the President*, 109.

120 **"If a cabinet member or Stan Turner":** Carter, telephone interview by the author.

120 **"There was no way anything from the president":** Turner, interview by the author.

120 **he corrected spelling errors:** Frank Carlucci, interview by the author, August 2012.

120 **a question mark did not require:** Donald Gregg, telephone interview by the author, January 2012.

120 **"highly impressed":** Untitled notes from April 12, 1977, Cabinet "Family Talk," 1977, undated (CIA-RDP80M00165 A002200050001-5), CREST.

121 **"a superb job":** Jimmy Carter, comments at the CIA, August 16, 1978, available at https://www.cia.gov/library/center-for-the-study-of-intelligence /csi-publications/books-and-monographs/our-first-line-of-defense -presidential-reflections-on-us-intelligence/carter.html.

121 **"professionalism and the competence":** Jimmy Carter, "United States Foreign Intelligence Activities Remarks on Signing Executive Order 12036," January 24, 1978. *Public Papers of the Presidents: Jimmy Carter, 1978, Book One,* available at http://www.presidency.ucsb.edu/ws/?pid=31089.

121 **had *all* made specific reference:** "Usefulness of Agency Product to Top Policy-makers," Memorandum for the Director, National Foreign Assessment Center from Stansfield Turner, March 6, 1978 (CIA-RDP05T00644 R000200650010-1), CREST.

121 **"very helpful to the president":** Zbigniew Brzezinski, "Former National Security Advisor's Recollections and Recommendations for CIA," address to CIA's conference on "CIA's Analysis of the Soviet Union, 1947–1991," Princeton University, March 9–10, 2001, available at CIA's Center for the Study of Intelligence site: https://www.cia.gov/library/center-for-the -study-of-intelligence/csi-publications/books-and-monographs/watching -the-bear-essays-on-cias-analysis-of-the-soviet-union/article08.html#4.

121 **"the Carter team worked most conscientiously":** Robert M. Gates, "An Opportunity Unfulfilled: The Use and Perceptions of Intelligence Analysis at the White House," *Studies in Intelligence* 24 (Winter 1980): 21, available at http://www.foia.cia.gov/sites/default/files/DOC_0000617580 .pdf.

121 **Carter relayed his concerns and criticisms directly:** Ibid.

121 **"disappointed" with analysis:** "Comments of President Carter on the Intelligence Community," Memorandum for the Record, March 11, 1977 (CIA-RDP80M00165 A002200040011-5), CREST.

121 **"Carter sent a note to us":** Dick Kerr, telephone interview by the author, October 2011.

122 **"What struck me about the PDBs":** Brzezinski, "Former National Security Advisor's Recollections and Recommendations for CIA."

122 **"broad, sweeping, bold insights into the future":** Ibid.

122 **"too much gisting of cables":** "Conversation with Dr. Brzezinski, 18 October 1978."

122 **"Very often we were critical":** Brzezinski, "Former National Security Advisor's Recollections and Recommendations for CIA."

122 **"the Agency would have been more helpful":** Ibid.

122 **"We had spent the past few years":** Richard J. Kerr and Peter Dixon Davis, "Mornings in Pacific Palisades: Ronald Reagan and the President's Daily Brief," *Studies in Intelligence* 42, 5 (Winter 1998–99): 51.

123 **"Carter and Brzezinski":** Winston Wiley, interview by the author, April 2011.

123 **Agency analysts joined his own experts:** Cyrus Vance, *Hard Choices* (New York: Simon and Schuster, 1983), 325–26.

123 **"Our intelligence apparatus":** Brown, telephone interview by the author.

123 **"material about Iran":** Mondale, correspondence with the author.

123 **He urged Carter to write a personal note:** Brzezinski, *Power and Principle*, 367.

123 **"I was dealing with China normalization":** Carter, correspondence with the author.

123 **"To Cy, Zbig, Stan":** Brzezinski, *Power and Principle*.

123 **"The attached note makes clear":** "Political Intelligence," Memorandum to the Secretary of State and Director of Central Intelligence from National Security Advisor Zbigniew Brzezinski, November 13, 1978, RAC collection, JCL.

124 **Political Intelligence Working Group:** Gates, "An Opportunity Unfulfilled," 21–22.

124 **"I was very upset":** Turner, interview by the author.

124 **"When people write":** Carter, telephone interview by the author.

124 **"We in the CIA were not well enough versed":** Stansfield Turner, comments during "Carter Administration and Middle East Policy" panel, University of Georgia School of Public and International Affairs, January 20, 2007, available at www.c-spanvideo.org.

124 **"There was nothing I could do":** Turner, interview by the author.

124 **"It was just a year ago":** "Security Review of Director's Address and Remarks Made at In-House Speakers Program," Memorandum for the Deputy Director of Public Affairs by Chief, Information Services Staff, Directorate of Administration, November 14, 1979 (CIA-RDP99-00498 R000300090002-1), CREST.

125 **"I read the PDB":** Clift, interview by the author.

125 **Mondale would occasionally raise items:** Ibid.

125 **"He's a very conscientious man":** Ibid.

125 **"I found the PDB to be flatly inadequate":** Ibid.

126 **"This is what was being given":** Ibid.

126 **a new approach toward the PDB's content:** Ibid.

126 **senior DI officers invited him:** Ibid.

127 **"it sounded in recent months":** "Conversation with the Secretary of Defense," Memorandum for the Record from Director Stansfield Turner, March 12, 1980 (CIA-RDP81B00401 R002300080001-1), CREST.

127 **"Their reaction to me":** Clift, interview by the author.

127 **"we thought he was more interested in detail":** Kerr, telephone interview by the author.

127 **"Today's News Today":** "Staff Meeting Minutes of 26 March 1980," March 26, 1980 (CIA-RDP84B00130 R000600010252-0), CREST.

127 **"a significant departure from the publication":** Note to Bruce Clarke, Director, National Foreign Assessment Center from DCI Stansfield Turner April 4, 1980 (CIA-RDP80B01554 R003300150021-1), CREST.

127 **The new book stood out enough:** "March 1980 Turner comments," notations on White House letterhead, March 1980, National Security Adviser collection, Zbigniew Brzezinski's CIA President's Daily Brief files, JCL.

127 **"I want you to be aware":** Letter to the Vice President from Director of Central Intelligence Stansfield Turner, March 25, 1980 (CIA-RDP80B01554 R003300160016-6), CREST. See also A. Denis Clift, *With Presidents to the Summit* (Fairfax, VA: George Mason University Press, 1993), 191–92.

128 **"the changes that you introduced":** Clift, interview by the author.

128 **"My recollection is that I was pleased":** Carter, correspondence with the author.

128 **"the PDB was fundamentally improved":** Mondale, correspondence with the author.

SEVEN: WRITE ONE FOR THE GIPPER

129 **Carter authorized the CIA:** John L. Helgerson, *Getting to Know the President: Intelligence Briefings of Presidential Candidates, 1952–2004*, 2nd ed. (Washington, DC: CIA, 2012), 114.

129 **Lehman reached out to the Reagan camp:** Richard J. Kerr and Peter Dixon Davis, "Mornings in Pacific Palisades: Ronald Reagan and the President's Daily Brief," *Studies in Intelligence* 42, no. 5 (Winter 1998–99): 51.

129 **CIA officers began briefing Allen:** Ibid.

129 **Turner showed the PDB to Reagan's advisors:** "DCI Meeting with President-Elect's Staff," Memorandum for the Record by National Intelligence Chairman Dick Lehman, November 14, 1980 (CIA-RDP83B0014 R000200030012-8), CREST.

130 **Allen invited Agency briefers:** Kerr and Davis, "Mornings in Pacific Palisades," 52.

130 **"extremely alert":** Helgerson, *Getting to Know the President*, 114.

130 **Bush's sessions were animated and loose:** Kerr and Davis, "Mornings in Pacific Palisades," 52.

130 **encourage Reagan to accept daily PDB briefings:** Ibid., 52–53.

130 **"I felt it was very important for the President":** George H. W. Bush, correspondence with the author, April 2012.

130 **Ed Meese informed the CIA:** Kerr and Davis, "Mornings in Pacific Palisades," 52–53.

130 **His plane landed early enough:** Ibid., 53.

131 **After meeting Nancy Reagan:** Ibid.

131 **an unlikely-looking pair:** Interviews by the author, 2011–13, of several former colleagues of Kerr and Davis.

131 **little supervision from CIA headquarters:** Ibid., 54–55.

132 **more than two dozen briefings:** Nicholas Dujmovic, "Ronald Reagan, Intelligence, William Casey, and CIA: A Reappraisal," in *Ronald Reagan, Intelligence, and the End of the Cold War,* supplement to the conference of the same name at the RRPL, November 2, 2011.

132 **"Reagan was a studious reader":** Kerr and Davis, "Mornings in Pacific Palisades," 54.

132 **"knew what he thought about everything":** Dixon Davis, interview by John Helgerson, April 26, 1993, cited in Helgerson, *Getting to Know the President,* 121.

132 **"The only things we were going to pass back":** Dick Kerr, telephone interview by the author, October 2011.

133 **first in-flight intelligence briefing:** Kerr and Davis, "Mornings in Pacific Palisades," 54; Helgerson, *Getting to Know the President,* 121.

133 **Agency officers came up with a list:** "Background Briefings for the President-Elect," Note for the DCI, December 12, 1980 (CIA-RDP81B00401 R002400110002-5), CREST.

133 **PDB itself continued to treat:** Helgerson, *Getting to Know the President,* 119–20.

133 **the president-elect seemed most interested:** Dujmovic, "Ronald Reagan, Intelligence, William Casey, and CIA: A Reappraisal."

133 **Bush encouraged the Agency's briefers:** Helgerson, *Getting to Know the President,* 119–20.

133 **"completely satisfied with the briefings":** Ronald Reagan, interview by John Helgerson, July 26, 1993, cited in Helgerson, *Getting to Know the President,* 117.

133 **"an interesting situation":** Kerr and Davis, "Mornings in Pacific Palisades," 51.

134 **"source of very interesting information":** Richard Allen, telephone interview by the author, March 2012.

134 **sat down with Kerr to review:** Helgerson, *Getting to Know the President,* 122.

134 **Reagan said that its current format:** Ibid.

134 **"By Inauguration Day":** Kerr and Davis, "Mornings in Pacific Palisades," 56.

134 *he* **would deliver the President's Daily Brief:** Helgerson, *Getting to Know the President,* 122.

134 **"We had a very good relationship with Allen":** Kerr, telephone interview by the author, October 2011.

134 **avid customer of intelligence:** Kerr and Davis, "Mornings in Pacific Palisades," 51.

134 **"Allen was one-on-one":** Dick Kerr, telephone interview by the author, November 2011.

135 **"On a typical morning":** Richard Allen, telephone interview by the author, March 2012.

135 **The familiar 8-by-10½-inch book:** "Printing and Photography Division, Weekly Report for Period Ending 28 April–4 May 1985," (CIA-RDP87-00352 R000100050036-4), CREST. Descriptions of the PDB's structure in the Reagan era are from Ed Meese, interview by the author, August 2012; Rod McDaniel, telephone interview by the author, December 2011; and Doug MacEachin, interview by the author, December 2011.

135 **supplement the core six-to-ten-page book:** John Hedley, interview by the author, July 2011.

135 **"Can I have these?":** Nicholas Dujmovic, interview by the author, February 2012.

136 **"straightforward presentation":** Richard Allen, telephone interview by the author, April 2012.

136 **Secretary's Morning Summary:** Allen, telephone interview by the author, March 2012.

136 **joined Allen's national security session:** Ibid.

136 **Baker remembers:** James Baker, interview by the author, May 2012.

136 **"more like *Reader's Digest*":** Meese, interview by the author.

136 **"The Vice President learned early on":** Robert McFarlane, interview by the author, October 2011.

137 **"He read it, he wrote on it":** MacEachin, interview by the author.

137 **Bush and an assistant or two:** Hedley, interview by the author, July 2011.

137 **"If I saw":** Donald Gregg, telephone interview by the author, January 2012.

137 **"very down-to-earth":** Hedley, interview by the author.

137 **"I've got to go downstairs":** MacEachin, interview by the author.

137 **CIA briefers delivered PDB copies:** Hedley, interview by the author.

138 **Although nearly opposite in style:** Interviews by the author, 2011–2013, of several former colleagues of Peters and Hedley.

138 **They first tried trading off:** Hedley, interview by the author.

138 **first two additional PDB customers:** Kerr and Davis, "Mornings in Pacific Palisades," 56; Helgerson, *Getting to Know the President*, 122.

138 **frequent earfuls from Haig:** Kerr, telephone interview by the author, November 2011.

138 **"There are the Soviets doing it again":** Ibid.

139 **"the most useful product":** "Producer-Consumer Relations Seminar: Summary of Discussions," by Helene L. Boatner, Chief of the Product Evaluation Staff, July 13, 1982 (CIA-RDP83M00914 R002700040022-9), CREST.

139 **"wonderful guy":** Hedley, interview by the author.

139 **Weinberger's overseas trips:** Caspar W. Weinberger with Gretchen Roberts, *In the Arena: A Memoir of the 20th Century* (New York: Regnery, 2001), 314, 316.

139 **Allen arrived just before:** See Richard V. Allen, "The Day Reagan Was Shot: An Exclusive First-Hand Account," *Constitution Daily*, March 30, 2011, available at http://blog.constitutioncenter.org/the-day-reagan-was -shot-an-exclusive-first-hand-account; and Del Quentin Wilber, *Rawhide Down: The Near Assassination of Ronald Reagan* (New York: Henry Holt, 2011), Chapter 3.

140 **he was flying to Texas:** Wilber, *Rawhide Down*, 49.

140 **Reagan's daily schedule came to a standstill:** James A. Baker III with Steve Fiffer, *"Work Hard, Study—and Keep Out of Politics!": Adventures and Lessons from an Unexpected Public Life* (New York: G. P. Putnam's Sons, 2006), 161.

140 **only one national security briefing:** Allen, telephone interview by the author, March 2012.

140 **the president should resume his national security briefing:** Ibid.

142 **declined the DI's offer to brief him:** "Staff Meeting Minutes of 21 January 1981," Memorandum for the Record, January 21, 1981 (CIA-RDP84B00130 R000600010422-1), CREST.

142 **Casey read the PDB:** Joseph E. Persico, *Casey: From the OSS to the CIA* (New York: Viking, 1990), 221.

142 **late items that had not appeared:** "Staff Meeting Minutes of 21 January 1981."

143 **"I warned Casey":** Robert Gates, telephone interview by the author, August 2012.

143 **Casey ended up devoting:** Persico, *Casey*; Robert M. Gates, *From the Shadows: The Ultimate Insider's Story of Five Presidents and How They Won the Cold War* (New York: Touchstone, 1996), 202.

143 **"We would always come back":** Hedley, interview by the author.

143 **The director used these:** "DCI's Meeting with the PFIAB," Draft presentation, May 12, 1982 (CIA-RDP84B00049 R001102690001-7), CREST.

143 **private messages to the president:** Rod McDaniel (National Security Council executive secretary under President Reagan; acting Deputy National Security Advisor in 1986), telephone interview by the author, December 2011.

143 **the two rarely met:** Dujmovic, "Ronald Reagan, Intelligence, William Casey, and CIA"; see also Gates, *From the Shadows*, 218.

143 **"Casey's closeness to Reagan has been exaggerated":** Robert M. Gates, interview by Timothy J. Naftali et al., July 23, 2000, George H. W. Bush Oral History Project, Miller Center, University of Virginia, available at http://millercenter.org/president/bush/oralhistory/robert-gates.

144 **he planned to engage fully on policy:** Persico, *Casey*, 203.

144 **disliked Casey's in-your-face style:** Gates, *From the Shadows*, 207.

144 **"academic, soft":** "Progress at the CIA," memorandum from William J. Casey to President Reagan, May 6, 1981, declassified and released for inclusion in the *Ronald Reagan, Intelligence, and the End of the Cold War*

supplement to the conference of the same name at the RRPL, November 2, 2011.

144 **ducking the CIA's duty:** Persico, *Casey*, 219.

144 **"pure bunk":** Quoted in ibid., 389.

145 **reorganized the DI:** Gates, interview by Naftali.

145 **split into two sections:** John H. Hedley, "Intelligence and the Presidency," *SpyCast: The Podcast of the International Spy Museum*, posted August 1, 2008.

145 **"Analysis and evidence were jumbled together":** Gates, telephone interview by the author.

145 **"the question was not their judgment":** Ibid.

145 **"most far-reaching reorganization":** "DDI Remarks," January 13, 1983 (CIA-RDP85B00652 R000100010037-4), CREST.

145 **"No other single change we have made":** Ibid.

146 **"coolheaded, evenhanded, affable guy":** Hedley, interview by the author, July 2011.

146 **"I'm going in to see the president":** John Hedley, interviews by the author, July 2011 and October 2011.

146 **Clark usually just left the PDB:** McFarlane, interview by the author.

146 **Reagan was so interested:** "Current Intelligence Items of Interest During Your Absence," memorandum from Acting Deputy Director for Intelligence to DCI, August 25, 1982 (CIA-RDP83M00914 R0029 00040032-6), CREST.

146 **a special supplement:** Carl Bernstein, "The Holy Alliance: Ronald Reagan and John Paul II," *Time*, February 24, 1992, available at http://www.time.com/time/magazine/article/0,9171,974931-1,00.html.

146 **the same basic approach to the PDB:** McFarlane, interview by the author.

147 **"For those who are allowed to read it":** Richard V. Allen, "An Intelligent Thing to Do," *New York Times*, November 14, 2003.

147 **"one for the *Washington Post*":** Allen, telephone interview by the author, March 2012.

147 **Senior White House staffers:** McDaniel, telephone interview by the author.

147 **"I read it every morning":** Mike Bohn, interview by the author, January 2012.

147 **copies of the book in his home garage:** Allen, "An Intelligent Thing to Do."

147 **He asked Casey:** "Leaks," Memorandum from the Director of Central Intelligence to the Deputy Director of Central Intelligence, April 9, 1981 (CIA-RDP88B00444 R001003870058-3), CREST.

148 **people who had access to the PDB:** Gregg, telephone interview by the author.

148 **"Some West Wingers left it lying around":** Bush, correspondence with the author.

148 **made the CIA more hesitant:** Helgerson, *Getting to Know the President*, 123.

148 **Casey's staff lobbied him:** "Topics for Your Meeting with Judge Clark, 16 April 1983," Memorandum from DCI staff to the Director of Central Intelligence, April 15, 1983 (CIA-RDP85M00363 R001102430007-8), CREST.

148 **Vessey should indeed start getting PDB briefings:** "DCI and DDCI Meeting with Judge Clark, 27 July 1983," Memorandum for the Record, August 1, 1983 (CIA-RDP85M00364 R000601010073-7), CREST.

148 **"pretty much letting it go":** Kerr, telephone interview by the author, November 2011.

148 **Casey told Bud McFarlane:** "DCI/DDCI Meeting with the Assistant to the President for National Security Affairs, 7 November 1985," Memorandum for the Record from Deputy Director for Central Intelligence John N. McMahon, November 12, 1985 (CIA-RDP87M00539 R000800990004 -9), CREST.

148 **"It was explicit":** Bruce Pease, interview by the author, December 2012.

149 **the three words "President's Daily Brief":** John Bellinger, interview by the author, September 2011.

149 **the fact of the existence of the PDB:** "Reagan Library Unveils Spies: Secrets from the CIA, KGB and Hollywood Exhibit," *What's News at CIA* no. 1017, February 26, 2002, available at http://www.foia.cia.gov/docs /DOC_0001243290/DOC_0001243290.pdf.

149 **McMahon mentioned the PDB:** McMahon wrote, "Regarding your concerns about the Soviet CW briefing, I'm told a paper—and possibly a PDB item—is in the works that will specifically lay out the issues and any areas of disagreement." Letter from Deputy Director of Central Intelligence John N. McMahon to Defense Intelligence Agency Director James A. Williams, May 29, 1984 (CIA-RDP86M00886 R001800080012-5), CREST.

150 **Gates referred to the PDB:** Gates wrote, "Early each morning a written briefing is delivered to the White House for the president. As directed by President Reagan in 1981, officers of the CIA's analysis directorate also fan out across Washington each morning to share copies of the president's briefing with the vice president, the secretaries of state and defense, the national security adviser, and the chairman of the Joint Chiefs of Staff." Robert M. Gates, "The CIA and American Foreign Policy," *Foreign Affairs* 66, no. 2 (Winter 1987/1988), 217.

150 **senior policy makers had referenced the PDB publicly:** The media did not treat the name of the President's Daily Brief as some great scoop. In 1986, William Safire of the *New York Times* referred to the PDB explicitly, but casually, in a piece about the National Intelligence Daily, the sub-PDB intelligence daily publication that went to a couple of hundred senior administration officials instead of a handful. William Safire, "Spilling the NID," *New York Times*, May 12, 1986.

150 **"daily, unabbreviated and without a covering summary":** See the excerpt of Kissinger's press conference in "The SALT Debate," *Washington Post*, December 28, 1975, 27.

150 **Jimmy Carter and his national security advisor:** Jimmy Carter, *Keeping Faith: Memoirs of a President* (New York: Bantam Books, 1982), 51, 55; Zbigniew Brzezinski, *Power and Principle: Memoirs of the National Security Adviser, 1977–1981* (New York: Farrar Straus Giroux, 1983), 64.

150 **"I don't remember anything about declassifying":** Gates, telephone interview by the author.

150 **His first four national security advisors:** Allen, telephone interview by the author, March 2012; William Clark, telephone interview by the author, October 2012; McFarlane, interview by the author, October 2011; John Poindexter, interview by the author, December 2012.

150 **he often wrote notes:** McDaniel, telephone interview by the author.

150 **public misstatements about the title of books:** See Lou Cannon, *President Reagan: The Role of a Lifetime* (New York: PublicAffairs, 1991), 252–53.

150 **markings or notations in the president's hand:** Dujmovic, "Ronald Reagan, Intelligence, William Casey, and CIA."

151 **in the margins of his PDB copy:** Ibid.

151 **Defense Intelligence Supplement:** McDaniel, telephone interview by the author; Dujmovic, interview by the author.

151 **The product, which typically ran six to eight pages:** A. Denis Clift, interview by the author, December 2011.

151 **"They were talking about having DIA":** Gates, telephone interview by the author.

152 **Reagan's daily intelligence packages:** Douglas F. Garthoff, *Directors of Central Intelligence as Leaders of the U.S. Intelligence Community, 1946–2005* (Washington, DC: Potomac Books, 2007), 175 n. 3; Dujmovic, interview by the author.

152 **The Directorate of Intelligence's managers and editors:** The following three paragraphs are based on interviews by the author, 2011–13, of several former CIA analysts and managers of the Reagan era.

152 **Gandhi had been assassinated in India:** Mike Barry, interview by the author, June 2011.

152 **opened his copy of the President's Daily Brief:** Ibid.

152 **"I wanted to know":** Gates, telephone interview by the author.

152 **Carmen had her first PDB article:** Carmen Medina, interview by the author, May 2013.

154 **he had seen parts of the PDB:** "Briefings for Secretary-designate Shultz," Memorandum for the Record by Assistant to the DDI for Current Support, June 28, 1982 (CIA-RDP83M00914 R002200160052-8), CREST.

154 **"The PDB was one of the first things":** George Shultz, interview by the author, April 2012.

154 **a senior DI officer told Casey:** "Current Intelligence Items of Interest During Your Absence."

154 **"he had too much of an agenda":** George Shultz, interview by James Sterling Young et al., December 18, 2002, Ronald Reagan Oral History Project, Miller Center, University of Virginia, available at http://miller center.org/president/reagan/oralhistory/george-shultz.

154 **sending personal notes:** See Gates, *From the Shadows*, 290.

154 **The two sat down in January 1986:** Shultz and Gates each found this meeting important enough to address at length in their memoirs, but they disagree on when it occurred. Gates says they met on January 9, while Shultz says it was on January 20. Gates, *From the Shadows*, 337; George P. Shultz, *Turmoil and Triumph: My Years as Secretary of State* (New York: Charles Scribner's Sons, 1993), 865.

154 **he felt manipulated:** Shultz, *Turmoil and Triumph*, 865–66.

154 **Gates listened carefully:** Gates, *From the Shadows*, 337.

155 **covert operations managers:** Shultz, *Turmoil and Triumph*, 867.

155 **"I suspect no senior CIA official":** Gates, *From the Shadows*, 337.

155 **failed to change either man's mind:** Shultz, *Turmoil and Triumph*, 866–67; Gates, *From the Shadows*, 337.

155 **renewed mutual admiration:** Shultz, *Turmoil and Triumph*, 867.

155 **"I had a very good relationship":** Shultz, interview by the author.

155 **"best senior user of intelligence":** Gates, *From the Shadows*, 287.

155 **"Policymakers may not like the message":** Gates, "The CIA and American Foreign Policy," 229.

155 **short films of foreign places and leaders:** Jimmy Carter, clearly not an actor, had also watched such films while in the Oval Office, according to Zbigniew Brzezinski, his national security advisor. Phil Gailey, "Reagan Views Films to Get the Diplomatic Edge," *New York Times*, December 24, 1981.

155 **it was the CIA itself:** Dujmovic, "Ronald Reagan, Intelligence, William Casey, and CIA."

156 **"Reagan always focused":** McFarlane, interview by the author.

156 **reporting from his first year:** Gailey, "Reagan Views Films to Get the Diplomatic Edge."

156 **"Would it be better for me":** Allen, telephone interview by the author, March 2012.

156 **asked for a video before every visit:** McFarlane, interview by the author.

156 **"a sense of having met him before":** Ronald Reagan, *The Reagan Diaries*, ed. Douglas Brinkley (New York: Harper Collins, 2007), 333. See also Dujmovic, "Ronald Reagan, Intelligence, William Casey, and CIA."

156 **"There are two visual images":** Former senior CIA officer, interview by the author, June 2012.

157 **"the movies were very helpful":** Meese, interview by the author.

157 **"He was very appreciative":** William Webster, telephone interview by the author, October 2011.

157 **would not be "necessary or desirable":** "Meeting with Judge William Webster," Memorandum of Conversation on March 23, 1987, in the Oval Office, April 1, 1987, declassified and released for inclusion in the *Ronald Reagan, Intelligence, and the End of the Cold War* supplement to the conference of the same name at the RRPL, November 2, 2011.

157 **"I got the PDB at 10:00":** Webster, telephone interview by the author.

157 **"enormous respect and affection"**: Gates, interview by Naftali.

158 **"easy, relaxed person"**: Garthoff, *Directors of Central Intelligence as Leaders of the U.S. Intelligence Community*, 172.

158 **"In contrast with Casey"**: John Gannon, interview by the author, October 2011.

158 **"accurate, illuminating, and timely"**: House Permanent Select Committee on Intelligence—Review Committee, An Evaluation of CIA's Analysis of Soviet Economic Performance, 1970–1990, November 18, 1991, cited in Douglas J. MacEachin, "CIA Assessments of the Soviet Union: The Record Versus the Charges," *Studies in Intelligence* (1997), available at https://www.cia.gov/library/center-for-the-study-of-intelligence/csi-publications/csi-studies/studies/97unclass/soviet.html, 57–58.

158 **analysts' estimates of economic growth**: MacEachin, "CIA Assessments of the Soviet Union."

158 **"Every President from Lyndon Johnson on"**: Gates, interview by Naftali.

158 **"The Department of Defense"**: Ibid.

159 **tried to answer crucial intelligence questions**: MacEachin, "CIA Assessments of the Soviet Union."

159 **CIA products in the Reagan years**: Ibid.

159 **the Soviet economy would be unable**: Douglas F. Garthoff, "Assessing the Soviet Challenge," in *The Directorate of Intelligence: Fifty Years of Informing Policy, 1952–2002*, expanded ed. (Washington, DC: CIA, 2002), 25.

159 **"the system can't last"**: Gates, interview by Naftali.

159 **"Precisely how these internal problems"**: "Soviet Society in the 1980s: Problems and Prospects," December 1982, in *The Directorate of Intelligence*, 65.

160 **"could employ various options"**: "Gorbachev's Economic Agenda: Promises, Potentials, Pitfalls," September 1985, in *The Directorate of Intelligence*, 73.

160 **"The reports we got from CIA"**: Shultz, interview by Young.

160 **"There was a distinct difference of opinion"**: Shultz, interview by the author.

160 **"Frank, I didn't know"**: Frank Carlucci, interview by the author, August 2012.

161 **"I'm never speaking"**: Gates, interview by Naftali.

161 **"passion and intensity"**: Caspar Weinberger, *Fighting for Peace: Seven Critical Years in the Pentagon* (New York: Warner Books, 1991), 29.

161 **man of high principles**: Shultz, *Turmoil and Triumph*, 864.

161 **"Howard Baker is one of the finest"**: Carlucci, interview by the author.

161 **"One of the things"**: Ken Duberstein, interview by the author, April 2013.

162 **"When Colin succeeded me"**: Frank Carlucci, interview by Philip Zelikow et al., August 28, 2001, Ronald Reagan Oral History Project,

Miller Center, University of Virginia, available at http://millercenter.org
/president/reagan/oralhistory/frank-carlucci.

162 **"he would take out his earphones":** Carlucci, interview by the author.

162 **the president's daily routine:** John Negroponte, interview by the
author, May 2011.

163 **deputy national security advisor had highlighted:** Ibid.

163 **citing the 40 percent figure:** Reagan, *The Reagan Diaries*, 661.

163 ***"that's* why he remembered it":** Negroponte, interview by the author.

163 **Duberstein drove:** Duberstein, interview by the author.

163 **"pretty bare":** Reagan, *The Reagan Diaries*, 692.

163 **"I don't need this anymore":** Duberstein, interview by the author.

164 **"the world is quiet today":** Ronald Reagan, *An American Life* (New
York: Simon and Schuster, 1990), 722.

EIGHT: THE SPYMASTER PRESIDENT

165 **"When I was President":** George H. W. Bush, correspondence with the
author, November 2012.

165 **"I think it helped":** George H. W. Bush, luncheon remarks at the "US
Intelligence and the End of the Cold War" conference at Texas A&M University, College Station Texas, November 19, 1999, available at http://
www.foia.cia.gov/sites/default/files/document_conversions/89801
/DOC_0001445131.pdf.

165 **"The real payoff":** George H. W. Bush, interview by John Helgerson,
May 6, 1993, cited in *Getting to Know the President: Intelligence Briefings of
Presidential Candidates, 1952–2004*, 2nd ed. (Washington, DC: CIA, Center
for the Study of Intelligence, 2012), 128.

165 **"He would start at page one":** William H. Webster, interview by Stephen Knott and Marc Selverstone, August 21, 2002, George H. W. Bush
Oral History Project, Miller Center, University of Virginia, available at
http://web1.millercenter.org/poh/transcripts/ohp_2002_0821_webster
.pdf.

165 **The briefer would:** Helgerson, *Getting to Know the President*, 127; George
Bush and Brent Scowcroft, *A World Transformed* (New York: Alfred A.
Knopf, 1998), 30.

166 **the president welcomed such a dialogue:** Brent Scowcroft, interview
by the author, January 2012.

166 **"the president took a quick look":** John Sununu, interview by the
author, October 2011.

166 **once Bob Gates's branch chief:** Robert Gates, telephone interview by
the author, August 2012.

166 **"You're the analyst":** Former senior CIA officer, interview by the author,
July 2011.

166 **"He would make you exceedingly uncomfortable":** Former senior
CIA officer, interview by the author, December 2012.

166 **"incredibly intimidating":** Michael Morell, interview by the author,
January 2015.

166 **"Hank was always such a gentleman":** Former senior CIA officer, interview by the author, December 2012.

166 **"very skilled, outstanding people":** Scowcroft, interview by the author.

166 **"I would have been pretty daunted":** Gates, telephone interview by the author.

166 **it must have been difficult:** Sununu, interview by the author.

167 **"They quickly realized":** Gates, telephone interview by the author.

167 **"Chuck rewrote almost everything":** John McLaughlin, interview by the author, February 2011.

167 **"I'm standing there in this smoke-filled room":** Rodney Faraon, interview by the author, January 2013.

168 **"Hank was so predictable":** Former CIA officer, interview by the author, March 2012.

168 **"I'm walking around":** McLaughlin, interview by the author.

168 **"not always as exciting":** Scowcroft, interview by the author.

168 **"rewrote every single word":** Pete Alvarez, interview by the author, April 2012.

168 **After the snowflakes:** John Helgerson, interview by the author, November 2011; William Webster, telephone interview by the author, October 2011; Scowcroft, interview by the author.

168 **"We almost never got any complaints":** Helgerson, interview by the author.

168 **"I always assumed":** Scowcroft, interview by the author.

168 **the CIA briefers earlier:** Webster, telephone interview by the author.

168 **"real grilling":** Robert M. Gates, interview by Timothy J. Naftali et al., July 23, 2000, George H. W. Bush Oral History Project, Miller Center, University of Virginia, available at http://millercenter.org/president /bush/oralhistory/robert-gates.

169 **Scowcroft sometimes queried Bush's briefer:** Bush, luncheon remarks at the "US Intelligence and the End of the Cold War" conference.

169 **principals would chat about policy:** Scowcroft, interview by the author; Webster, interview by Knott and Selverstone.

169 **"you know what Mitterrand just did":** Brent Scowcroft, interview with Bradley Thompson, January 11, 1999, cited in Bradley H. Patterson Jr., *The White House Staff: Inside the West Wing and Beyond* (Washington, DC: Brookings Institution Press, 2000), 57.

169 **Scowcroft called:** Gates, interview by Naftali.

169 **"the way you handled this issue":** Scowcroft, interview by the author.

170 **he asked the CIA:** Ibid.

170 **when Bush traveled:** Gates, interview by Naftali.

170 **"Why is that there?":** Helgerson, interview by the author.

170 **"Don't let anybody else tell you":** Bush, interview by Helgerson, cited in Helgerson, *Getting to Know the President*, 128.

170 **"most honest broker I ever knew":** Webster, telephone interview by the author.

170 **"There is nobody":** Bush, luncheon remarks at the "US Intelligence and the End of the Cold War" conference.

170 **"We never got enough information":** Sununu, interview by the author.

170 **"it wasn't designed for that":** Scowcroft, interview by the author.

171 **"You need to know":** Dan Quayle, telephone interview by the author, December 2012.

171 **"We had made arrangements":** Webster, telephone interview by the author.

171 **His daily briefer ensured:** Former CIA officer, interview by the author, March 2012; Carnes Lord, interview by the author, April 2011.

171 **"The people who briefed me":** Quayle, telephone interview by the author.

171 **"When I asked questions":** Ibid.

172 **Bush used such informal meetings:** Dan Quayle, interview by James S. Young et al., March 12, 2002, George H. W. Bush Oral History Project, Miller Center, University of Virginia, available at http://millercenter.org/president/bush/oralhistory/danforth-quayle.

172 **"The PDB was thorough":** Quayle, telephone interview by the author.

172 **"Powell was always very well informed":** Michael McConnell, interview by the author, May 2011.

173 **"So the PDB was never left":** Gates, interview by Naftali.

173 **help prevent inadvertent disclosures:** Charles Peters, interview by John Helgerson, January 31, 1994, cited in Helgerson, *Getting to Know the President*, 126–27.

173 **"We tried to protect":** Bush, luncheon remarks at the "US Intelligence and the End of the Cold War" conference.

173 **"I want you and Dick and Colin Powell":** James Baker, interview by the author, May 2012.

173 **Cheney elected to look at his copy:** Dick Cheney, interview by the author, November 2011.

173 **"I went up and knocked":** Former senior CIA officer, interview by the author, March 2012.

174 **"The first time with [secretary of state Lawrence] Eagleburger":** Carmen Medina, interview by the author, May 2013.

174 **A different logistical challenge:** Ibid.

174 **"We collected them all":** Webster, telephone interview by the author.

175 **"I won't refer by name":** Bush, luncheon remarks at the "US Intelligence and the End of the Cold War" conference.

175 **"we brought in imagery":** Webster, telephone interview by the author.

175 **"advanced disguise systems":** Jonna Mendez, interview by the author, January 2012.

175 **"In the right places":** Webster, telephone interview by the author.

175 **"Let's take this to the White House":** Mendez, interview by the author.

176 **"It wasn't all that perfect":** Webster, interview by Knott and Selverstone.

176 **"We went out to the car":** Mendez, interview by the author.

177 **young "courier" sat quietly:** Webster, interview by Knott and Selverstone.

177 **"He was the only one":** Webster, telephone interview by the author.

177 **Webster played it straight:** Mendez, interview by the author.

178 **"She did it very well":** Webster, telephone interview by the author.

178 **"The president got a big kick out of it":** Webster, interview by Knott and Selverstone.

178 **"You must have the best job":** Mendez, interview by the author.

178 **"I'll bet you an ice cream cone":** Gates, telephone interview by the author; Gates, interview by Naftali.

179 **"The Office of Comic Relief":** Charles A. Peters, "Serving Our Senior Customers," *Studies in Intelligence*, undated, available at http://www.foia. cia.gov/sites/default/files/DOC_0001407022.pdf.

179 **"Signs of the Times":** Nicholas Dujmovic, interview by the author, February 2012.

179 **"Tanks for the Memories":** Former CIA officer, interview by the author, March 2012.

179 **"We tried":** Peters, "Serving Our Senior Customers."

179 **"Club of Kings":** Dujmovic, interview by the author.

180 **"a serious and avid consumer":** Scowcroft, interview by the author.

180 **"He was the easiest brief":** John Gannon, interview by the author, September 2011.

180 a **"Red Book" PDB:** Dick Kerr, telephone interview by the author, November 2011.

181 **"We followed that pretty well":** Ibid.

181 **"We had been assured":** Cheney, interview by the author.

181 **"he would not be foolish enough":** Baker, interview by the author.

181 **Shevarnadze came back from lunch:** Ibid.

181 **Overnight on August 1:** Bush and Scowcroft, *A World Transformed*, 302–3.

182 **Bush and Scowcroft called Baker:** Ibid., 314.

182 **"beginning of the coalition":** Baker, interview by the author.

182 **Webster stuck around:** Bush and Scowcroft, *A World Transformed*, 315.

182 **"like clockwork":** Former CIA officer, interview by the author, March 2012.

182 **Throughout the buildup:** Winston Wiley, interview by the author, April 2011.

182 **The president read:** Peters, "Serving Our Senior Customers."

182 **substantially degrade Iraqi forces:** Scowcroft, interview by the author.

182 **"half of the Iraqi armor":** Cheney, interview by the author.

182 **Agency analysts fed battle-damage assessments:** Robert D. Vickers Jr., "Desert Storm and the BDA Controversy," *Studies in Intelligence*, undated, available at http://www.foia.cia.gov/sites/default/files/DOC_0006122350.pdf, 7.

183 **the gap in these estimates expanded:** Ibid., 8.

183 **Differences emerged:** Vickers, "Desert Storm and the BDA Controversy, 8; Wiley, interview by the author.

183 **"it was larger than DIA was saying":** Bruce Riedel, interview by the author, February 2013.

183 **different conclusions in the PDB and in the NID:** Vickers, "Desert Storm and the BDA Controversy," 8; Wiley, interview by the author.

184 **"we'd still be in Saudi Arabia":** H. Norman Schwarzkopf with Peter Petre, *It Doesn't Take a Hero* (New York: Bantam, 1992), 432.

184 **"We reported on what we were seeing":** Webster, telephone interview by the author.

184 **"I don't think we understood the political risk":** Kerr, telephone interview by the author.

184 **"It was not hostile":** Webster, interview by the author; Vickers, "Desert Storm and the BDA Controversy," 8.

184 **"pilot euphoria":** Webster, interview by the author.

184 **"I got a hurry-up phone call":** Cheney, interview by the author.

184 **CENTCOM judged:** Vickers, "Desert Storm and the BDA Controversy," 8.

184 **"It got to be a heated argument":** Scowcroft, interview by the author.

185 **The conflicting assessments leaked:** Vickers, "Desert Storm and the BDA Controversy," 8.

185 **"Someone in Congress":** Webster, telephone interview by the author.

185 **A CENTCOM draft paper in November 1991:** Vickers, "Desert Storm and the BDA Controversy," 9.

185 **Some participants in this saga:** Schwarzkopf, *It Doesn't Take a Hero*, 432.

185 **Powell asserts:** Colin Powell with Tony Koltz, *It Worked for Me: In Life and Leadership* (New York: HarperCollins, 2012), 114–15.

185 **"we were right and the Agency was wrong":** Cheney, interview by the author.

185 **exhaustive survey of the theater:** Vickers, "Desert Storm and the BDA Controversy," 8–9.

185 **"We were right, and time proved that we were right":** Riedel, interview by the author.

185 **"CIA turned out to be more accurate":** Scowcroft, interview by the author.

186 **"so much information coming in":** Jonathan Howe, telephone interview by the author, October 2012.

186 **"let them set forth their theses":** Brent Scowcroft, interview by Philip Zelikow et al., November 12–13, 1999, George H. W. Bush Oral History Project, Miller Center, University of Virginia, available at http://miller center.org/president/bush/oralhistory/brent-scowcroft.

186 **"The Agency's forecast of serious trouble":** Robert M. Gates, "Intelligence in the Reagan and Bush Presidencies," in Kenneth W. Thompson, ed., *The Bush Presidency: Ten Intimate Perspectives of George Bush* (Lanham, MD: University Press of America, 1997), 154.

186 **Gates remembers eating pancakes:** Gates, interview by Naftali.

187 **The PDB piece concluded:** Michael R. Beschloss and Strobe Talbott, *At the Highest Levels: The Inside Story of the End of the Cold War* (Boston: Little, Brown, 1993), 421.

187 **"Should I take this seriously?":** Gates, interview by Naftali; Bush and Scowcroft, *A World Transformed*, 519.

187 **within twenty-four hours of that briefing:** Bush and Scowcroft, *A World Transformed*, 519.

187 **"We did the coup":** Kerr, telephone interview by the author.

187 **"a complete surprise":** Scowcroft, interview by the author.

187 **"they did their job":** Scowcroft, interview by Zelikow et al.

187 **"we just didn't know it":** Baker, interview by the author.

187 **"the biggest puzzle for all of us":** Gates, interview by Naftali.

188 **"I didn't see that particular PDB":** Cheney, interview by the author.

189 **measures that exist to this day:** Christopher Andrew, *For the President's Eyes Only: Secret Intelligence and the American Presidency from Washington through Bush* (New York: Harper Collins, 1995), 535.

189 **"I wanted a brick wall there":** Gates, telephone interview by the author.

189 **"Bob had gone through so much":** Helgerson, interview by the author.

189 **"John would do for me what I did for Casey":** Gates, telephone interview by the author.

189 **once in a while there would be an article:** Helgerson, interview by the author.

189 **"I'd just drop in":** Gates, interview by Naftali.

189 **Bush did not intrude:** Gates, "Intelligence in the Reagan and Bush Presidencies," 147.

190 **"the most important thing that a DCI brings":** Gates, interview by Naftali.

190 **"I wouldn't have wanted to try":** Bush, luncheon remarks at the "US Intelligence and the End of the Cold War" conference.

190 **"My relationship with these men and women":** Bush, correspondence with the author.

190 **George Bush Center for Intelligence:** "FLASHBACK: April 26, 1999: CIA Headquarters Named George Bush Center for Intelligence," article posted on CIA's News and Information page, May 1, 2014, available at https://www.cia.gov/news-information/featured-story-archive/2014-featured-story-archive/flashback-cia-headquarters-named-george-bush-center-for-intelligence.html.

Nine: Ebb and Flow

191 **"obviously intrigued":** John L. Helgerson, *Getting to Know the President: Intelligence Briefings of Presidential Candidates, 1952–2004*, 2nd ed. (Washington, DC: CIA, 2012), 134–35.

191 **they took almost an hour:** Ibid., 135.

191 **proliferation, Somalia, Bosnia, and especially Haiti:** Ibid., 134–35.

191 **"ripping their roofs off":** Sandy Berger, interview by the author, December 2012.

192 **"I became convinced early on":** Bill Clinton, telephone interview by the author, March 2013.

192 **more widely than his predecessor:** Helgerson, *Getting to Know the President*, 134–35.

192 **While in Little Rock:** Ibid., 136, 141.

192 **"an interest in everything":** Colin L. Powell with Joseph E. Persico, *My American Journey* (New York: Random House, 1995), 563.

192 **first PDB briefing after the inauguration:** Charles A. Peters, "Serving Our Senior Customers," *Studies in Intelligence*, undated, available at http://www.foia.cia.gov/sites/default/files/DOC_0001407022.pdf.

193 **"The president had a great natural tendency":** Thomas "Mack" McLarty, telephone interview by the author, July 2011.

193 **many other days to follow:** Peters, "Serving Our Senior Customers."

193 **"We just sat outside the Oval Office":** R. James Woolsey, interview by the author, September 2011.

193 **the CIA director simply stopped going:** R. James Woolsey, interview by Russell L. Riley et al., January 13, 2010, William J. Clinton Presidential History Project, Miller Center, University of Virginia, 18, available at http://millercenter.org/president/clinton/oralhistory/r-james-woolsey; Peters, "Serving Our Senior Customers"; Walter Pincus, "PDB, the Only News Not Fit for Anyone Else to Read," *Washington Post*, August 27, 1994.

194 **"As I got more comfortable":** Clinton, telephone interview by the author.

194 **"quite an avaricious consumer of intelligence":** Berger, interview by the author.

194 **"He would underline things":** John Podesta, interview by the author, February 2013.

194 **the president took the book seriously:** Former senior CIA officer, interview by the author, December 2012.

194 **"See attached magazine article":** Woolsey, interview by the author.

194 **"By reading the PDB":** Clinton, telephone interview by the author.

194 **in Clinton's regular national security meeting:** McLarty, telephone interview by the author.

195 **"On the days when":** Clinton, telephone interview by the author.

195 **"all the time":** Ibid.

195 **Secretary's Morning Summary:** Thomas A. Kean and Lee H. Hamilton with Benjamin Rhodes, *Without Precedent: The Inside Story of the 9/11 Commission* (New York: Vintage Books, 2007), 187.

195 **"more snapshots than movies":** Berger, interview by the author.

195 **"The frustration that I felt":** Clinton, telephone interview by the author.

195 **As he chatted on the phone:** Senior Clinton administration official, interview by the author, January 2012.

196 **"the most effective, engaged vice president":** McLarty, telephone interview by the author.

196 **"The vice president was always present":** Ibid.

196 **"There were days when":** Clinton, telephone interview by the author.

196 **"I read it religiously every morning":** Al Gore, interview by the author, July 2013.

196 **often during his car ride:** Ibid.

196 **"He wanted to sit down":** Pete Alvarez, interview by the author, April 2012.

196 **Saturdays felt more comfortable:** Gore, interview by the author.

197 **"The briefers were typically people who":** Ibid.

197 **passing the VP a classified report:** Denny Watson, interview by the author, March 2013.

197 **"When there *was* a question":** Ibid.

197 **"If it was weak":** Gore, interview by the author.

197 **create a mock PDB:** Ibid.; Watson, interview by the author.

198 **The worst part of the daily drives:** Watson, interview by the author.

198 **"If I had known that":** Gore, interview by the author.

198 **the vice president's limo made its way:** Watson, interview by the author.

199 **"Knock knock":** Ibid.

199 **"Black Hawk Down":** See Bill Clinton's account in his memoirs, *My Life* (New York: Knopf, 2004), 549–54.

199 **policy makers received warnings:** William Crowe, interview by Charles Stuart Kennedy, June 8, 1998, Association for Diplomatic Studies and Training Foreign Affairs Oral History Project, available at http://lcweb2.loc.gov/service/mss/mfdip/2004/2004cro04/2004cro04.pdf; Paul Quinn-Judge, "UN Position in Somalia Called Dire," *Boston Globe*, September 30, 1993, 1; Kenneth Michael Absher et al., *Privileged and Confidential: The Secret History of the President's Intelligence Advisory Board* (Lexington: University Press of Kentucky, 2012), 286–87.

199 **"The intelligence failure in Somalia":** Crowe, interview by Kennedy; Quinn-Judge, "UN Position in Somalia Called Dire"; Doug MacEachin, interview by the author, December 2011.

199 **flow of intelligence to Clinton was in flux:** MacEachin, interview by the author.

200 **"Aidid had 20 percent of Mogadishu":** Clinton, telephone interview by the author.

200 **getting the PDB delivered personally again:** MacEachin, interview by the author.

200 **"It was a very sobering moment for me":** Clinton, telephone interview by the author.

200 **regularized the national security briefing:** Pincus, "PDB, the Only News Not Fit for Anyone Else to Read."

200 **allocated more time:** Bill Clinton, interview with Dan Goodgame and Michael Duffy, in "Blending Force with Democracy: Bill Clinton," *Time*, October 31, 1994, 35.

201 **delivered the goods in his daily intelligence:** John McLaughlin, "Remarks of the Deputy Director of Central Intelligence," address to CIA's conference on "CIA's Analysis of the Soviet Union, 1947–1991," Princeton University, March 9–10, 2001, available at https://www.cia.gov/library/center-for-the-study-of-intelligence/csi-publications/books-and

-monographs/watching-the-bear-essays-on-cias-analysis-of-the-soviet
-union/article08.html.

201 **"I used to sit":** Former senior CIA official, interview by the author,
August 2011.

201 **enabled** *something* **from the CIA briefer:** Berger, interview by the
author.

201 **"I didn't have a** *bad* **relationship":** Woolsey, interview by the author.

201 **"Tony Lake was basically my boss":** Ibid.

201 **NSC meeting about Somalia:** Ibid.

203 **"I do not think we have been successful":** William Nolte, "A Wealth
of Experience: An Interview with William O. Studeman," *Studies in Intelligence*, undated, available at http://www.foia.cia.gov/sites/default/files
/DOC_0006122348.pdf, 12–13.

203 **205 appointments on Capitol Hill in 1993:** R. James Woolsey, testimony to the Senate Committee on Governmental Affairs, August 16,
2004, available at www.c-spanvideo.org.

203 **"good and sound":** Woolsey, interview by the author.

203 **aircraft down on the South Lawn:** Maureen Dowd, "Crash at the
White House," *New York Times*, September 13, 1994.

203 **Woolsey trying to get an appointment with Clinton:** Woolsey,
interview by the author; R. James Woolsey, comments during "CIA and
Intelligence Reform" panel, C-Span Washington Journal, November 22,
2004, available at www.c-spanvideo.org.

204 **Clinton sent the skeptical John Deutch:** Douglas F. Garthoff, *Directors
of Central Intelligence as Leaders of the U.S. Intelligence Community, 1946–2005*
(Washington, DC: Potomac Books, 2007), 235.

204 **not being impressed:** John Deutch, interview by the author, April 2011.

204 **Gore's annoyance with the overlapping content:** Alvarez, interview
by the author.

204 **"I asked them so many damned questions":** Gore, interview by the
author.

204 **bilateral commissions that Gore was responsible for:** "Gore Speaks
on His Role as First Shepherd of Policy; Vice President Takes Credit for
Host of Initiatives," *Baltimore Sun*, June 18, 1997; Leon Fuerth's webpage at George Washington University, available at http://elliott.gwu.edu
/fuerth; Alvarez, interview by the author.

204 **articles in the new publication:** Watson, interview by the author.

205 **"Once we figured out what the sweet spot was":** Alvarez, interview
by the author.

205 **"If there was something weak":** Gore, interview by the author.

205 **"he learned, and he remembered":** Ibid.

205 **"What was shown to the vice president":** Leon Fuerth, interview by
the author, July 2012.

206 **"most thoughtful, most engaged":** George Tenet, interview by the
author, June 2011.

206 **"most demanding and most sophisticated":** Marty Petersen, interview by the author, June 2011.

206 **"Leon could efficiently direct my inquiries":** Gore, interview by the author.

206 **Clinton was acting on its content:** Watson, interview by the author.

206 **lack of regular, direct access:** John Gannon, interview by the author, September 2011; Woolsey, interview by the author.

206 **tended toward the negative:** Michael Morell, interview by the author, January 2015.

206 **analytic leaders decided to reengineer the PDB:** Gannon, interview by the author.

206 **"we were writing this book largely for ourselves":** Morell, interview by the author.

207 **lacked a consistent connection:** Gannon, interview by the author.

207 **"It was not what you would have expected":** Ibid.

207 **spur from national security advisor Tony Lake:** Roger Z. George, "Central Intelligence Agency: The President's Own," in Roger Z. George and Harvey Rishikof, *The National Security Enterprise: Navigating the Labyrinth* (Washington, DC: Georgetown University Press, 2011), 165.

207 **he required thinking beyond that likely to emerge:** Mike Barry, interview by the author, June 2011.

207 **"We interviewed a lot of people":** Ibid.

207 **"First Customer" campaign:** Ibid.

208 **"For the first time":** Ibid.

208 **"changed the mentality":** Morell, interview by the author.

208 **"there is no such thing as a second page":** Barry, interview by the author.

209 **"How are you going to get analysts to buy in":** Ibid.

209 **streamlined the directorate's organization:** John Hollister Hedley, "The DI: A History of Service," in *The Directorate of Intelligence: Fifty Years of Informing Policy, 1952–2002*, expanded ed. (Washington, DC: CIA, 2002), 16.

209 **"I wanted our expertise":** Gannon, interview by the author.

209 **the CIA's analytic cadre had shrunk:** John McLaughlin, "Remarks of the Deputy Director of Central Intelligence," address to CIA's conference on "CIA's Analysis of the Soviet Union, 1947–1991," Princeton University, March 9–10, 2001, available at https://www.cia.gov/library/center-for-the -study-of-intelligence/csi-publications/books-and-monographs/watching -the-bear-essays-on-cias-analysis-of-the-soviet-union/article08.html.

209 **First Customer campaign:** Barry, interview by the author.

209 **"throwing darts while blindfolded":** Andy Liepman, interview by the author, October 2012.

209 **"We were still missing the mark":** Morell, interview by the author.

209 **"It didn't change things overnight":** Ibid.

209 **Corporate culture started rewarding analysts:** Barry, interview by the author.

209 **"particular value":** National Commission on Terrorist Attacks upon the United States, *The 9/11 Commission Report* (Washington, DC: National Commission on Terrorist Attacks upon the United States, 2004), 90.

210 **briefings became even less regular:** Former senior CIA official, interview by the author, August 2011.

210 **"the longer I stayed there":** Clinton, telephone interview by the author.

210 **Clinton consumed more intelligence:** Samuel R. Berger, interview by Russell L. Riley et al., March 24, 2005, William J. Clinton Presidential History Project, Miller Center, University of Virginia, 41, available at http://millercenter.org/president/clinton/oralhistory/samuel-r-berger.

210 **"You guys are the only ones in government":** Former senior CIA official, interview by the author, August 2011.

211 **"Where's my PDB?":** Ibid.

211 **Clinton chuckled at the Agency's salesmanship:** Barry, interview by the author.

211 **"As your first customer":** Bill Clinton, "Remarks on the 50th Anniversary of the Central Intelligence Agency in Langley, Virginia," September 16, 1997, *Public Papers of the Presidents, William J. Clinton—1997*, 2, 1170, available at http://quod.lib.umich.edu/p/ppotpus/4733182.1997.002/296?rgn=full+text;view=image.

211 **"They tried to convince me":** Clinton, telephone interview by the author.

211 **"incredibly valuable, steadily better over time":** Ibid.

211 **distributed more widely within the White House:** Walter Pincus, "Under Bush, the Briefing Gets Briefer," *Washington Post*, May 24, 2002.

211 **more than two dozen people:** John McLaughlin, interview by the author, February 2011.

211 **"I'm so proud of myself":** Barry, interview by the author.

212 **ripped pages out of the book:** Pincus, "PDB, the Only News Not Fit for Anyone Else to Read."

212 **tended to rely more on products:** Strobe Talbott, correspondence with the author, January 2013; see also "Lessons from the Frontline: Increasing CIA's Value Added to the Policymaker," *Studies in Intelligence* 42, no. 2 (1998), available at http://www2.gwu.edu/~nsarchiv/NSAEBB/NSAEBB431/docs/intell_ebb_006.PDF.

212 **reading the PDB mostly to ensure:** Madeleine Albright, *The Mighty and the Almighty: Reflections on America, God, and World Affairs* (New York: Harper Perennial, 2007), 48.

212 **not having enough time to read every word:** Madeleine Albright, comments during "Carter Administration and Middle East Policy" panel, University of Georgia School of Public and International Affairs, January 20, 2007, available at www.c-spanvideo.org.

212 **"I used to get irritated":** Ibid.

212 **Briefers also made their way to the Pentagon:** Pincus, "PDB, the Only News Not Fit for Anyone Else to Read"; interviews with CIA leaders and briefers, 2011–12.

212 **one of the best listeners:** Alvarez, interview by the author.

212 **"PDB editors had a tendency to chase the news":** John Hamre, correspondence with the author, May 2013.

212 **"I seldom got stuff in the PDB":** telephone interview by the author, February 2012.

213 **asking his briefer for clarifications on PDB items:** Hugh Shelton with Ronald Levinson and Malcolm McConnell, *Without Hesitation: The Odyssey of an American Warrior* (New York: St. Martin's Press, 2010), 329–30.

213 **Even the Joint Chiefs' intelligence guru:** Alvarez, interview by the author.

213 **"The PDB distilled down":** Podesta, interview by the author.

213 **expanded-distribution customer in the West Wing:** Former senior CIA official, interview by the author, August 2011.

213 **Neither Woolsey nor Deutch:** Woolsey, interview by the author; Deutch, interview by the author.

213 **"The PDB was irrelevant":** Deutch, interview by the author.

213 **the White House chief of staff stopped his briefer:** Watson, interview by the author.

214 **Tenet served as acting director:** Garthoff, *Directors of Central Intelligence as Leaders of the U.S. Intelligence Community*, 257.

214 **no direct role in the irregular PDB briefings:** George Tenet with Bill Harlow, *At the Center of the Storm: My Years at the CIA* (New York: Harper Collins, 2007), 136.

214 **"make sure the president was treated differently":** Tenet, interview by the author; former senior CIA official, interview by the author, August 2011.

214 **"Clinton used to write lots of questions":** Tenet, interview by the author.

215 **"I should pay more attention to the PDB":** Former senior CIA officer, interview by the author, December 2012.

215 **his briefer showed him the PDB:** Tenet, *At the Center of the Storm*, 30; Faraon, interview by the author.

215 **"He was always a reader":** Faraon, interview by the author.

215 **answers ready for Tenet's typical questions:** Tenet, *At the Center of the Storm*, 30; Faraon, interview by the author.

215 **multimillion-dollar compensation figure:** Tenet, "DCI Statement on the Belgrade Chinese Embassy Bombing," testimony to the House Permanent Select Committee on Intelligence, Open Hearing, July 22, 1999, available at https://www.cia.gov/news-information/speeches-testimony/1999/dci_speech_072299.html; see also Kerry Dumbaugh, "Chinese Embassy Bombing in Belgrade: Compensation Issues," *Congressional Research Service Report for Congress*, undated, available at http://congressionalresearch.com/RS20547/document.php.

215 **Later that morning in the car:** Faraon, interview by the author.

215 **"This piece doesn't make any sense":** Ibid.

217 **"On many days the book is very good":** Tenet, interview by the author.

217 **informing policy makers for decades:** "Terrorism Analysis in the CIA: The Gradual Awakening (1972–1982)," *Studies in Intelligence* 51, no. 1 (2007), available at http://www2.gwu.edu/~nsarchiv/NSAEBB /NSAEBB431/docs/intell_ebb_017.PDF.

217 **highlighted the growing threat from al Qaida:** *The 9/11 Commission Report*, 119.

217 **"Bin Ladin Preparing to Hijack US Aircraft and Other Attacks":** Ibid., 128–29.

219 **"I am not aware of any specific threats":** Bill Clinton, "Remarks Following Discussions with Prime Minister Kjell Magne Bondevik," November 1, 1999, *Public Papers of the Presidents, William J. Clinton—1999*, 2:1943, available at http://quod.lib.umich.edu/p/ppotpus/4733182.1997.002/296.

219 **Gore wrote years later:** Al Gore, *The Assault on Reason* (New York: Penguin, 2008), 179–80.

219 **"it might have brought much more attention":** *The 9/11 Commission Report*, 344.

219 **personal letters to the president:** Tenet, *At the Center of the Storm*, 122.

220 **"*that* ought to scare the world":** Clinton, telephone interview by the author.

220 **the rivals could unleash unparalleled destruction:** Bruce Riedel, "American Diplomacy and the 1999 Kargil Summit at Blair House," Policy Paper Series of the Center for the Advanced Study of India, University of Pennsylvania, 2002, 2–3.

220 **Sharif found himself in a tight bind:** Ibid., 2–3, 6.

220 **Sharif desperately sought a middle ground:** Ibid.

220 **Pakistani forces had to move back:** Clinton, *My Life*, 865.

220 **Sharif came to Washington:** Riedel, "American Diplomacy and the 1999 Kargil Summit at Blair House," 2002, 6–7.

220 **"He knew he had messed up":** Clinton, telephone interview by the author.

220 **Clinton confronted Sharif with his apprehensions:** Bruce Riedel, *Avoiding Armageddon: America, India, and Pakistan to the Brink and Back* (Washington, DC: Brookings Institution Press, 2013), 133–34; Riedel, "American Diplomacy and the 1999 Kargil Summit at Blair House," 8–9.

220 **"Sharif seemed taken aback":** Riedel, "American Diplomacy and the 1999 Kargil Summit at Blair House," 11.

221 **it would be a "catastrophe":** Ibid., 11–12.

221 **Clinton pledged to encourage India:** Clinton, *My Life*, 865.

221 **the Pakistani military arrested the prime minister:** Riedel, "American Diplomacy and the 1999 Kargil Summit at Blair House," 15.

221 **"I felt particularly well served":** Clinton, telephone interview by the author.

221 **"While the election results were open":** Podesta, interview by the author.

221 **"No one anticipated how long that would take":** Ibid.

222 **Clinton authorized the CIA to start:** Helgerson, *Getting to Know the President*, 157.

222 **"I was standing in my office":** Jami Miscik, interview by the author, June 2011.

TEN: "THE GOOD STUFF"
223 **"Make sure he reads the PDB":** Andy Card, interview by the author, May 2012.
223 **CIA briefing earlier in the campaign:** John L. Helgerson, *Getting to Know the President: Intelligence Briefings of Presidential Candidates, 1952–2004*, 2nd ed. (Washington, DC: CIA, 2012), 152–53; National Commission on the Terrorist Attacks upon the United States, *The 9/11 Commission Report* (New York: W. W. Norton, 2004), 198.
224 **"I remember thinking":** Helgerson, *Getting to Know the President*, 151.
224 **"the briefing cannot fail":** Ibid., 163.
224 **near the governor's mansion:** Ibid., 156.
224 **receiving the PDB electronically:** Ibid., 164.
224 **a weekly rotation for the transition:** Marty Petersen, interview by the author, June 2011.
224 **officials quickly settled:** Helgerson, *Getting to Know the President*, 158.
225 **the ceiling collapsed:** Ibid.
225 **"I'd give Governor Bush a PDB":** Winston Wiley, interview by the author, June 2011.
225 **supplemented Bush's PDB:** Helgerson, *Getting to Know the President*, 159.
225 **The Austin support team struggled:** Ibid., 164–65.
226 **"Would you like me to leave":** Ibid., 158.
226 **"I can trust you guys":** Petersen, interview by the author.
226 **"I had great respect for the CIA":** George W. Bush, correspondence with the author, November 2012.
226 **the cat crawled into the Christmas tree:** Petersen, interview by the author.
226 **"Good morning, Mr. President-elect":** Ibid.
226 **"We went over an hour sometimes":** Wiley, interview by the author.
226 **had just selected Michael Morell:** Ibid.; Jami Miscik, interview by the author, June 2011; Petersen, interview by the author.
226 **Wiley introduced Morell to the president-elect:** Wiley, interview by the author; Michael Morell, interview by the author, January 2015; Helgerson, *Getting to Know the President*, 166.
227 **Morell handled the next day's session:** Morell, interview by the author.
227 **"We will make the articles":** Ibid.
227 **"It's been a pleasure":** Wiley, interview by the author.
227 **"I've obviously thought a lot":** Ibid.
227 **"breaking the back of the book":** Ibid.
228 **"Saying 'a generally reliable source'":** Petersen, interview by the author; Helgerson, *Getting to Know the President*, 168.
228 **"I was long an advocate":** James Pavitt, interview by the author, July 2011.

228 **the briefing team for the Oval Office:** Wiley, interview by the author.

228 **"we are off to a strong start":** Helgerson, *Getting to Know the President*, 167.

228 **"When I started":** Morell, interview by the author.

228 **"teeing up" the first article:** Dick Cheney, interview by the author, November 2011; Michael J. Morell, "11 September 2011: With the President," *Studies in Intelligence* 50, no. 3 (2006), available at http://www2 .gwu.edu/~nsarchiv/NSAEBB/NSAEBB493/docs/intell_ebb_022.PDF, 24; George Tenet with Bill Harlow, *At the Center of the Storm: My Years at the CIA* (New York: Harper Collins, 2007), 32.

229 **"The presence of these people":** Morell, "11 September 2011," 24.

229 **Bush routinely asked questions:** Cheney, interview by the author; Morell, "11 September 2011," 24; Tenet, *At the Center of the Storm*, 32.

229 **"color commentary":** Cheney, interview by the author; Morell, "11 September 2011," 24; Tenet, *At the Center of the Storm*, 32.

229 **six to eight short analytic articles:** *The 9/11 Commission Report*, 254.

229 **"I'm going to fly down to Mexico":** Morell, interview by the author.

230 **"The president wanted it":** Card, interview by the author.

230 **"The setting was different":** Bush, correspondence with the author.

230 **he remained on Air Force One:** Morell, "11 September 2011," 30.

230 **Barney had picked a fight:** Petersen, interview by the author.

230 **more relaxed than the White House sessions:** Morell, interview by the author.

230 **"I learned best through the Socratic Method":** Bush, correspondence with the author.

231 **"raised the bar, constantly":** Morell, interview by the author.

231 **"I challenged analysts":** Ibid.

231 **briefers should move on:** Tenet, *At the Center of the Storm*, 31.

231 **two-briefer system for the president:** Miscik, interview by the author.

231 **"All my PDB briefers were excellent":** Bush, correspondence with the author.

231 **"the combination of what we did":** Wiley, interview by the author.

231 **had been shocked to see:** Card, interview by the author.

231 **narrowed the distribution:** *The 9/11 Commission Report*, 533 n. 2.

231 **Bush initially restricted:** Card, interview by the author; Miscik, interview by the author.

232 **His first PDB briefing:** Helgerson, *Getting to Know the President*, 160.

232 **"It was a calculated risk":** interview by the author, July 2011.

232 **armed with a thin book:** Ibid.

233 **"I asked a lot of questions":** Cheney, interview by the author.

233 **"The briefers would put material there":** Ibid.

233 **"His memory was phenomenal":** Interview by the author.

233 **Cheney's PDB sessions:** Cheney, interview by the author.

233 **the briefer would hop in the limo:** Interview by the author.

233 **"I was vice president now":** Cheney, interview by the author.

233 **began taking his PDB briefer:** Interview by the author; Cheney, interview by the author.

234 **"When the president asks them":** Miscik, interview by the author.

234 **"It's helpful":** Donald Rumsfeld, interview by the author, April 2012.

234 **"It's like publishing a newspaper":** Tenet, interview by the author.

234 **"the system was blinking red":** George Tenet, interview with the 9/11 Commission, January 2004, cited in *The 9/11 Commission Report*, 259.

235 **had been warning in intelligence publications:** *The 9/11 Commission Report*, 254–60.

235 **more than forty pieces in the PDB:** Ibid., 254.

235 **the president several times asked Morell:** Ibid., 260.

235 **"I had asked the CIA":** George W. Bush, *Decision Points* (New York: Crown, 2010), 135.

235 **"in response to questions of the president":** Condoleezza Rice, testimony to the 9/11 Commission, cited in Steven Strasser, ed., *The 9/11 Investigations* (New York: PublicAffairs, 2004), 223.

235 **"Mike asked our analysts":** Tenet, *At the Center of the Storm*, 158.

235 **Morell recalls it similarly:** Michael Morell with Bill Harlow, *The Great War of Our Time: The CIA's Fight Against Terrorism—From al Qa'ida to ISIS* (New York: Twelve, 2015), 42–43.

235 **"When it was first presented to me":** Barbara S., interview by the author, June 2013.

235 **to get officials at the White House:** Anthony Summer and Robbyn Swan, *The Eleventh Day: The Full Story of 9/11 and Osama bin Laden* (New York: Ballantine Books, 2011), 331.

235 **eager to put a piece into the book:** Richard Ben-Veniste, *The Emperor's New Clothes: Exposing the Truth from Watergate to 9/11* (New York: Thomas Dunne Books, 2009), 319.

235 **title and lead sentence clearly present:** *The 9/11 Commission Report*, 261–262.

236 **called a contact of hers at the Bureau:** Ibid., 535 n. 37; Barbara S., interview by the author.

237 **the report would have included:** Mark Riebling, *Wedge: From Pearl Harbor to 9/11, How the Secret War Between the FBI and CIA Has Endangered National Security* (New York: Touchstone, 2002), 470.

237 **didn't see the PDB article at all:** Thomas Pickard, testimony to the 9/11 Commission on April 13, 2004; available at http://www.washington post.com/wp-dyn/articles/A9088-2004Apr13.html#pickard.

237 **version in the Senior Executive Intelligence Brief:** *The 9/11 Commission Report*, 260–62, 535 n. 38.

237 **gives her editors credit:** Barbara S., interview by the author.

237 **Morell went to bed early:** Morell, "11 September 2011, 23.

238 **assassination on September 9:** Summer and Swan, *The Eleventh Day*, 358.

238 **before boarding Air Force One:** Morell, "11 September 2011," 24.

238 **Loewer served as the replacement:** Deborah Loewer, interview by the author, February 20, 2012.

238 **Morell arranged to meet her:** Morell, "11 September 2011," 25.

238 **had gotten to know her:** Ibid.; Loewer, interview by the author.

238 **didn't rise with his alarm:** Morell, "11 September 2011," 23.

239 **met Loewer at 7:30:** Loewer, interview by the author.

239 **made their way up to the hallway:** Ibid.; Morell, "11 September 2011," 25.

239 **from the Situation Room's morning report:** Loewer, interview by the author.

239 **The material that day:** Bush, *Decision Points*, 126.

239 **"uneventful":** Morell, interview by the author; Morell, "11 September 2011," 25.

239 **Morell had wrapped up:** Loewer, interview by the author.

239 **"When I hung up the phone":** Ibid.

239 **Morell jumped into the staff minivan:** Morell, interview by the author.

240 **White House Situation Room called Loewer:** Loewer, interview by the author.

240 **the briefer told Fleischer:** Morell, interview by the author.

240 **"I ran up to the president's car":** Loewer, interview by the author.

240 **Loewer spoke on the phone again:** Ibid.

240 **"quiet and just struck by the sight":** Cullen Murphy and Todd S. Purdum, "Farewell to All That: An Oral History of the Bush White House," *Vanity Fair*, February 2009, available at http://www.vanityfair.com /politics/features/2009/02/bush-oral-history200902.

240 **Morell finished up his call:** Morell, interview by the author.

240 **she heard shouts:** Loewer, interview by the author.

241 **"I had to get past the Secret Service agent":** Ibid.

241 **"He believed me":** Ibid.

241 **noticed Card's motion:** Murphy and Purdum, "Farewell to All That."

241 **Card's voice echoing the words:** Bush, *Decision Points*, 127.

241 **"There's not a doubt in my mind":** Vimal Patel, "Andrew Card Recalls Delivering News of Attacks to President Bush," *The Eagle* (Bryan/College Station, Texas), April 16, 2012, available at http://www.theeagle.com /news/local/andrew-card-recalls-delivering-news-of-attacks-to-president -bush/article_11c950d3-1440-5822-8942-db369367ec94.html.

241 **"I was just 7":** Tim Padgett, "The Interrupted Reading: The Kids with George W. Bush on 9/11," *Time*, May 3, 2011, available at http://content .time.com/time/magazine/article/0,9171,2069582,00.html.

241 **saw the iconic images:** Bush, *Decision Points*, 127.

241 **Loewer proceeded to tell him:** Loewer, interview by the author.

242 **Morell stayed with the entourage:** Morell, "11 September 2011," 27.

242 **an order to the communicators:** Loewer, interview by the author.

243 **Bush asked him about:** Tenet, *At the Center of the Storm*, 166; Morell, "11 September 2011," 28.

243 **Morell replied that he had no doubt:** Morell, "11 September 2011," 31.

243 **six-page fax from Langley:** Ibid., 33; Bush, *Decision Points*, 136.

243 **"played a big role on 9/11":** Card, interview by the author.

243 **NSC video teleconference at Offut Air Force Base:** Morell, interview by the author.

243 **"I had at least half an hour":** Watson, interview by the author.

243 **began asking his briefer about topics:** Rumsfeld, interview by the author; Steve Cambone, interview by the author, April 2013.

244 **Watson woke in the middle of the night:** Watson, interview by the author.

244 **had just arrived at his office:** Donald Rumsfeld, *Known and Unknown: A Memoir* (New York: Sentinel, 2011), 335–36.

244 **"you need to just cancel this":** Watson, interview by the author.

244 **"That damn helicopter":** Ibid.

245 **the secretary's security detail barged in:** Ibid.

245 **made his way to the crash site:** Rumsfeld, *Known and Unknown*, 336–37.

245 **"Everything went on":** Rumsfeld, interview by the author.

246 **bounced his car off the ground:** Morell, "11 September 2011," 27.

246 **"the most classified document in the US government":** Watson, interview by the author.

246 **CTC officers stayed at their desks:** "In the Counterterrorism Center on 9/11," *SpyCast: The Podcast of the International Spy Museum*, posted September 9, 2011.

247 **"Everything had to be coordinated with everyone":** Barbara S., interview by the author.

247 **"We didn't stop the plot":** "In the Counterterrorism Center on 9/11."

247 **delivered a pep talk:** Ibid.

248 **The president expanded his daily briefings:** Card, interview by the author.

248 **incorporating FBI information more regularly:** Morell, interview by the author.

248 **"We were a nation that had been attacked":** Bush, correspondence with the author.

248 **Card called him:** Card, interview by the author.

248 **"I expect the FBI to determine":** Robert Mueller, remarks to the National Symposium for United States Court of Appeals Judges, Washington, DC, November 4, 2011, available at http://www.fbi.gov/news/speeches/the-importance-of-the-rule-of-law.

248 **Card remembers Mueller looking over:** Card, interview by the author.

249 **feeling like a "chastened schoolboy":** Mueller, remarks to the National Symposium for United States Court of Appeals Judges.

249 **"As soon as we get back":** Card, interview by the author.

249 **shifting some two thousand agents:** Mueller, remarks to the National Symposium for United States Court of Appeals Judges.

249 **for a US-focused session:** Condoleezza Rice, *No Higher Honor: A Memoir of My Years in Washington* (New York: Crown Publishers, 2011), 79.

249 **this new "homeland" audience:** Tenet, *At the Center of the Storm*; Walter Pincus, "Under Bush, the Briefing Gets Briefer," *Washington Post*, May 24, 2002.

249 **expansion of the PDB's distribution:** Helgerson, *Getting to Know the President*, 168.

249 **a new document called the Threat Matrix:** Tenet, *At the Center of the Storm*, 231–32, 235–36; Garrett M. Graff, *The Threat Matrix: The FBI at War in the Age of Terror* (New York: Little, Brown, 2011), 392.

249 **"joint product of the two agencies":** Robert Mueller, comments before the Senate Committee on Governmental Affairs, June 27, 2002, available at http://www.fbi.gov/news/testimony/homeland-security.

249 **they got better over time:** Tenet, interview by the author.

249 **tended to brief too much:** Tenet, *At the Center of the Storm*, 236.

249 **"You never knew which attack":** Miscik, interview by the author.

250 **"You knew 95 percent of it":** Former senior CIA officer, interview by the author, December 2012.

250 **"It was a real challenge":** Morell, interview by the author.

250 **"As our plane landed at LaGuardia":** Cheney, interview by the author.

250 **Ritz-Carlton hotel room:** Bush, *Decision Points*, 152–53; Cheney, interview by the author.

251 **tests soon confirmed they were all safe:** Cheney, interview by the author.

251 **"One of the things I worked hard at":** Tenet, interview by the author.

Eleven: Under Investigation

253 **"make a full and complete accounting":** Public Law 107-306, November 27, 2002, available at http://govinfo.library.unt.edu/911/about/107-306.pdf.

253 **Bush had already invoked:** Neil A. Lewis, "Bush Claims Executive Privilege to Response to House Inquiry," *New York Times*, December 14, 2001.

253 **managed to get White House consent:** Thomas A. Kean and Lee H. Hamilton with Benjamin Rhodes, *Without Precedent: The Inside Story of the 9/11 Commission* (New York: Vintage Books, 2007), 89.

254 **CBS News had reported in May 2002:** David E. Sanger, "Bush Was Warned bin Laden Wanted to Hijack Planes," *New York Times*, May 16, 2002.

254 **"That Presidential Daily Brief":** Alison Mitchell, "Cheney Rejects Broader Access to Terror Brief," *New York Times*, May 20, 2002.

254 **"My strong feeling is that we should not":** Dick Cheney, comments on *Fox News Sunday*, May 19, 2002.

254 **The commission requested PDB articles:** Kean and Hamilton, *Without Precedent*, 91.

254 **"When the PDB request came in":** John Bellinger, interview by the author, September 2011.

254 **"If we're going to take the PDB":** Cheney, comments on *Fox News Sunday.*

255 **"You can quickly get to the point":** Dick Cheney, interview by the author, November 2011.

255 **guarding more Clinton-era PDBs than its own:** Kean and Hamilton, *Without Precedent,* 102.

255 **stepping-stone approach:** Ibid., 91.

255 **the commissioners asked the CIA:** *The 9/11 Commission Report,* 533 n. 3.

255 **"In the minds of the families":** Kean and Hamilton, *Without Precedent,* 90.

256 **the commissioners filed their first request:** Ibid.

256 **"I remember the discussion":** Lee Hamilton, telephone interview by the author, November 2011.

256 **State of the Union address:** Available online at http://georgewbush -whitehouse.archives.gov/news/releases/2003/01/20030128-19.html.

256 **"Anything that's committed to an electron":** John Brennan, interview by the CIA Center for the Study of Intelligence, in "Organizational Innovation: An Interview with TTIC Director John Brennan,'" *Studies in Intelligence* 48, no. 4 (2004), available at http://www.foia.cia.gov/sites /default/files/DOC_0005618307.pdf.

257 **Brennan admitted:** Brennan, interview by the CIA Center for the Study of Intelligence.

257 **President's Terrorism Threat Report:** Douglas Jehl, "Intelligence Briefing for Bush Is Overhauled," *New York Times,* July 20, 2005.

257 **expanded the TTIC's cadre of analysts:** Andy Liepman, interview by the author, October 2012.

257 **conflicts arose quickly:** Former senior CIA official, interview by the author, July 2011.

257 **look at the bigger picture:** Ibid.

258 **"That's why we would come out":** Bellinger, interview by the author.

258 **"Any document that has to do with this investigation":** Philip Shenon, "9/11 Commission Could Subpoena Oval Office Files," *New York Times,* October 26, 2002.

258 **"I absolutely sympathized":** Bellinger, interview by the author.

258 **White House officials first offered:** Kean and Hamilton, *Without Precedent,* 95–96.

259 **"The 9/11 Commission report":** Hamilton, telephone interview by the author.

259 **two members stridently opposed the deal:** Kean and Hamilton, *Without Precedent,* 96–98.

259 **"This was less than we wanted":** Ibid., 98–100.

260 **"As a result of the 9/11 Commission's insistence":** Bellinger, interview by the author.

260 **Senior US officials who did not routinely see the book:** Andrew Card, interview by the author, May 2012; Josh Bolten, interview by the author, October 2012.

260 **"It was a way":** Bolten, interview by the author.

260 **"It was a personal diplomacy tool":** Stephen Hadley, interview by the author, June 2011.

260 **invitation to Bush's briefing in Crawford:** George W. Bush, *Decision Points* (New York: Crown Publishers, 2010), 232.

260 **"The president wanted to show it":** Card, interview by the author.

261 **"That wasn't unusual":** George Tenet, interview by the author, June 2011.

261 **virtually like regular business:** Winston Wiley, interview by the author, June 2011.

261 **"With Tony Blair, it was easy":** Jami Miscik, interview by the author, June 2011.

261 **when a few others:** David E. Sanger, "Meanwhile, Back at the Ranch," *New York Times*, May 28, 2003.

261 **"We heard it from the president":** Michael Morell, interview by the author, January 2015.

261 **"a work of art":** Card, interview by the author; Wiley, interview by the author.

261 **signing his copy of the book:** Morell, interview by the author.

261 **"we have a book like this, too":** Tenet, interview by the author; Card, interview by the author.

261 **A historically unique visitor to the PDB briefings:** John L. Helgerson, *Getting to Know the President: Intelligence Briefings of Presidential Candidates, 1952–2004*, 2nd ed. (Washington, DC: CIA, 2012), 165.

261 **"his son was president and he wasn't":** Hadley, interview by the author.

261 **"He would politely excuse himself":** John Negroponte, interview by the author, May 2011.

262 **"There was huge mistrust":** Porter Goss, interview by the author, September 2011.

262 **the Agency's seventh-floor leadership cadre:** Douglas F. Garthoff, *Directors of Central Intelligence as Leaders of the U.S. Intelligence Community, 1946–2005* (Washington, DC: Potomac Books, 2007), 283.

262 **"support the administration":** Douglas Jehl, "New CIA Chief Tells Workers to Back Administration Policies," *New York Times*, November 17, 2004.

262 **"More often than not":** Goss, interview by the author.

262 **five hours every day with the PDB:** Ibid.

263 **"it was on to the rest of the world":** Ibid.

264 **"It's a dangerous weapon":** Ibid.

264 **"He had used them on his own people":** Peter Pace, telephone interview by the author, November 2011.

264 **"getting some forecasts wrong":** George Tenet, remarks at Princeton

University, March 2001, cited in Charles E. Lathrop, *The Literary Spy: The Ultimate Source for Quotations on Espionage and Intelligence* (New Haven: Yale University Press, 2004), 15.

264 **"well over two hundred articles":** Mike Leiter, interview by the author, November 2012.

264 **"the Intelligence Community was dead wrong":** Letter from the commissioners to President Bush, October 31, 2005, available at http://www.gpo.gov/fdsys/pkg/GPO-WMD/pdf/GPO-WMD.pdf.

265 **"The daily intelligence briefings given to you":** Ibid.

265 **"Even though the daily reports the president saw":** Tenet, *At the Center of the Storm*, 336.

265 **"They were simply wrong":** Letter from the commissioners to President Bush, October 31, 2005.

265 **"old assumptions and inferences":** *The Commission on the Intelligence Capabilities of the United States Regarding Weapons of Mass Destruction, Report to the President of the United States*, March 31, 2005, 9, available at http://www.gpo.gov/fdsys/pkg/GPO-WMD/pdf/GPO-WMD.pdf.

265 **"dubious reliability":** Ibid., 10.

265 **"explained away or disregarded":** Ibid.

265 **"Curveball" . . . "a serious failure":** Ibid., 11, 105.

265 **"did not encourage skepticism":** Ibid, 11.

266 **"loosely reasoned, ill-supported":** Ibid., 12.

266 **"nuance and uncertainty":** Leiter, interview by the author.

266 **"always more alarmist":** Ibid.

266 **what Rice had routinely pointed out:** Morell, interview by the author.

266 **"attention-getting" PDB titles:** *The Commission on the Intelligence Capabilities of the United States Regarding Weapons of Mass Destruction, Report to the President of the United States*, 14.

266 **"We found things that were disturbing":** Miscik, interview by the author.

266 **the DNI would run the PDB process:** Walter Pincus, "CIA to Cede President's Brief to Negroponte," *Washington Post*, February 19, 2005.

266 **A senior intelligence official said:** Scott Shane and David E. Sanger, "Daily Intelligence Briefings Are Vague, Officials Say," *New York Times*, April 3, 2005.

266 **"The confidence levels":** Richard Myers, interview by the author, September 2011.

267 **"very critical of the policy":** Hadley, interview by the author.

267 **"He'll be responsible":** Pincus, "CIA to Cede President's Brief to Negroponte."

267 **"I did it for the signal":** Card, interview by the author.

268 **regular discussions of clandestine operations:** Goss, interview by the author.

268 **"I'm not interesting in spending any time":** Thomas Fingar, interview by the author, April 2012.

268 **largely an Agency process:** Thomas Fingar, *Reducing Uncertainty: Intelligence Analysis and National Security* (Stanford: Stanford Security Studies, 2011), 113.

268 **"How did the PDB become mine?":** Negroponte, interview by the author.

268 **briefers remained CIA careerists:** Goss, interview by the author; Negroponte, interview by the author.

268 **Agency authors still contributed:** Fingar, *Reducing Uncertainty*, 113.

268 **"hugely expensive irrelevance":** Ibid., 16–17.

268 **he realized that the president:** Fingar, interview by the author.

268 **"I'm going to leave it where it is":** Ibid.

269 **"I don't think anybody else":** Former senior DI officer, interview by the author, June 2012.

270 **"still written by CIA authors":** Michael Hayden, interview by the author, April 2011.

270 **stayed almost unchanged:** Former senior DI officer, interview by the author, June 2012.

270 **Key articles came from:** Jehl, "Intelligence Briefing for Bush Is Overhauled."

270 **had to get directly involved:** Interview by the author, July 2011.

270 **lambasted the turf battle:** *The Commission on the Intelligence Capabilities of the United States Regarding Weapons of Mass Destruction, Report to the President of the United States*, 17.

270 **"Bush was *so* focused":** Leiter, interview by the author.

270 **"Terrorism Tuesdays":** Garrett M. Graff, *The Threat Matrix: The FBI at War in the Age of Terror* (New York: Little, Brown, 2011), 544.

270 **"I don't remember seeing any changes":** George W. Bush, correspondence with the author, November 2012.

270 **"One thing that I was confident in":** Bolten, interview by the author.

270 **"who was very well informed":** Ibid.

270 **"deep dive" briefings:** Michael McConnell, interview by the author, May 2011.

270 **"I wanted some of the analysts":** Bush, correspondence with the author.

270 **"I like this":** McConnell, interview by the author.

270 **more than two hundred analysts:** Thomas Finger, comments to the Intelligence National Security Alliance (INSA) Analytic Transformation Conference, Orlando, Florida, September 4, 2008, available at http://cryptome.org/0001/ddni090408.htm.

270 **"Mike McConnell and I would go over the agenda":** Hadley, interview by the author.

271 **"You've got two chairs by the fireplace":** Hayden, interview by the author.

271 **The president so regularly asked:** Helgerson, *Getting to Know the President*, 169–70.

271 **"They would all read the analytic piece":** Hadley, interview by the author.

271 **"They were tough questions":** Robert Gates, *Duty: Memoirs of a Secretary at War* (New York: Knopf, 2014), 94.

271 **Hayden compared the average PDB article:** Hayden, interview by the author.

271 **"The analysts loved it":** Liepman, interview by the author.

271 **"sharp and engaged":** Bolten, interview by the author.

271 **"We got more in-depth stuff":** Cheney, interview by the author.

271 **Paulson attended the deep dives:** Henry Paulson, telephone interview by the author, December 2012.

272 **"How great is this for these analysts":** Robert Kimmitt, interview by the author, October 2012.

272 **"very intellectually stimulating":** Bush, correspondence with the author.

TWELVE: THE PDB, TODAY AND TOMORROW

273 **first PDB session, on November 6, 2009:** "Obama to Receive First Daily Intel Briefing," CNN.com, November 5, 2008, available at http://politicalticker.blogs.cnn.com/2008/11/05/obama-to-receive-first-daily-intel-briefing.

274 **non-PDB intelligence presentations:** Michael Morell, interview by the author, January 2015.

274 **a misunderstanding surfaced:** Ibid.

274 **"We should have just done it":** Ibid.

274 **"I was very adamant":** John Podesta, interview by the author, February 2013.

274 **his briefing with Obama on December 9:** Michael Hayden, interview by the author, April 2011.

275 **"I didn't realize, and I should have":** Mike Leiter, interview by the author, November 2012; Garrett M. Graff, *The Threat Matrix: The FBI at War in the Age of Terror* (New York: Little, Brown, 2011), 534.

275 **"They didn't want to be without a DNI":** Michael McConnell, interview by the author, May 2011.

275 **a few differences from the Bush sessions:** Sheryl Gay Stolberg, "The White House Loosens Its Buttoned-Up Style," *New York Times*, January 29, 2009; Dennis Blair, interview by the author, March 2013.

276 **"Let me read":** McConnell, interview by the author.

276 **directed the intelligence officers to leave:** Ibid.

276 **"completely uninformed by dialogue":** Blair, interview by the author.

276 **Blair was surprised to find:** Ibid.

276 **"In our pre-briefs":** Ibid.

276 **focused on intelligence linked to policies:** Dennis Blair, media roundtable on March 26, 2009, transcript available at http://www.dni.gov/files/documents/Newsroom/Speeches%20and%20Interviews/20090326_interview.pdf.

276 **changing the timing of pieces' publication:** Ibid.

277 **Having the PDB out of rhythm:** Blair, interview by the author.

277 **delaying some articles:** Blair, media roundtable on March 26, 2009.

277 **holding the briefing sessions less regularly:** Blair, interview by the author.

277 **Economic Intelligence Brief:** Tom Gjelten, "What's Still Top Secret? Economic Briefings," *NPR*, September 15, 2009, available at http://www.wbur.org/npr/112829960; Mark Hosenball, "Obama's New Daily Economic Intelligence Briefing," *Newsweek*, February 24, 2009, available at http://www.newsweek.com/obamas-new-daily-economic-intelligence-briefing-82443.

277 **"We have to know":** Bobby Ghoush, "Obama's New Daily Briefing: Economic Intel," *Time*, February 25, 2009.

277 **"Terrorism Tuesdays":** Graff, *The Threat Matrix*, 544.

278 **Mueller focused Obama's attention:** Anne E. Kornblut, "Obama Gets Weekly Tutorials in Terrorism," *Washington Post*, May 6, 2010.

278 **typically placed on the agenda:** Ibid.

278 **intense US government effort:** See "White House Review Summary Regarding 12/25/2009 Attempted Terrorist Attack," January 7, 2010, available at http://www.whitehouse.gov/the-press-office/white-house-review-summary-regarding-12252009-attempted-terrorist-attack.

278 **"The session became very different":** Leiter, interview by the author.

278 **"much more focused on the specific details":** Kornblut, "Obama Gets Weekly Tutorials in Terrorism."

278 **Leiter briefing the president:** Leiter, interview by the author.

278 **human errors and systematic breakdowns:** "White House Review Summary Regarding 12/25/2009 Attempted Terrorist Attack."

278 **"actions taken":** Leiter, interview by the author.

279 **"80 percent about the PDB":** Andrew Liepman, interview by the author, October 2012.

279 **"the NTB was, in many ways, more important":** Leiter, interview by the author.

279 **"What are you trying to do with this":** Blair, interview by the author.

280 **"The PDB should give more on warning":** Ibid.

280 **signals from White House officials:** David Ignatius, "Obama Seeks to Reshape Intel Operations with Choice of Clapper," *Washington Post*, June 9, 2010.

280 **Clapper often delegated:** Philip Zelikow, "The Evolution of Intelligence Reform, 2002–2004," *Studies in Intelligence* 56, no. 3 (September 2012), available at https://www.cia.gov/library/center-for-the-study-of-intelligence/csi-publications/csi-studies/studies/vol.-56-no.-3/pdfs/Zelikow-Reflections%20on%20Reform-18Sep2012.pdf.

281 **Clapper or Cardillo answered any questions:** Morell, interview by the author.

281 **"I've gotten to know Robert really well":** Quoted in Nancy M. Rapavi, "Cardillo Takes Over as New NGA Director," *Belvoir Eagle*, October 9, 2014, available at http://www.belvoireagle.com/news/article_ef05a114-4fb6-11e4-af33-001a4bcf6878.html.

281 **claim from the Government Accountability Institute:** "Presidential Daily Briefs: A Time-Based Analysis," Government Accountability Institute, September 2012, available at http://www.g-a-i.org/wp-content /uploads/2012/09/GAI-Report-Presidential-Daily-Brief-A-Time-Based -Analysis-FINAL-DOC.pdf.

281 **briefing attendance rates decreased:** Marc A. Thiessen, "Why Is Obama Skipping More than Half of His Daily Intelligence Meetings?" *Washington Post*, September 10, 2012.

281 **"not particularly interesting or useful":** Ibid.

281 **calculation appears to include Sundays:** "Presidential Daily Briefs."

281 **"he absorbs information best by reading":** Morell, interview by the author.

282 **"I was impressed in NSC meetings":** Ibid.

282 **"It was clear to everyone":** Former senior CIA official, interview by the author, October 2012.

282 **"The impression that a lot of the analysts had":** Ibid.

282 **"A long-time sine wave":** Morell, interview by the author.

282 **Requests for additions:** Blair, interview by the author.

282 **more than thirty recipients:** C. Lawrence Meador and Vinton G. Cerf, "Bringing New Tools to the White House: Rethinking the President's Daily Intelligence Brief," *Studies in Intelligence* 57, no. 4 (December 2013), 11, available at https://www.cia.gov/library/center-for-the-study -of-intelligence/csi-publications/csi-studies/studies/vol-57-no-4/pdfs /Meador-Cerf-Rethinking%20the%20PDB-Dec2013.pdf.

282 **The book went to customers like:** "40 Under 40: Ben Rhodes," *Time*, October 14, 2010, available at http://content.time.com/time/specials /packages/article/0,28804,2023831_2023829_2025191,00.html.

283 **both Principals Committee** *and* **Deputies Committee meetings:** Morell, interview by the author.

283 **Kissinger passed up the chance:** "Evaluation of the Process Leading to the President's Morning Intelligence Package," memo from A. W. Marshall to Henry A. Kissinger, March 18, 1970, RNL, November 28, 2007, materials release. Available online at http://www.nixonlibrary.gov/virtual library/releases/nov07/031870_pdb.pdf.

283 **Turner considered options:** Memorandum to the Director of Central Intelligence from the Chairman of the DCI Intelligence Information Handling Committee, May 17, 1977 (CIA-RDP80M00165 A000300021003-6), CREST.

283 **Turner continued to explore:** Memorandum to the Director of Central Intelligence from PB/NSC Coordination Staff, February 8, 1980 (CIA-RDP81B00401 R002400110044-9), CREST.

283 **"If I was in the White House now":** Jimmy Carter, interview by John Helgerson, June 23, 1993, cited in John L. Helgerson, *Getting to Know the President: Intelligence Briefings of Presidential Candidates, 1952–2004*, 2nd ed. (Washington, DC: CIA, 2012), 181.

283 **head bent down over an iPad:** White House Photo of the Day, White House website, January 31, 2012, available at http://www.whitehouse.gov /photos-and-video/photogallery/january-2012-photo-day.

283 **"proof positive":** Bob Gourley, "President's Daily Brief: There's an App for That: iPad Used to Deliver President's Daily Briefing," CTOvision.com, February 2, 2012, available at https://ctovision.com/2012/02/presidents -daily-brief-theres-an-app-for-that-ipad-used-to-deliver-presidents-daily -briefing.

283 **"A more radical future vision":** Meador and Cerf, "Bringing New Tools to the White House," 3, available at https://www.cia.gov/library/center -for-the-study-of-intelligence/csi-publications/csi-studies/studies/vol -57-no-4/pdfs/Meador-Cerf-Rethinking%20the%20PDB-Dec2013.pdf.

284 **direct access to reference documents:** Ibid., 9.

284 **"Access to original source intelligence":** Ibid.

284 **Daily briefers in the Obama administration:** Ibid., 12.

285 **CIA presses:** "The Evolution of the President's Daily Brief," CIA public website's "Featured Story Archive," February 27, 2014, available at https:// www.cia.gov/news-information/featured-story-archive/2014-featured -story-archive/the-evolution-of-the-presidents-daily-brief.html.

285 **"Because of its importance":** Former senior CIA officials, interview by the author, December 2012.

286 **"The key question is":** Robert Gates, telephone interview by the author, August 2012.

287 **there were few days when he felt:** Bill Clinton, telephone interview by the author, March 2013.

287 **"No one's going to tell me":** John Negroponte, interview by the author, May 2011.

288 **"That's a hell of an investment we made":** Blair, interview by the author.

288 **"One of the greatest values of the PDB":** Gates, telephone interview by the author.

289 **"I can't imagine any president not taking it seriously":** Clinton, telephone interview by the author.

INDEX

Dr. David Priess served during the Bill Clinton and George W. Bush administrations as an award-winning intelligence officer, manager, and daily intelligence briefer at the CIA as well as a desk officer at the State Department. He obtained his PhD in political science from Duke University and has published articles in journals such as *Security Studies, Middle East Policy,* and the *Mershon International Studies Review* as well as book reviews and eclectic articles in outlets ranging from *Foreword* to *Skeptic.* Priess is currently director of analytic services for Analytic Advantage, Inc., offering specialized training, mentoring, and consulting services to the intelligence community, other government offices, and the private sector.

PublicAffairs is a publishing house founded in 1997. It is a tribute to the standards, values, and flair of three persons who have served as mentors to countless reporters, writers, editors, and book people of all kinds, including me.

I. F. STONE, proprietor of *I. F. Stone's Weekly*, combined a commitment to the First Amendment with entrepreneurial zeal and reporting skill and became one of the great independent journalists in American history. At the age of eighty, Izzy published *The Trial of Socrates*, which was a national bestseller. He wrote the book after he taught himself ancient Greek.

BENJAMIN C. BRADLEE was for nearly thirty years the charismatic editorial leader of *The Washington Post*. It was Ben who gave the *Post* the range and courage to pursue such historic issues as Watergate. He supported his reporters with a tenacity that made them fearless and it is no accident that so many became authors of influential, best-selling books.

ROBERT L. BERNSTEIN, the chief executive of Random House for more than a quarter century, guided one of the nation's premier publishing houses. Bob was personally responsible for many books of political dissent and argument that challenged tyranny around the globe. He is also the founder and longtime chair of Human Rights Watch, one of the most respected human rights organizations in the world.

•   •   •

For fifty years, the banner of Public Affairs Press was carried by its owner Morris B. Schnapper, who published Gandhi, Nasser, Toynbee, Truman, and about 1,500 other authors. In 1983, Schnapper was described by *The Washington Post* as "a redoubtable gadfly." His legacy will endure in the books to come.

Peter Osnos, *Founder and Editor-at-Large*

—